Born in 1962, Nigel ... ersity
College, Lampeter, ... hristi
College, Oxford. In ... War
Museum as an arch... ents,
responsible for colle... War
manuscripts. In June ... of the
Museum's Research a... Department. He is the
author of two books about the Gallipoli battlefields.

Peter Hart was born in 1955, and went to Liverpool University before joining the Sound Archive at the Imperial War Museum in January 1981. As the museum's Oral Historian his work primarily involves him in interviewing war veterans.

Together, Nigel Steel and Peter Hart have previously written two other highly acclaimed books: *Defeat at Gallipoli* (1994) and *Tumult in the Clouds* (1997).

The three of us, plastered up to our ears with glutinous mud, listened to the venomous shriek of the five-nines and looked out upon that chaotic gas poisoned sea of slime with dull hatred in our hearts and a dull longing to escape. 'Vimy Ridge was a picnic to this,' said one with an uneasy grin. And yet, Vimy Ridge was anything but a picnic. There were unhealthy sectors of the British line of which ex-servicemen still speak with a queer homely affection. But I have never met a British soldier who really liked the Salient.[1]

A.J. CUMMINGS

PASSCHENDAELE

THE SACRIFICIAL GROUND

NIGEL STEEL
AND PETER HART

CASSELL

Cassell Military Paperbacks

Cassell, an imprint of Orion Books Ltd, Orion House,
5 Upper St Martin's Lane, London WC2H 9EA

This Cassell Military Paperbacks edition published 2001

A catalogue record for this book is available from the British Library

ISBN 978-1-4072-1467-2

Printed in Great Britain by Mackays of Chatham plc, Chatham, Kent

The Orion Publishing Group's policy is to use papers that are natural, renewable and recyclable products and made from wood grown in sustainable forests. The logging and manufacturing processes are expected to conform to the environmental regulations of the country of origin.

www.orionbooks.co.uk

CONTENTS

LIST OF ILLUSTRATIONS

All illustrations have been reproduced courtesy of the Imperial War Museum photographic archive. The authors would like to thank the keeper for her permission to include them in this book.

Maps

PREFACE

Historical military analysis of the First World War has developed a passing similarity to the theatrical and intellectual reassessment of the works of Shakespeare. Just as his timeless Elizabethan verse is frequently reinterpreted according to the fashions or convictions holding sway amongst the latest school of producers and actors, so the battles that raged on the Western Front have become the testing ground for the theories of military historians. Individuals, events and themes are given prominence according to the latest historical trend or socially accepted political orthodoxy. With the increasing pace and commercial motivations of modern life, the struggle has been hard and occasionally bitter. But the terrible battles of the First World War are not plays to be performed on stage with no risk to life and limb other than some mishap with falling scenery. The Third Battle of Ypres, better known now as 'Passchendaele', was a life and death struggle involving millions of armed men trained to kill or maim their enemies. Each soldier was a painfully vulnerable individual who suffered in awful conditions while waiting with heavy foreboding to discover his fate. Hundreds of thousands of men lost their lives, their limbs or their sanity in this vortex of despair. It was an experience most survivors never forgot until death or the confusions of extreme old age brought down the curtain on their minds.

We do not claim that this book stands as a 'pure' history of the Third Battle of Ypres. Inevitably it is polluted by the times in which we live and our own shallow experience of life. Our method is straightforward: into the simple textual mould which outlines the tragic historical events we have poured the personal experiences of the men who had to endure the consequences of command decisions that they could not possibly influence. Perhaps some strange modern phenomenon, in which the individual demands his own right to speak, leads us to focus on just a few of the millions who suffered; to bring their thoughts and deeds to light as recorded in their diaries, letters and oral history interviews; to allow them to stand for the silent majority. But we hope they form a truly representative sample that will act as a tribute to all those men who strove together in a common cause – the defence of their country. Poor and downtrodden many of them may have been in terms of political, economic or social justice; but all sections of society fought side by side in the man-made Slough of Despond that was Passchendaele. Like John Bunyan's Pilgrim they travelled alone but as one with a greater power – in this case the secular ability of men to bind themselves together in the face of the most awful horrors then imaginable. By 1917 most soldiers had long since lost any warlike enthusiasm that they may have possessed earlier in the war. But in the absence of any other personal options the vast majority fought on, unable to swim against the tide of history. In the end they were just sticking it out as best they could with their pals. Their all too frequent sacrifice has a simple grandeur that seems awfully remote as we drift into the twenty-first century.

In the course of writing this book we have been helped directly and indirectly by a great many people but in particular we would like to thank John Terraine, who has towered above all other historians in his measured interpretation of the conduct of campaigns on the Western Front. We would recommend his ground-breaking *Douglas Haig: the Educated Soldier* (first published in 1963, but available in a new edition from Cassell). More recently the cool analytical work of Robin Prior and Trevor Wilson in their brilliant book *Passchendaele: the Untold Story* (published by Yale University Press in 1996) has also been of great value in raising ideas and themes which might otherwise have escaped us. Paddy Griffiths has explored and exploded many of the populist myths of British military incompetence in his influential *Battle Tactics of the Western Front* (also published by Yale University Press in 1994). Three specialist historians have been of great help in amassing and making original source material publicly available. Alex Revell's masterpiece of research, *High in the Empty Blue* (published by Flying Machines Press in 1995) was of great help in providing a coherent account of the last fight of Werner Voss in September 1917. Our work would have been considerably more difficult had we not been able to rely upon the definitive chronology of the campaign written by our friend and colleague, Chris McCarthy, *The Third Ypres: Passchendaele – The Day by Day Account* (Arms & Armour, 1995). Bryn Hammond, also our colleague in the Imperial War Museum, has been generous to a fault in making available some of the masterly research for his thesis into tank tactics in the First World War.

Any history based heavily on diaries, letters, memoirs and oral history leaves the authors incredibly indebted to the people who created those sources and who actually experienced what we can only write about. We acknowledge our debt to all these people and hope that this book will encourage more people to delve into the archives. For us, the curators of these collective memories are the superb staff of the Imperial War Museum. Grateful thanks are due as ever to Rod Suddaby and his staff in the Department of Documents: Simon Robbins, Stephen Walton, Tony Richards, Wendy Lutterloch, Amanda Mason, and, of course, the late, great David Shaw. We are also heavily indebted to Margaret Brooks and her glorious team at the Sound Archive: Jo Lancaster, Nigel de Lee, Richard McDonough, Lyn Smith, the sublime Rosemary Tudge and Conrad Wood. Thanks are due too to Bridget Kinally and her staff in the Photographic Archive for their patient help and their permission to use the photographs included in this book. Malcolm Brown, who is now as permanent a fixture in the Museum as Edith Cavell's dog, has also, as ever, been most helpful in his suggestions.

Outside the IWM, we would like to thank Lyn Macdonald, both for her example in setting the standard in personal, experience-based histories and for allowing us to quote from the memoir of Bertram Stokes; Simon Moody of the RAF Museum; and our agent Peter Robinson of Curtis Brown who has guided us through many of the pitfalls of publishing. Keith Lowe and Angus MacKinnon of Cassell have been exemplary in their encouragement and patience with us over the difficult last few months when our deadlines and babies seemed to arrive in conjunction with awesome precision. Special thanks are due to Polly Napper and Bryn Hammond for checking early versions of the script, and to Tony Richards for undertaking valuable research on our behalf. As usual our partners have been wonderful and this book would not exist but for the wonderful support of Polly and Marion.

The original quotations that are such an important part of this book have where necessary been lightly edited for readability. Punctuation and spellings have been largely standardized, material has occasionally been reordered and irrelevant material has been omitted without any indication in the text. However, changes in the actual words used in our original sources have been avoided wherever possible. We would also like to thank all those people who have generously given us permission to include extracts from sources in which they hold the copyright.

CHAPTER ONE

GESTATION

The Third Battle of Ypres, someone has called it: but there is only one battle of Ypres. It has lasted from October 1914 and, with Verdun, it is the biggest battle of all.[1]

Captain Harry Yoxall, 18th Battalion, King's Royal Rifle Corps

The Ypres Salient was an accident of history that became the most potent symbol of British resistance to the German invasion of Belgium. The First World War had begun in August 1914 with a campaign of violent movement as the great conscript armies of France and Germany clashed in the Battle of the Frontiers. The first movement was made on 5 August by the Germans under the overall command of General Helmuth von Moltke, when he put into operation an amended version of the plan finalized in 1905 by his predecessor as Chief of the German General Staff, Graf von Schlieffen. This envisaged a huge encircling movement intended to burst through the Belgian frontier and sweep down and round towards Paris to get behind the French armies, forcing a quick and comprehensive victory, before the German Army turned its attention to the threat from the much-vaunted Russian steamroller on their eastern border.

The French, humiliated by their earlier defeat at the hands of the nascent German Empire in 1870, had originally put their faith in an intricate plan of national defence based on a series of powerful fortresses built from Switzerland to Luxembourg which complemented the natural defensive features of the heavily wooded, river-crossed country around them. It was precisely this solid defensive line which the Schlieffen Plan had been intended to circumvent. Yet in 1912 the Chief of the French General Staff, General Joseph Joffre, abandoned this concept of deliberate defence and adopted instead the more romantic alternative of the offensive. Plan XVII, which was put into action on 12 August, was little

The Western Front 1914–1918

more than a blind charge into the provinces of Alsace-Lorraine that the French had been forced in defeat to cede to Germany.

Direct involvement in such a clash of the continental titans was not in the traditional British style. The vast French and German armies were based on systems of compulsory service for civilians in order to provide the state with the necessary human resources to maintain its defences against the threats posed by its immediate neighbours. However, safe behind the English Channel and protected by the supremacy of the Royal Navy, the British had never developed a similar system. The British Army was a small professional body largely geared to service outside Britain. For nearly 100 years, since the final defeat of Napoleon in 1815, there had been no direct threat to the British Isles. Instead, the preoccupation of the armed services had been the security of the burgeoning British Empire. Imperial defence had been based upon the command of the seas and the ability of the Royal Navy to move a well-trained military force quickly along secure sea-routes to any threatened colony or dependency. Within this strategy, the army fulfilled the role of an Imperial garrison. A significant part of it was always based overseas; but the remainder was also available to be sent out at short notice whenever necessary.

Service within the Empire, and particularly in India, bred a different kind of soldier from those produced by the armies of continental Europe. British soldiers were more used to small-scale conflicts in isolated parts of distant countries than preparing to fight battles on their own borders. It had only been in the years immediately prior to the Great War that political associations with Russia and France had slowly drawn Britain into the grand strategic confrontations of the continent. As a result of these prewar plans Britain had undertaken a commitment to send to any war that broke out between France and Germany as large a body of troops as it could from its standing military resources at home. But these were very limited and, known as the British Expeditionary Force, or BEF, on mobilization in 1914 it consisted of just one cavalry and four infantry divisions, although this was quickly augmented by four more infantry divisions as reservists were called back to the colours. The size of this contribution can be gauged by comparison with the French strength of some seventy divisions. On arrival in France the BEF, commanded by Field Marshal Sir John French, was to provide part of a screen covering the French left flank against the threat of attack.

Within a fortnight the foolhardy French assault on the Alsace-Lorraine border had been defeated, with extraordinarily heavy casualties that left them thoroughly debilitated, while the Germans in accordance with the Schlieffen Plan moved steadily through Belgium to envelop the French extreme left flank. Here they were directly facing the BEF, which by the middle of August had moved up into position beyond Maubeuge into the southern corner of Belgium. The arrival there of the British troops was unknown to the Germans who, as they attempted to encircle the French armies, instead of finding open space found the BEF. On 23 August, with the French forces in the south already falling back, the British made a stand at Mons, holding the line there until nightfall. Here the British regulars proved beyond doubt that they could shoot fast and straight with their trusty Lee Enfield rifles; but there were just too few of them to stop the German advance. A retreat to the River Marne followed as the British and French reeled back. For a while it appeared that nothing could stop the Germans. However, a combination of French resilience and German errors led to an unlikely Allied triumph at the Battle of the Marne that forced a rapid German retreat in mid-September. The Germans turned and made their stand on the heights behind the River Aisne and, after a series of sanguinary battles, primitive trench systems were established on both sides. The grandiose schemes of the opposing French and German General Staffs had both proved to be ineffective. The final phase of the war of movement had the feel of a comic opera, despite the intensity of the fighting, as the two armies made successive desperate lunges to the north in vain attempts to turn each other's flank and break the stalemate imposed by the developing trench lines. As they repeatedly crashed into each other, further trenches were scratched out at each point of contact. And so, gradually, the Western Front came into being. The final climactic clash came at the old Belgian city of Ypres some 22 miles from the sea.

Ypres was a prosperous agricultural and commercial centre that dominated the maritime plain of Western Flanders. It lay in a shallow basin only 66 feet above sea level and dominated to the east by a series of low wooded ridges rising mostly to about 160 feet but peaking at around 265 feet to the south. From these 'hills' small streams ran down to join the canalized River Yser. It should perhaps be emphasized that this was not some strange nightmare swamp country, but a typical European maritime plain that had been drained and irrigated for several centuries. Despite its sleepy appearance it was no stranger to war, existing as it did in an area coveted, dominated and fought over in turn by France, Austria, Spain and the Netherlands. The ever 'perfidious Albion' had played no small part in the wars that had raged across Flanders for hundreds of years, culminating in the final triumph of Wellington and Blücher over Napoleon just 65 miles away at Waterloo in 1815. On the dissolution of the French Napoleonic Empire, Belgium reverted to the Netherlands until finally in 1831 the Kingdom of Belgium was formed and commerce reigned supreme. Yet distant echoes of the violent past remained evident in the strong ramparts that surrounded Ypres; while the magnificent Cloth Hall symbolized the population's hopes for a continued peaceful and commercial future.

The First Battle of Ypres began with a fast-flowing encounter on 19 October. The BEF managed to get to Ypres before the Germans and as the latter's numerically superior forces began to range against them, they took up scratch defensive positions in a broad semicircle on the low ridges to the east of Ypres. Inspired by the presence of the Kaiser himself, the Germans flung all their immediately available reserves into a last determined effort to batter their way right through the British line. Their aim was to capture the Channel ports of Dunkirk and Calais whose loss would fatally compromise British communications and bring an early end to their effective participation in the war. Failure would mean that the parallel lines of trenches finally reached the sea, ensuring that the war of movement and manoeuvre would be replaced by siege operations on a scale never before witnessed.

With a heroic, if rash, disregard for casualties the Germans flung themselves repeatedly against the British line. Time and time again, it seemed that the Germans would prevail, time and time again, plain dogged determination or counter-attacks against near impossible odds prevented a final breakthrough. Inestimably proving their worth, and defying the Kaiser's sarcastic dismissal of them as a 'contemptible little army', outside Ypres the original BEF fought their last battle as a homogeneous entity in the field.

> The night came on rather misty and dark, and I thought several times of asking for reinforcements, but I collected a lot of rifles off the dead, and loaded them and put them along the parapet instead. All of a sudden about a dozen shells came down and almost simultaneously two machine guns and a tremendous rifle fire opened on us. It was the most unholy

din. The shells ripped open the parapet and trees came crashing down. However, I was well underground and did not care much, but presently the guns stopped, and I knew then that we were for it. I had to look over the top for about 10 minutes, however, under their infernal maxims before I saw what I was looking for. It came with a suddenness that was the most startling thing I have ever known. The firing stopped, and I had been straining my eyes so, for a moment I could not believe them, but fortunately I did not hesitate for long. A great, grey mass of humanity was charging, running for all God would let them straight on to us not 50 yards off – about as far as the summer-house to the coach-house. Everybody's nerves were pretty well on edge as I had warned them what to expect, and as I fired my rifle the rest all went off almost simultaneously. One saw the great mass of Germans quiver. In reality some fell, some fell over them, and others came on. I have never shot so much in such a short time, could not have been more than a few seconds and they were down. Suddenly one man, I expect an officer, jumped up and came on; I fired and missed, seized the next rifle and dropped him a few yards off. Then the whole lot came on again and it was the most critical moment of my life. Twenty yards more and they would have been over us in thousands, but our fire must have been fearful, and at the very last moment they did the most foolish thing they possibly could have done. Some of the leading people turned to the left for some reason, and they all followed like a great flock of sheep. We did not lose much time I can give you my oath. My right hand is one huge bruise from banging the bolt up and down. I don't think one could have missed at the distance and just for one short minute or two we poured the ammunition into them in boxfuls. My rifles were red hot at the finish, I know, and that was the end of that battle for me. The firing died down and out of the darkness a great moan came. People with their arms and legs off trying to crawl away; others who could not move gasping out their last moments with the cold night wind biting into their broken bodies and the lurid red glare of a farm house showing up clumps of grey devils killed by the men on my left further down. A weird, awful scene.[2]

Captain Harry Dillon, 2nd Battalion, Oxfordshire and Buckinghamshire Light Infantry

Although the line buckled and fell back, step by step, it did not break. Whenever the situation seemed most hopeless, just enough British and French reserves or reinforcements always seemed to arrive in time to thwart the Germans. Although they lost the high ground of the Messines–

Wytschaete Ridge to the south, the low ridges to the east and the flat ground to the north, the British held on to the centre of the line and Ypres itself. Thus the Ypres Salient was born, as it would continue, in a welter of blood and despair. Lieutenant General Sir Douglas Haig, who commanded the I Corps in the northern sector of the Salient, felt that just one more push by the Germans would have finished the job.

> The opinion on all sides is that the troops are very exhausted . . . Landon and Fitzclarence assure me that if the enemy makes a push at any point, they doubt our men being able to hold on. Fighting by day and digging by night to strengthen their trenches has thoroughly tired them out.[3]
>
> Lieutenant General Sir Douglas Haig, Headquarters, I Corps

Haig never forgot the lessons of this battle and resolved he would never miss such an opportunity to seize victory should it ever be presented to him.

The beleaguered city of Ypres thus became a symbol of British resolve to honour their pledge to restore the national integrity of Belgium and defeat Imperial German ambitions. However unlikely both seemed in the autumn of 1914, the BEF never wavered in their belief that both would ultimately be achieved. Ypres would not be given up. The Salient that so many had died to preserve could not be abandoned to create a straighter, more logical line of defence. As every yard of earth had been fought for, it had to be preserved at all costs. The Germans did not accept their reverse gracefully and in November began a deliberate artillery and aerial bombardment of Ypres that caused considerable damage and burned out the imposing Cloth Hall on 22 November. Although the First Battle of Ypres is formally considered to have finished in mid-November, the fighting continued sporadically well into December as each side tried to improve their position ready for the next attempt to break through. The winter rains, combined with a drainage system already disrupted by shells and trenches, soon precipitated the appearance of the dreaded mud that had dogged generals and their long-suffering troops throughout the long history of warfare on the Flanders plains. Unfortunately the exigencies of total war meant that there could be no break in the campaigning season and so the troops remained huddled in their shallow water-filled trenches throughout the freezing winter of 1914–15. The fighting at Ypres would not stop for four long years.

The spring of 1915 saw the first attempts by both sides to break free from the iron grip of trench warfare. At the Battle of Neuve Chapelle in March the British tried an intensive artillery bombardment followed by a simple, but vigorous, infantry attack. Although the German line gave a little under the pressure, it did not give way and the assault was held. On 22 April the Germans made their first major attempt of the year at Ypres, earning an iniquitous entry in the pantheon of war by becoming the first nation to use poisonous gas in a major offensive. This terrible new development marked the beginning of the Second Battle of Ypres. The blow fell first against a French colonial regiment whose line broke amidst considerable panic and the situation was only contained by the resolute stand of the nearby, newly arrived Canadians.

> It was on the afternoon of my birthday that we noticed volumes of dense yellow smoke rising up and coming towards the British trenches. My company was not in the firing line and we did not get the full effect of it but what we did was enough for me. It makes your eyes smart and then I became violently sick. But it passed off fairly soon. By this time the din was something awful where we were. We were under a cross-fire of rifles and shells. We had to lie flat in the trenches. The next thing I noticed was a horde of those Turcos (French colonial soldiers) making for our trenches. Some were armed, some unarmed. The poor devils were absolutely paralysed with fear. They were holding a trench next to a section of the 48th. So the 48th had to hold it also until some of their officers came and made them all go back.[4]
>
> Lance Corporal James Keddie, 15th Canadian Battalion

Following the initial rupture of the French line, the pursuing German infantry made some gains and for a moment the situation seemed very precarious. Once again, things were all but hopeless, but before the Germans could exploit this success, the front line was re-established through a combination of literally last-gasp stands, bolstered by counter-attacks from both Canadian troops and fresh British territorial divisions who were rushed into the line. The battle, which continued well into May, increased the bloody reputation of the Ypres Salient.

Further British attempts in 1915 to smash the German lines at Aubers Ridge, Festubert and Loos were to fail amidst a welter of heavy casualties and recriminations as the theoretical and practical problems of trench warfare became increasingly apparent, but the actual solutions remained elusive. Lessons were learnt, but often far too late in the day to be put into action in the circumstances for which they were relevant. Each step forward in the tactics of attack seemed to be more than matched by effective defensive counters. It was soon evident that both sides faced a unique state of siege warfare that had hitherto been seen as a highly technical discipline within the martial arts. Now it was the prevailing state of war from the English Channel to Switzerland. The language initially seemed archaic, as terms like parados, parapet, revetting, barricades, saps, breastworks, grenades and mortars reappeared in the everyday language of soldiers. Some terms had mutated slightly in their meaning, but the overall language recalled the epic sieges of fortress towns in the past and would have been understood by the sapper generals of Marlborough or Wellington.

Trenches had long existed in warfare, but the application of modern weapons technology and mass industrial production to the inherent strength of malleable earth fortifications transformed them into a formidable defensive system. Line after line of trenches protected by barbed wire entanglements were linked by communication trenches that allowed the relief troops to approach under cover. The front line infantry could project a veritable hail of bullets from their bolt-action rifles and heavy machine guns into any attacking force that dared to show its face in No Man's Land, yet they remained relatively invulnerable to any return fire. But the real threat lay in the awesomely destructive power of modern artillery. Masses of field artillery guns and howitzers were dug in and concealed behind the lines where they were invulnerable to all infantry weapons, but could rain down scything storms of shrapnel and high explosive to form a deadly curtain through which no attacker could pass unscathed. Even if an attacker got through the enemy front-line system, then the reserve trench lines and the arrival of counter-attack divisions meant that it all had to be done again and again and again, if there was to be any prospect of a breakthrough beyond the trenches to force a renewal of open warfare. To make a successful attack, all the links of this defensive chain had to be destroyed. This was the tactical conundrum which faced the British generals.

Following the failure of the Loos Offensive in 1915, Sir John French was placed in an impossible position by a combination of his failure to meet the expectations of success cherished by the British government and general public, the intrigues of an ambitious subordinate and his own personal inadequacies as a military leader. On 19 December 1915 that former subordinate, General Sir Douglas Haig, took up the baton as Commander in Chief of the BEF. Douglas Haig was born on 19 June 1861, the son of a whisky distiller of some renown. He enjoyed a privileged education at Clifton College and at Brasenose College, Oxford, before he found his true vocation on entering the Royal Military College, Sandhurst as a cadet in 1884. Here he did well, disciplining himself to master his new profession with the chilling single-mindedness that was to prove his hallmark. He was commissioned into the 7th Hussars in 1885 and served as a regimental officer at home and in India for nine years. After a period as the aide de camp of the Inspector General of Cavalry and then as a staff officer serving under the command of Sir John French, he had a useful spell at the Staff College in Camberley from 1896 to 1897. One of his contemporaries has recorded a telling anecdote.

> If a scheme interested him, he took tremendous pains with it; if he thought there was no profit in working it out, he sent in a perfunctory minimum. I remember a road reconnaissance sketch on which most of us lavished extreme care, marking all the letterboxes, pumps, gateways into fields and such like. Haig handed in a sheet with a single brown chalk line down the centre, the cross roads shown and the endorsement, 'twenty miles long, good surface, wide enough for two columns with orderlies both ways.' [5]
>
> Brigadier General Sir James Edmonds

After passing out of the Staff College, Haig had his first experience in the heat of battle in a skirmish with a party of Dervishes whilst serving as a staff officer during the Sudan Campaign of 1898. He responded well to the stress of combat, betraying no nerves, and was evidently more than eager to accept responsibility without any prevarication or qualms. His subsequent analytical accounts of engagements were as cool and measured as his staff college assignments had been. Haig next served as a Brigade Major, again under the command of Sir John French, with the Aldershot Cavalry Brigade. On the commencement of the Boer War in October 1899, he went out to South Africa with French who was promoted to command the Cavalry Division. Late in 1900 Haig was then given command of a small column of troops, one of many attempting to suppress the guerrilla activities of the Boer commandos. Next he assumed command of the 17th Lancers and at the end of the war returned with them to Edinburgh in September 1902. His appointment as ADC to King Edward VII was a further mark of official approval. In October 1903 came another great step in his career, when he was called to India by Lord Kitchener, the Commander-in-Chief of the Indian Army. Although only a colonel, Haig had been cherry-picked to modernize cavalry training in the grand-sounding capacity of Inspector General of Cavalry. Haig threw himself into his work, participating fully in arcane controversies over the relative merits of cavalry and mounted infantry, but also attempting to instil professional standards into the training of cavalry officers.

In 1906, he returned to Britain as a Major General, to take up the position of Director of Military Training at the War Office. Here he reported directly to the dynamic Liberal Secretary of State for War, Richard Haldane, who was then engaged in the root and branch reform of the whole British Army. Haig's particular responsibility was in overseeing the creation of the Territorial Army that would organize all Britain's disparate and disjointed volunteer units into one coherent structure that would mirror the Regular Army. It was evident from this time that Haig was being prepared for the rigours of High Command. From 1909 to 1912 he served as Chief of Staff in India. At that time the Indian Army was resistant to modernization and blessed with a labyrinthine system of control and command that rendered it incapable of any meaningful contribution in a modern war. Like many others, Haig made little impact on the overall system, but he did successfully address the issue of directing his officers' thoughts to the implications of directly engaging in the imminent European conflict. Finally, in 1912, Haig was given the plum posting of Commander-in-Chief at Aldershot, with the rank of Lieutenant General. The Aldershot Command contained within it two full divisions and on mobilization of the army, following the outbreak of war, these would form the I Corps of the BEF. Haig was fully conscious of the approach of war and he concentrated his energies in training hard to prepare his command for the coming trial. When the war broke out I Corps was in the thick of the fighting, sharing in all the major battles of the 1914 campaign. Promoted to full General on 20 November, Haig was appointed to command the newly formed First Army as part of the reorganization which expanded the BEF into two armies in December. As such, he was responsible for carrying out the attacks at Neuve Chapelle and Loos before taking the final step to Commander-in-Chief on the fall from grace of his old chief, Sir John French.

Haig's adamantine personality is difficult to assess, as his primary characteristic was an astonishing degree of self-control, clearly apparent in almost everything he did. Self-revelation was therefore not his forte in either his reported speech or writings. His working days were based around a routine that betrayed a formidable appetite for sheer hard work and an addiction to the concept of clearing his desk leaving nothing over to clog up the next day. Throughout his career he met triumph and disaster with an equal calm, providing an example to his more excitable colleagues in moments of great stress. Strangely inarticulate for such an obviously intelligent man, he was aware of this weakness and therefore stiflingly cautious in his conversation, preferring to encapsulate his thoughts in closely argued memoranda. Although easily offended by what he regarded as inappropriate conduct in others, he rarely seems to have shown his feelings and had a reputation for quiet courtesy in his overall personal behaviour to others. It is easy to see why Haig is often caricatured as a strait-laced hidebound Scot. Fiercely rejecting any form of excess in the joyous twin temptations of alcohol and women, his sincere religious piety and exemplary personal life were an important part of his character. But Haig also had a formidable analytical and flexible turn of mind. He may not have thought up new and radical schemes himself, but he could assess their merits in the work of others and suck out those elements that were of value to him in his overall purpose. Early on, Haig clearly saw the value of machine guns; recognized the overwhelming power of artillery; accepted the need for aerial reconnaissance; encouraged the use of aerial artillery observation and backed the use of the first tanks. If he retained a seemingly anachronistic trust in the power of cavalry to exploit a breakthrough, this was because in the absence of the reliable, fast armoured fighting vehicle that lay a generation in the future, the cavalry was the only rapid mobile reserve he had.

Haig had an absolute belief in the primacy of the Western Front. In this his chief ally was General Sir William Robertson, who had been appointed Chief of Imperial General Staff (CIGS) in December 1915 at the same time that Haig had taken over command of the BEF. Blessed with a clear analytical brain, masked to a certain extent by a degree of social gaucheness and an overly brusque manner, he had risen all the way to the pinnacle of his profession having enlisted as a regular private soldier in 1877. As CIGS, Robertson was responsible for the global prosecution of the war and was the accepted primary conduit of military advice to the War Cabinet. Although he recognized the importance of defending the British Empire from the threats posed by Germany's eastern ally Turkey, he also realized that once the integrity of the Empire had been secured there was no point in wasting more resources in conflicts that could not affect the main issue.

The 'Westerners', as they have become known, believed that to win the war the main force of the enemy had to be brought to battle in the field and defeated. In this case, that meant that the German Army had to be defeated on the Western Front before the war could be won. This seemingly obvious point has been obfuscated by the sheer verbal dexterity employed by the two main 'Easterners', those twin stars in the political firmament, Winston Churchill and David Lloyd George. As First Lord of the Admiralty, Churchill had been instrumental in initiating the disastrous campaign at Gallipoli intended to knock Turkey out of the war in 1915. This laudable aim, however, would only have been possible if sufficient resources had been deployed to ensure success from the start. But as the Gallipoli landings were begun three days after the Germans launched the Second Battle of Ypres, it can be seen that the Westerners had a point when they claimed that such largesse would risk the whole security of the Western Front. The usual messy compromise ensued and, although large numbers of troops were eventually sent to Gallipoli, they arrived too late to be of any real value. Consequently the worst of both worlds was achieved. Simultaneously, on the opposite flank of the Ottoman Empire, limited operations in Mesopotamia originally launched to safeguard British oil supplies from the Persian Gulf had developed into a full-blooded campaign. Despite initial successes this led to a humiliating surrender of a considerable body of British forces in April 1916 after the protracted siege of Kut el Amara. A third option started in September 1915, strongly favoured by David Lloyd George, then Minister of Munitions, was a Balkan campaign directed against Bulgaria from the Allied base in Salonika. The common attraction of these schemes was that for relatively modest investments of resources and lives they seemed to offer far greater results than could be achieved on the Western Front. But it was not the Turks or Bulgarians who were threatening France and Belgium.

The Easterners relied on a complicated 'domino effect' that they believed would, through a series of collapses, eventually destabilize Germany. Few of the Allied military High Command were convinced by these arguments. But as thousands died to gain just a few yards on the Western Front, the Easterners' claims had an increasingly seductive siren effect on politicians who were accountable to their electorates and hence sought an easier or less costly solution.

From the moment the Western Front became static, both sides set about evolving new strategies and tactics. But so much was new and strange that there was a great deal of confusion over the best means to ensure success. The scale of the conflict was also growing exponentially as the great warring empires mobilized the full weight of their manpower reserves from every corner of the globe to serve the mother countries. In 1916 both sides took a deep breath and launched a devastating war of attrition with pulverizing offensives that would have seemed inconceivable in scale just two years before. The Germans struck first in February 1916. They chose their battleground carefully at Verdun and sought to bleed the French Army dry by forcing it to fight on a narrow concentrated front where pride and military considerations would combine to make sure that a tactical withdrawal was impossible. At the end of 1915 the British, constrained by the considerations of their French allies, committed themselves to an offensive on the Somme. This was originally conceived as being a joint offensive, but as a result of Verdun the British assumed the greater burden of the battle which finally commenced on 1 July 1916. The British perspective of the First World War has been partially warped by the effects of both the passage of time and the work of some able propagandists. Thus for the last thirty years the Battle of the Somme has been seen as the epitome of useless sacrifice; of gallant soldier pals – 'lions' – led by dim-witted and callous generals and their uncaring red-tabbed staff officers – 'donkeys'. It is doubtful if this highly distorted and unrepresentative image will ever change, burned as it now has been onto our national consciousness by constant repetition. Rational assessment is made even more difficult by the undeniable fact that the first day of the Somme was indeed an absolute disaster for the British Army.

The Battle of the Somme was conceived with the intention of rupturing the German line along a wide front so that it could not be re-established, and thus allowing the cavalry through to exploit the victory in traditional style. The main weapon was to be a pulverizing artillery bombardment intended to erase the front-line German defences from the face of the earth. Unfortunately the bombardment, although impressive by the standards of the day, failed to deliver. Spread over an ambitiously wide front, the large number of guns were in fact more thinly spread than at the Battle of Neuve Chapelle and the British had severely underestimated the strength of the German defences. The guns fired far too great a proportion of shrapnel shells, which had little effect against men well under cover. High explosive shells, preferably of a heavy calibre, were essential to clear away the barbed wire, smash the trenches and cave in the dugouts on the heads of the garrison. The fire plans also lacked subtlety, with the sudden lifts to new targets giving time for the defenders to rush up from their underground lairs to pour bullets into the attacking troops. The supreme importance of counter-battery work to silence the German artillery had also not been addressed. To undertake the offensive, the men of the British Fourth Army were largely drawn from Kitchener's volunteer armies. Although brave and keen as individuals, they were simply not well enough trained. The result was the catastrophe of the opening day with 57,470 casualties including 19,240 dead. The legend of the 'pals battalions' marching to their slaughter was born. In criticizing the simple tactics employed that day, it is sometimes forgotten that in just two years the British Army had grown in size from a small professional body to an army numbered in millions. There were just not enough regular officers and NCOs to go round, to train the men and lead them in battle. This was exacerbated by the unfortunate fact that many of the regulars who had survived the first two years of the war unscathed were intellectually or temperamentally unsuited for such rapid promotion. In addition, the specialist arms such as the Royal Artillery, Royal Engineers and Royal Flying Corps had been massively expanded and their role changed beyond all recognition. Gunners, engineers and pilots all needed time to acquire knowledge and learn their skills.

After the horrendous débâcle of 1 July the rest of the Battle of the Somme was marked by a steady if painful learning curve for the British Army. As the troops battered their way across the scarred chalk downs and matchstick woods, the artillery gradually developed new techniques of bombardment: ever-increasing concentrations of guns, more high-explosive shells rather than shrapnel, heavier calibres of gun, creeping barrages, standing barrages, counter-battery work, sound and flash spotting methods of ranging, improved pre-registration of targets and increasing use of aerial artillery observation. At the same time the infantry introduced more sophisticated attack tactics and began to place more emphasis on consolidation when gains were made. All these slow steps forward were taken during the summer and autumn of 1916. In the process the British Army suffered dreadful casualties, but so too did the Germans. The combination of the relentless British hammering on the Somme and the mincing machine of Verdun meant that the German Army was badly drained and the impact was obvious to Field Marshal Hindenburg and his Chief of Staff, General Erich Ludendorff.

> GHQ had to bear in mind that the enemy's great superiority in men and material would be even more painfully felt in 1917 than in 1916. They had to face the danger that 'Somme fighting' would soon break out at various points on our fronts, and that even our troops would not be able to withstand such attacks indefinitely, especially if the enemy gave us no time for rest and for the accumulation of material. Our position was uncommonly difficult, and a way out hard to find. We could not contemplate an offensive ourselves, having to keep our reserves available for defence. There was no hope of a collapse of any of the Entente Powers. If the war lasted our defeat seemed inevitable. Economically we were in a highly unfavourable position for a war of exhaustion. At home our strength was badly shaken. Questions of the supply of foodstuffs caused great anxiety, and so, too, did questions of morale.[6]
>
> General Erich Ludendorff, German GHQ

In such circumstances the German High Command were determined to try and conserve their strength and believed they had found a new weapon – unrestricted submarine warfare – that would bring Britain to her knees by cutting off her ocean highways. Yet that in turn risked disturbing the brooding neutrality of the United States. It was a high risk to take.

At the end of 1916 Haig had become convinced that the next major British offensive effort should take place in Flanders and, specifically, in the Ypres Salient. His belief was emphatically not based on reasons of sentiment; there were many practical reasons for launching an offensive at Ypres. This was in stark contrast to the selection of the Somme area that had essentially been chosen only because the French and British fronts joined there and the French could therefore keep their eye on the British efforts. The main strategic importance of the Ypres area lay in its proximity to the Channel ports. Whilst the Germans threatened Ypres they also threatened the main British cross-Channel routes that ended at Dunkirk, Calais and Boulogne. These could not be considered entirely secure until the Germans had been driven back. But the reverse was also true. Operations in Flanders would benefit from shortened supply lines back to Britain, and from the British perspective, Ypres lay tantalizingly close to the German-controlled ports of Ostend and Zeebrugge that were linked by canal to Bruges. Since their capture in 1914 these had become major German naval bases from which destroyers, submarines and mine-layers could emerge into the English Channel. The submarine menace was especially grave as hundreds of thousands of tons of Allied shipping were being sunk every month, to the consternation of the Admiralty. Thus a successful offensive from Ypres would both remove the threat from the British-controlled Channel ports and eject the Germans from their vital naval bases. An independent combined operation on the German bases was too expensive and risky an undertaking, while an assault directly along the coast was impossible due to the flooding in 1914 of the River Yser along the coastal segment of the Western Front from Nieuport to Dixmude. Haig's answer was a general advance from the Ypres Salient coupled with a coastal landing once the main attack had been successful in overcoming the successive German lines of defence which lay on the ridges east of Ypres.

A second strategic attraction of a Flanders campaign was that the German Army would surely have to stand and fight. Retirement would be impossible if they were not to lose both the Channel ports and the important railway junction town of Roulers that lay just 5 miles beyond the Passchendaele Ridge. Haig believed, not without justification, that the German Army had suffered terrible losses during the fighting on the Somme and at Verdun and he was optimistic that further shattering blows delivered by twin British and French offensives would break down their remaining resistance. It was this belief that would be tested in 1917.

A third factor was the sheer inconvenience of the British tactical situation in the Ypres Salient. Born in the heat of desperate battle, the British trenches were overlooked from every vantage point by an enemy who were able to fire directly into them from three sides. Logically, the British should have evacuated the Salient and thus straightened their line along tactically superior positions; but logic did not allow for the emotional significance of the blood-soaked ground. Nevertheless, the drip, drip, drip of casualties in the Ypres Salient was a never-ending painful drain on British manpower resources. A successful offensive would hopefully eradicate the problem of the Salient.

For these reasons Haig had favoured a Flanders offensive since his appointment as Commander-in-Chief, but had been forestalled by the increased requirements of the Somme offensive in 1916. Nevertheless, extensive planning and preparations had been got under way. The German positions on the Messines Ridge lying to the immediate south of Ypres posed an obvious threat to any operations driving east from the Salient onto the Gheluvelt Plateau and Pilckem Ridge. As early as July 1915 General Sir Herbert Plumer, commander of the Second Army, had sanctioned the commencement of a series of mines designed to blast the Germans from their perch, prior to any main offensive that might be launched. The planning process continued throughout 1916 until it crystallized at the Chantilly Conference called on 15 November to discuss the Allied plans for 1917. This conference and subsequent high-level meetings endorsed a series of key decisions. The main Allied effort was to be centred on British and French offensives launched on the Western Front, but simultaneous offensives were to be launched on the Russian and Italian fronts in an attempt to prevent the Germans from using their central strategic position to switch their reserves in turn from front to front. The British were to renew the Somme offensive in the spring, but then switch their main effort to Flanders in the summer. This complied not only with Haig's long-standing plans, but also with instructions received from the War Committee of Prime Minister Herbert Asquith's British Cabinet, which indicated that there was no operation of war they regarded as of greater importance than the expulsion of the Germans from the Belgian coast.

Following the Chantilly Conference, Haig requested Plumer to submit his plans for an attack at Ypres as soon as possible. However, when Plumer responded with his detailed proposals on 12 December they were to be a disappointment to Haig. The naturally cautious Plumer had restricted his horizons to the capture of the Messines Ridge and the low-lying Pilckem Ridge immediately to the east of Ypres. This was hardly the broad-ranging offensive to clear the Belgian coast that Haig envisaged.

He sought a second opinion and called in General Sir Henry Rawlinson, the commander of the Fourth Army that had borne the brunt of the Somme offensive, with the intention of giving him responsibility for the northern sector of the attack.

However, these nascent plans for a Flanders offensive were to be rudely disrupted by political and military developments on both sides of the Channel. Firstly, General Joseph Joffre, the enigmatic French Commander-in-Chief since the outbreak of war, finally paid the price for his many failures and was dismissed. On 12 December the French government selected as his successor General Robert Nivelle, who had attracted great admiration for two successful counter-attacks launched in the closing months of the Battle of Verdun. These limited attacks had restricted themselves to an advance of just 2,500 yards following a concentrated artillery bombardment that had smashed the German front-line defences. Nivelle believed he could extrapolate from this experience a magic formula for success without tears – a complete breakthrough following an intensive, scientifically targeted bombardment on a wide front – all without the punitive casualties that had befallen previous Allied offensives.

In the same month, in Britain the faltering Asquith administration finally fell. The new Prime Minister, David Lloyd George, although a Liberal, had attained his position through successfully attracting Conservatives, dissatisfied with the supine Asquith, by promising to prosecute the war more vigorously – including the pursuit of the 'knockout blow'. It had been a tortuous process for Lloyd George to attract the support he needed for his premiership from men who had loathed him in his former incarnation as Liberal Chancellor of the Exchequer. Part of the price they extracted was a definitely 'tongue in cheek' promise from Lloyd George to abstain from interference in the generals' military conduct of the war. Yet Lloyd George had been appalled by the Somme battles and was determined to reduce the level of British casualties. His preference had moved from an increased commitment in the Balkans to making the main Allied effort against the Austro-Hungarian Army in north-eastern Italy. He reasoned that this would force the Italian Army into bearing a far greater share of the war effort than had hitherto been the case, reinforced by a contribution of British and French artillery and troops.

> Had the Austrians been beaten on the Italian Front it would have been imperative for them to withdraw several divisions and batteries from their

> Eastern Front. The Germans would therefore have to extend and thus weaken their lines on the same front. That would have eased the position for the hard-pressed Russians and Rumanians and would have given them time to reform and recover their fighting strength. In the alternative the Germans would have withdrawn divisions from France and made a break-through on that front a more feasible operation.[7]
>
> David Lloyd George, Prime Minister

This 'Italian plan' was pursued by Lloyd George at the Allied Conference held in Rome in January 1917. The combination of professional military scepticism from the British and French High Commands, coupled with the Italians' forthright rejection of their proposed central role in this scheme of things, meant that the plan was stillborn. This left Nivelle putting forward his proposals as the only real alternative worth considering. After the Somme Lloyd George distrusted Haig and his offensive plans, and to him Nivelle's proposals seemed exactly the kind of imaginative scheme he preferred. Lloyd George's overriding priority was to avoid British casualties and the best method he could see to achieve this was to inveigle others to take up the brunt of the fighting. Here were Nivelle and the French government offering to pick up the poisoned chalice and Lloyd George was more than happy to pass it to them. Haig had his doubts about Nivelle but he was impressed by his intellectual vigour and he also saw the advantages of letting France take the lead in a major offensive on the Western Front. After all, if it succeeded, much would be achieved; but even a failed French offensive would further drain German stamina and make them more vulnerable to the hammer blows Haig still had planned for Flanders. With Haig and Lloyd George both agreeable, even if for different reasons, the Nivelle plan was accepted.

Nevertheless, planning for an Ypres offensive continued and in January 1917 Plumer was prodded to spice up his plan to take account of the opportunities that it was presumed would follow the launch of the Nivelle offensive. The overall intention was to break out towards Roulers before turning the main thrust towards the German naval bases on the coast. A second attack would be launched from the area of Nieuport directly along the coast in conjunction with a combined operation to land troops on the coast near Ostend. On 30 January Plumer again responded with caution, proposing a simultaneous attack on the Messines Ridge, the Pilckem Ridge and part of the Gheluvelt Plateau as the first stage of the operation. He then envisaged a series of thrusts across the Gheluvelt Plateau leading up onto the Passchendaele Ridge before instigating the right hook to the Belgian coast that would trigger the advance from Nieuport and the sea landings. Plumer, from long experience, was very conscious of the logistical restrictions imposed on any operations by the cramped conditions in the Ypres Salient and Rawlinson, in commenting on the plans, was in full agreement with these concerns. Taking a position broadly in support of Plumer's plans, Rawlinson was extremely wary of the prospects for any attack on the Pilckem Ridge whilst the Germans remained in control of the Gheluvelt Plateau. He therefore proposed that an accelerated assault on the Messines Ridge be followed forty-eight to seventy-two hours later by a combined attack on the Gheluvelt Plateau and Pilckem Ridge. This was the bare minimum time needed to allow the artillery to move into new positions ready to support the next attacks.

Haig had another option in mind, one proposed on 14 February by a special planning section under Colonel C. N. Macmullen of the General Staff at GHQ. This scheme proposed a simultaneous assault on Messines, Gheluvelt and Pilckem but overcame the logistical difficulties this would entail for the artillery by assigning the capture of the Gheluvelt Plateau to the Tank Corps. It envisaged an attack without artillery preparation by massed tanks. Unfortunately, this novel scheme did not withstand serious scrutiny as it soon became apparent that the combination of bad terrain, unsuitable for tanks, and their excessive vulnerability to artillery fire whilst passing through the narrow defiles between the woods that littered the Plateau, rendered the scheme utterly unfeasible as a serious operation of war.

Haig seems to have been torn between his desire to attack simultaneously along the whole Ypres front and the logistical imperatives imposed by the nature of the Salient. After the collapse of the tank plan, he seems to have accepted the rationale of the arguments put forward by Plumer and Rawlinson, but he was obviously unhappy with what he saw as their lack of real offensive spirit. His response, in effect, was to 'shoot the messenger' and once again he began to look elsewhere amongst his senior army commanders to find one more sympathetic to his own overall aspirations.

Meanwhile Nivelle had centre stage. The essence of his plan was for the French Army to launch a surprise attack supported by a crushing artillery barrage that would rupture the German front line along the

Chemin des Dames, focusing on the Soissons–Rheims area. The confidently predicted breakthrough would allow a vigorous exploitation leading to the collapse of the whole German front, rendering the proposed Flanders operations unnecessary and presaging a rapid and victorious end to the war. The British role was confined to taking over responsibility for a further section of the Western Front from the French and the commitment to launch a diversionary offensive at Arras to draw German reserves away from the critical area.

Any illusion of harmony between the British and French did not last long, as tensions between Lloyd George, Haig and Nivelle simmered not far below the surface. On 26 February, at the Calais Conference held between the British War Cabinet and the French Government, Lloyd George made a decisive intervention that appalled his own generals and soured his relationship with them for the rest of the war. Without warning he gave wholehearted support to Nivelle's position and, furthermore, took the unprecedented action of subordinating Haig to Nivelle for the duration of the offensive. Haig was naturally dumbfounded and took serious umbrage. He fought back, exploiting his many personal contacts in the military establishment, the press, sympathetic politicians and even the royal family. At first Lloyd George was disposed to face Haig down, and he even secretly canvassed support amongst the War Cabinet for a proposal to dismiss him out of hand. To his horror he found that his ministers were not openly willing to risk the public opprobrium that would be aroused if Haig, who just a few months before had been promoted to Field Marshal, were now to be dismissed in such controversial circumstances. Thus Haig remained in place and, as a sop to his pride, was granted definite permission to launch his Flanders offensive should Nivelle fail in his grand scheme.

In March 1917 the plans for the British diversionary offensive at Arras were partially compromised by the German tactical withdrawal to the Hindenburg Line from the precarious salient they had occupied between Arras and the old Somme battlefields. This retirement to a shorter, better sited and meticulously prepared series of defensive lines meant that the chances of any serious breakthrough were greatly reduced. It was also an illustration of what the British should have done to remove the Ypres Salient. Nevertheless, the Battle of Arras was launched on 9 April and the capture of Vimy Ridge crowned a day of great success built on the foundations of an artillery bombardment almost three times the strength and weight of that which presaged the attack on the Somme. However, despite this promising start, the operations soon bogged down in a series of minimal advances achieved at an increasing cost in casualties.

Finally, on 16 April, after delays caused by bad weather, the Nivelle offensive itself was launched against the Chemin des Dames. The result was catastrophic to the Allied cause. Nivelle's previously effective use of surprise in his relatively minor counter-attacks at Verdun proved impossible to replicate in a gigantic offensive deploying hundreds of thousands of men. French security was breached and the Germans, forewarned and forearmed, were ready for the French *poilus*. In reality, for all his plausible manner, Nivelle had nothing new to offer. The casualties were dreadful, adding up to some 115,000 men in just ten days, and French morale collapsed in the most spectacular fashion. The flame of mutiny, flickering at first but growing increasingly strong, spread through the disaffected French troops. Whole units disobeyed their officers and it was clear that the French would be incapable of serious offensive action for the near future, although it seemed the troops were willing to act in a defensive capacity to protect their homeland. This disastrous state of affairs was not made immediately apparent to either Haig or the British government. Nivelle paid the price of his monstrous failure and was summarily dismissed. His replacement was General Philippe Pétain, whom many saw as the real hero of Verdun; the man who had organized the grim defence when everything seemed lost was now cast as the saviour of all France.

Another factor in the progressively worsening situation was the developing consequences of the Russian Revolution in March 1917 and subsequent formation of a Liberal/Socialist Provisional Government under Alexander Kerensky. Although Russia remained in the war and indeed as a swan song launched a last disastrous offensive in July, it became increasingly obvious that Russian support could not be relied upon in the longer term. A separate peace treaty was always a distinct possibility following the fall of the Tsar.

On 1 May Haig summarized his views on the overall position on the Western Front in a paper sent to the War Cabinet.

> The guiding principles are those which have proved successful in war from time immemorial, viz., that the first step must always be to wear down the enemy's power of resistance and to continue to do so until he is

> so weakened that he will be unable to withstand a decisive blow; then with all one's forces to deliver the decisive blow and finally to reap the fruits of victory. The enemy has already been weakened appreciably, but time is required to wear down his great numbers of troops. The situation is not yet ripe for the decisive blow. We must therefore continue to wear down the enemy until his power of resistance has been further reduced. The cause of General Nivelle's comparative failure appears primarily to have been a miscalculation in this respect, and the remedy now is to return to wearing down methods for a further period, the duration of which cannot yet be calculated.[8]
>
> Field Marshal Sir Douglas Haig, GHQ

Haig was left in a powerful position by the failure of Lloyd George's protégé Nivelle and he pressed home his advantage. On 4 and 5 May, at the Franco-British Military and Inter-Allied Conferences held in Paris, it was agreed that the decisive rupture of the German lines was no longer likely, but that future attacks should concentrate on limited objectives strictly within the zone that could be dominated by the mass of supporting artillery. Lloyd George, from his equal and opposite position of weakness, could do little other than to exhort the French to keep on attacking alongside the British and piously to support the supremacy of generals in deciding the time, place and methodology to be employed in such attacks. Haig accepted his victory gracefully enough in his diary, but even he must have felt some flickering of emotion at this abject climb-down.

> Mr Lloyd George made two excellent speeches in which he stated that he had no pretensions to be a strategist, that he left that to his military advisors, that I, as C. in C. of the British Forces in France had full power to attack where and when I thought best. He (Mr L. G.) did not wish to know the plan, or where or when any attack would take place. Briefly, he wished the French Government to treat their Commanders on the same lines. His speeches were quite excellent.[9]
>
> Field Marshal Sir Douglas Haig, GHQ

The overall policy was to cause maximum damage to the Germans whilst conserving Allied strength ready for the decisive offensive in the following year. Although the state of Russia remained of great concern, the entry into the war of the United States of America in April, provoked by the German policy of unrestricted submarine warfare, offered the hope of new armies of willing soldiers in 1918.

Haig considered that he now had a free hand for his Flanders offensive and by then he had identified the man he considered to have the thrusting qualities needed to take advantage of any opportunities that might arise if the German resistance suddenly cracked under successive hammer blows. His choice, General Sir Hubert Gough, commander of the Fifth Army, was relatively young for such a senior figure at 47, with a reputation for impatience and a willingness to push on at all costs. Haig regarded him as ideal to press on relentlessly in the face of the difficulties that were bound to arise in clearing the Ypres ridges, whilst as a cavalryman he would ensure that any exploitation after a breakout was carried out with the necessary vim and vigour. These qualities were considered sufficient to outweigh his lack of familiarity with the prevailing conditions and topography of the Ypres Salient. As a result of his selection to command the main operations, Rawlinson was left solely with responsibility for the coastal operations, whilst Plumer took charge of the capture of the Messines Ridge.

On 7 May, at a meeting of his army commanders at Doullens, Haig unveiled his final plans.

> The objective of the French and British will now be to wear down and exhaust the enemy's resistance by systematically attacking him by surprise. When this end has been achieved the main blow will be struck by the British forces operating from the Ypres front, with the eventual object of securing the Belgian coast and connecting with the Dutch frontier.[10]
>
> Field Marshal Sir Douglas Haig, GHQ

The offensive at Arras, originally a diversion for Nivelle's ill-fated attack, would be continued to keep up the overall pressure and, of course, hopefully divert German attention from the imminent Flanders operations. On 7 June Plumer would launch his attack on the Messines Ridge. Some weeks later Gough would then launch the main offensive from the body of the Ypres Salient onto the Pilckem Ridge and the Gheluvelt Plateau. In the interval the French, Italians and Russians had promised to launch limited offensives to help exhaust the German reserves and fighting spirit. On 16 May Haig was finally given express approval from the War Cabinet on condition that the French co-operated fully in launching limited but powerful offensives to play their part in the overall scheme.

Unfortunately it was now clear to the French just how dire their situation was as the spread of mutinies accelerated towards the end of May. It was soon apparent to British liaison officers that the French did not regard their promise to launch a subsidiary attack as a firm commitment. This left Haig in a quandary. His Flanders offensive had been conceived with due allowance for diversionary attacks from the French to confuse the German High Command as to where the main thrust was being planned. If he cancelled the offensive through lack of proper French support, then he feared that the Germans might prove curious as to why the Allies were not attacking – and in their curiosity uncover the dreadful malaise afflicting the French Army of which they would surely take full advantage. Although the French claimed that their men would fight to defend their homeland if attacked, their troops surely could not be relied upon under the extreme stresses and all the attendant horrors of a full-scale German offensive on their lines. On the other hand, if Haig continued his offensive alone then the Germans would be able to concentrate all their resources to throw him back in Flanders.

At a meeting on 18 May Haig tried to pin down Pétain as to what exactly he intended. Pétain promised a series of summer attacks that would be generally helpful to the British aims; but, with some justification, pointed out that the distant objectives of the Flanders offensive were hardly in line with the attacks for limited objectives that had been agreed in Paris. Haig replied that he intended successive attacks each with limited objectives.

> As the wearing down process continues, advanced guards and cavalry will be able to progress for much longer distances profiting by the enemy's demoralisation until a real decision is reached.[11]
>
> Field Marshal Sir Douglas Haig, GHQ

Haig was dissembling, of course, but in Pétain's fraught circumstances he was more than willing to let the British attack and as an encouragement offered the use of six French divisions to join in the main Ypres offensive. This was enough to convince Haig and the British government that their French allies really would play their part. The stage was set for the curtain to go up on the Battle of Messines as the overture to the Flanders offensive that would eventually be known by the reviled name of Passchendaele.

CHAPTER TWO

MESSINES

Every gun opened fire at once and the mines were exploded. The very earth swayed with the force of the explosions. The ground appeared to open, flames shot up into the sky, making night like day and it seemed as though we were looking into the bowels of the earth. The machine guns opened fire. It was veritable inferno, a hell upon earth.[1]

Signaller George Stewart, 16th Divisional Signal Company, Royal Engineers

The Messines Ridge had been lost to the Germans in the First Battle of Ypres in 1914. Although not particularly high at 260 feet above sea level, in a land of hillocks it still provided the Germans with an excellent observation platform from which their artillery observers could peer down behind the British lines, gazing right into the innards of the Ypres Salient as it stretched away northwards. The attack on Messines was to be conducted by the Second Army and masterminded by General Sir Herbert Plumer. Having been a tutor when Haig attended Staff College in 1896, he had to endure being called 'old man' by his former pupil – even though he was in fact only four years older. Plumer had a sound mind that allowed him to apply basic military principles to a given situation without becoming overexcited and, above all, with an eye for the common-sense solution. Army commanders responsible for hundreds of thousands of men were of necessity remote figures, yet Plumer was successful in creating at least the illusion of close, personal contact with the men under his command, whilst still maintaining the strict discipline essential to overall efficiency. His avuncular nature was illustrated by an amusing, if dangerously apocryphal, story circulating amongst his officers.

> The Army Staff under Plumer had a conference on discipline at which dissatisfaction was expressed at the saluting of the Canadians. 'Plum' let it go on for a while and then broke in with, 'Well, gentlemen, I don't

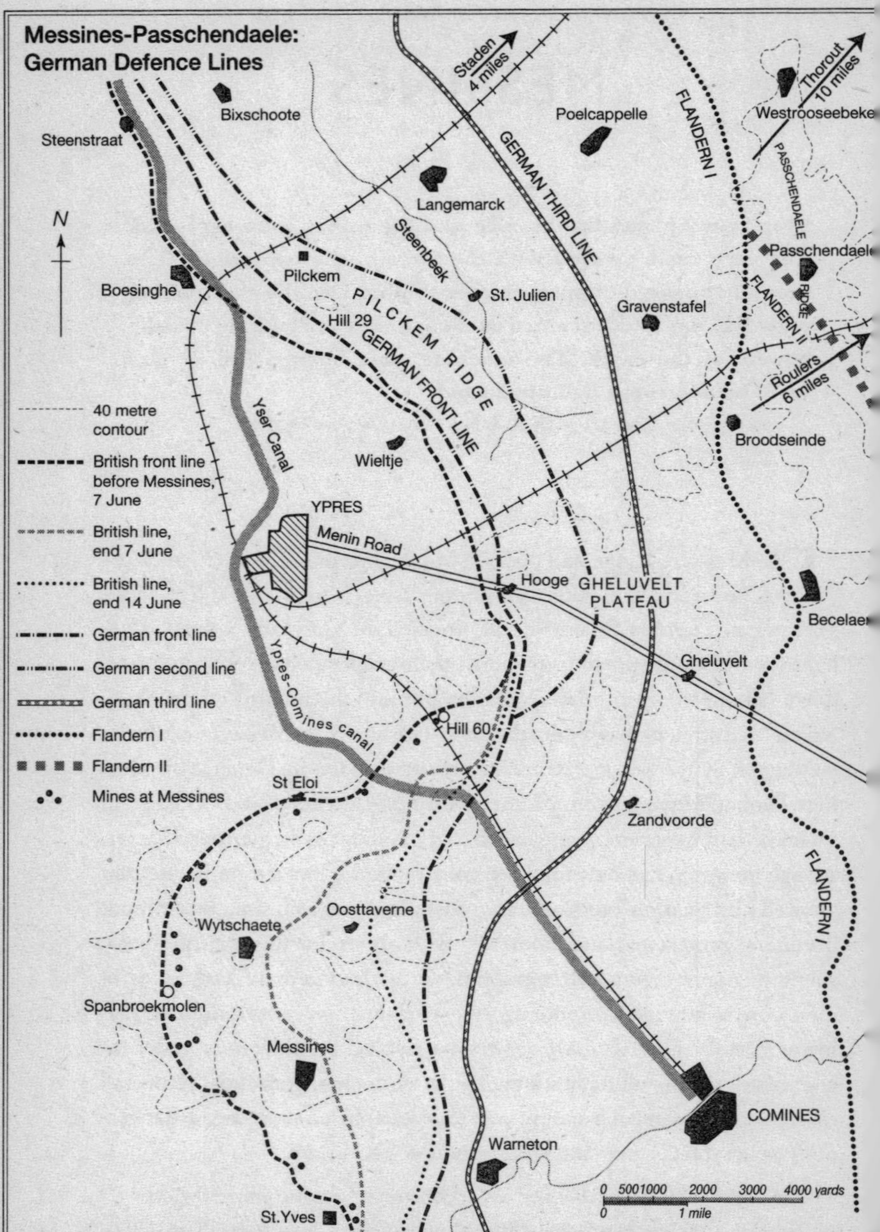

Messines-Passchendaele:
German Defence Lines
Steenstraat
Bixschoote
Staden 4 miles
Poelcappelle
FLANDERN I
Thorout 10 miles
Westroosebeke
Langemarck
GERMAN THIRD LINE
PASSCHENDAELE
Steenbeek
Passchendaele
Pilckem
Boesinghe
St. Julien
Gravenstafel
PILCKEM RIDGE
Hill 29
GERMAN FRONT LINE
FLANDERN II
RIDGE
Roulers 6 miles
Broodseinde
Yser Canal
Wieltje
40 metre contour
British front line before Messines, 7 June
British line, end 7 June
British line, end 14 June
German front line
German second line
German third line
Flandern I
Flandern II
Mines at Messines
YPRES
Menin Road
Hooge
GHELUVELT PLATEAU
Becelaer
Gheluvelt
Ypres-Comines canal
Hill 60
St Eloi
Zandvoorde
FLANDERN I
Oosttaverne
Wytschaete
Spanbroekmolen
Messines
COMINES
Warneton
0 500 1000 2000 3000 4000 yards
0 1 mile
St.Yves

think there's very much wrong with the saluting of the Canadians. Nearly every Canadian I salute returns it!' That brought it to an end.[2]

Major Roderick Macleod, 240th Brigade, Royal Field Artillery

Plumer formed an extremely close and harmonious working relationship with his chief of staff, Major General Charles Harington, also known as Tim, who had been with him since June 1916. Together they had built up a reputation for meticulous preparation and attention to detail in all their headquarters staff work.

They are a wonderful combination, much the most popular, as a team, of any of the Army Commanders. They are the most even-tempered pair of warriors in the whole war or any other war. The troops love them. When a division is rattled for any reason, either because of heavy casualties or because it thinks it has had unfair treatment, it is sent to Second Army and at once becomes as happy as sandboys. The two men are so utterly different in appearance. Plumer, placid and peaceful looking, rather like an elderly grey-moustached Cupid. Harington, always rather fine drawn and almost haggard. Neither has ever been known to lose their temper.[3]

Brigadier General John Charteris, Intelligence Section, GHQ

The seeds of their plan to take the Messines Ridge lay in the series of mines planted under the German front line as early as 1915. These had been assiduously extended over the years until by spring 1917 there were twenty-one mines fully primed for action containing nearly a million pounds of high explosive. At the culmination of a preliminary four-day artillery bombardment, these were finally to be detonated amidst a hurricane of shellfire. At zero hour, nine infantry divisions from the X, IX and II Anzac Corps, supported by seventy-two tanks, would attack on a broad front stretching from Mount Sorrel in the north to St Yves 10 miles to the south. Three further divisions would provide a tactical reserve. An advance of 1,500 yards to capture the German defensive positions on the front crest of the Messines Ridge – or what remained of them – was all that Plumer's original plan for the first day had envisaged. Haig, however, sought to capitalize on the opportunities he felt sure would appear. He insisted that the German second line, based on the back crest of the ridge and the village of Wytschaete, should also be seized in the first thrust. Furthermore, after a short phase of consolidation in the afternoon, the advance was to be continued down the rear slope of the ridge with the intention of capturing the German guns and grabbing the German defensive positions of the Oosttaverne Line. In all this entailed a fairly ambitious advance of some 3,000 yards.

By 1917 the German defences were no longer based on successive lines interlinked by communication trenches and bolstered by occasional strongpoints and switch lines as had been the norm in 1916.

> The course of the Somme battle had also supplied important lessons with respect to the construction and plan of our lines. The very deep underground forts in the front trenches had to be replaced by shallower constructions. Concrete 'pillboxes', which, however, unfortunately took long to build, had acquired an increasing value. The conspicuous lines of trenches, which appeared as sharp lines on every aerial photograph, supplied far too good a target for the enemy artillery. The whole system of defence had to be made broader and looser and better adapted to the ground.[4]
>
> General Erich Ludendorff, German GHQ

As a result, a new and much more flexible format had arisen as the foundation of German tactical defensive thinking.

> In sharp contrast to the form of defence hitherto employed, which had been restricted to rigid and easily recognised lines of little depth, a new system was devised, which, by distribution in depth and the adoption of a loose formation, enabled a more active defence to be maintained. It was of course intended that the position should remain in our hands at the end of the battle, but the infantryman need no longer say to himself: 'Here I must stand or fall,' but had, on the contrary, the right, within certain limits, to retire in any direction before strong enemy fire. Any part of the line that was lost was to be recovered by strong counter-attacks.[5]
>
> General Erich Ludendorff, German GHQ

The forward zone that would inevitably be devastated in any attack was now 'expendable' and to be only lightly held in terms of the number of German troops deployed. However, those holding the forward positions were to be concentrated in a network of strongpoints and machine gun posts, not in formal unified lines, but scattered across the whole of the zone. The forward garrison troops would resist to the utmost of their abilities until they were relieved by local counter-attack troops who would move forward as circumstances dictated to attack the British troops who themselves would be severely disrupted by the interlocking fire from the strongpoints. Behind these German front-line divisions lurked further counter-attack divisions held in reserve specifically to enter the battle wherever required when the British threatened to break through the front-line zone.

Despite the increasing sophistication of the German defences, the techniques employed by the British artillery had also advanced greatly in concept and scale since the early days of the Somme offensive. Gunnery was rapidly becoming a science with the precise weight of shells required to suppress the German artillery and destroy a given yardage of their front line established by a combination of theory and practical experience. The initial success of the Arras operations in April 1917, particularly the spectacular *coup de main* in capturing Vimy Ridge, had shown without doubt what could be achieved against the new pattern of German defences. In essence the plan was simple: the German strongpoints and barbed wire defences were to be swept from the face of the earth by the preliminary bombardment; the front-line troops were to be harassed and exhausted by constant artillery and indirect machine-gun fire on all communication routes; the German artillery was to be engaged from the outset in a duel designed to break their power to respond in any meaningful manner when the attack was launched and finally, when the battle commenced, the counter-attacks were to be broken up by having to pass through a maelstrom of bursting shells from protective barrages which formed a solid screen protecting the new British forward line.

One crucial problem facing the artillery was the difficulty of gaining effective observation of the German hinterland 'over the hill'. The Royal Flying Corps was charged with overcoming the disadvantages of geography by providing aerial reconnaissance and artillery observation. But in spring 1917 the RFC had undergone a severe trial of strength with the German Air Force when their obligations during the Arras offensive had unfortunately coincided with a period of German aerial supremacy. However, the advent of a whole new generation of British aircraft stabilized the position, engendering growing optimism that the tide was turning. Both sides began to concentrate their aerial forces and soon some 500 British and 300 German aircraft faced each other in the Flanders skies. As the reconnaissance aircraft plied their risky trade photographing every inch of ground behind the German lines, the artillery observation machines flew endlessly up and down providing the wireless corrections essential for the gunners below to guide the shells unerringly onto their targets. Meanwhile bombing squadrons targeted the German billets and lines of communication. The main role of the scout squadrons was to stop the opposing German scouts interfering with the British observation aircraft as they flew over the German lines while, at the same time, preventing the German observation machines from crossing the vertical equivalent of the front line.

The total number of guns and howitzers available to Plumer was 2,266. The ordinary field artillery consisted of 1,158 18-pounders and 352 4.5-inch howitzers. These two guns were the workhorses of the British Army throughout the First World War. It was estimated that 341 heavy guns would be required to neutralize the German batteries that had been identified as lying immediately opposite the attack zone or within effective range on the flanks. In addition it was calculated that one medium or heavy howitzer was required for every 45 yards of front, which meant a further 378 guns. Experience had indicated that 5 per cent of the total number of guns should be 'super heavy' pieces, which meant a further thirty-eight of these monster guns should be included in the fire programme. Thus the total requirement for heavy artillery was some 757 guns and Plumer was to be only one gun short when the day arrived.

One by one the batteries were moved into the Messines area with as much secrecy as was possible under the eyes of the Germans on their ridge. The bombardment began on 21 May, increasing gradually in pace and deadly intent. The Germans soon realized that a British offensive was imminent and brought in additional gun batteries until they had some 630 guns in the area. The artillery duel was hard fought, but the British numerical superiority was crucial and as each German battery position was identified they were deluged in high explosive and gas shells until they were well and truly neutralized. Two rehearsals of the final creeping barrage were successful in provoking retaliation from hitherto concealed batteries and they too were eliminated. During this preliminary bombardment 3,561,530 shells were fired. At the same time some 144,000 tons of shrapnel and high-explosive ammunition were laboriously brought up ready for the final effort on 7 June. Each 18-pounder was allotted 1,000 shells, the 4.5-inches had 750 and the heavy guns had 500. This did not include another 180,000 gas and smoke shells. In addition the machine guns and mortars lashed the German positions mercilessly. The exact location of many of the machine-gun posts, strongpoints and local headquarters had been revealed from detailed examination of the RFC aerial reconnaissance photographs and these were the specific targets for the Special Gas Brigade. Livens projectors designed to hurl drums directly into the German front line were installed and camouflaged in narrow trenches behind the front line and then thousands of drums filled with phosgene gas or highly inflammable oil were launched over into the German lines. The deadly gas claimed its victims as men struggled to put on their gas masks, while the exploding oil drums caused further panic amongst the front-line troops.

The artillery plan for 7 June was for the mass of 18-pounders to fire a creeping shrapnel barrage timed to land just in front of the advancing infantry; the rest of the guns and the 4.5-inch howitzers would fire standing barrages on identified German strongpoints some 700 yards ahead of the creeping barrage, lifting onto the next target as the infantry approached within 400 yards of the objective. When each objective was attained the creeping barrage would move forward and settle in position as a protective barrage some 150–300 yards ahead of the new British line to thwart any potential German counter-attacks. Meanwhile over 700 massed machine guns would fire indirectly over the attacking troops, laying down a hail of machine-gun bullets ahead of the creeping barrage. The heavy and super-heavy artillery would lay down standing barrages on the German rear lines and communications.

But it was the mines that made Messines unique. Mines had been used before and indeed many of greatly varying sizes had been exploded before the infantry went over the top on the Somme on 1 July. Yet it is the sheer, unimaginable scale of the explosive force secreted in the galleries under the German lines in the Messines sector that catches the imagination. No one in truth had any real idea of what the effects of such a simultaneous detonation of concentrated mines would be like. They were to find out at 03.10 on 7 June. The first British tunnelling had been started in July 1915, when the 175th Tunnelling Company of the Royal Engineers sank a drift mine in the side of a railway cutting near the front. The mine was aimed directly at the German positions on Hill 60 which lay just to the north of the Messines Ridge.

We just drifted in the hillside in this big cutting that had gone through the hill. It meant we were very deep without sinking for it. It was mainly pick and shovel work, mainly clay. It was good to work in. They used to keep you going with the bags that were being filled. We put a railway track down and all the sandbags were filled and put on the truck. It saved all the dragging of bags and it was quicker. You would get 40 or 50 bags onto an iron-wheeled bogie and bring that out on one run. We pushed it along, it would only be about four feet in height. Mind you, you were doubled over but it was quicker than dragging them out by hand. It was close timbered all the way, bottom, sides and top. You could put it up making very little noise, it fastened itself as the earth fell around it and it didn't need any hammering. Once you'd got it timbered there was no more earth fell in to remove – it was sealed up like being in a box. It was one of the longest tunnels constructed. We had never been so far underground; we were very deep. We were a mile past the German front line when we left it.[6]

Sapper George Clayton, 175th Tunnelling Company, Royal Engineers

These mining operations steadily increased in scale as both sides struggled to establish underground supremacy. Sometimes on detecting German workings a camouflet mine would be hurriedly charged, tamped and exploded in a spur with the intention of directing the explosive force towards the German galleries and destroying them, hopefully without damaging the British tunnels too much.

From the 15th onwards the sound of the enemy's work could be heard with the unaided ear and the position was so critical that orders were given to charge the mine. At 4 a.m. on the 18th with Lieutenant Clinton I took up a position in the chamber and then commenced an endless chain of tins of high explosive which we placed in position. We placed two sets of independent electric leads to the mine and in each set there were 4 detonators in series. While the work of charging the mine was in progress the position became most exciting. The vibrations arising from the enemy's work caused small flakes of clay to fall from the roof of the lightly timbered chamber and we were forced to place sandbags on top of the tins containing the explosive. It seemed that at any moment we could expect the bottom of the enemy's shaft to fall away and precipitate earth and enemy on top of us.[7]

Captain Oliver Woodward, 1st Australian Tunnelling Company, Australian Engineers

Of course the Germans were engaged in exactly the same process and the miners were painfully aware that if they lost the race to detonate the first camouflet, then at any moment they could be overwhelmed as the roof collapsed around them. The tension of this underground battle of wits and nerve was exacerbated by awful working conditions as the miners toiled in the bowels of the Messines Ridge. Tunnels frequently filled with gas, flooded or collapsed even without German intervention. The Germans frantically tried to locate the mineshaft entrances and when they were successful exposed them to heavy shelling. Still the miners grafted on. Tactics evolved as it became obvious that concealment of workings was the most effective defence against counter-mining.

> Spanbroekmolen was the largest mine which I had helped to charge. It was driven 1,707 feet from its entrance, finished off by 171 Tunnelling Company who chambered, charged it and detonated it. Its depth according to the ordnance map was 92 feet – if you added on the rubble on top of an ancient windmill, it was 110 feet! The Germans were down below at 130 and every now and again caused us trouble. The essence of mining in a clay area was silence and secrecy. We wore felt slippers, rubber-wheeled trolleys, wooden rails and we spoke in whispers. When the Germans 'blew' us we never answered back, we suffered casualties and did nothing, tried not to give away where we were. We listened for them with very delicate instruments, the geophone and the Western Electric. One of our officers was once so near to a German sinking shaft that he recorded and translated a series of anecdotes that the German NCO told his shift! [8]
>
> Lieutenant Bryan Frayling, 171st Tunnelling Company, Royal Engineers

As the mines were completed, one by one, they lay *in situ* but dormant for a whole year. This was a further nightmarish problem for the tunnelling officers who had to ensure that the electrical connections were still working, despite the all-pervading dampness, and the charge itself remained in operational order.

> I linked this very large charge not only by electric detonators, but by cordodetonon which is TNT in a lead tube, the first time that that technique was used. I had hoped very, very much that I would push in the switch that blew up Spanbroekmolen, instead I was ordered to get up on Kemmel Hill that night and act as official observer for all the Tunnelling Companies. I had two subalterns with me, we put out lining

sticks on the correct bearings, and waited in pitch dark. My anxiety of course was that some of the mines had been sitting in extremely wet ground for nearly a year and the explosive was ammonol which doesn't go off when it's wet. It was in soldered waterproof tins but we wondered how they'd fared.[9]

Lieutenant Bryan Frayling, 171st Tunnelling Company, Royal Engineers

The British preparations had been impressively thorough, but certainties rarely exist in war and certainly not for the individuals involved in an attack. Just before dawn on 7 June the artillery fire seemed to slacken into an unnatural calm that belied the inner turmoil in the hearts and minds of thousands of soldiers. As the minutes ticked by the men of the 1st Australian Tunnelling Company stood ready to detonate their mine under Hill 60.

Everything was in order. The Commanding Officers had been called back to Headquarters and each one had been issued with a synchronised watch. They were sent back to their units and we went up to the line. Then we were definitely told when it would be, which was 3.10 a.m. on the 7th June. Well, everyone was in a bit of a jitter that morning, we didn't know what was going to happen. The night had been absolutely calm, fewer shots than I'd ever heard.[10]

Sapper Roll, 1st Australian Tunnelling Company, Australian Engineers

Although testing had been more or less continuous, the final connections had to be made and the circuits checked one last time.

I approached the task of final testing with a feeling of intense excitement. With the Wheatstone Bridge on an improvised table, I set out to check the leads and as each one in turn proved correct I felt greatly relieved. At 2.25 a.m. I made the last resistance test and then made the final connections for firing the mines. This was a rather nerve wracking task as one began to feel the strain and wonder whether the leads were correctly joined up. Just before 3 a.m., General Lambart took up his position in the firing dugout. It was his responsibility to give the order, 'Fire!'[11]

Captain Oliver Woodward, 1st Australian Tunnelling Company, Australian Engineers

Two of the mines failed the engineers' tests, but nineteen of the mines were in full working order.

There we were all waiting and ready. We manned our posts about a quarter of an hour before the time. I don't know whether any of you have had to wait a quarter of an hour in a dentist's room – well, this felt four times as long as that. Fifteen minutes to go. We started talking about what we'd do on leave, how was 'Mademoiselle of Armentières', anything we could think of! [12]

Sapper Roll, 1st Australian Tunnelling Company, Australian Engineers

General Lambart began his countdown. After months, even years of preparation and effort, the moment of truth, both for the mines and the men, had finally arrived.

Watch in hand he stood there and in a silence that could almost be felt he said, 'Five minutes to go'. I again finally checked up the leads and Lieutenant Royle and Bowry stood with an exploder at their feet ready to fire should the dynamo fail. Then the General, in what seemed to be interminable periods called out, 'Three minutes to go!' 'Two minutes to go!' 'One minute to go!' [13]

Captain Oliver Woodward, 1st Australian Tunnelling Company, Australian Engineers

Whilst Woodward nervously checked and rechecked his equipment, Lambart's voice counted down to destiny.

Then 45 seconds, 30 seconds, 15 seconds, 10 seconds, 5 seconds, 4, 3, 2, 1 . . . GO![14]

Sapper Roll, 1st Australian Tunnelling Company, Australian Engineers

On receiving the command Woodward reacted instantly, but in his excitement made an elementary mistake.

I grabbed the handle firmly and in throwing the switch over my hand came in contact with the terminals, so that I received a strong shock that threw me backward. For a fraction of a second I failed to realise what had happened, but there was soon joy in the knowledge that Hill 60 mines had done their work.[15]

Captain Oliver Woodward, 1st Australian Tunnelling Company, Australian Engineers

Simultaneously, along the length of the line underneath the Messines Ridge, tunnelling officers detonated their mines. An unprecedented explosion of energy ripped through the earth.

When zero came the first thing we knew was a terrific tremor of the ground, it was quite fantastic. Further down the hill the Commander-in-Chief was in a dugout with lots of steel girders on top of him for safety and we remarked that it must be like dice in a pot being shaken! It was as

> bad as that. After the tremor we saw the flames. I think Kruisstraat was the first, Spanbroekmolen, almost simultaneously with it. A sheet of flame that got tongued in the end. It went up higher than St Paul's – I estimated about 800 feet. It was a white incandescent light, we knew that the temperature was about 3,000 degrees centigrade. The Germans there went up as gas. The biggest bit of German I found afterwards was one foot in a boot. Some of the 'common' mines were much less spectacular, Ontario Farm was a sort of deep orange glow with a lot of smoke. A common mine is a mine so charged that it lifts up the ground and drops it back into the hole it came from. In one of the common mines there were a lot of Germans dropped back and they were alive when one of the chaps went to have a look at them. But before the ambulance men went up they were all dead because of the carbon monoxide gas. Over a range of miles to east and west there was all this lot going up. When the mines went up the first remark made by anybody was the chaplain who said, 'The earth opened and swallowed them up!' [16]
>
> Lieutenant Bryan Frayling, 171st Tunnelling Company, Royal Engineers

At the same moment the guns burst back into life.

> At exactly 3.10 a.m. Armageddon began. The timing of all batteries in the area was wonderful, and to a second every gun roared in one awful salvo. At the same moment the two greatest mines in history were blown up – Hill 60 and one immediately to the south of it. I cleared everyone out of the dugouts and was watching for it. Never could I have imagined such a sight. First, there was a double shock that shook the earth here 15,000 yards away like a gigantic earthquake. I was nearly flung off my feet. Then an immense wall of fire that seemed to go halfway up to heaven. The whole country was lit with a red light like in a photographic darkroom. At the same moment all the guns spoke and the battle began on this part of the line. The noise surpasses even the Somme; it is terrific, magnificent, overwhelming. It makes one almost drunk with exhilaration and one simply does not care about the fact that we are under the concentrated fire of all the Hun batteries. Their shells are bursting round now as I write at 3.40 a.m., but it makes one laugh to think of their feeble little efforts compared to the 'Ausgezeichnete Ausstellung' that we are providing. We are getting our revenge for 1914 with a vengeance.[17]
>
> Major Ralph Hamilton, 106th Brigade, Royal Field Artillery

For the officers responsible for the mathematical precision needed to direct the guns, it was a cathartic release as the guns blazed in unison all along the line.

> What an intoxicating and exhilarating noise is a 'full steam' barrage. It reminds one somehow of the glorious thunder of hoofs down a hard polo ground. Once it had started all cares and troubles vanished, and beyond strolling round to visit each gun there was nothing to do. But the concussion of the myriad guns stirred up all the latent gas lying in the shell holes and that, mixed with the cordite fumes and the dense clouds of dust, made the atmosphere like nothing on earth.[18]
>
> Major Neil Fraser-Tytler, 150th Brigade, Royal Field Artillery

The horrific technology of war moved forward another inevitable step with the firing by the Special Gas Brigade of 300 of the new thermit bombs from Stokes mortars onto what little remained of the German front line. Thermit was a caustic mixture of powdered aluminium and iron oxide which when ignited caused a startling chemical reaction generating thousands of degrees of raw heat as the air bursts scattered the molten metal on the hapless heads of the Germans. Men suffered horrible burns as their clothing caught fire and even wood used as revetting in trenches and dugouts burst into flames; flames which were still burning and smouldering hours later.

> The whole hillside, everything rocked like a ship at sea. The noise from the artillery was deafening, the thunder from our charges was enormous. The infantry dashed forward under a barrage and kept sending back thousands and thousands of prisoners, I couldn't tell you how many. They came back through our dugouts, we saw them and they were absolutely demoralised. We were all so happy that we didn't know what to do! Then when we got a look at the craters there were lumps of blue clay as big as a small building lying about. Our Hill 60 crater was 100 yards across from lip to lip and still 45 yards deep although a lot of the stuff had naturally fallen back into the crater. We thought the war was over.[19]
>
> Sapper Roll, 1st Australian Tunnelling Company, Australian Engineers

Out of the dark, dew-drenched mist the infantry surged forward to their first objectives, encountering minimal resistance from the dazed and confused survivors left alive in the German front-line defence zone.

> There was a fearsome explosion and the ground was rocking to such a degree that one more or less spread-eagled on the ground rather than fall

down. An enormous noise and a blaze of yellow light in every direction. The whole thing was a spectacular show. We then began to dash forward. We reached the lip of this enormous crater and lying around were many German bodies. Later we found a German sergeant major and he told us he'd got a company of 220 men in that area and not one of them had survived this enormous explosion. Those actually near to it still had been blown down and in some cases killed by the force of the explosion. We went round this great crater and then up the pathway through to White Chateau. As we went a bit further along, they began to come out from deep dugouts and throw their stick bombs. I got near enough to the entrance of the dugout to call down to them in German to surrender and they came up, hands up, quite calmly. My little corporal was standing there ushering them out and helping himself to their watches and other equipment – on the basis that somebody would get it and it might as well be him. He was a real Bermondsey boy![20]

Second Lieutenant Arthur Hemsley, 12th Battalion, East Surrey Regiment

Following behind the steadily advancing creeping barrage, the leading troops worked forward, surrounding and isolating remaining strong-points which were then pinched out by mopping-up parties deploying a combination of Lewis gun fire, hand grenades and rifles. With them went the signallers whose task was to maintain communications during the advance.

I was given a job with about 30 signallers from various battalions to go up some mineshaft, directly the mines had blown up, which would take me under our own front line which was by then expected to be bombarded by the enemy and come up the other side of it, to then go and do some signalling. I dressed myself up very carefully and polished my Sam Browne belt to be 'on parade' looking the part of a well-dressed British officer on the occasion – and to impress the Germans suitably if they saw me. At ten minutes past three the mines all went up. I didn't see them going up, because I was somewhere underground. It was like a minor earthquake, the whole ground shook. I went along underneath in a horizontal trench which had been used for mining under the front lines. We came up a mineshaft, vertically, got to the top. When we emerged from the bowels of the earth there was a very grim sight. The Headquarters of the 7th Battalion, The Leinster Regiment had just received a shell to itself and there were a number of casualties in a very

> confined space. There was one officer there – a very good Irish chaplain called Father Rafter who must have been nearer 60 than 50 – a very good chap. He made the classic remark to me, 'Jourdain, have a drink!' It was the most sensible remark a man could have made.[21]
>
> Lieutenant F. W. S. Jourdain, 6th Battalion, Connaught Rangers

The lumbering tanks also moved off. Their initial approach to the line had been masked by the sound of low-flying aircraft cruising above the German lines.

> Our officer made us get out of the tank and get in a little slit trench at the side of the Australians. The bombardment started and the mines went up. It was a tremendous crash – we saw all the flames. We jumped in the tank and off we went and as we went the mist got lighter and the Australians, there was no holding them, they were gone. But we caught them up. We were sailing along nicely when all of a sudden there was a tremendous thump right in the belly of the tank, outside. A shell had hit our tank. I was the second driver so the other chap was driving. I sat there pulling the gears in for when they wanted to turn. The place was full of smoke, gas and everything else – but the shell didn't come through. The bottoms of the tanks were steel – it bent that up about two and half feet. This chap on the six-pounder, he stood there, he'd got hit and it had fetched two great lumps out of his hand. The next chap standing with the machine gun, his leg was black. The officer shouted, 'See if you can get any stretcher bearers!' We didn't know where we were. It was all smoke, terrible inside the tank, we didn't know who else was hit. But that's all the damage it had done – if it had gone through I shouldn't have been here now. It hit like a glancing blow, bent it up. We couldn't open the door, we tried, we were in a trap until another man came and we opened it. There happened to be stretcher bearers and they came and took these two chaps out, put them on the stretcher. We closed the door again and the officer said, 'See if we can start the engine, we're going to carry on!' They started the engine again. I was as white as a sheet so they told me. I should think I was as well! We carried on, quietly. The Germans had run like rabbits when the mine went up. At last we came to the mine, we were about 20 yards away. Everywhere was quiet. Thompson said, 'We'll get out and have a look!' We all got out of the tank and walked over to this huge crater. You'd never seen anything like the size of it; you'd never think that explosives would do it. But I saw about 150 Germans laid there, in different positions, throwing a bomb, a

gun on their shoulder, all laid there dead. The mine had killed them. The crew stood there for about five minutes and looked. It made us think. That mine had won the battle before it started. We looked at each other as we came away and the sight of it remained with you always. To see them all laid there with their eyes open.[22]

Private Frederick Collins, B Battalion, Tank Corps

The first objectives were captured in accordance with the artillery timetable and the infantry pushed on towards the forward crest of the Messines Ridge. The veritable fortress that was the village of Messines itself was taken after a brutish but short engagement and although more resistance was encountered the troops seemed to be all but unstoppable. By 05.00 the German defensive positions all along the ridge had been captured.

It was just like a field day, everything seemed to go according to plan. Streams of German prisoners kept on coming back. In the early part of the day I had a little local difficulty with my signallers who got hold of a jar of rum from somewhere or other and were beginning to help themselves to it at about 08.00 with potentially disastrous results. I did the bravest thing I ever have done because I got hold of that said jar of rum and poured it on the ground with about 50 or 60 Irish soldiers! They made suitable noises but I lived to tell the tale. The signallers did not mutiny but did their stuff for the rest of the day and as a result collected one DCM and ten MMs between them![23]

Lieutenant F. W. S. Jourdain, 6th Battalion, Connaught Rangers

A short pause allowed the troops to consolidate whilst their protective artillery barrages shredded the ground ahead of them to rule out all possibility of an effective German counter-attack.

The pace of our fire varied according to what was going on, e.g., during the periods of consolidation of each captured line, it would drop to a round per gun per minute, which gave us the chance of resting the guns and doing small repairs. Then as soon as the Infantry were ready to move on the barrage reformed in front of them, and having gradually worked up to intense, crept forward once more.[24]

Major Neil Fraser-Tytler, 150th Brigade, Royal Field Artillery

Fresh battalions moved forward and a new creeping barrage crashed out to support them in the next phase of the attack launched at 07.00.

The German soldiers encountered that morning appeared to be unable to cope with the sheer enormity of what was happening to them. Physically shocked and transfixed by the mines and shells, harassed by low-flying RFC aircraft spitting machine-gun bullets, they were in no competent mental state to provide the sort of coherent organized opposition that would have held up the advancing British troops and as a result they surrendered in droves. The fortified village of Wytschaete, which had been almost razed to the ground, was quickly over-run and by 09.00 the British front line had crossed the crest and was moving down the eastern slopes. Artillery observation parties were afforded the rare privilege of an unfettered view of the German rear areas.

> We spotted a German battery down in the valley and it had just got all their horses up and was going to pull out. We ran through to Brigade Headquarters and got every gun we possibly could on them. It was all synchronised together. We opened out and I don't think there was a damned horse or man got out – we just shot them right up. It was terrible, terrible – flashes, dust and rubble.[25]
>
> Signaller Jim Crow, 110th Brigade, Royal Field Artillery

Another phase of consolidation was completed before the final attack timed for 15.10 was launched to capture the Oosttaverne Line. Yet still no German counter-attack materialized, as their reserve divisions had been located so far back that they were unable to intervene in time. Those minor attacks that did occur were almost effortlessly swatted aside by the combined power of concentrated machine-gun and artillery fire.

Ironically, British casualties were beginning to mount due to the very success of the attack. Estimates of over 50 per cent losses in the initial phases had been widely out and there was consequently considerable congestion as the infantry milled about on top of the ridge which rendered them vulnerable to what remained of the German artillery. Furthermore, the confusions of war meant that the situation on the far side of the ridge was unclear to the British artillery and their support began to lose some of its former precision. As a result some shells fell short and on several occasions bombardments were actually directed in error onto British formations. Despite these problems most of the Oosttaverne Line was safely in British hands before nightfall and after further tidying-up operations the whole of the British objectives were attained by 14 June.

The attack on Messines was a *pièce de résistance* of methodical generalship. The German fortress looming over the southern plane of the Ypres Salient had been taken. No fewer than 7,354 German prisoners were captured along with 48 guns, 218 machine guns and 60 trench mortars. Meticulous planning, marked by obsessive attention to detail, had been coupled with dogged hard graft by thousands of men over the years of preparation. All this had culminated in an attack designed to achieve limited objectives that could be measured in just two or three thousand yards. It was as far removed as possible from the sweeping arrows promising fantastic breakthroughs which had scorched across Rawlinson and Haig's maps depicting the Somme battlefield just a year before. There were no false visions at Messines of cavalry troopers ransacking their way to Berlin. Prosaic it may have been – but it worked. However, the inevitable temptation to capitalize as much as possible on the labour invested in the plans meant that although few casualties were lost in the actual capture of the ridge itself, the attempt to seize the Oosttaverne Line, instigated by Haig, ultimately saddled the operations with a heavier casualties bill than would otherwise have been necessary, totalling over 24,500 in all. Nevertheless, the Battle of Messines stands out as a testament to the value of hard work and limited ambition.

CHAPTER THREE

PLANS AND PREPARATIONS

If our resources are concentrated in France to the fullest possible extent, the British Armies are capable and can be relied on to effect great results this summer – results which will make final victory more assured and which may even bring it within reach this year.[1]

Field Marshal Sir Douglas Haig, GHQ

After Messines Sir Douglas Haig originally intended a further strike, if possible, while the iron was still hot. He wanted the triumphant storming of the ridge to be immediately exploited by an attempt to seize the western portion of the Gheluvelt Plateau to give Gough the best possible start in his offensive. It offered, in theory at least, a broken German flank south of Ypres, a point of weakness, which might crumble if an attack was launched before they could properly revise their defensive arrangements. In response to Haig's expressed intention, Plumer intended the II and VIII Corps to advance some 1,200 yards across the Gheluvelt Plateau to seize the high ground around Westhoek, but on 8 June he asked Haig for a further three days to allow for the transfer of the all-important medium and heavy artillery from Messines to the Salient. This was not an unreasonable request and indeed he may have been erring a little on the optimistic side given the inherent difficulties in moving, siting and registering guns in the battlefield conditions that existed in the Salient. Yet Haig rejected the request and immediately handed over control of the II and VIII Corps to Gough to form part of his Fifth Army. Gough was inherently sceptical of the possibilities for a 'rushed' attack and requested a delay while he examined the scheme. Perversely Haig allowed this, even though it meant a greater total delay than Plumer had indicated might be

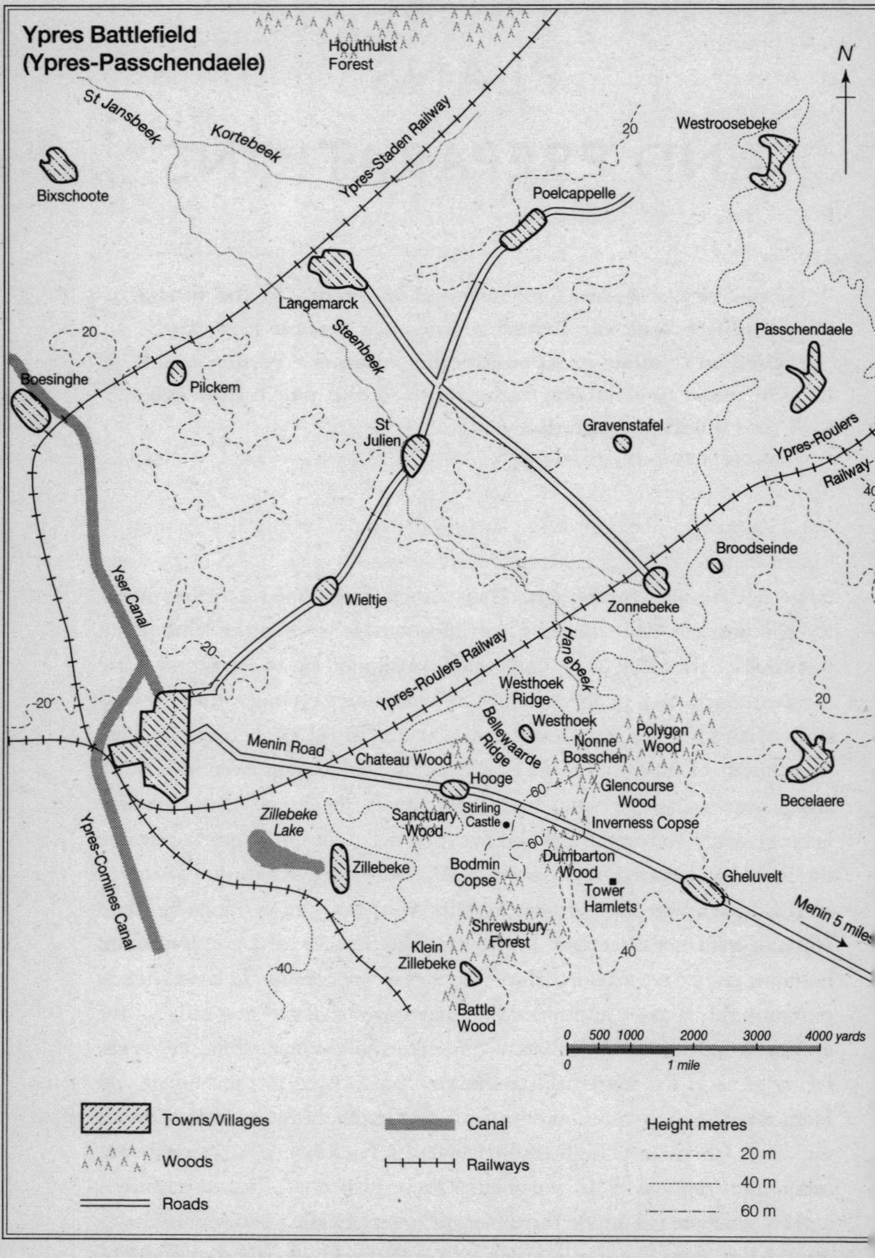
Ypres Battlefield
(Ypres-Passchendaele)
Houthulst
Forest
N
St Jansbeek
Kortebeek
Ypres-Staden Railway
20
Westroosebeke
Bixschoote
Poelcappelle
Langemarck
20
Steenbeek
Passchendaele
Boesinghe
Pilckem
Gravenstafel
St
Julien
Ypres-Roulers
Railway
40
Broodseinde
Yser Canal
Wieltje
Zonnebeke
Ypres-Roulers Railway
Hanebeek
20
20
Westhoek
Ridge
20
Westhoek
Bellewaarde
Ridge
Polygon
Wood
Nonne
Bosschen
Menin Road
Chateau Wood
Hooge
Glencourse
Wood
Becelaere
60
Stirling
Castle
Inverness Copse
Sanctuary
Wood
Zillebeke
Lake
60
Dumbarton
Wood
Zillebeke
Bodmin
Copse
Tower
Hamlets
Gheluvelt
Ypres-Comines Canal
Shrewsbury
Forest
Menin 5 miles
Klein
Zillebeke
40
40
Battle
Wood
0 500 1000 2000 3000 4000 yards
0 1 mile
Towns/Villages
Woods
Roads
Canal
Railways
Height metres
20 m
40 m
60 m

needed. Gough had only shifted his headquarters from Arras to take formal command of the Ypres front on 10 June. Though he duly considered the proposals as best he could, given his unfamiliarity with the ground, his heart was not really in it. In the end he decided not to pursue it, as he did not want to push his troops into what would in effect be a further exposed salient pushed out from a salient. After all, he considered, the Gheluvelt Plateau would be captured in the main offensive when it came.

This failure to exploit the flickering opportunity opened up by the capture of Messines is frequently regarded as a blunder; but exploitation is a difficult concept to differentiate from rashness. The extra push to seize the Oosttaverne Line following the capture of the Messines Ridge is often seen by the selfsame critics as provoking needless casualties by 'over-egging the pudding'. The eternal verities of warfare mean that artillery and troops cannot be effortlessly switched between battlefields; defences do not necessarily crumble by some process of osmosis and a successful frontal assault in one part of the line does not predicate success in another frontal assault a few miles away in different tactical circumstances. In essence, Haig was probably perfectly right in prodding his commanders to try and get what he could from the situation as it developed in Flanders, but his subordinates' caution was equally justified.

The great offensive at Ypres was now all that remained of the Allied strategy as defined at the Paris Conference of May 1917. However, since the number of mutinies in the French Army had risen quickly with some eighty serious 'acts of collective indiscipline' between 25 May and 10 June, Pétain was determined to nurse his grievously wounded forces back into rude health before exposing them to further risk and he was forced to admit to Haig that he would be unable to launch the supporting offensives scheduled for the summer. This activated the concern of the War Cabinet who on 16 May had tied permission to proceed with the Flanders offensive to full-blooded French co-operation. A special Cabinet War Policy Committee was established to review the situation, consisting of David Lloyd George, Lord Milner, Lord Curzon, Sir Andrew Bonar Law and Lieutenant General Jan Christian Smuts. This Committee held an extensive series of meetings in June to which the service experts were invited to contribute their specialist knowledge as appropriate. These discussions went to the heart of the British strategic dilemma in the middle of 1917. The French were in a seriously debilitated state and any British operations would have to be carried out virtually independently. Yet not to proceed risked exposing the French weakness.

Haig, in preparing his positional paper for the Cabinet War Policy Committee, was heavily influenced by a series of Intelligence Reports provided by the chief of his GHQ Intelligence Section, Brigadier General John Charteris. These reports were essentially optimistic in outlook, as Charteris was convinced that the after-effects of the Somme offensive, coupled with the German casualties during the spring offensives of 1917, were seriously draining Germany's reserves of manpower. This, he believed, could not be completely offset by the possible transfer of divisions from the Eastern Front due to the enfeebled state of revolution-torn Russia.

> It is a fair deduction that, given a continuance of the existing circumstances and of the effort of the Allies, Germany may well be forced to conclude a peace on our terms before the end of the year.[2]
>
> Brigadier General John Charteris, Intelligence Section, GHQ

It is indisputable that this intelligence appreciation greatly influenced Haig in his belief that Germany was near to collapse and it underpinned his whole strategy throughout 1917. As he reported to the Cabinet War Policy Committee:

> The German Army, too, shows unmistakeable signs of deterioration in many ways and the cumulative effort of further defeats may at any time yield greater results in the field than we can absolutely rely on gaining.[3]
>
> Field Marshal Sir Douglas Haig, GHQ

He went on to warn that a relaxation of the intense Allied effort in 1917 could lead to a German revival and a corresponding increase in Allied vulnerability.

> Waning hope in Germany would be revived, and time would be gained to replenish food, ammunition and other requirements. In fact many of the advantages already gained by us would be lost, and this would certainly be realised by, and would have a depressing effect on, our Armies in the field, who have made such great efforts to gain them. The depressing effect in France would be especially great and especially dangerous. At the present crisis of the war French hope must have something to feed on. The hope of American assistance is not sufficient for the purpose. It is still too far distant and the French at the moment

> are living a good deal on the hope of further British successes. They can and will assist in these by keeping the enemy on their front fully employed, wearing him down, and preventing him from withdrawing divisions to oppose us. But they feel unable to do more at present than this, and it is useless to expect it of them – although any considerable British successes and signs of a breakdown in the German power of resistance would probably have an electrifying effect.[4]
>
> Field Marshal Sir Douglas Haig, GHQ

He further expressed absolute confidence in his ability to deliver such a success as long as British strength was not dissipated on other campaigns away from the Western Front.

> If our resources are concentrated in France to the fullest possible extent, the British Armies are capable and can be relied on to effect great results this summer – results which will make final victory more assured and which may even bring it within reach this year. On the other hand, I am equally convinced that to fail in concentrating our resources in the Western theatre, or to divert them from it, would be most dangerous. It might lead to the collapse of France. It would certainly encourage Germany. And it would discourage our own officers and men very considerably. The desired military results, possible in France, are not possible elsewhere.[5]
>
> Field Marshal Sir Douglas Haig, GHQ

With hindsight it can be seen that Haig's conclusions were based on an over-optimistic appreciation of the immediate effects of what was, more accurately, a desperate long-term strategic situation for the Germans. However, at the War Office the Director of Military Intelligence reporting direct to Sir William Robertson had drawn the exact opposite conclusions from the intelligence his department had amassed. It was his opinion that the release of German divisions from the Russian front would allow the Germans to gain an actual superiority in both raw numbers and artillery on the Western Front in 1917.

> It is obvious that offensive operations on our front would offer no chance of success; and our best course would be to remain on the defensive, strengthen our positions, economise our reserves in manpower and material, and hope that the balance would be eventually redressed by American assistance.[6]
>
> Major General Sir George Macdonogh, Director of Military Intelligence, War Office

In this clash of the intelligence chiefs, Haig loyally backed his own man, Charteris, and must thus bear the responsibility for the effects that his faulty appreciation had on his conduct of operations in 1917. However, it was Macdonogh's report that was passed to the War Cabinet and Robertson offered Haig sage advice in presenting his case.

> Don't argue that you can finish the War this year or that the German is already beaten, but argue that your plan is the best plan.[7]
>
> General Sir William Robertson, Chief of Imperial General Staff, War Office

Noticing the discrepancy between the overall tone of Haig's positional paper and the Macdonogh intelligence report, Lloyd George emerged from his chastened post-Nivelle state to launch another broadside against the 'Westerners'.

> The Cabinet must regard themselves as trustees for the fine fellows that constitute our army. They are willing to face any dangers, and they do so without complaint, but they trust to the leaders of the nation to see that their lives are not needlessly thrown away, and that they are not sacrificed on mere gambles which are resorted to merely because those who are directing the War can think of nothing better to do with the men under their command. It is therefore imperative that before we embark upon a gigantic attack which must necessarily entail the loss of scores of thousands of valuable lives, and produce that sense of discouragement which might very well rush nations into premature peace, that we should feel a fair confidence that such an attack has a reasonable chance of succeeding. A mere gamble would be both a folly and a crime.[8]
>
> David Lloyd George, Prime Minister

Here then was the nub. Lloyd George considered Haig's plan an irresponsible gamble based on optimistic intelligence reports.

> It is therefore proposed that we should rush into the greatest battle of the War, against an enemy almost equal in number, quite equal in equipment, still the greatest army in Europe in everything that constitutes an efficient fighting force, with larger reserves than our own, to make up the deficiency during this year, holding formidable defensive positions which he has taken three years to strengthen and to perfect; and we are to launch this attack with doubtful support from our most powerful and important ally.[9]
>
> David Lloyd George, Prime Minister

Even the successes achieved by the new British offensive tactics, used first at Vimy Ridge and more recently at Messines, did not allay his fears.

> I ask whether the CIGS anticipates anything better than Vimy and Messines can ensue as the result of this attack. Brilliant preliminary successes followed by weeks of desperate and sanguinary struggles, leading to nothing except perhaps the driving of the enemy back a few barren miles – beyond that nothing to show except a ghastly casualty list.[10]
>
> David Lloyd George, Prime Minister

With reasonable logic Lloyd George argued that if attacks were to be made on the Western Front, he wanted them to be limited to swift surprise strikes to cause maximum casualties and damage to the Germans with minimum British casualties. However, he fatally undermined this position by re-submitting his strategic 'red herring' of reinforcing the Italians, mainly with heavy artillery rather than masses of troops, for an assault intended to knock Austria-Hungary out of the war. Once again Haig and Robertson made short work of this proposal, and trotted out their usual arguments pointing out the key importance of the Western Front and the sheer unfeasibility of the Italian option. Haig further reiterated his view that Germany was near to collapse and that they could not transfer enough divisions from the Eastern to the Western Front in time to affect his summer plans. He also insisted that he intended to proceed in a flexible 'step by step' approach allowing operations to be suspended if there appeared to be little chance of success.

The debate in the Cabinet War Policy Committee was thus hanging in the balance when the Government's leading naval adviser, Admiral Sir John Jellicoe, the First Sea Lord, made a dramatic intervention that explicitly outlined the direct threat to Britain's security caused by the resumption of the German campaign of unrestricted submarine warfare in February 1917.

> It was necessary to be very outspoken to the War Cabinet on the subject of the submarine danger even at the risk of being accused of pessimistic views, for it was very difficult during the first half of 1917 to get the magnitude of the danger realised. The facts of the situation had to be faced, and faced boldly, not ignored or minimised. There was a tendency in high quarters to ignore the danger and to delay taking the action necessary to meet it.[11]
>
> Admiral Sir John Jellicoe, First Sea Lord

The German submarine offensive had been biting increasingly deep into British reserves of shipping and the steady inexorable erosion of Britain's traditional maritime strength had placed Jellicoe under severe pressure. Losses were tremendous and he made clear his deeply pessimistic outlook.

> A most serious and startling situation was disclosed today. At today's Conference, Admiral Jellicoe, as First Sea Lord, stated that owing to the great shortage of shipping due to German submarines, it would be impossible for Great Britain to continue the war in 1918. This was a bombshell for the Cabinet and all present. A full enquiry is to be made as to the real facts on which this opinion of the Naval Authorities is based. No-one present shared Jellicoe's view, and all seemed satisfied that the food reserves in Great Britain are adequate. Jellicoe's words were, 'There is no good discussing plans for next Spring – we cannot go on.'[12]
>
> Field Marshal Sir Douglas Haig, GHQ

It should be borne in mind that this was in essence merely re-stating, in somewhat extreme terms, the long-standing Admiralty policy. Certainly Haig and Lloyd George, from their radically different perspectives, both thought that Jellicoe was exaggerating. Nevertheless, coming as it did from the nation's most senior naval officer, this revelation had a dramatic effect on the Committee and undoubtedly influenced the discussions that followed. In the end neither side was able to claim victory. Smuts and Curzon supported Haig, whilst Milner and Bonar Law travelled with Lloyd George, but all hesitated to overrule their senior service advisers. After a considerable delay, the result was a compromise. On 20 July the Flanders offensive was finally given explicit War Cabinet approval, but only on the condition that it would be called off *if* the first stages did not come up to expectations. In that event Haig was to make all necessary arrangements to support an Italian offensive. By this means the War Cabinet intended to keep strategic control over the whole operation. Having agreed this caveat the real question was whether they would have the nerve to take action if, and when, the going got tough.

THROUGHOUT ALL the protracted and bitter discussions the preparations had been proceeding apace at Ypres. When Gough had handed over his responsibilities at Arras, the troops formerly under his command were transferred to the Third Army under General Sir Julian Byng. Gough's 'new' Fifth Army in Flanders consisted of the XIV Corps (Guards, 20th, 29th and 38th Divisions); the XVIII Corps (11th, 39th, 48th and 51st Divisions); the XIX Corps (15th, 16th, 36th and 55th Divisions) and the II Corps (8th, 18th, 25th and 30th Divisions). Two further 'Corps' were kept in reserve: the VIII Corps (61st Division) and the V Corps (56th Division). To the left of the Fifth Army was the French First Army whilst on their right was Plumer's Second Army. Rawlinson's Fourth Army retained responsibility for the coastal operations that would only be triggered by a successful advance to the Roulers–Staden Ridge. Until then the Fourth Army was to remain on standby.

Even without their view from the Messines Ridge, the Germans still had excellent observation into the Ypres Salient from the Pilckem Ridge and the Gheluvelt Plateau. They could not help but be aware of the movements of troops and artillery taking place below them and the time allowed for offensive preparations proved equally valuable to the Germans for strengthening their defences. The German defensive principles had not at this point changed since the débâcle they had suffered at Messines. The front line and thinly defended forward zone stretched along the Pilckem Ridge and across the westward fringes of the Gheluvelt Plateau. Behind this was a Second Line sited on the reverse slope of the Pilckem Ridge and running across the centre of the Gheluvelt Plateau. This marked the start of the battle zone stretching back to the Third Line that ran along the lower slopes and spurs of the Passchendaele Ridge and across the eastern half of the Gheluvelt Plateau. Finally, the rear zone lay between the Third Line and the Flanders I Line that ran along the front of the Passchendaele Ridge and the rear of the Gheluvelt Plateau. Behind this, protecting the approaches to Menin and Roulers, there still lay the new Flanders II and Flanders III Lines. The Germans used the time to construct yet more extra defensive lines and create in effect two super fortresses out of the key Gheluvelt Plateau and the Houthulst Forest which protected the northern approaches to the Passchendaele Ridge. If these two bulwarks could survive relatively intact on either side of the British axis of advance, then it would in effect drive itself into an even worse salient. Furthermore, the German artillery batteries concentrated on the rear slopes of the Gheluvelt Plateau would remain easily within range to offer support for any German counter-attacks.

The Germans worked hard to increase massively the number of strong-points littered across the whole of the defensive lines. These largely took the form of newly built concrete pillboxes and heavily fortified existing farm buildings. The pillboxes were to be the *bête noire* of the British infantry. Their low elevation made them a difficult target for artillery operating at long range, whilst their reinforced concrete construction meant that, even when they did suffer a direct hit, they were not necessarily put out of action. Just a few German soldiers armed with a machine gun in one of these pillboxes could hold up a considerable body of troops. Each one was meticulously sited to provide mutual support and together could combine to create a deadly pattern of interlocking fire. They were intended to act as a focus for the initial resistance of the defending troops, designed to break up the flow of the British attacks and render them vulnerable to the German counter-attack divisions when they finally arrived from their billets away from all but the longest-range British guns. In essence, the German intention was to ensure that the attacking British troops faced increasingly strong resistance the further they got from the support and security of their guns.

Gough and his chief of staff, Major General Neill Malcolm, set to work on refining the outline scheme that had been passed to them by Haig and GHQ. The original plan developed by Plumer and Rawlinson had intended an initial advance on the first day of about a mile to the German Second Line, thus overrunning the Pilckem Ridge and gaining a foothold on the Gheluvelt Plateau. There was then to be a two-day pause to allow the field artillery to move forward to ensure the same power of bombardment before the next leap forward. This was deemed too slow by Gough the 'thruster'. Instead he planned to telescope the whole attack into one day with only short breaks between each stage to allow consolidation and reorganization before the next thrust forward. The first stage would take the German front line along the Pilckem Ridge and establish the British on the Gheluvelt Plateau (this advance was later identified in the orders and on the maps as the Blue Line objective). After a pause of just thirty minutes, the advance would resume to capture the German Second Line on the reverse slopes of the Pilckem Ridge and push further across the Gheluvelt Plateau (the Black Line). There would then be a four-hour gap to allow some of the artillery to move forward before the third phase advanced the British line across the Steenbeek Valley and the Gheluvelt Plateau to the German Third Line (the Green Line). At this point, local divisional commanders were to use their own powers of judgement to determine whether further advances were feasible with a view to moving up onto the main Passchendaele Ridge as far as Langemarck and Broodseinde (the Red Line). This extended the advance anticipated on the first day to a massive 5,000 yards which meant that the final stages would be well beyond the range of most of the supporting artillery. After a three- or four-day interval the next attack would seize control of the whole Passchendaele–Staden Ridge.

Haig approved these plans but, fresh from the grilling that had been meted out to him by Lloyd George at the Cabinet War Policy Committee, even he sounded a clear note of caution at Gough's vaulting ambitions for the advances on the first day. One of his senior staff officers cogently expressed such doubts in a memorandum and recommended that the Black Line objectives would be quite far enough for the first day in what, after all, was supposed to be a limited, staged offensive and not an attempt at a breakthrough.

> We should not attempt to push infantry to the maximum distance to which we can hope to get them by means of our artillery fire, our tanks, and the temporary demoralisation of the enemy. Experience shows that such action may, and often does, obtain spectacular results for the actual day of operations, but these results are obtained at the expense of such disorganisation of the forces employed as to render the resumption of the battle under advantageous circumstances at an early date highly improbable. An advance which is essentially deliberate and sustained may not achieve such important results during the first day of operations, but will in the long run be much more likely to obtain a decision. By a deliberate and sustained advance, I refer to a succession of operations each at two or three days' interval, each having as its object the capture of the enemy's defences, strongpoints, or tactical features, to a depth of not less than 1,500 yards and not more than 3,000 yards. It has been proved beyond doubt that with sufficient and efficient artillery preparation we can push our infantry through to a depth of a mile without undue losses or disorganisation.[13]
>
> Brigadier General John Davidson, Operations Section, GHQ

In other words, it was the effort to go the extra mile that both caused the bulk of the casualties and so disorganized the troops that the German counter-attack divisions were then able to strike them when they were at their most vulnerable – which, as has been noted, lay at the heart of the

German defensive plan. Davidson also commented that in undertaking a deliberate and limited advance:

> Since the zone of preparation will not be so deep, the artillery fire for the purposes of destruction will be more concentrated.[14]
>
> Brigadier General John Davidson, Operations Section, GHQ

This was a crucial point. The degree of concentration of artillery fire was of paramount importance, particularly given the nature of the German defences, reliant as they were on numerous pillboxes spread out across the battle zones. In trying to advance double the distance Gough was, crudely speaking, halving the number of shells falling in the vicinity of each pillbox or fortified farmhouse in the contested area during the preliminary and opening bombardments. This in fact meant that he was correspondingly less likely to succeed in capturing any of his objectives.

Davidson's memorandum was circulated amongst Gough's Corps commanders of which one, Lieutenant General Sir Ivor Maxse, wrote vigorous marginal comments on his copy, still preserved in the Imperial War Museum. Maxse took issue with almost every point raised by Davidson.

> No: the battle is not resumed by the same troops! You cannot do it in three days either!! What about communication trenches? . . . But suppose the Hun has fled from the 'next zone' as at Arras? Are we not to occupy it? . . . Yes, but it will not kill so many Huns? . . . Yes, but limiting the objective to 2,000 yards will not much reduce ragged fronts. They are caused by obstinate Huns or by weak British leadership. . . . He will go 'Scot free' on first day!! . . . The time when we can take most risks and with greatest results in Hun casualties is at the end of the first day's successful assault.[15]
>
> Lieutenant General Sir Ivor Maxse, Headquarters, XVIII Corps

He summed up his opinion on Davidson's carefully considered paper, rather vulgarly, in a single word – 'Balls!!' Gough, too, was unmoved by the arguments for caution on the first day.

> Should we go as far as we can the first day, viz: certainly up to the Green Line, and possibly the Red Line, or should we confine ourselves to the Black Line on the first day and attack again in three days to gain the Green Line, and again to gain the Red Line at a further interval of three days? It is important to recognise that the results to be looked for from a well organised attack which has taken weeks and months to prepare are great, much ground can be gained, and prisoners and guns captured

during the first day or two. After the first attack, long prepared, one cannot hope to gain similar results in one attack as long as the enemy can find fresh reserves, and the depth of ground gained and guns captured usually decline in subsequent attacks. I think therefore it would be wasteful not to reap all the advantages possible resulting from the first attack. If we only go as far as the Black Line on the first day and then make two more attacks with intervals on the Green and Red Lines, we would have to move many guns at least twice instead of only once as would be the case if we can take the Red Line on the first day.[16]

General Sir Hubert Gough, Headquarters, Fifth Army

To which remarks Maxse enthusiastically commented in the margins of his copy, 'Hear, hear!!'[17] Yet Gough and Maxse were not by any standard fools – they had clear military reasons for their opinions based on their hard-won practical experience. Maxse, who was one of the most outstanding divisional and corps commanders of the war, had a particular interest in the minutiae of tactics and had already won a formidable reputation as a brilliant trainer of the men in his command. He was definitely not some reactionary old buffer baffled by proposals far beyond his intellectual grasp. On the contrary, he had been deeply concerned at the lost opportunities at the start of the Battle of Arras and sought to use that hard-won experience to avoid making the same mistakes in Flanders.

After discussing these issues face to face with Plumer and Gough, Haig seems to have accepted Gough's viewpoint that it was worth trying to seize as much ground as possible on the first day. In this he was undoubtedly influenced by his core belief that the Germans were approaching a state of collapse. However, Haig had his own reservations about the proposed conduct of operations. Gough envisaged an attack spread evenly all along the Pilckem Ridge and across the Gheluvelt Plateau. There was no concentration of extra divisions or artillery to help smash through the intimidating series of German defences criss-crossing the Gheluvelt Plateau. Haig therefore re-emphasized the vital importance of the Plateau but, despite this, Gough failed to alter his dispositions and Haig failed to pursue the point. This lapse in command authority was to prove crucial.

GOUGH PREPARED his troops for battle in a thoroughly meticulous manner, attempting to use all the lessons so expensively learnt in the previous three years. It may have taken time, but there is no doubt that by 1917 almost all senior commanders and their staffs understood the absolute necessity for detailed preparations and extensive tactical training.

> General principles for the conduct of the troops in the battle were elaborated, and a very clear distinction was made between the necessity and importance of quickness and initiative by subordinate commanders in seizing unoccupied tactical points or those which were only lightly held, and the totally different situation which arises when the enemy is holding his ground strongly. Here impetuous and disordered action was to be avoided and every step forward was to be the result of thorough preparation and organisation, which might require intervals of from three to seven days.[18]
>
> General Sir Hubert Gough, Headquarters, Fifth Army

The problem for Gough's subordinate commanders was the near impossibility of determining in the heat of battle exactly where the German lines were and whether or not strongpoints were destroyed, dormant or active. At corps and divisional headquarters, large-scale models were prepared of the local front lines illustrating the exact location of identified German fortifications.

> Models enabled the leaders of the attacking troops to know the ground over which they were to advance, to recognise where they were, and the objectives they were to seize. They were made of earth, and compiled from air photographs strictly to scale. Any features still standing, as well as the trenches, were accurately copied. We found this method of showing the leaders what they might expect to see and what they had to do was very helpful.[19]
>
> General Sir Hubert Gough, Headquarters, Fifth Army

The models offered a chance for men to grasp the interrelationship between topography and man-made defences; to see the contours and lines hitherto only previously seen in one dimension on maps made 'flesh'.

> We went past the model of the 'advance' area – a huge model of the area covered by my map all done to scale by the Royal Engineers and with a staging round it from which a whole company could be lectured at a time. The children at home would have loved to have seen the trenches, farms, cottages and water all done in miniature.[20]
>
> Reverend Maurice Murray, 12th & 13th Battalions, Royal Sussex Regiment

The necessity for secrecy was impressed on all ranks and had amusing consequences on at least one occasion when Maxse was making a tour of the scale model of the trenches.

> In the course of this instruction a young Second Lieutenant was conducting his platoon round these trenches when he met a General Officer with every outward sign of high rank, and a pleasant and attractive manner. After a few words the General asked the subaltern what part he was taking in the scheme. 'Very sorry, Sir, I'm afraid I can't tell you. Commanding Officer's orders and I don't know you.' 'But you must,' came the quick response, 'I am your Corps Commander. I command 100,000 men.' 'Very sorry, Sir, I am a Second Lieutenant and I command 50 men. I don't know you, Sir, and my orders are to maintain secrecy.'[21]
>
> Anon source, 4th Battalion, Seaforth Highlanders

The men were also given the opportunity to practise on battle training grounds far behind the front line which had been adapted as far as possible to mirror the landscape of the battle zone. These enabled them to practise the flexible new battle formations with which they were to attack, to gain an idea of the physical nature of the task ahead and the distance between objectives in real feet and inches.

> Dummy trenches were constructed so that we could familiarise ourselves with the layout of the enemy position that we were to over-run. When it came to the actual attack, there did not seem to be much resemblance, but it was a help to know roughly the distance one had to go and to keep in mind the fact that there was an intermediate trench to be crossed between the enemy front line and the trench that was to be our ultimate objective.[22]
>
> Captain Thomas Owtram, 1/5th Battalion, King's Own Royal Lancaster Regiment

Despite every effort of the military authorities, exercises could never be fully realistic as they lacked the crescendos of shellfire and general mayhem of battle; but they still gave officers at all levels a chance to learn how to avoid the relatively trivial mistakes that could be fatal in action.

> We sat about in wringing wet crops then attacked at dawn – the whole Brigade. I thought the 'waves' seemed a bit muddly. Kitchener's Wood was funny, being a few boughs. The barrages were represented by the beating of a big drum which was rather a scream. We ruined acres of

growing crops and the men ate green peas as they lay in them. Of course it was impossible for me to judge the whole thing.[23]

Reverend Maurice Murray, 12th & 13th Battalions, Royal Sussex Regiment

Some units had the unsettling experience of treading in the footsteps, and hence across the graves, of their predecessors who had gone before them as part of Kitchener's Army, the brave but hopelessly inexperienced 'pals' who had borne the brunt on the battlefields of the Somme.

We marched into the old No Man's Land, facing Gommecourt. Here, much equipment, and many steel helmets (some with hair still adhering to their linings) were still lying where they had been left on July 1st, 1916. There were many graves, the crosses of which bore that date. Some of the crosses had no names on them, but merely tin strips bearing the words 'Soldat Anglais, Inconnu', and 'Mission Français'. The Battalion rehearsed an attack, we signallers with flags representing the barrage, and advancing just in front of the 'first wave'. Passed over the old enemy trenches. These and their barbed wire were still in good condition – much better than our trenches at their best. It is no wonder that our attack failed here.[24]

Signaller Sydney Fuller, 8th Battalion, Suffolk Regiment

In Rawlinson's Fourth Army, the 1st Division was earmarked for the assault landing on the coast and they therefore required a great deal of new and specialist training. The division went into a special camp under 'impenetrable' security cover pretending that they were all in quarantine owing to an outbreak of some fearsome infectious disease.

We were withdrawn from the line and we were in camp at a place called Clippon between Nieuport and Dunkirk. We were going to make a landing the other side of Ostend to coincide with the Passchendaele attack. We had the monitors in Dunkirk with the Navy. We had tapes on the sand dunes representing the barge. We were all lined up on these tapes and then as the whistle went we had to dash off these 'barges' and run as fast as we could. We had to get off the barges, which the monitors were going to push up on the beach, dash up on the sands and attack the fortifications, if there were any left because the fleet were going to bombard the coast for us. They had a replica of the sea wall built. The fittest of our crowd had the job of carrying a rope with a hook on the other end. I was one of the silly idiots that volunteered. Our job was to scramble up this wall and hook this on whatever we could find up above, throw the rope down to drag the machine guns up over the wall. We wouldn't have had a chance to do that but that was what we were supposed to do. The Colonel told us, 'If it's a secret, we'll all get the VC! But if the Germans know about it, we'll be annihilated.' And we would have been! If the fleet hadn't managed to smash everything up we wouldn't have got off the barges. It never came off, or else I shouldn't be here today to talk about it.[25]

Private Walter Grover, 2nd Battalion, Royal Sussex Regiment

Tanks were to assist in charging the formidably high concrete sea walls and defences that lined the Belgian coast. This was a startlingly modern concept in combined operations.

I was sent to take part in a demonstration with a view to being employed for an attack on the sea wall somewhere near Ostend. At Erin, which was one of the villages near by, there was a mock-up of the sea wall done in concrete and the tanks had to come off the sea from landing craft, crawl over the sand and climb up the sea wall. This was a very difficult thing to do because the sea wall was made of concrete, it had a very steep slope for about 20 feet and then there was an edge jutting out, half rounded above it, the purpose being to break the force of the wave and stop them at the very top. The interesting thing was to watch the tank tackle this. The tank was provided with a wooden framework of crib, which it pushed in front of it up the slope. The tank got a grip on the slope, which it normally couldn't have done because it had fixed to its tracks slabs of wood with steel spikes in them. These steel spikes dug into the cement and enabled the tank to crawl up. By the time the tank had reached the top, which was at a pretty steep angle, then the crib reached as far as it could go, which was under the edge of this lip, which stuck out. It was shaped so that it would do so. The next thing was that the tank started to crawl up on the crib, which it had pushed in front of it, rather like a baby chimp being crawled over by its mother. However, the studs on the bottom of the crib bit into the cement, and the spikes on the bottom of the tank bit into the crib – and so it crawled up – up and up and up and up. When it got as far as it could go before it toppled over onto the ground the driver was literally lying on his back. It was an extremely brave thing to do I think for the driver. So it was proved perfectly possible to surmount those concrete coastal defences in that manner. In the same way lorries were pulled up with a rope and over the crib. I was going to be one of the party who were going to take part in this attack and a

> separate company was formed with a view to doing so. I was one of the members of this suicide squad. I was bubbling over with enthusiasm, I thought it was a marvellous thing. With all the futility of one's feeling at the time I thought it would be the end of the war and so on.[26]
>
> Lieutenant Mark Dillon, B Battalion, Tank Corps

The coastal landings had been conceived in conjunction with an attack along the coast from the positions that the British had recently taken over from the French in the bridgehead on the eastern bank of the Yser in the Nieuport sector. The Yser at this point was deep and wide and the Germans saw their chance to strike a telling blow. From 6 July a German artillery bombardment began concentrating on the exposed pontoons and bridges across the Yser with the intention of physically isolating the bridgehead. At 20.00 on 10 July the German assault troops went in and swept over the garrison on the right bank which was almost wiped out, suffering 70 to 80 per cent casualties. Most of the vital bridgehead in the Dunes sector was lost. An immediate counter-attack was ordered in haste by Rawlinson, but then cancelled as the inherent difficulties in such an operation were recognized. It was instead proposed to wait until the main offensive had started and then to launch a flanking attack to the coast to retrieve the bridgehead before proceeding as originally planned with the coastal attack and landing operations when the moment was right.

As the troops poured into the Ypres Salient in preparation for the coming offensive, many could not hide their fear inspired by the awful reputation of that dread locality.

> He said to me, 'I hope I never go up to Ypres. I don't know why, but I dread that place – it must be a terrible place.' We were a good way from Ypres and he went on leave. No sooner had he gone on leave than we had orders to go up to Ypres. We never thought a word about it. When he came back from leave he nearly went mad. He said, 'I didn't want to come up here!' He was like a different chap, he said, 'I don't want to die, I've got two lovely little boys and a lovely wife – I want to be with them . . .' The next day I thought about him, I said, 'Where's Fitzjohn?' They said, 'He's had a direct hit! He got killed.'[27]
>
> Private Frederick Collins, B Battalion, Tank Corps

Many of the men passed through the haunting remnants of the city of Ypres.

> Presently we reached the Square, where stands the famous Cloth Hall. I've heard of the Taj Mahal by moonlight – but for me it could never be so impressive as this ruin. The stones and masonry gleamed snowy white and the massive tower stood there, raising its jagged turrets against the dark sky like some huge iceberg. Its base emerged from a vast heap of fallen masonry that had been brought down from above and levelled off into a sea of brick and stone rubble all around the cobbled square. There it stood, the shattered but invincible emblem of all that the Ypres Salient means – awe inspiring and unforgettable. There was just time to notice by the stump of a lamp post the crumpled body of a dead soldier. Then I had to get busy as we passed on towards the Menin Gate.[28]
>
> Lieutenant Huntly Gordon, 112th Brigade, Royal Field Artillery

The pallid inspiration of the blasted townscape was soon dispelled by grim reminders of the history of the Salient. Macabre place names assigned by long-dead soldiers marked out various crossroads which continued to act as magnets for speculative German shellfire. Such symbols of fear and devastation did nothing to reassure the tremulous new arrivals.

> The chap who decided on the names of these places must have had a morbid mind. It's easy enough to get the wind up without the map making your flesh creep with such names as 'Hell-Fire', 'Hell-Blast' and 'Shrapnel Corner'. The lunar-cratered landscape, with its tortured trees, flooded shell holes and putrefying carcasses of horses among tangles of barbed wire, seen by the fitful light of the moon on a blustery rainy night, surely this is enough without the implication that shrapnel may be expected to burst over you at any minute. Now if only they had called it 'Sunny Bank', 'Bluebell Corner' – or since we are in a foreign land – 'Sans Souci' or 'Mon Repos', I for one would find it a little more reassuring. Though admittedly a dead horse smells the same in any language.[29]
>
> Lieutenant Huntly Gordon, 112th Brigade, Royal Field Artillery

Although most of the men destined to fight and possibly die in the Salient had no idea of the reasons for their presence, some did grasp the essential importance of Ypres to both sides.

> The Bosche has orders to defend every inch of ground here and he is fighting desperately: because he cannot go back without surrendering vital ground here. He could lose thirty miles on the Somme and ten at Arras and not be much the worse for it: but if he is forced back here he

> loses the coast and Lille – both of which are essential to him. That is why I believe we are working up for the last great period of battle on the Western Front.[30]
>
> Captain Harry Yoxall, 18th Battalion, King's Royal Rifle Corps

Ypres was a terrible place at the best of times, but the ever-increasing pace of trench warfare as the offensive loomed meant that acclimatization was not a gentle experience for the troops who moved into the line. The 1/5th Battalion, Seaforth Highlanders of the 51st Division crossed the Yser Canal and moved up on 4 July. It was already disturbingly wet as the disrupted drainage took its toll.

> We entered a communication trench. This was a fairly good one for a considerable distance but as we drew near the reserve and front trenches it became very wet and muddy, being for the most part knee deep and had been blown in every few yards causing blocks in the trench. The result was we had to be constantly climbing out of the trench, running on the top past the block and dropping into the trench again. Each time this occurred we, of course, got splashed up to the eyes with mud and water and on several occasions rolled into shell holes full of water so that we were soon wet to the skin and everything we carried was caked in mud. It was a very miserable journey and was not made any the pleasanter by the constant shelling which was taking place. In addition, each time a flare light went up, we had to lay flat and keep perfectly still whether in mud or water so that we should not be observed. The trenches were in a wretched state with the constant shelling being a mass of broken duckboards, deep holes, barbed wire and broken, jagged bits of corrugated iron, all of which in the dark proved very big obstacles and put us in the worst of tempers.[31]
>
> Signaller Stanley Bradbury, 1/5th Battalion, Seaforth Highlanders

From this miserable start things just got worse. The front line lay some 2,000 yards across the other side of the Yser Canal. At this point it was just a disjointed and inadequate breastwork line, the parapet often overgrown with weeds. The support line, such as it was, resembled a series of grouse butts intermingled with fortified farm buildings. In fact it is fair to say that British defensive positions and tactics had not really developed since 1915. Trenches were still regarded as mere temporary resting places prior to the next big offensive. This mindset persisted despite the fact that, if anything, for the past three years at Ypres it had been the Germans on the attack. This may have been the Third Battle of Ypres but it was in fact the first British offensive in the Salient. As Bradbury reached the front line he took shelter in the Turco Farm dugout. All that night and into the next day German shelling and mortaring continued, remorselessly pounding the sector. It was a grim welcome.

> Just before teatime, two trench mortars dropped simultaneously one on each of the two entrances to the dugout. The result was terrific. The whole of the heavy cement blocks crashed in burying those under and near them and the dugout was reduced to a heap of dirt and debris. The dugout had been full of men all sitting on the steps from the top to the bottom, I and two more being sat right at the bottom. We were blown amongst a heap of wreckage onto the floor of the dugout but beyond the shock had not suffered any injury although from the cries and groans of those who had been on the steps it seemed that many were terribly injured. A state of panic then existed as with intense darkness and the only entrance whereby fresh air could enter the dugout being completely blocked there appeared to be a grave fear that we should suffocate. However, as no-one appeared to know what was best to do, I temporarily took command and assured those who were capable of listening that we still had our box respirators which could last us in case of emergency for a full 24 hours. I then requested all those who were capable of shouting to shout as hard as they could so as to attract attention of any passers by in the trench or those in the distant trenches. This appeared to be of no avail but after what seemed to be an eternity (it was really only about 15 minutes) we heard digging going on at the entrance. Plenty of willing helpers were soon engaged in removing the debris and very soon there was a small hole through which we could see daylight. This gradually became larger and larger until it was possible to wriggle through. By the light which streamed through the aperture we were able to see what damage had been done. The interior of the dugout was unrecognisable. Where there had once been steps, now dead and wounded men lay half buried in the debris. With the aid of those outside, we were all in turn extricated, that is, those it was possible to extricate, as one or two were pinned under solid blocks of concrete. Once out in the daylight we were able to take note of our casualties: which were three killed and 32 wounded out of a total of 38 occupants of the dugout.[32]
>
> Signaller Stanley Bradbury, 1/5th Battalion, Seaforth Highlanders

Turco Farm soon had to be abandoned when it became obvious that the Germans were likely to shell the position heavily, with or without provocation, and that the shelter offered by its concrete walls was illusory under the relentless pounding impact of heavy shells. New arrivals were astonished at the sheer power of artillery for which their training had in no way prepared them.

> People who have never seen or heard a shell burst have very little idea what it is like and cannot imagine it. A high explosive shell bursts immediately on contact with the ground and makes a tremendous noise throwing up stones and dirt quite 30 yards high leaving a big hole in the ground several feet deep and 5 to 8 yards in diameter. The splinters from these shells will fly 200 yards and kill any person they may hit at that distance. There are two types of shrapnel shells, one bursts in the air and the other on the ground. Both kinds make a very big noise on exploding and the shrapnel will fly in all directions for a distance of at least 50 yards. By the screech of a shell it is possible to tell whether it will explode near to you. When the trenches are heavily shelled we have to lie down close to the sides or crouch very low and trust to luck hoping that one will not drop in our particular traverse. If in the open, it is necessary to fall flat and the shell splinters will pass over you, but you will be covered with dirt or mud. [33]
>
> Signaller Stanley Bradbury, 1/5th Battalion, Seaforth Highlanders

Shortly after the 15th Division moved into the line they found that the Germans had once again racked up the pitch of technological horror. Captain Philip Christison, commanding D Company of the 6th Battalion, Cameron Highlanders, was in the line to the left of C Company under Captain Harry Rowan.

> At about 08.00 hours I was going forward to my forward trench when the Germans started shelling steadily but with small stuff and we could not understand why the shells all seemed to be duds; they just made a plop. Then 77mm stuff came over mixed with the others. One shell landed in my trench almost beside me and did not burst – just a sort of plop. I felt a burning sensation just above my right knee and heard the man next to me cough and retch. I realised this was something very odd and shouted, 'Gas!' and quickly put on my respirator. The gas alarm immediately sounded and, as we were very good at our gas drill, only 5 or 6 of my company were gassed. Captain Rowan heard the gas alarm and his men

> put on respirators. After wearing them for some time in the heat of the morning and no attack developing he took his Company down into a deep German dugout, a vast place, so the men could take off their masks. He went up to the anti-gas sentry in the trench above, removed his mask and shouted down, 'Gas clear!' Masks were thankfully removed and up they came. But they thought the original alarm was false as no gas had been smelt. What they didn't know was that this was mustard gas, had no smell and delayed action. The C Company trenches were saturated with the stuff and the whole Company was struck down. My D Company was clear except for an odd shell. By nightfall every Officer and man of C Company was either dead or in hospital. The Battalion lost 5 Officers and 135 men dead. The Commanding Officer ordered me to take over C Company's front and this I did still in our gas masks. I think this was one of my worst days. Stuffed up in sweaty respirators with eye-pieces constantly misting up so that one had no clear vision and expecting to be attacked any moment. But the Germans did not attack. I could not understand why they used this surprise weapon and did not follow it up. Were they afraid of their own deadly gas? [34]
>
> Captain Philip Christison, 6th Battalion, Cameron Highlanders

For Scottish units dressed in the traditional style the new gas posed a particularly serious threat; one which could unman even the hardiest of privates, accustomed as they were to the icy shafts of fate. However, their officers were well used to turning every wartime eventuality into yet one more testament to the efficacy of the kilt.

> When we first learned of its power of burning the skin, it was thought that we would probably suffer badly in the kilt. However, it is satisfactory to know that the kilt once again proved its efficiency as a fighting garment. While we have no statistics, we believe it is true that we did not suffer more than the trousered regiments in this respect, the reason being that it was generally the parts of the body where the skin was tender that got burnt. The skin of the legs having got hardened by exposure to the weather, was generally able to withstand the effects of gas in the same way as the hands and the face. Again, most of the cases of burning were caused by men sitting down on the ground which was saturated with gas. The kilt being thick, the gases could not easily penetrate it, and no doubt its swinging in the air, when the men got up, helped dispel them.[35]
>
> Lieutenant Colonel Norman Macleod, 7th Battalion, Cameron Highlanders

Truly it seems the Camerons were 'Devils in Skirts'! Nevertheless the new German poison gas was by no means a joking matter. The stretcher bearers soon grew familiar with the symptoms suffered by mustard gas victims.

> The shell used to burst with a PLOP, that's all you heard. The shell burst open and the liquid came out and the moment it met the air it became gaseous. Of course it soaked the ground where the shell had fallen and if some unfortunate soldier happened to sit in that small shell hole he'd have everything burnt away very quickly. Mustard gas attacked all the vesicular parts of the body. The under-arm, between the elbow, by the ear – all where the lymphatic glands are. It was a very, very nasty gas, a very bad invention that.[36]
>
> Sergeant William Collins, Royal Army Medical Corps

The British gas specialists were immediately contacted to see if they could identify the precise chemical composition of the new gas and then develop an effective method of countering its effects.

> They were blind, the men, they couldn't see at all. They were choking and in thousands they had to leave the line. Fortunately one or two of the shells had not exploded and I got one of these and nursed it on my knee all the way back to the research station. But it took our best chemists some weeks to find out what this new substance was – dichloretyl sulphide. It was an oily liquid which evaporated very slowly and because it had such a faint smell the troops tended to take no notice of it. And when they did feel their eyes smarting they were too late. It was a dreadful substance.[37]
>
> Captain J. C. Hill, Special Gas Company, Royal Engineers

The appropriate countermeasures were taken swiftly and within a couple of weeks everyone was briefed on the dangers posed by the new gas – for which a distinctive smell had now been identified.

> An extension was fitted to our box respirators. This extension contained 'lime permanganate' granules, and was fitted to give protection against a new kind of gas which the enemy was using. This new gas, we were told, was invisible, and smelt like mustard, rotten oranges etc. The only effect, at first, was to cause much sneezing, but 5 to 10 hours afterwards the victim's eyelids swelled, the eyes became very inflamed, blindness followed and great pain was suffered, morphia having to be administered. The blindness continued for about 10 days.[38]
>
> Signaller Sydney Fuller, 8th Battalion, Suffolk Regiment

However, even an extra filter did not entirely remove the threat. The new gas was a pernicious and penetrative foe. The Germans used different combinations of high explosive, shrapnel and gas shells to cause the maximum possible inconvenience to the long-suffering British infantry.

> The Germans mixed gas shells with ordinary shells and so compelled us practically to live wearing our respirators. We rigged anti-gas blankets on frames at the entrances to dugouts and behind each blanket was placed a flat tin containing chloride of lime; the men stood in this, crossed a further anti-gas blanket and could then remove masks and get food and rest. Unfortunately, heat generated gas out of the men's clothing and some got gassed even with all precautions.[39]
>
> Captain Philip Christison, 6th Battalion, Cameron Highlanders

The bulk of the artillery concentrated for the Messines attack was moved north into the Salient and every available gun that could be spared along the whole Western Front was earmarked for Ypres. The mass arrival of guns on this scale demanded major preparatory works. Railway and road communications had to be radically improved to carry both the guns themselves and the enormous numbers of shells that had to be stockpiled. Many of the heavier guns needed special platforms to give them the stability that was essential for accuracy in the muddy conditions and shifting clays that prevailed in the Salient. All of this had to be done under the eye of the German artillery observation officers peering down from the surrounding ridges. The Germans were also moving in guns and they tried their best to disrupt the Allied preparations. In this they were at least partially successful. The date of the offensive was originally set for 25 July but the commander of the French First Army, General Anthoine, encountered greater than expected problems in organizing his artillery build-up. He asked for more time to prepare and as Gough was also experiencing difficulties Haig agreed to an extension of three days, moving the attack date to 28 July. The French continued to have severe problems and, although Haig was extremely unwilling to delay further, it was eventually agreed to grant another three days' grace, which meant the troops were to go over the top on 31 July. This lost time was to prove vital.

The securing of aerial supremacy over the intended battlefield was now considered an essential preliminary to any serious operations of war. Artillery observation and detailed reconnaissance work to identify German batteries and strongpoints had to be carried out relentlessly, all day, every day. Unfortunately the efforts of the Royal Flying Corps were hampered by the insistence of the government that experienced scout squadrons be assigned to the Home Front to bolster the defence of London. On 13 June a daylight Gotha bomber raid had caused serious casualties, including one direct hit on a crowded infant school with the inevitable heart-rending results. Public outrage demanded immediate action, but Haig, with considerable justification, claimed that his entire offensive was threatened by this weakening of his aerial forces.

> Two good fighting squadrons will proceed to England tomorrow as ordered. Request following facts may be laid before War Cabinet at once in connection with this decision. Fight for air supremacy preparatory to forthcoming operations was definitely commenced by us this morning. Both enemy and ourselves have concentrated fighting machines for this struggle in the air which will undoubtedly be the most severe we have yet had. Success in this struggle is essential to success of our operations. Withdrawal of these two squadrons will certainly delay favourable decision in the air and render our victory more difficult and more costly in aeroplanes and pilots.[40]
>
> Field Marshal Sir Douglas Haig, GHQ

Haig's comments highlight the crucial importance that the new aerial dimension had already attained. Many at the front fumed at a perceived lack of courage back in England.

> Fritz is no doubt superior to us in the air, and is getting bolder and more cheeky every day. One cannot help wondering whether the Government at home are keeping aeroplanes there instead of sending them here. The Londoners howl over 250 casualties; we have three or four thousand a day. There is a very nasty feeling here that we are not supported in the air as we should be.[41]
>
> Brigadier General W. R. Ludlow, Area Commandant, Ypres

The fluctuations of the air war were watched nervously by the gunners, who were all too aware of its importance for their continued existence and the success of their efforts. Good observation was crucial and the British kite balloons from which the British observers peered over the Pilckem Ridge were an obvious target for the aggressive German scouts.

> The Hun planes were especially offensive against the chain of sausages which haunt the sky near our wagon line, looking like a row of aerial

sentry boxes. Five of these were brought down in three days. On one occasion three Hun planes attacked the three balloons nearest us. As soon as the planes began to swoop down, the six occupants of the balloons jumped out and came floating down below their white parachutes, but none of the balloons caught fire, and the Huns cleared off suddenly and made for home. A moment later a squadron of our new fighting planes dropped out of the blue on to them and after a real good scrimmage two of the Huns whirled down in flames and the remaining fellow was forced to within 50 feet of the ground and then headed back over our heads. His speed was at least 120 mph and in close pursuit, about 100 yards higher up, were two of our planes with their machine guns going like blue murder. It was a real tally-ho chase. Though the dust was being flicked up in every direction around us, none of our horses were hit by the bullets from the planes. The Hun made a marvellous landing at full speed on a parade ground behind us among the mass of infantry camps.[42]

Major Neil Fraser-Tytler, 150th Brigade, Royal Field Artillery

Everyone in the area made for the German aircraft, driven by curiosity, or a lust for instant vengeance.

Another officer and I ran across and found a huge crowd gathering round the machine. We got close enough to see the airman as he climbed out of the cockpit, taking his helmet off. He was fair haired and not more than 19 or 20. If we could have got hold of him, we would have killed him. Everyone was savage at the machine-gunning, we being so helpless in the wagon-lines. However some senior officers got him into a tent.[43]

Lieutenant Huntly Gordon, 112th Brigade, Royal Field Artillery

When Major Fraser-Tytler arrived at the scene, he found a raging mob baying for blood.

Jack and I and most of the battery tore after him to be in at the death, which proved to be very nearly true, as when we reached the spot there was a raging crowd of several thousand men round the tent in which the prisoner had been placed. Feeling was running pretty high, for everyone thought that he had machine-gunned the camp on landing, though probably our own machines had done it! As we could not get anywhere near we returned home. We heard later that soon after we had left someone cried, 'Remember London,' and the tent ropes were cut. In the ugly rush which followed the two British officers with the prisoner had a very thin time of it. From our wagon lines a mile away we could hear the

> mob howling for blood. The Hun was eventually rescued by a small body of Colonels armed with thick sticks! I fear this is not a very creditable incident, but it is indicative of the trend of feeling out here. In a few years we shall doubtless have got down to cannibalism.[44]
>
> Major Neil Fraser-Tytler, 150th Brigade, Royal Field Artillery

The barrages planned by Major General H. C. C. Uniacke, in overall command of the Fifth Army artillery, were truly gargantuan in scale. Although the softening-up artillery duel had begun in June the preliminary bombardment itself was originally intended to start on 16 July and last for nine days, but, as we have seen, this subsequently had to be extended to fifteen days. The counter-battery work was of prime importance and it was intended to reach a crescendo in the week running up to Zero Day. The last day would be spent on a gas shell bombardment that would deluge all remaining identified German batteries. The German trenches and strongpoints were to be destroyed four days before the assault and the barbed wire was to be cut by mortars and howitzers. The roads lying behind the German lines were not to be shelled as they would be needed to facilitate the move forward of the guns once the infantry had advanced. Once Zero Hour had arrived, a creeping barrage of high-explosive and shrapnel shells was to be fired just ahead of the attacking troops moving forward at a rate of 100 yards every four minutes. Calculations had allowed for one 18-pounder gun per 15 yards of front and one heavy howitzer every 50 yards. Once objectives had been captured, it was an absolute priority to protect the infantry whilst they consolidated before their next attack. To this end, a protective barrage would be fired some 500 yards ahead of the new front line searching backwards and forwards for any German counter-attack troops. Arrangements were made to ensure prompt response to any emergency requests for extra artillery support and RFC patrols and artillery observation aircraft were to report on the ongoing situation and identify worthy targets. Meanwhile designated batteries were ordered to move forward quickly into the former No Man's Land and beyond ready to support the infantry on the next move forward.

To carry out this ambitious programme the Fifth and Second Armies deployed 2,092 18-pounder guns and 4.5-inch howitzers, 718 medium pieces and 281 heavy guns. In total 3,091 guns were employed in around 450 batteries. They were faced by 1,556 German guns, but superior German observation from the ridges meant that it was an extremely hard-fought battle. One by one, the batteries were moved into their gun positions until they were almost wheel to wheel in the cramped confines of the Salient. Whether they were new to the Ypres area or old hands being reorganized ready for the bombardment it was already apparent that life for the gunners was not going to be easy.

> The road to the new position is a mere apology for a road and as we are taking down the first gun at night the road surface collapses and the gun sank to its cradle. It has lain there for three days now and we have not been able to shift it – two caterpillars failed to move it. Now we have had heavy rain so it is very doubtful if we will get the guns to their new place at all. The result of three nights' work is to get one gun into a hole and another off to a workshop. Tonight I am to get the gun out of the ditch and another to the workshop if possible. The Hun shelled the Battery all afternoon, broke another limber and badly damaged the road again. About midnight he again shelled and set off more ammunition but all the men got clear. I got the gun out of the ditch with two engines and into the new position. It was difficult to get the gun away to the workshop owing to the road being cut up but we succeeded without mishap about 3 a.m.[45]
>
> Lieutenant Robert Blackadder, 152nd Siege Battery, Royal Garrison Artillery

The gunnery duel was intense as both sides sought to erase each other from the face of the earth. When the German gunners were certain of the location of a British battery they would order a concentrated shoot to destroy the position.

> *29 July*: At night, about 11 p.m., the old Hun began to strafe us and all around. The guns got it first of all so I ordered all to clear out. Then he worked up towards the fighting post, a concrete erection left by the Hun. Several of the gunners had come up here for shelter, some very badly shaken. The shells were falling very near now, the concussion putting out the lights several times, then, all of a sudden, a tremendous crash and all darkness and smoke almost suffocating us – a direct hit on the post! We lit the candles again, but could hardly see for the smoke. After ascertaining all were untouched I tried to get out, the shelling having moved to the guns again, but found the entrance blocked with debris. All wires had been broken too so we were out of touch with the guns and headquarters. We soon worked a passage out and set to work to get into communication. Meantime some of the ammunition on No. 3 gun had been set on fire

and the limber and stores were burning merrily. I got this gunner to come with me to put the fire out, this we did without mishap and returned to the concrete post. About 2 a.m. the shelling stopped and at dawn we reckoned up the damage done. Casualties, nil, material destroyed, very little. The fighting post was only slightly damaged and will stand many more hits thanks to the excellent work of the Hun.[46]

Lieutenant Robert Blackadder, 152nd Siege Battery, Royal Garrison Artillery

The 18-pounder and 4.5-inch field artillery pieces were under constant bombardment.

It is quite impossible to sleep if one is lying under a tarpaulin with 5.9s and 8″ shells falling within a 100 yards. To begin with, there is the suspense of waiting between shells, which may vary from five seconds to ten minutes. Then there is the four or five seconds beginning with the first faint whine of the shell in the far distance, which rapidly rises to the well known rushing scream; then there is the crash as it lands, which makes the whole place shake for a couple of 100 yards, and finally the angry 'zip' of the flying splinters, which may be any size from a match to the size of a large meat-chopper, weighing up to 20lb, and with jagged edges like fish-hooks all over them. As soon as the pieces have finished flying, one looks out and inquires, 'Where did that one go?' Or, 'Are you all right over there?' One sees heads popping out of the ground everywhere, just like rabbits in a burrow.[47]

Major Ralph Hamilton, 106th Brigade, Royal Field Artillery

The flying, scything splinters could cause deadly wounds in an instant, smashing into the body or peppering it with multiple wounds. A typical case occurred as Major Hamilton attempted to put out a threatening fire that had broken out in one of their ammunition dumps.

I turned round to get another sandbag and saw a man lying beside me. He appeared to be quite dead, so I went on with the work. However, Ryves, who is a medical student, discovered that he was still alive, so we put him on a stretcher and carried him under cover. It was quite hopeless and he died in under five minutes. My own impression is that he was dead all the time and only the muscles moving. He was hit in the heart, head, stomach, both legs and both arms, and his neck was broken as well.[48]

Major Ralph Hamilton, 106th Brigade, Royal Field Artillery

The artillery had many complicated preparations to make for their part in the actual attack.

The plan for the attack has now come out – about 100 pages of typed foolscap which had to be read through, digested and from which the battery programme had to be extracted and the calculations made. After two hours' bombardment our artillery brigade was to move to forward positions to continue supporting the advance of the infantry. From our OPs we selected positions in No Man's Land near Hill Top Farm from which to move but they also had to be reconnoitred in detail. The problem was to choose the time to do it.[49]

Major Roderick Macleod, 241st Brigade, Royal Field Artillery

The Brigade arranged a rendezvous at Hill Top for just after dawn.

The night we chose was pitch black, low cloud and with the Germans gas shelling. I started from the battery at midnight, wearing a respirator, on a compass bearing to one of the crossings over the canal. I had to remove my mask occasionally to read the compass. Unfortunately there was a large pond, or lake, short of the canal and into this I fell. The compass was jerked out of my hand, sunk and lost. I scrambled out and tried to find my way to the bridge, but must have lost my sense of direction, for after an hour I found myself walking into the back of our artillery positions. I felt humiliated, but on ringing up brigade headquarters was told that neither the CO nor the other battery commanders had managed to get to the rendezvous.[50]

Major Roderick Macleod, 241st Brigade, Royal Field Artillery

They were finally successful in reconnoitring the intended advance gun positions but then the real work began for the struggling gunners.

We now had to get sufficient ammunition onto these forward positions for further bombardments, barrages and answering SOS calls when we moved up to them. I reckoned we should need at least 600 rounds per battery and as much more as could be managed afterwards. The problem was how to do it. The German night shelling of roads and tracks on our side was severe, particularly at the bottlenecks of the few bridges over the canal. Every morning there was a shambles at each of them. Smashed up wagons, dead horses and men, and through these one had to pick one's way. I decided that to send up ammunition wagons would be asking for trouble, so asked for, and got, pack saddles with attachments for carrying ammunition. Each pack saddle took eight rounds, four on each side. The horses and mules with their drivers went up every night up to Zero day and luckily there were few casualties.[51]

Major Roderick Macleod, 241st Brigade, Royal Field Artillery

One of the main problems of attacking from the northern section of the Salient was the necessity of crossing the Yser Canal before the German front line could be assaulted. Although the partially drained canal was not usually deep, depending on the rainfall situation, it was still a considerable obstacle. This crucial sector of the line was assigned to the Guards Division. After lengthy experimentation it was decided that the men would carry mats made of canvas reinforced by wire and wooden slats. However, through constant patrolling and raiding across the canal, the Guards discovered that the Germans were in the habit of evacuating their front line at night. During the morning of 27 July it was discovered that the Germans had not returned to their positions and Major General Feilding, who commanded the Guards Division, ordered the 3rd Coldstream Guards to cross the Yser Canal in broad daylight without any preliminary bombardment, to take the Germans by surprise. Exploratory patrols used their mats to cross the canal and then found the German lines were still deserted. Moving carefully forward, they managed to establish and consolidate a new defensive line linking with the 38th Division on their right and with the French on the left. By 28 July the eastern bank was secure and a major problem had been overcome by local initiative and pluck.

Although the scheme to deploy them in action unsupported by artillery in a mass attack on the Gheluvelt Plateau had been abandoned, tanks were still allotted a considerable role in the forthcoming attack – which would be by far the biggest tank operation yet attempted. Though hindsight has called into question the use of tanks in the quagmires and smashed woods of the Salient, it was absolutely inconceivable at the time that any credible weapon of war should not be flung into the melting pot of what was then perceived as the main Allied offensive of the year. Yet the ground conditions did undoubtedly pose pronounced difficulties for the tanks; as indeed did the task of concealing their approach.

The main problem was in finding somewhere where you wouldn't get ditched on your way up to the line. Behind the lines the roads were wanted for essential purposes so therefore tanks couldn't use them because they chewed the road surface up. So you had to find a route

> which enabled you to waddle along and get into your position without ditching, disturbing the roads or upsetting other people who were also fighting the war – such as gunners and signallers. You used to trip over signal wires, they were all over the countryside, like a spider's web, wherever you went. Sometimes they were up on poles if they had to cross a road. You tried to avoid disrupting signal wires because they were part of the essential framework of the battle. We did this by personal reconnaissance; we got up as far as one could then walked. So that the tanks could find their way one laid down white tape with a black mark in the middle. Having found my route up to the front trenches I used to start my tape from the front trench and lay it back, follow your route backwards. There might be half a mile of this – you'd dodge in and out of various obstacles.[52]
>
> Lieutenant Mark Dillon, B Battalion, Tank Corps

In the evening gloom the infantry watched the tanks making their ponderous way across the rear areas.

> I saw 12 huge tanks crawling away out of the wood where they had been so well hidden, that we had not seen them. The officers in charge of each looked like boys and the men inside were looking out of the flaps and joking with everybody. They all seemed to be Scots. This was the first tank I had seen. Their line to the front has been taped with very broad tape and they are not to keep to the roads but go all across the marsh. These are the tanks which are to go over with us behind them tomorrow.[53]
>
> Reverend Maurice Murray, 12th & 13th Battalions, Royal Sussex Regiment

As the crews took the tanks forward to their jumping-off positions, Reginald Beall was serving aboard a 'male' Mark IV tank proudly named 'Lion', and armed with two 6-pounder guns.

> We moved off towards a gap in the canal which had been sand-bagged. All the tanks of two battalions crossed over this part of the canal and beyond that there was a track pegged out and it was straight sailing from there while the daylight lasted. We got to a spot almost opposite Zillebeke Lake and hadn't got beyond the confines of the Lake when this dense shelling came on, very, very, very heavy indeed and darkness with it. We realised that we were in for a very serious time by the complaints the other members of the crew made that it was not to be compared with the experiences they had on the Somme – the Somme was far easier – so I

guessed it must be pretty savage. We picked up stragglers, one of them was a captain. On ordinary routine parade work, you would bank on him taking you into the jaws of hell. But suddenly he broke down and cried. There was a lieutenant with us also at this time and he said his prayers. This had a very demoralising effect on the remainder of the crew. The captain and the lieutenant kept whimpering and one of the gunners shouted, 'Shut up, you ruddy twerps!' And they shut up! Apparently they couldn't see and our officer tried to lead the tank with a special signalling device he carried on his back. The guns were almost touching axle to axle. To pick your way through was a real work of art and this officer was endeavouring to do that when he disappeared into a gun pit! The tank stopped and we decided to call a halt for an hour or so. But the shelling went on for three to four hours. Ultimately we got to the jumping off point in front of Zillebeke Lake where there was supposed to be a row of trees. Actually there was tree stumps probably ten feet high but no foliage, shells had taken the tops off. So we covered the tank with tarpaulin and camouflage net and made our way back to rendezvous with our lorries. We got back to camp and we slept the clock around I should think.[54]

Private Reginald Beall, A Battalion, Tank Corps

During the last few days before the attack many men found that the comforting old certainties of their civilian life could still be found in the liturgy of the Church of England, though twisted to reflect the common cause.

The Archbishop of York gave the 53rd Brigade an address or sermon, his 'text' being a part of the 20th verse of the 6th Chapter, 1st Epistle to Timothy – 'Keep that which is committed to your trust'. He said, 'You must all do your best in the coming operations, which may, if successful, bring about the end of the war in a short time.' His address was given from an old wagon, the Brigade forming three sides of a hollow square in front of him.[55]

Signaller Sydney Fuller, 8th Battalion, Suffolk Regiment

Forgotten childhood beliefs were often dusted off and revived by men who knew that they were about to go into the uncertainty of battle. The padres were almost swamped in the rush by the unwonted number of men seeking solace in the holy sacrament.

There were so many communicants that Crawley and I decided to have the Celebration of the Holy Communion (a veritable viaticum) in

> the big Church Army hut adjoining. I went back on Thom's bicycle to my tent and got my robes and helped to administer to over 200 communicants, and Thom gave out hymn after hymn and took some prayers. Crawley celebrated at the end. The hut was so hot that I had to keep wiping my face.[56]
>
> Reverend Maurice Murray, 12th & 13th Battalions, Royal Sussex Regiment

Men bargained with themselves, their consciences and their creator as they strove to hold their fears at bay.

> My twentieth birthday was to be on July 29th and I had a compelling longing to live until that day. How I would have liked to tell General Jacob, 'But I am twenty years old, Sir.' I had given up asking God to see that I wasn't killed soon after I reached the front in 1914. It seemed selfish and unreasonable to expect him to take special steps on my behalf when I was only one in about ten million soldiers in the various armies. But I felt so strongly about being allowed to live until I was twenty that I started praying, 'Please let me live until I am twenty!' Well, I was still alive on Sunday, July 29th, 1917 and twenty years old. I celebrated with a good swig of whisky.[57]
>
> Lieutenant M. L. Walkinton, 24th Machine Gun Company, Machine Gun Corps

Showing scant respect for conscience or naked fear the inexorable timetable of the offensive beckoned as zero hour approached. Blessed or otherwise, the men of the assault battalions made their way up to the front line. As ever, they bore a heavy burden, physically as well as psychologically.

> Haversacks on the back containing 3 days' rations and folded waterproof sheet. Water bottle, tin hat, entrenching tool, rifle and bayonet, 4 grenades, gas mask, full pouches of ammunition plus spare bandolier making 220 rounds per man. I weighed the load to be carried by each man. It came to 102 pounds. How can we manoeuvre or carry out the moves we have been practising on exercises under such a handicap?[58]
>
> Captain Philip Christison, 6th Battalion, Cameron Highlanders

On the night of Monday 30 July 1917 hundreds of thousands of nervous men approached what they knew would be the greatest moment of truth in their mostly short lives, their own personal Armageddon. For some units the way was clearly signposted.

> The track for our Division was marked by small direction posts at

intervals and at short intervals were small iron rods on top of which were small iron discs, painted white, with the Divisional Sign painted in black. The Battalion's Scouts had been posted at intervals along the track as a further precaution against our going astray in the darkness. Our guns, especially the 'heavies' were very active. So were the enemy's, and the shells were flying all over the place, many being gas shells.[59]

Signaller Sydney Fuller, 8th Battalion, Suffolk Regiment

The Germans were restless. The usual harassing shells fell and gas took its toll during the long approach to the front line.

As long as the respirator was being worn eyes and lungs were safe but not the skin. Pip realised that his back was hurting him and when he squatted down and rested it against a trench side it pained him very much. He opened his tunic and slid his hand under his shirt and under his arm and felt a huge blister. Further probing made him realise that he had many such blisters especially under the other arm and at the top of his thighs; the weak, tender parts of his skin. His tunic and trousers showed no signs of anything being abnormal.[60]

Signaller Gerald Dennis, 21st Battalion, King's Royal Rifle Corps

More and more troops moved into the front line: thousands and thousands of men, each allocated his place in the plans of attack.

It was now nearly 10 p.m. We were going to start over into No Man's Land at about 11 o'clock to get into our 'kicking off' positions. This last hour was spent in final instructions – cautions as to silence etc. No Man's Land at this place was about 400 yards wide – there was a track marked by small boards leading out towards the Boche front lines for about 100 yards. We looked upon No Man's Land as ours because at night it was patrolled by us from dusk to dawn. At 11 p.m. we started out into No Man's Land, C Company leading. We sent a small covering party out in front of us and went along slowly towards the Boche lines. We had to cross a small but fairly deep stream on the way. This we did by jumping on an old willow tree which had fallen half across the stream. Soon we reached the 'kicking-off' trench. It was 'some' trench; it was battered about – waterlogged in many places and it was not continuous.[61]

Major Cecil Barton, 1st Battalion, Worcestershire Regiment

With some difficulty Barton and his men took up their allotted positions – or so they believed.

> The officers of A Company and my own Company, with an officer of the Machine Gun Corps, had a pow wow; nearly all of them were convinced that we were in the wrong place, but after a great deal of arguing I managed to persuade them we were in the right place. Of course everyone wanted to consult their maps but it was impossible to use a flashlight, so we tried to read them by the occasional fitful glare of a Verey Light.[62]
>
> Major Cecil Barton, 1st Battalion, Worcestershire Regiment

The officers toured their lines checking that their men were properly in place and ready for the dawn.

> My watch told me it was past midnight, the hands moving inexorably into 31st July. Normally the hour or so before dawn is occupied with what might be called trench house-keeping – sorting and storing what the ration party has brought up, re-stocking ammunition, minor repairs to dugouts and so on. This night we had no such tasks to distract us: shortly we should leave Image Crescent for ever, our next quarters Jehovah or Jordan. The men stood about in twos and threes waiting, nothing to do, listless, for the most part silent. I knew and shared their common thought – that half of us would be dead before the first glint of sun peeped over the horizon. What can men talk about, knowing what all are thinking? I walked up and down along the trench wanting to show insensibility, knowing I was watched by all. I decided I must walk the whole length of Image Crescent stopping a moment to exchange a few words with every man.[63]
>
> Lieutenant Bernard Martin, 1st Battalion, North Staffordshire Regiment

Some officers found things were amiss but were more than capable of resolving any disciplinary problems they encountered without recourse to higher authority.

> On rounds alone tonight I come on a sentry fast asleep although trench routine allows of all getting sufficient rest before battle. If court martialled he is liable to be shot. My fingers at once close on the fellow's neck and I give him a rough shake. He looks up indignantly and says in reply to me that he is not unwell. I tell him I shall forward to High Command any complaint he cares to make about me, and that, having taken the law into my own hands, I will not report him. I have not the heart to charge the man just before action in any case.[64]
>
> Lieutenant Colonel James Jack, 2nd Battalion, West Yorkshire Regiment

With the infantry and tanks in place, the gunners in their dugouts behind them struggled to make their final, all-important mathematical calculations for the barrage tables on which their part of the battle depended.

> It is now after midnight and I have just got zero time and filled in all the barrage tables. There are no less than 45 'lifts', each involving a different range and angle for each gun. It would be simple enough if one had a room with a table and good light to work with, but here in a mud hole and with a guttering candle it is very difficult indeed.[65]
>
> Major Ralph Hamilton, 106th Brigade, Royal Field Artillery

By the early hours of 31 July, after months of planning and weeks of preparation, with the men all in position, Gough's Army was as ready as it ever would be for the dawn.

CHAPTER FOUR

PILCKEM RIDGE, 31 JULY 1917

It was still practically dark, and exactly at the appointed time all the batteries opened fire – hundreds of them – batteries of all sorts and sizes from 12 inch to 18 pounders. The darkness was at once dispelled by the flash of guns, and the stillness of early dawn was rent by the sudden roar. Anyone who has not seen a gun fired by night, I believe, has no idea of the brightness of the flash. It does not give one the idea of fire, but rather of an electric flash. The flash from one gun fired at night will light up the sky like a flash of lightning, and will be visible from miles away.[1]

Lieutenant E. C. Allfree, 111th Siege Battery, Royal Garrison Artillery

Although the battle was set to start at 03.50, less than four hours after midnight, for the waiting men these hours and minutes seemed interminable. Minute by minute the designated Zero Hour, the crucial moment which would mark the formal opening of the offensive, drew nearer. The assembly and jumping-off trenches in the narrow front lines were inevitably terribly crowded with men and very vulnerable to the effects of any German counter-bombardment.

Late at night, we lined up in the places where we were to go over and other troops came up from the supports to fill the gaps with the result that we were packed in the trench and had several hours to spend in a very cramped position. Fritz was evidently very nervous as his flare lights were going up every two minutes to try and find out if anything was doing. About two o'clock he commenced shelling but to our amusement he dropped them all in his own front line, which made his men in the trench send up a couple of lovely golden fountains which is the signal for

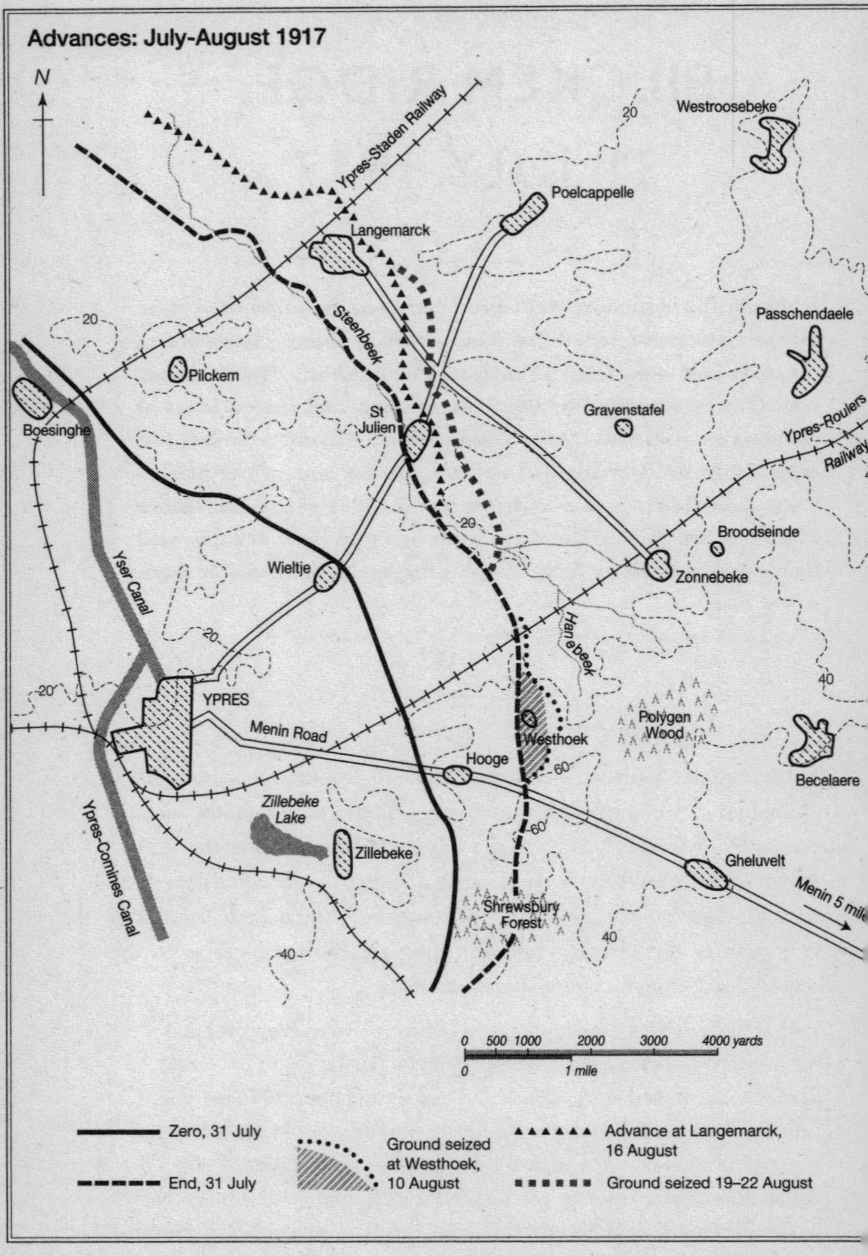
Advances: July-August 1917
N
Ypres-Staden Railway
20
Westroosebeke
Poelcappelle
Langemarck
Passchendaele
20
Steenbeek
Pilckem
Gravenstafel
St
Julien
Boesinghe
Ypres-Roulers
Railway
20
Broodseinde
Wieltje
Zonnebeke
Yser Canal
Hanebeek
20
40
20
YPRES
Polygon
Wood
Menin Road
Westhoek
Becelaere
Hooge
60
Zillebeke
Lake
60
Zillebeke
Gheluvelt
Ypres-Comines Canal
Menin 5 mi
Shrewsbury
Forest
40
40
0 500 1000 2000 3000 4000 yards
0 1 mile
Zero, 31 July
End, 31 July
Ground seized
at Westhoek,
10 August
Advance at Langemarck,
16 August
Ground seized 19–22 August

the artillery to lengthen their range. This he did and we had a terribly hot time. Calls were made for stretcher-bearers on the right and then on the left but the trench was too full for them to come so the men who had been hit would bear their pain until the trench was less congested, knowing by so doing they would not cause a commotion in the trench and give the show away – which might have meant us all being wiped out.[2]

Signaller Stanley Bradbury, 1/5th Battalion, Seaforth Highlanders

Throughout the salient final briefings were being conducted at every level of command.

At 02.30 a.m. on the 31st I personally reported to Brigade Headquarters that the 2/West Yorks were ready to attack. The other three battalion commanders of the 23rd Brigade and Commanders of attached units made similar reports. General Grogan asked me in my turn, 'And you, Colonel Jack, do you understand your orders?' I replied, 'Yes, Sir.' He then read out the latest news from the Divisional front, saying in conclusion, 'That's all, gentlemen; thank you and good luck.' We reciprocated the good wishes, saluted and returned to our units.[3]

Lieutenant Colonel James Jack, 2nd Battalion, West Yorkshire Regiment

Last-minute details were checked and double-checked to ensure that everyone knew exactly what they were to do when the moment came.

Company Commanders struggled along the trench to the deep headquarters dugout where we had cups of cocoa and a final briefing from the CO. Then, returning to our respective Companies, we led our men out into No Man's Land and disposed them lying down in two lines just in front of our own wire. It was about 1 a.m., so for nearly three hours we lay there in the darkness of a night that was overcast though as yet there was no rain. The silence was broken by the intermittent firing of distant guns and the occasional passage overhead of a salvo of heavy shells.[4]

Captain Thomas Owtram, 1/5th Battalion, King's Own Royal Lancaster Regiment

In the oppressive dark of night, the weather soured, matching the dismal mood of the men. Facing the darkest of dawns, the tardy sun seemed unwilling to cast its light on the hellish prospect that beckoned with the new day.

It began to drizzle, increased to a fine wetting rain, when, next morning at quarter to four, which was Zero Hour, we went 'over the top'. It was planned for the attack to start at the first light of dawn, but under a nimbus cloud, with the rain pouring down, it was indeed as 'black as night'. The tense, ominous hours spent during the night waiting for Zero Hour, caused some men to pray, others to curse, and some to think and talk of home and loved ones, but I had a splitting headache, which, with the fear, put me to sleep. Awakened for the final 'stand to', one is oppressed by the deathly silence that always precedes a battle. The calm before the storm. Even the enemy seemed to be saving his ammunition for the imminent cataclysm.[5]

Company Sergeant Major John Handley, 1/6th Battalion, King's Liverpool Regiment

In many units the rum ration, traditional for men about to risk their lives for King and Country, was issued. Most emphatically, this was not to make them drunk. It was intended to be just enough of a panacea to relax their inhibitions a little for the trials that lay ahead and to ease their way from relative passivity into violent action.

They had their rum ration, the Quartermaster was always good on these occasions, it was practically a double, because he'd filched or watered or done something to it to let us have some more. Then you gave the men your last orders. They had brief ladders, two bit of wood nailed together with three or four cross pieces to help them get out. Five minutes before the actual time of going over, that was the worst time for the troops, that's when their feelings might break.[6]

Lieutenant Ulrich Burke, 2nd Battalion, Devonshire Regiment

The racking tension was too much for Colonel Jack, who left his designated post at battalion headquarters to get a little closer to his men.

At 03.40, after shaving, a last polish and brush up by Holden, then a light breakfast, I proceeded with Palmes and our orderlies to a previously selected mound of sandbags outside Junction Trench, a couple of hundred yards from the front line. Although orders forbade battalion headquarters to quit their headquarters during an assault lest the 'chain of command' were interrupted, I thought it right to see my companies start off correctly, and considered this post secure enough for a minute or two after 'Zero'.[7]

Lieutenant Colonel James Jack, 2nd Battalion, West Yorkshire Regiment

The officers' carefully synchronized watches ticked the seconds away in perfect uniformity, drawing the whole army into a bond of shared experience.

The trench was crowded with men, all of them tense, because in a few minutes we were to go over the top. The officer looked at his watch and began counting down to Zero!'[8]

Private Alfred Warsop, 1st Battalion, Sherwood Foresters

As the moment of reckoning finally approached, last-minute preparations were made.

The order to fix bayonets was passed along. A faint streak of greenish gold light showed up in the East to our right front. I looked at my watch and thought of a saying of the men: 'Another minute, and we'll be for it!' It is almost time.[9]

Major Cecil Barton, 1st Battalion, Worcestershire Regiment

All along the line hundreds of young subalterns were quietly marking time, almost chanting as if in unison, although each remained individually isolated, as they counted down the remaining few minutes that remained for many of the men under their personal command.

'Five minutes to go!' You'd shout it down the left and right of your sector. Then, 'Four minutes', 'Three minutes', 'Two minutes' and 'Half a minute!' [10]

Lieutenant Ulrich Burke, 2nd Battalion, Devonshire Regiment

At last the moment could be delayed no longer. The time had come. The ultimate test of a man's courage, his character, his nerve was upon each and every one of them.

Just as the luminous dial of one's wrist watch indicated 3.50 a long jagged line of flame burst from the ground some way in front of us followed by a hollow roar which was followed by a tremendous crack as our field guns opened fire and the whistling of the barrage of shells as it passed over our heads. I blew my whistle and shouted. Men struggled stiffly to their feet and we advanced until the shells were bursting only about fifty yards in front of us.[11]

Captain Thomas Owtram, 1/5th Battalion, King's Own Royal Lancaster Regiment

The stupendous bombardment was awesome, reassuring and terrifying – all three combined in one. It was more powerful than any one of them could have imagined; more than any sane person would ever choose to experience.

There was the most terrible noise going on from masses of artillery. They were wheel to wheel, thousands of artillery pieces, smashing the trenches, smashing the wire right where we went over.[12]

Lieutenant Ulrich Burke, 2nd Battalion, Devonshire Regiment

Some of the more poetically inclined tried to convey the nature of that awful barrage skimming over their heads.

A flooded Amazon of steel flowed roaring, immensely fast, over our heads and the machine gun bullets made a pattern of sharper purpose and maniac language against that diluvian rush. Flaring lights, small ones, great ones, flew up and went spinning sideways in the cloud of night; one's eyes seemed not quick enough; one heard nothing from one's shouting neighbour and only by the quality of the noise and flame did I know that the German shells crashing among the tree stumps were big ones and practically on top of us.[13]

Lieutenant Edmund Blunden, 11th Battalion, Royal Sussex Regiment

Faced with this overwhelming experience, some soldiers just could not cope and the façade of their manhood, so carefully constructed and cherished all their adult lives, fell to pieces in front of their more stoical comrades.

As the barrage opened it was terrific. One person he broke down, he started screeching, like a pig. You've heard a pig screeching, well he screeched like a stuck pig. He was sent back. It was no fault of his; it wasn't cowardice. We knew the fellow, he wasn't the type of boy who played football or roughed it up a bit. He was temperamental, a brilliant pianist and in fact he shouldn't have been in the army at all. His nerves just went. I suppose we had faith in those people who were leading us otherwise it would have been scaring. Our training made us have faith, in whoever was leading us: our officer, section leader, sergeant or a corporal.[14]

Private Ivor Watkins, 15th Battalion, Welsh Regiment

Men who had known each other all their lives, or men recently thrown together by the vagaries of military life, all went forward together into a maelstrom of bursting shells and seemingly inevitable corporeal dissolution.

We scrambled out of the trench and every one there must have been dumbfounded. We knew we had been sending up guns, guns and more guns, until they must have been standing wheel to wheel; and the

> Germans must have been doing the same. We knew they would all fire at once and concentrate on a line so many yards in front. It was still dark but then suddenly it was illuminated by a line of bursting shells, but what was astonishing still was that we must all have been quite deafened by the noise. I looked at Herbert, I could see his lips move – I shouted but I couldn't hear myself at all. I wanted to tell him that we would keep together so I grabbed his hand and we went over together as we had gone to Sunday School – hand in hand.[15]
>
> Private Alfred Warsop, 1st Battalion, Sherwood Foresters

United they went into their modern-day valley of death.

THE OBJECTIVES along the line had been simply delineated. First the Blue Line (the German First Lines and immediate support works), then the Black Line (the German Second Line), beyond that lay the Green Line (the next German system of trenches and linked pillboxes) and finally the Red Line of theoretical objectives only to be attempted if everything was going really well.

On the left of the attack, two divisions of the French First Army moved forward with consummate ease buoyed by the sheer power of their artillery support. Pushing aside the almost non-existent opposition, they moved beyond their final objectives, even reaching the outskirts of the village of Bixschoote. On the French right flank lay the British XIV Corps set to attack on either side the Ypres–Staden railway deploying the Guards Division and 38th (Welsh) Division. Their task had been considerably simplified by the Guards' success in crossing the Yser Canal only a few days before. In front of XIV Corps was the low rise of the Pilckem Ridge and beyond it the Steenbeek Valley. As the barrage crashed out with awesome precision at 03.50, they moved into No Man's Land.

> I should think the guns could have been easily heard in England. The noise on the Somme was terrific, but the noise during today and all through last night was still more stupendous. I should like some of the munitions workers to come over and see the results of their efforts at home. I have just been thinking of the millions of people who have been working day and night for months for a victory like this. It would do them good to see us here.[16]
>
> Captain Arthur Gibbs, 1st Battalion, Welsh Guards

At first the men of both divisions met little effective resistance as they advanced to their Black Line objectives along the 'top' of the Pilckem Ridge.

> I am afraid we have not killed many Huns, as they ran too fast for us long before we came up to them. With the exception of the short check at Colonel's Farm the French went through each objective side by side with our troops, and farther to the left went considerably beyond their last objective. The artillery support throughout the battle was magnificent; the creeping barrage was a uniform and unmistakable line behind which our troops advanced at a distance of only 50 yards; the counter-battery work was so effective that the Germans never put down an effective barrage.[17]
>
> Captain Arthur Gibbs, 1st Battalion, Welsh Guards

The support brigades moved up behind the first wave to continue the assault, but faced a much more difficult task as the German resistance gradually stiffened with heavy machine-gun fire from blockhouses and pillboxes sited on the Ypres–Staden railway and around Langemarck village. Casualties began to mount.

> I suddenly felt a tremendous blow in the chest. Then I fell to the ground, nearly unconscious. But I could think enough to realise that I had been wounded. How badly I didn't know, but I remember wondering whether this was it. Was I dead or not? If so, what was going to happen? Then the blackness gave way to light, apparently of this earth. Glory be to God, I was alive. But was I? For the next object of definition to crystallise out was my red-headed Company runner and he was saying with the utmost clarity, 'Gawd, Sir, you're a goner. It's plumb through your bloody 'eart!' By this time I was getting a little mixed up and feeling not a little aggrieved that he should put things quite as he did. But nothing seemed to happen, and I was quite relieved when my runner, who had himself been wounded by the same shell, handed me over to two Germans who had surrendered and hoped they would not be shot if found carrying a wounded British officer to the rear. But my troubles were not at an end. For as they were carrying me on the stretcher, the sounds of battle seemed to be getting louder. Summoning such powers of assessment as my enfeebled state permitted, I came to the conclusion that the Germans were completely confused and were carrying me back into the front line – a more heroic gesture than I intended![18]
>
> Lieutenant Lord Gage, 2nd Battalion, Coldstream Guards

Fortunately Gage had a fair grasp of German and was able to redirect them to the dressing station where his wounds could be tended. Behind him the XIV Corps had been broadly successful in securing the Green Line along the Steenbeek, an advance of some 3,000 yards. This was no mean achievement.

Immediately to their right the XVIII Corps, made up of the 51st and the 39th Divisions, attacked across the Pilckem Ridge, passing through what remained of a series of woods to reach the Steenbeek and capture the village of St Julien. The 51st Division were supported by hundreds of flaming oil drums projected into the German front line.

> The order, 'Get ready, A Company!' was soon passed along and with bayonets fixed we prepared to clamber over the parapet. Two more minutes passed and then the sky was lit up by a tremendous sheet of flame from the boiling oil emitted from our trench. It was ten minutes to four on the morning of July 31st, a memorable morning indeed. It was quite dark and the sky overcast, but we had no time for contemplating, 'Over the top!' was the order – and over we went. Behind us over 2,000 guns were blazing as hard as they could go, forming a splendid barrage which crept along in front of us and a 100 machine guns rattled incessantly making a curtain of fire about 30 yards in front of us. The noise was tremendous and shout as hard as you could it was impossible to make the man next to you hear. It was each man for himself. I had only got two yards beyond the parapet when I tripped up on the broken barbed wire and fell full length. I got up and after another yard or two the lad on my side was struck down by a shell bursting very near and I again found myself sprawling on the ground. I thought I had been hit as my arm felt bruised – but it was only caused by a large lump of mud or dirt striking it, so I kept on. Fritz had put on a big barrage immediately ours opened, with the result that shells were bursting everywhere and it was impossible to tell which were ours and which his. Our objective consisted of the enemy's first two lines of trenches but in the dark and excitement we had passed over these and were still progressing. What men the enemy had left in his first two lines must have been wiped out by our artillery but on reaching his third line we encountered a few snipers and machine gunners. These were soon 'napooed' by short sharp rushes till we reached them. Then of course it was 'Hands up!' and a cry for mercy which they got – I don't think! Fritz's next line had many machine gun emplacements and the guns rattled away until they saw that the

game was up, then they caved in and received the same treatment as their comrades in front. At this line we thought it best to get back to our objective whilst the troops who were to take objectives farther on proceeded, so we set off to return. There were five of us together, but as the shells seemed to burst all around in every direction, we rested awhile in a large shell hole where one of the chaps (who had a bottle of rum and had already indulged too much in it!) handed the bottle all round and we had a good 'swig'.[19]

Signaller Stanley Bradbury, 1/5th Battalion, Seaforth Highlanders

To their right the men of the 39th Division charged towards St Julien.

We went over the top. It was all quite nice, we didn't have anybody firing at us, not for the first quarter of an hour or so anyway. We were getting strung out in what we called open formation, a couple of yards between each man and we came under long distance machine gun fire. As we were going along the man on the right of me was hit in the heart, he died – he probably died – we weren't allowed to stop anyway. It missed me altogether, that was just the luck of the war. We were told that we'd got to get a stream called Steenbeek. We got there and were told to lie down prone. We were all lying there and I suddenly felt an object fall at my side. I looked around and it was a tin of Woodbines. I looked again and there was a padre. I'd never seen a padre taking part in an attack and whoever he was he was worthy of the very highest praise because he was in a very dangerous position. We hadn't had too many casualties at that time and then we saw a pillbox, not far away, about a couple of hundred yards. We were told to make for that. We got up and got another 50 yards and we were told to get down again. Then we were told to get up. As we got up we came under very heavy machine-gun fire from quite a distance and practically the whole of our platoon was wiped out with machine-gun fire. It got most of them in the heart. It's just a matter of luck really. The earth was all up and down all over – I must have been standing on lower ground, or higher ground, or God knows what – anyway the one that hit me caught me in the shoulder joint.[20]

Lance Corporal Clifford Lane, 1st Battalion, Hertfordshire Regiment

Having made good progress in the initial assault the men began to consolidate their captured positions along the Steenbeek and around St Julien.

> The battalion headquarters soon advanced from the old British front line, still conspicuous with the tall tree stumps and crushed itself into a little concrete dugout with a cupola over it, formerly used for a perfect survey of the British defences. I tried to throw up enough earth to protect an annexe next door, but was driven from the work by a machine gun, hanging on no great way off. Road making parties had lost no time and, strung out among the shell bursts, were shovelling and pummelling tracks across old No Man's Land. And then the Brigade headquarters came, beautiful to look upon, and their red tabs glowed out of several shell holes. This was more than the German observers could endure and in a short time there was such a storm of high explosive on that small space that the brains of the Brigade withdrew, a trifle disillusioned, to the old British trenches. [21]
>
> Lieutenant Edmund Blunden, 11th Battalion, Royal Sussex Regiment

The 51st and 39th Divisions were supported by several tanks from the 1st Tank Brigade. The tank commanded by Lieutenant Birks slowly moved towards Mousetrap Farm.

> This was the first time I'd actually commanded a tank in action and I was petrified. I hoped the whole way up that I should sprain my ankle or something like that so that we should never get there or that the whole thing would be called off. We had no such luck at all and the ghastly hour got nearer and nearer. The worst moment of all was when we started up our engines and they would backfire – we got a sheet of flame out of the exhaust – everybody calling each other a bloody fool and waiting to know what was going to happen. However nothing did happen and we climbed into the tank. The gearsmen got into their places, then the side gunners, then the driver and then the officer gets in through the top. We started off. [22]
>
> Lieutenant Horace Birks, D Battalion, Tank Corps

Close by, Sergeant J. C. Allnatt was in a 'female' tank which was armed with multiple machine guns rather than 6-pounder guns and rather ominously named 'Gravedigger'.

> Dawn was beginning to break and I could see from my half closed shutter the dark forms of the other tanks. I quickly joined them and made for the German front line across Admiral's Road which ran down the middle of No Man's Land. The artillery barrage was terrific. Many five gallon drums of oil were hurled into the front line and set fire by an

automatic device. The Germans responded first by sending up the artillery support alarm and then their own gun fire. The noise of the shrieking and bursting shells was quite fearful.[23]

Sergeant J. C. Allnatt, G Battalion, Tank Corps

Conditions inside the tanks were pretty frightful.

We had to close down because we were within very comfortable machine gun range and once we were shut down we were completely isolated from the world, we had no means of communication at all. The thing got hotter and hotter and hotter. The only ventilation was concerned with the engine and not with the crew. You could only see forward through a little slit in the front visor and if you wanted to see out of the side you looked through steel periscopes which gave you a sort of translucent outside light all distorted. The tank inside was just steeped in Stygian gloom – gloomy, hot and steamy. My particular tank never went until the engine had boiled, once it had boiled you kept it boiling and it was jolly good. The noise inside was such that you could hear nothing outside at all and people made little gestures to you, rude or otherwise, that was all you could do, your sole means of communicating. When this barrage came down you could distinguish that quite easily because any shell bursting within a few yards of the tank you got tremendous back pressure and you felt it all the way through. In fact a shell bursting between the horns of the tank seemed to lift it up in the air. And then the machine guns started, they were quite easy to discern because they were just like peas in a tin can rattling away.[24]

Lieutenant Horace Birks, D Battalion, Tank Corps

The severely limited visibility, deafening noise and lack of any easily discernible landmarks made for absolute confusion as the tanks crawled towards their objectives.

It began to rain as we reached the first German trenches. They did not present any great difficulty, although slimy with mud and covered with considerable quantities of partly destroyed barbed wire. Tanks were facing in all directions and already some were in trouble. I suddenly became aware of someone standing in front of my tank and beckoning me with his walking stick. It was Captain Powell, my Section Commander. He was trying to help me to find a passage between the shell holes which were filled with water and mud. He was almost up to his knees in mud and he was probably finding it more difficult to get

> about than I was. After helping us for some 20 minutes he signalled me to stop and got into the tank by the side door and sat next to me at the end of the engine. 'That's too bloody hot out there for me, Sergeant', he said. We continued our journey and each time we went in to or passed through a shell hole the muddy water came sluicing into the floor of the tank, making everything into a filthy mess.[25]
>
> Sergeant J. C. Allnatt, G Battalion, Tank Corps

Things got worse as they approached the River Steenbeek, which they had been warned was about 10 feet across.

> I found that the banks were non-existent and that the stream had spread itself to about 40 feet wide. I had grave doubts as to whether I should be able to get over. I had a try, in fact I had three tries, at the spot where I thought I could get over but with no success. I was, however, fortunate in being able to back out and decided to look for a crossing a little up-stream in the village of St Julien.[26]
>
> Sergeant J. C. Allnatt, G Battalion, Tank Corps

After this diversion 'Gravedigger' managed to cross the Steenbeek and headed for their rather appropriate objective of Springfield Cemetery on the Langemarck–Winnepeg Road. So far, despite all their efforts, they had made little concrete contribution to the battle.

The neighbouring XIX Corps also suffered mixed fortunes in its attack across the Pilckem Ridge towards the German defensive positions on the Gheluvelt–Langemarck Line in front of the London Ridge, which reached out to from the main Passchendaele–Gheluvelt Ridge. Initially at least the 55th and 15th Divisions were tremendously successful. Company Sergeant Major Handley went over the top with D Company of the 1/6th Battalion, King's Liverpool Regiment. They were to attack Camel Trench and then move on to the Jasper Farm pillboxes that formed the Blue Line objectives.

> We wait, tense, resigned, each and every one of us, to meet his end or whatever pain and anguish fate holds in store for him. One gun breaks the heavy silence and in a split second comes ear-splitting thunder, as thousands of our massed guns fire simultaneously and continue firing as we go forward into the attack. The whole battalion went forward in four waves or lines, with each Company Headquarters in the centre of formation, but first we had to get through our own barbed wire. During

the waiting period parties, at intervals, went out, cut lanes through the wire and laid white tapes for the men to follow; then on getting beyond our wire they would spread out in waves. The first wave went forward at Zero, immediately after the guns fired, the second wave went half a minute after, then over the parapet I climbed leading the Company HQ; the other waves followed at half minute intervals. Following the white tape, I was horrified to find myself tangled up in our own wire. Knowing from experience that the enemy would rain a deluge of blasting shells on our front line within three minutes – at the most – I frantically tore myself through the obstructing wire, hurrying forward out of the most dangerous area. When I felt clear I looked about me, but in the darkness could see no-one. There was no sign of those who should have been following me i.e. the acting captain (the full captain stayed behind on 'nucleus'), his servant, signallers, first aid men, stretcher bearers and so forth. As far as I could make out I was alone. But I went forward, till, suddenly I fell, tripped up by the German wire. As I plunged into the mud several rifle shots flashed and cracked from the enemy trench just in front of me. The bullets whizzed past my head and incidentally, for weeks afterwards, I was partially deaf in the left ear. My rifle was useless, choked with mud. Pulling out a hand grenade, I released the lever and lobbed it as near as I could to the area from which the shots came. Bobbing up to see the explosion, I saw several heads silhouetted against the flash. I had aimed well. At that moment one of our Lewis gun teams came up and I led them into the German trench where, in the half light of dawn, we only found one badly wounded Hun.[27]

Company Sergeant Major John Handley, 1/6th Battalion, King's Liverpool Regiment

To their left the 1/5th Battalion, King's Own Royal Lancaster Regiment had also reached the German front line. On they surged.

In the trench just in front of us a number of Germans could be seen in the faint light. They appeared to be throwing things at us. There was a sound of bursting hand grenades. Then the Germans got out of the trench and ran back. As quickly as I could, I got my men over the trench and moved forward again (leaving the so-called mopping up parties to deal with any of the enemy who might be skulking in their dugouts). I could only see about twenty yards in either direction, so hoped that the platoon commanders on my right and left were doing likewise. We resumed the advance. To the best of my knowledge it was only as we were getting near the reserve line that constituted our final objective that we ran into the curtain of machine gun fire that caused us such heavy casualties. I saw my runner who was close beside me fall apparently lifeless without a sound and at the same moment I received a blow where my left leg joined my body that knocked me over as though a horse had kicked me. Bullets were flicking the earth all around me. The parapet of the trench at which our advance was to terminate was about five yards in front of me. I got up and made a dash for it. As I was crossing the parapet, another bullet hit me, piercing my right knee joint.[28]

Captain Thomas Owtram, 1/5th Battalion, King's Own Royal Lancaster Regiment

Meanwhile Handley had also moved forward towards his next objective. But on ground literally torn apart, it was not easy to be certain of direction.

I had to find Jasper Farm and set up the Company HQ, situated roughly in the centre of the ground allotted for our capture. On the map it was shown as halfway down a central communication trench. Going down the first connecting trench I failed to find it, so came back to the German front line and went down the next one. As trenches they were difficult to discern, for our bombardment had almost erased them. It was a case of plodding through shell holes and round small earth mounds. Skirting one mound I came into full view of Jasper Farm. It was a huge mound of bare concrete with gun slits – a pillbox. Stark and bare, it looked grotesque, our bombardments having blown away the earth which concealed it. I was surprised and even more so when I saw six Germans lined up in front of it. They immediately put their hands up in surrender. Pointing my useless rifle at them, I released an arm to wave them forward in the direction of the British lines. On reaching the old German front line I handed them over to one of my sergeants for escorting back to captivity.[29]

Company Sergeant Major John Handley, 1/6th Battalion, King's Liverpool Regiment

It is perhaps an amusing aside to note the comments of Major Stanley Gordon, who had been left out of the battle as part of the nucleus intended to act as the focal point for rebuilding the Battalion once the attack was over.

A number of prisoners (about 100) were captured especially near Jasper Farm, one German officer actually complained to Captain Tyson that our men spoke roughly to him.[30]

Major Stanley Gordon, 1/6th Battalion, King's Liverpool Regiment

At Jasper Farm itself, Handley was concerned to find that the rest of his Company headquarters were conspicuous by their absence.

> Returning to Jasper Farm I waited for the other members of Company HQ to appear, but none arrived until after some considerable time, when only an odd man or two reported. They too had been caught in our own wire and by the German shells as well. Ultimately it transpired that the acting Company Captain and others had been killed; the rest wounded, and Company HQ virtually wiped out, because they lost valuable time getting through the wire. What I had feared actually happened and I had escaped, by what, premonition or experience?[31]
>
> Company Sergeant Major John Handley, 1/6th Battalion, King's Liverpool Regiment

The plight of the wounded Captain Owtram of the 1/5th King's Own Lancasters was symbolic of the disproportionately high number of casualties amongst officers and non-comissioned officers. Both of the other officers of his company had been killed and command had, of necessity, devolved onto the corporal who was the sole surviving NCO. As Owtram lay helpless, the second wave of the attack formed by the Liverpool Scottish passed through at 11.30 a.m. to launch their attack on the Black Line.

> I remember being struck by the determined and intent look of the men as they went through our line. At this stage at any rate they did not encounter the same hail of machine gun bullets that had cost us so many lives. But soon after they had passed, the Germans, having presumably now realised that the whole of their front trench system was in enemy hands, began systematically shelling our position with high explosive. The trench was of sufficient depth to give us good protection and nothing short of a direct hit could harm us, but several bursts were near enough for the blast to jangle the nerves of my wounded knee very painfully. The shelling had only stopped a few minutes before someone stopped outside of my tiny shelter and I discerned the now familiar features of the Liverpool Scottish Medical Officer Chavasse, whose tunic was now decorated with the ribbon of the VC he had won on the Somme the previous year.[32]
>
> Captain Thomas Owtram, 1/5th Battalion, King's Own Royal Lancaster Regiment

The 55th and 15th Divisions both succeeded in exploiting their initial successes and they managed to advance to their Green Line objectives approaching the low London Ridge. Consolidation was all important and Company Sergeant Major Handley immediately recognized the onerous responsibilities that had fallen to him in the absence of any surviving officers.

> As no officers could be found, I set about locating the troops of the Company. I reorganised them and set them to work on the necessary duties, one of which was to improve and reverse the old German trenches we had captured. This done, I set to work, after getting the necessary information from sergeants and corporals, to prepare the various reports which were overdue at Battalion HQ; such as known killed and wounded, the number of active men, amount and conditions of weapons and ammunition and that we had occupied our objective etc. Having completed the reports, I was about to sign it when a young Second Lieutenant, newly out of England, arrived in a demented state. 'Look what I've got!' he said to me, showing a collection of German helmets and other booty. Obviously he was 'crackers'! Should I get him to sign the report? I wondered! If I signed, the honours would be mine, but on the other hand he would have to explain his absence and neglect of duty with, possibly, serious consequences. Deciding on the more honourable, unselfish actions, for his protection, I said, 'Never mind those, sign this report for HQ!' He signed, without reading and knowing what he was authorising. After the battle, when the honours were allotted he got the Military Cross and my reward was the Croix de Guerre (Belgian).[33]
>
> Company Sergeant Major John Handley, 1/6th Battalion, King's Liverpool Regiment

On the southern flank of the Fifth Army, the II Corps were entrusted with the attack on the Gheluvelt Plateau ranging from the Westhoek Ridge through to Shrewsbury Forest. This area formed the crucial high ground that Haig had emphasized to Gough *must* be captured or the success of the whole offensive would be endangered. Although Gough and his II Corps Commander, Lieutenant General Sir Claud Jacob, were aware of the difficulties that faced them, it is clear that they were still overly sanguine in their assessment of the situation given the formidable strength of the German defences, even though four divisions, the 8th, 30th, 18th and 24th, were assigned to this Herculean task. The 8th Division directly faced the Westhoek Ridge, with the 2nd Battalion, Devonshire Regiment heading to the left of Bellewaarde Lake.

When you get out on top you try and keep as straight line as possible. You were spaced at 3 to 4 yards' interval, going forward at the high port, that is with the rifle diagonally across your chest with the bayonet pointing up at the sky. We reckoned to do a minute to a minute and a half per hundred yards. We knew we could run it in nine seconds. But with the shell holes, the men had to go round them, at the same time being fired on and trying to keep their distance between one another and to keep their alignment.[34]

Lieutenant Ulrich Burke, 2nd Battalion, Devonshire Regiment

From his illicit forward position Colonel Jack cheered off his men as they leaped forward and promptly encountered a situation which made it plain why he had been ordered to remain at battalion headquarters behind the front line itself.

Our barrage had opened; the inferno was deafening. There was now nothing more to be done; so, cheering, 'Forrard away, the West Yorks,' I turned back for my headquarters. Presently a small fragment of shell scratched my leg; then, as if in answer to my contemptuous, 'Pouf! They can't really damage me', a heavy shell, whose explosion I neither saw nor heard, buried me in the trench I was about to enter, wounded me severely and knocked me unconscious.[35]

Lieutenant Colonel James Jack, 2nd Battalion, West Yorkshire Regiment

The 2nd Battalion, Northamptonshire Regiment advanced directly towards Bellewaarde Lake. Newly 20-year-old Lieutenant Walkinton and two machine-gun teams were in close support.

Everyone was very excited and elated. Bursting shells gave light to see by and it was thrilling to see the Northampton bayonets flashing as the troops advanced. Surely nothing could stop us. As we crossed the German support line their barrage fell on us. Shells screamed down and burst all around. I felt as if I had been kicked hard in the backside by an elephant. I was lifted high into the air and fell with a crash, unable to move my left leg. I felt no pain but my leg was completely numb. A little blood came through my trouser leg. Sergeant Carter shouted, 'You alright, Sir? 'Yes', I said, 'keep going.' On he went into the smoke, flame and dust taking the men with him.[36]

Lieutenant M. L. Walkinton, 24th Machine Gun Company, Machine Gun Corps

In between intermittent bouts of unconsciousness, Walkinton dragged himself into a shell hole and looked round for stretcher bearers to take him to safety.

> I saw a small group of men with rifles and fixed bayonets searching for wounded or shamming Germans. They were 'moppers up' whose job it was to kill off any who looked likely to cause trouble. Experience in other battles had shown that this horrible job was necessary. I waved and one of them came towards me and to my astonishment pointed his rifle at me and demanded my watch! His Corporal was only a few yards behind and I said, 'Your Corporal's shouting at you. What does he want?' He looked round and the corporal did shout. By the time he turned round again, I had him covered with my revolver and he dropped his rifle. The Corporal came up and I told him what had happened. I said, 'Now take him forward and I hope he gets killed!'[37]
>
> Lieutenant M. L. Walkinton, 24th Machine Gun Company, Machine Gun Corps

On the right of the 8th Division front, the 1st Battalion, Worcestershire Regiment advanced towards Chateau Wood.

> We are moving slowly towards that reddish line. I suddenly see some wicker revetments sticking up amidst the jumbled earth – it is the Boche front line. We are almost in our own barrage now – a shell bursts just in front of me (I don't know whether it was one of Fritz's but probably our own). I expect at any moment to see a Boche aiming at me and keep wondering if I shall be quicker than he. For some reason or other the men are all cheering off to the left.[38]
>
> Major Cecil Barton, 1st Battalion, Worcestershire Regiment

As they reached the German front line, the British troops made their charge.

> It was only when you got to within 20 yards of the trench that you said, 'Charge!' They then brought their rifles facing the enemy and charged into the trench, killing and bayoneting. It only lasted a few seconds. If there weren't many troops about you knew there must be more so you threw bombs down the dugouts, that wasn't so much to kill them, it was to keep them there.[39]
>
> Lieutenant Ulrich Burke, 2nd Battalion, Devonshire Regiment

The 8th Division was making steady progress despite the difficult terrain.

> We went fairly well. We got through the German front line, got through their local support line and we were passing a place called Lake Farm –

> there was a huge lake in front of our battalion sector, the Bellewaarde Lake, and beyond that was Lake Farm. There our commanding officer was killed, the second in command took over and we went on a tiny bit further. When you get to the trench, up to the last moment you're seeing if your men are there and if you've got any left. Then you jump into the trench. This German put his bayonet up and I'm afraid I caught it in the right shoulder, right across my back and just missing my spine – I was impaled on this. My only fear was that he would press the trigger which would have made a hell of a mess. My sergeant, who was near me, saw me, he came in close, shot the fellow and then hoisted me with the help of another man off the bayonet because I was on top of the German – he was dead and it wasn't pleasant. A bayonet wound hurts directly it goes in and the withdrawal is more anguish than the 'putting in' because the 'putting in' is instantaneous. If you get hit by a bullet or bomb splinter it's so hot that it cauterises the wound and you don't feel anything for a minute or so.[40]
>
> Lieutenant Ulrich Burke, 2nd Battalion, Devonshire Regiment

The 1st Worcesters moved through Chateau Wood towards Westhoek. By now Barton was becoming aware that he had an open flank to his right.

> I soon find that I am the right hand man, with my servant who has stuck to me all the time. I remember shouting and waving to the men to come to the right, but of course they could not hear. We are now on the second line but still no live and active Boche. One of my puttees comes undone in the wire in front of the parapet – my servant immediately rips it off. By now we are over the ridge and going down the slope. Machine guns and rifle fire started in front but they seem to be firing rather too high. Our guns are firing some shells which burst about 70 feet in the air in big flaming drops of burning oil. By their light I see a small lake in front of us and realise we are about 500 yards too much to our left. Just about this point my servant scrambles up into a shell hole – I wonder what is up until he says, 'I'm hit, Sir!'[41]
>
> Major Cecil Barton, 1st Battalion, Worcestershire Regiment

Barton collected together some of his company and set off to the right in an attempt to plug the gap opening up between them and the 30th Division which was meant to be coming up in parallel alongside the 8th Division. The fighting was becoming fragmented and confused as Barton led forward a party of men towards a group of German pillboxes.

By this time, the barrage is a long way ahead. The machine gun and rifle fire is getting more intense. Suddenly I see a Hun just in front in the remains of a wood. I remember shooting him and seeing him fall. As I was doing this, six Huns ran out from somewhere and went into a pillbox shelter behind me. I got a couple of bombs from a bomber and went up to the entrance and put a bomb in. It was rather awkward as the entrance was so constructed that one had to throw the bomb round a corner, which meant exposing oneself a bit, but luckily they were a tame lot of Huns and did not do anything vindictive. The first bomb did not seem to have much effect, so I put another one in. After that, four of them came running out all wounded – the other two must have been either killed or too hurt to come out. One of the four was an officer with an iron cross. He was slightly wounded in two or three places. He had an empty automatic holster. I wanted the pistol and got quite angry with him. He got annoyed and kept trying to make me understand that he had thrown it away in his fright.[42]

Major Cecil Barton, 1st Battalion, Worcestershire Regiment

As the support brigade came up to reinforce the attack one soldier at least was struck by one of those moments when a fleeting glimpse of natural beauty, ironically generated by weapons of hate and destruction, was sufficiently strong, just for an instant, to eclipse the chaos of battle.

I saw German shells falling into Bellewaarde Lake. They sent up fountains of water as they fell, with the colours of the rising sun reflected in the water. I stood for a little admiring this then found I was stuck in the mud but someone soon pulled me out.[43]

Private Alfred Warsop, 1st Battalion, Sherwood Foresters

The Foresters pushed on until they reached their objective of the village of Westhoek on the Black Line. Further progress was impossible because of heavy machine-gun fire emanating from the Hannebeek Valley in front of them and Glencourse Wood on their right flank.

All that was left was three or four groups of ruined houses, the basement of which had been turned into a reinforced concrete pillbox. I wanted to see what it was like over the Ridge and on the other side saw a strange sight: down in the valley, perhaps half a mile away, our barrage was still advancing, a line of shells moving forward 25 yards at intervals. In front just like a line of ants was a line of German troops getting away as fast as they could. I saw one of our men standing almost beside me, obviously in pain. I asked him if there was anything I could do. 'No,' he said, 'I'm done for, bleeding internally.' Then he asked me to get his water bottle. I have never forgotten him, among all the hundreds I saw die that day, alone and quietly dying.[44]

Private Alfred Warsop, 1st Battalion, Sherwood Foresters

As a runner, Warsop was ordered by his officer to take a message back to brigade headquarters to report their progress. As he walked back across the Westhoek Ridge towards Ypres, he gained a powerful insight into the tactical value of the ridge for which they were fighting. Ahead of him lay an astonishing vista.

Now in daylight, I could look back down the slope and see the ruins of the town. I could understand why it had been such a death trap for so long; every street seemed plain without binoculars, any movement an easy target for the Germans established on the top of the Ridge. At the Headquarters I found an officer who in the past had always seemed very cool and unruffled but who was now very agitated and almost in a panic. He gave me a message saying, 'For God's sake get it through!' I took it back and afterwards guessed what was in it – the reserves could not get through and we were to hold the Ridge at all costs.[45]

Private Alfred Warsop, 1st Battalion, Sherwood Foresters

On the right of the 8th Division frontage the Worcesters were having great difficulty in maintaining their front while simultaneously bending back to the right in an attempt to link up with the forward troops of the 30th Division who had fallen behind. It was of crucial importance that a unified front should be established and consolidated if the German counter-attacks were not to sweep them back from all their hard-won gains.

We were now the most advanced troops in the neighbourhood, with no-one to our right, and the troops to our left were to our left rear so far as we knew. We lined a slight rise formed by an old German parapet. This, with some old bits of trench gave us quite good cover. To our right front, about 200 yards away, the Huns had lined the ditch or trench on the side of the Menin Road. Most of them must have taken shelter in a tunnel which ran along under the road at this point, and come out when the barrage had passed. There were also six Huns holding out in a trench about 20–30 yards to our left front. Huns were moving across our front in twos and threes to reinforce the strong post on our right. I shot several of

> these at a range of about 200–300 yards. I had two Lewis guns with me at this time and started firing at the strong post. One gun was knocked out by a bullet and the other jammed after a few rounds, which was a pity as these Huns were holding up the advance on the right and we had perfect enfilade fire on them. So we carried on with rifle fire.[46]
>
> Major Cecil Barton, 1st Battalion, Worcestershire Regiment

Quite a vigorous firefight sprang up between Barton's small force and the two German posts he had identified.

> I then turned to have a bit of a strafe with the strong point on the left. I made a dash over the slight rise of the ground into the trench beyond, to see if I could get at them better. A Lewis gunner who followed me carrying some drums of ammunition, was shot through the stomach, the bullet passing through one of the magazine drums and setting the cordite on fire. I looked back as he dashed over the slight rise and wondered at the yellowish flare the cordite made. An officer of the Manchesters who tried to follow me was shot though the head. The only live person I saw here was a Jewish looking Hun with an awful wound in his back, crawling along. I beckoned to him to surrender and yelled to the men behind to get him in. I then saw one of our dead rifle Grenadiers by me so I took his grenades and started firing them alternatively right and left of the Huns. A Corporal of the Manchesters did likewise. I had quite a duel with one Hun on the left; we made alternate shots at each other. As only his head and rifle were showing and he was having shots at me as well, I didn't manage to get him.[47]
>
> Major Cecil Barton, 1st Battalion, Worcestershire Regiment

Adjoining the 8th Division, the 30th Division had indeed had a torrid time. It had been recognized that they faced the most difficult task of all. Confronted by heavy German shellfire when they started, in the morass of shell holes, mud, barbed wire and devastated woodland of Sanctuary Wood, they soon lost touch with the creeping barrage which progressed inexorably ahead of them, allowing the German defending troops to emerge in good time. Although they were successful in grasping the Blue Line objectives they were then held up by severe machine-gun fire emanating from the Stirling Castle pillbox complex. These problems were exacerbated by the loss of direction suffered by several units, and in particular the 2nd Battalion, Royal Scots Fusiliers who, on emerging from Sanctuary Wood, mistook Chateau Wood for their intended objective of

Glencourse Wood and therefore veered off to the left. Eventually Stirling Castle and Bodmin Copse were captured, but only after troops intended for the assault on Glencourse Wood and Inverness Copse had been thoroughly entangled in the bitter fighting. The situation was totally confused and made worse when the German barrage fell right across Sanctuary and Chateau Woods and cut all communications. It was obvious that the British counter-battery fire in this sector had completely failed to suppress the massed German batteries concealed on the reverse slopes and valleys of the Gheluvelt Plateau. The 30th Division's second wave moved forward without the support of a creeping barrage and soon became embroiled in the fighting as part of a *mélange* of miscellaneous battalions, although they were successful in establishing tenuous links with the 8th Division on their left near the Menin Road. As they passed the German front-line positions, they found the corpses of their enemies.

> There were two dead Germans, one lying on his face and the other leaning against a wall. He was a handsome bloke, he reminded me of my father a bit. A shell had dissected him nicely, it had taken the whole of the front off his chest down to his stomach. Neatly cut aside and laid apart as if he was in an anatomy school. I said, 'What a fantastic exhibition of anatomy!' It sounds heartless but then you're in an area of suppressed emotion so your mind tends to take over.[48]
>
> Corporal E. G. Williams, 19th Battalion, King's Liverpool Regiment

The 18th Division were due to leapfrog over the 30th Division once it had captured Glencourse Wood and push across the Gheluvelt Plateau. From their reserve positions they watched the attack begin at 03.50. They had a fine view as the awesome behemoths of B Battalion, Tank Corps rolled forward.

> It was just beginning to get light, and the tanks looked very queer as they crawled from their clumps of bushes and other hiding places and went forward. The enemy shelled our trench intermittently with 5.9s so we had to keep our heads down most of the time. I saw some of the Norfolks killed and wounded by a shell immediately in front of us. A tank which came forward on our right ran right over some of the men in front, who were lying on the ground either dead or wounded. We shouted ourselves hoarse, but it was of no use – the men in the tank could not hear us and the tank was over the men in a minute.[49]
>
> Signaller Sydney Fuller, 8th Battalion, Suffolk Regiment

As planned the 53rd Brigade of the 18th Division went forward in the tracks of the 30th Division. It was immediately apparent that something had gone very wrong as they moved through Sanctuary Wood.

> About 3½ hours after the barrage started the Battalion, according to plan, formed up in artillery formation and began to advance, to take up the advance from where the Division in front had halted. As soon as we began to move we were horribly shelled by the enemy, 4.2s and whizz-bangs and many of our men were killed and wounded. It was evident from the way that the shelling was done that we could be seen by the enemy. This was not 'as planned' for the Division in front of us should by now have captured the whole of the first ridge in front and the enemy should therefore have been unable to see the ground we were advancing over.[50]
>
> Signaller Sydney Fuller, 8th Battalion, Suffolk Regiment

The Suffolks crossed the breastwork of the former German front line and came under heavy rifle and machine-gun fire.

> The going was very heavy owing to the mud and we soon had to stop for a short rest. The enemy's built up trenches were almost obliterated by the heavy fire of our guns. Trunks of trees were lying across them, anyhow, and the whole of the ground had been pulverised by shells. One badly wounded German lay writhing in agony on the ground near where we stopped. He was evidently past help. One of the signallers who had managed to get a little more than his share of rum issue, was desirous of shooting the dying German. 'Bastard', he called him, but we put a stop to that business. I saw two bullets strike the wounded German immediately afterwards and he ceased to move so evidently someone had no scruples about it. Possibly (but not probably) someone shot him to 'put him out of his misery'. However, there were many men who shot down any of the enemy, regardless of circumstances – wounded or prisoners it made no difference – and it was noticeable that the men who did that sort of thing were loudest in condemning the German 'atrocities'. Two wrongs evidently made a right with them.[51]
>
> Signaller Sydney Fuller, 8th Battalion, Suffolk Regiment

After a short rest, they continued past Stirling Castle to the Menin Road embankment.

> We then discovered that we were at the limit of our advance – the first division had not captured anything like the amount of ground allotted to them, hence the reason why the enemy shelling and machine gun fire had been so deadly when we advanced.[52]
>
> Signaller Sydney Fuller, 8th Battalion, Suffolk Regiment

They also discovered that the tanks were having severe problems.

> Six of our tanks got stuck in the boggy ground immediately behind us. Four of them managed to struggle out again, but two sank so deeply in the mud that they were left. Four of these tanks were named Brian Boru, Boomerang, Bentley and Britannia. Two of them got up the bank onto the road and the enemy's bullets struck them by scores, but of course had no effect. When the tanks had gone a little way up the road, towards Inverness Copse, they were one after the other knocked out by small shells.[53]
>
> Signaller Sydney Fuller, 8th Battalion, Suffolk Regiment

Of the forty-eight tanks of the 2nd Tank Brigade deployed in front of the II Corps, only nineteen got through the mud into action and all but one became casualties. The seventeen tanks lying derelict by Clapham Junction earned it the sobriquet 'the tank graveyard'. They had achieved little to help the infantry. Eventually the Suffolks crossed the Menin Road by Clapham Junction and after advancing a few more hundred yards, they were forced to consolidate in front of the strongly held Glencourse Wood.

Meanwhile Barton had belatedly managed to establish contact with a few of the Manchester Regiment from the left-hand brigade of the 30th Division. He discovered to his astonishment that his troops were positioned exactly where they were supposed to be although his pride was tempered by the knowledge that, as far as he was concerned, it was a complete fluke! His view of the courageous attempts of the tanks to overcome the hostile terrain also showed what might have been possible in different circumstances.

> Eight or nine tanks came slowly up, but the ground was too heavy for them and a lot of them got stuck. One tank got tired of sticking so it got onto the Menin Road and went along clambering over fallen logs in fine style. It put a machine gun which was worrying our people on the right out of action, then it stuck.[54]
>
> Major Cecil Barton, 1st Battalion, Worcestershire Regiment

Unfortunately communications with his own battalion headquarters had by this stage completely broken down and Barton set off to find out where they were. Although he was successful in finding another twenty men under an NCO – which doubled his force – the rest were not to be found. Eventually he found a runner who was just as frantically looking for the forward companies. He carried orders that they were to withdraw from their positions and retire to Chateau Wood. The right flank of the 8th Division was being compromised by the failure of the 30th Division attack.

> Our way lay through a wood by the lake we had seen earlier. Suddenly I saw a shrapnel burst about 70 yards in front and felt a stinging pain in my left arm. I knew at once it was broken. I told Sergeant Moore to take the men on to Battalion Headquarters. A stretcher bearer who was by me cut away the sleeve of my tunic and put a first field dressing on my arm and we then started to walk back, the stretcher bearer carrying my pack for me.[55]
>
> Major Cecil Barton, 1st Battalion, Worcestershire Regiment

In the plan for the II Corps attack the 24th Division had been intended to form a defensive flank on the right of the advance. But the left-hand brigades of the division, after passing through Shrewsbury Forest, found themselves dragged down by the same problems as the 30th Division. The difficult terrain and vigorous German opposition caused them to become detached from their creeping barrage and they too stalled in front of the German second line. The combined efforts of the 30th and 18th Divisions had failed against the rock of the Gheluvelt Plateau.

South of the main thrust being carried out by Fifth Army, Plumer's Second Army was to make a simultaneous advance across the right-hand edge of the Gheluvelt Plateau pivoting on the new positions won at Messines six weeks earlier. Forging the link between the two armies was the 41st Division of the X Corps which was to advance on either side of the Ypres–Comines Canal. On the left the 123rd Brigade moved forward from Battle Wood.

> We were in the fourth wave, we were well back. Everybody got into trouble that morning. The first, second, third wave, all the lot of us because of these concrete pillboxes. This was the first time they'd been encountered. Concrete emplacements with a machine gun slot in the

front of them. There wasn't much artillery fire there. These pillboxes were so built that one covered another. If you were busy attacking one, you came under fire from another one, they all covered each other. The only way to really clear them, that some of our men used, was to creep underneath the machine gun slot, and put a Mills bomb through – one bomb was sufficient as a rule to clear the inside of them. We hadn't gone much further forward before I was hit, I saw the blood running down my hand, it was painful of course – and that's as much as I know of that battle![56]

Private George Thompson, 20th Battalion, Durham Light Infantry

The 21st Battalion, King's Royal Rifle Corps provided close support to the attack by the 123rd Brigade on the German trenches near the road to Klein Zillebeke.

The going was very heavy; water-filled shell holes; slippery craters; slimy mud – all helped to make it hard work lifting one's feet to progress, little by little. Yet, the troops went forward and despite the cloudy day with its threat of rain, the tasks set to the brigade were overcome satisfactorily, though with many casualties. A successful mission was achieved, though we did not realise it. We, in support, were now occupying some water-logged trenches, well over the ankles in mud. We struggled to keep our rifles clean, it was a problem finding somewhere to rest them that was not wet through. A drizzle had been falling for some time and was getting more like showers. By four o'clock the showers had turned to heavy rain, almost torrential. What ground, and little there was of it, that had not been churned up by our bombardment was fast becoming a quagmire – not a jot of help to us, but helping the enemy to reorganise and reinforce his defeated troops.[57]

Signaller Gerald Dennis, 21st Battalion, King's Royal Rifle Corps

Further progress was dependent on the success of II Corps' attack on the Gheluvelt Plateau immediately to the north, and in the light of what had happened there consolidation was the only option. Minor attacks along the rest of the Second Army front were intended simply to exploit the opportunity offered by the offensive to improve tactical positions secured after the Messines offensive and to add to the general pressure on the German front line.

Throughout the day, all over the Salient, the Royal Flying Corps whenever possible flew 'contact patrols' which were desperately needed to try and determine what progress the attack had made. Such information was vital in controlling the artillery and in directing reinforcement units into action where they were most needed. At dawn Lieutenant Jack Walthew and his observer, Lieutenant Woodstock, took off in an RE8 on this dangerous mission in terrible flying conditions.

> The weather was most hopelessly dud. The clouds were at 800 so we had to fly at 700. This was almost suicidal as a machine is a very big and easy target. However, as we were the contact patrol flight we had to go up and try to do something. The other flights have been on the ground all day. I left the aerodrome at 05.30 and scraped over houses and trees etc. until I got to our guns. Here the fun started as there was, so experts tell me, the worst barrage that has ever been known – and I had to fly through it. I could hear, and occasionally see, the shells and every minute I was expecting to see one of my wings vanish. However, nothing hit us until we got over the line (which had been pushed forward considerably) and here in 8 minutes we got 30 holes through the machine from machine guns. Ten of them passed within a few inches of Woodstock. The wireless transmitter valued at £200 disappeared, three spars on the wing were broken, and lastly a bullet went through the petrol tank. I smelt a smell of petrol and in a few minutes it all came rushing over my feet and legs. How we got back I don't know, it seemed the longest journey I have ever made but eventually we landed safely.[58]
>
> Lieutenant Jack Walthew, 4 Squadron, Royal Flying Corps

Once safe back on land, Walthew didn't even get a chance to have his breakfast before he was sent aloft again to track down the whereabouts of the struggling 30th Division.

> We called to the infantry to light flares for us; but as they wouldn't do this, we had to draw the fire of the Huns ourselves so as to discover where the enemy line was, and deduct ours' from it. We managed to do this fairly successfully and came back unhurt. Immediately we were put into a car and taken to Corps Headquarters where we interviewed several old Generals and Brass Hats. So altogether we had a pretty busy morning. This afternoon it has been raining, so we've had nothing to do. It is an awful shame the weather is so bad, as given fine weather we could have done much better work and chased the Hun for miles.[59]
>
> Lieutenant Jack Walthew, 4 Squadron, Royal Flying Corps

It was recognized as crucially important to get the relatively short-range field artillery of 18-pounder guns and 4.5-inch howitzers forward as soon as possible, if the artillery support was not to begin to falter as the infantry advanced beyond their effective range.

> We were due to cease firing and advance at 06.10 a.m., so at that hour, the backs of the gunpits having been previously been pulled down, we started the heavy labour of man-handling the guns out of their sunk pits. Luckily at that very moment a Highlander came down the track escorting 25 prisoners. I called to him to go into the cookhouse and have some tea, and to hand over his rifle and the prisoners to my tender mercies. The Hun was sending over some 8 inch shell and when I ordered the prisoners to man the drag-ropes they started to argue that they ought not to be made to do it, but the arguments only lasted 30 seconds; the well-known sound (almost 'Esperanto') of a rifle bolt going to full cock and a few well chosen words of abuse learnt on a Pomeranian barrack square, quickly got them to work, and meanwhile our gunners were safely under cover and able to have breakfast.[60]
>
> Major Neil Fraser-Tytler, 150th Brigade, Royal Field Artillery

Arrangements had been made for parties of gunners to move up with the infantry ready to prepare advanced positions for the guns to occupy immediately they could be brought forward.

> We were now struggling through the shell holes and the black mud which stuck to us like glue, until we reached a point near to where our first line trenches used to be before the attack opened out and our officer decided that our new gun position was to be at this spot. Each gun place was marked off and it was now hard graft with spades and entrenching tools, filling sandbags, with tunics and shirts off and the rain coming down like hell, and a thick mist covering the ground like a November morning. We commenced to build a double row of sandbags to form a gunpit and give a certain amount of protection from shell fire, which we were getting plenty of at the time being. We could see the sappers and engineers laying duckboards and plank roads along the shell shattered roads and fields.[61]
>
> Gunner A. J. Heraty, 241st Brigade, Royal Field Artillery

As soon as it was feasible the field guns were advanced into their new positions.

> Just as dawn broke, we moved off towards the line. The grand attack had

started. We encountered some pioneers, all elderly men, on either side of the road, where they had been doing repairs. They had a steam-roller with them and none of the horses could pass this. The first team went plunging into the ditch, dragging their gun with them, and then somebody gave the order to place sandbags over the horses, eyes and ears. We did this and somehow got through. We arrived at an old cemetery, when a heavy shell blew the first team and gun to smithereens – and this was the first time some of these men had been in action. How the remainder of us got through I do not know, but we did land near Pilckem Ridge and St Julien. On the track, we crouched down between our horses and cantered whenever possible. Lying on the ground was a great number of men of the Cheshire Regiment. Our horses jumped over them or stepped on them and the wheels went over their bodies, wounded or dead. It made no difference – it was advance. The German artillery was peppering us with shells of all calibres. The smell was horrible – combining gas shells, rotten apples and mustard gas – it just stank. Our eyes were watering and we were all coughing. Horses were snorting. Still the order was, 'Use your whips and get forward!' At last we reached some marked positions. We unlimbered our guns and left our gun limbers with ammunition for the gunmen and managed to canter back anywhere to get beyond the shellfire of the enemy. Two of my team horses had been hit and also the drivers. One was the wheel driver and we must have dragged these two horses at least fifty yards before we unhooked them from the traces.[62]

Driver Rowland Luther, 92nd Brigade, Royal Field Artillery

Despite the advances that had been made, as the guns moved forward they were vulnerable to German counter-battery fire once their new positions had been identified.

It was now about 10 a.m., the rain had eased off a bit and the mist had begun to clear up. Our guns had arrived and we were lining them up on our targets as messages began to come through from our observation post. We had built sandbags up to the height of our gun wheels and had covered the gun up with 'camouflage' we carried with us. We were ready for action when we heard a plane coming towards us and he suddenly appeared from nowhere, right on top of us. We could see he was a Jerry by the markings on his wings and, as he banked over us his wing tips were no more than six feet from the ground. Several of us immediately grabbed a rifle and had a pot at him, but I am afraid

> we were unable to hit him. It would have saved us a lot of trouble if we had been lucky enough to have brought him down because within half an hour, shells began to drop around us which came closer and closer. Jerry plastered us with his 5.9 howitzers both time bursting and high explosive with the result that we lost four gunners and an NCO within an hour. One of our men was hit with a large piece of shrapnel, it had scalped him and as we laid him down his brains were spewing over his forehead. I tried to smooth it back again and put the top of his scalp back again, thinking he might live – those are some of the things one tries to do in our state. Well it was 'action stations' as orders kept coming over the line from our OP and we commenced to give Jerry a bit back in return. We were in action for most of that day firing shells as quick as the mules could bring them up to us. Between our six guns we must have fired at least a 1,000 rounds of ammunition.[63]
>
> Gunner A. J. Heraty, 241st Brigade, Royal Field Artillery

The gunners did their best but it was physically impossible to duplicate the destructive power of the morning bombardment as the infantry moved over the ridge, out of sight, often out of touch and, for many batteries, even out of range of their intended targets.

ALONG THE front of the attack the thinly held German forward defensive zone had been taken. But the German counter-attack policy was based firmly on the premise that as the British infantry moved further forward, so artillery support for their attack formations weakened, just as the German strength correspondingly would grow as their specially designated counter-attack divisions moved up from their reserve billets. Positioned behind the Broodseinde–Passchendaele Ridge these counter-attack divisions were almost unscathed by the British bombardments and their thrust was directed squarely at the advanced brigades of the 39th, 55th, 15th and 8th Divisions in the centre of the attack. Even in success these formations had suffered inevitable casualties, increased physical and mental fatigue and a general breakdown in communications with both their artillery support and divisional commanders. At 14.00 a pulverizing German barrage fell upon the British line between the Ypres–Roulers railway and the village of St Julien. It presaged a serious German counter-attack directed initially on the left against the 39th Division which had moved forward from St Julien into positions on either side of the St Julien–Poelcappelle road. The tired troops were unable to hold onto all their hard-won gains, being forced back to a line along the Steenbeek which entailed losing control of the battered remnants of the village of St Julien itself. As the tide turned, Lieutenant Eric Walthew, whose brother Jack had earlier in the day flown his RE8 on contact patrols above the attack, found his luck had changed.

> I don't think I had ever enjoyed myself so much as I did while the show was on, till suddenly something hit me and when I woke up I was in a shell hole with a dead Herts man beside me and three or four Germans looking on. When they saw I was still alive and kicking, they took me along, having previously relieved me of all my kit including my glasses which had just arrived the day before! Apparently the Battalion lost heavily and were forced to fall back.[64]
>
> Lieutenant Eric Walthew, 1/1st Battalion, Hertfordshire Regiment

The tanks of G Battalion were caught up in the battle. Sergeant Allnatt was heading back to refuel at the tank rendezvous in Kitchener's Wood and had just managed to recross the Steenbeek.

> I had not gone more than 50 yards towards home when I saw a tank which had come up on the left and was firing in the direction of the enemy. I swung round and saw that an enemy counter-attack was in full blast and the Germans were only about 100 yards away. Although in a very sleepy condition the gunners opened fire. I patrolled up and down, giving each pair of gunners turns at the enemy. Unfortunately, at this time the other tank – 'Glamorgan' I think its name was – was standing still firing at the enemy, with all its guns. It was bound to happen, although they were unaware of it, enemy shells were falling all about it. I thought for a moment that I could send someone to tell them what was happening, but I knew it would probably mean the death of one of my crew. I turned away momentarily, and when I looked back, 'Glamorgan' had disappeared. The names of the crew are inscribed on the Menin Gate as 'Killed, but no known grave'.[65]
>
> Sergeant J. C. Allnatt, G Battalion, Tank Corps

The German success in driving back the British line exposed the left flank of the 55th Division who in turn were soon subjected to repeated attacks.

The men fought hard but the Germans had artillery superiority and greater numbers. Bit by bit they too were forced back.

> The day wore on with the enemy raining explosive shells on us in a leaden sky and in a steady downpour. The mud was appalling, the shell holes and trenches filled with water, adding discomfort to continuous danger. Fortunately, I was able to enjoy the comparative comfort of the concrete pillbox, but whenever an alarm of enemy counter-attack was signalled, we had to dash out and man a newly dug support trench, which was nearly waist deep in water. It was like jumping into a bath, a very cold bath, in which we had to stand for hours.[66]
>
> Company Sergeant Major John Handley, 1/6th Battalion, King's Liverpool Regiment

As the casualties mounted the medical officers and padres were busy, desperately trying to alleviate the physical and mental suffering of the wounded and dying.

> Piper and I went out and tried to collect wounded. We found one man pretty bad in our trench and got him along after a rather strenuous journey. We ought to have got him over the top of the trench to start with and then to have made across the open but we kept on and soon could not have got out if we had tried. The mud and loose duckboards made it fearfully difficult. In the end we got him to the aid post. We had been told of another man who had been seen up towards Garden Trench and we found the blood trail but never got him as he had evidently crawled out of the trench and been seen and evacuated.[67]
>
> Reverend Maurice Murray, 12th & 13th Battalions, Royal Sussex Regiment

The Sussex's original Regimental Aid Post was too far back to deal with casualties amongst the advancing troops. It was therefore moved forward to Calf Support Trench in the former German lines.

> Poor old Piper was hit at 3 p.m. A liaison officer told me where he was. He had taken shelter from the shelling with some others under the lee of a sort of low roofed shed. I told Gatchell and he did him up as soon as I had found him. He used the pointed stick which I had given Piper at Poperinghe as a splint and I kicked away another piece from the trench for another. I sat with him in a dip on the side of the shed which was 12th Battalion Headquarters till 8 p.m. when at last stretcher bearers came for him. He asked me to sing Hymns, 'Abide with me' and 'Sun of my soul'. He had lost a lot of blood before I found him

and was very white. His foot was nearly blown off and he was in great pain, and I put his head on my knees.[68]

Reverend Maurice Murray, 12th & 13th Battalion Royal Sussex Regiment

Thousands of wounded lay in the makeshift dressing stations, surrounded by suffering, but alone with their thoughts.

German shells were crashing around, the near ones making the whole place shake and spraying the tin roof over my head with stones and lumps of soil. I lay there feeling relaxed and happy. I had little fear of the German shell. After all, they'd been trying to hit me for three years and I didn't think they were likely to succeed twice in one day. But the main cause of my relief was my elation from the fear of being afraid.[69]

Lieutenant M. L. Walkinton, 24th Machine Gun Company, Machine Gun Corps

Captain Noel Chavasse VC of the Royal Army Medical Corps, the Medical Officer of the Liverpool Scottish, rescued Captain Owtram from his helpless predicament lying wounded in the captured German trench.

An hour later he reappeared with stretcher-bearers drawn from the Pioneer Corps. They were Welsh miners whose peacetime labours can scarcely have been more arduous than that of carrying human bodies across a thousand yards at least of shell pitted ground now being turned into a morass by the rain that was falling steadily. Their supply of epithets to describe the situation was copious and I felt with them, if not for them, as they slipped and slithered across the slimy and treacherous ground. At last we reached the shelter of the great Wieltje dugout where after receiving an injection of morphia, I remained through the night in a state of only intermittent consciousness.[70]

Captain Thomas Owtram, 1/5th Battalion, King's Own Royal Lancaster Regiment

Owtram was just one of the many who owed their lives to Chavasse over the next two days. As a result Chavasse was subsequently awarded a posthumous bar to his VC for his actions during this period. Although suffering from a head wound received on the first day of the battle, he went out again and again with his stretcher bearers into No Man's Land to rescue the wounded. Finally he was wounded again, this time mortally, on 2 August and died in hospital two days later.

As the day wore on the 15th Division faced increasing German counter-attacks on their positions along the London Ridge.

Nothing happened till afternoon when the German artillery opened up and local counter-attacks developed. One such, by I should say a battalion, penetrated a gap on my right and occupied some concrete pillboxes which we had captured previously. Then another came in on my left and drove in the Highland Light Infantry. My two forward platoons stayed where they were and were eventually surrounded and captured after hanging onto their positions till next day. Now my Headquarters and Reserve Platoons were pinned down by fire from right and left, but we were not attacked. I sent my runner, Private Kay, back to Battalion Headquarters to explain the position and to say I thought I was all right till dark, but what was I to do then? Kay carefully crawled back till he was in dead ground. About half an hour later he returned to say that Colonel Russell and Johnny Carrick, the Adjutant, had been killed by a shell and no one at HQ knew where the other Companies were. It was now getting late and would soon be dark. It was obvious we could not silence the pillboxes, the nearest only some 100 yards away. Every time a head went up for a look out it drew fire. So we had to wait until dusk. When bad light made it possible I tried to get in touch with my forward platoons but at that moment to my horror our guns brought down a heavy barrage on us, wiping out several of my Reserve Platoon. I with Private Kay and MacLean, my batman, were lucky enough to dive into a huge shell crater, but sad to say Kay had been hit and died in agony in my arms. As soon as it got dark MacLean and I tried to find B and C Company but could find no sign of them. Then the barrage was lifted and brought back behind us and we had the awful experience of seeing it approach from behind, sweep over us and settle on the ridge in front. As Senior Officer I now made for Battalion Headquarters, which I eventually found with great difficulty. I gathered a fresh attack was being mounted by another Division as our Brigade HQ thought we had failed to take our objective and were completely out of the picture, whereas we been on our sector of the objective all day. As we were making forward again to find the remnants of my Company, if I could, our new barrage opened intensively and MacLean and I had to dive for a shell crater and endure an agonising 30 minutes or so being shelled by our own guns. Then the fresh infantry attack came in the dark and we were all but bayoneted by English troops taking us for Germans. When moving back I collected what stragglers I could find and marched them back to Brigade Headquarters. Here I told Brigadier Allgood what had happened and he said how sorry he was that the troops on our flanks had failed to deal with the concrete pillboxes and so had left the Camerons out on a limb. Owing to Colonel Russell's death he could get no word of what had happened to the Camerons, or where they were, such is the fog of war; and after all our carefully rehearsed exercises. I brought out with me 41 men, and with others straggling back we mustered 3 Officers and 140 strong. I was officially reported missing, believed killed, and I never wish to go through such a terrible experience again.[71]

Captain Philip Christison, 6th Battalion, Cameron Highlanders

In such chaos and confusion, the calm controlled decisions of tactical exercises simply could not be reproduced. It was almost impossible to take firm, clear-cut decisions without any intelligence as to one's own position or reserves, no idea of the location of the enemy and no means of communication on a battlefield torn with screaming shell fragments and nerve-jarring detonations.

The German counter-attacks did not meet with universal success all along the line. Perversely, where things had not gone so well and the front had not advanced as far forward, the German attempts to hit back often met with a vigorous response from well-consolidated troops still in touch with their artillery.

About seven o'clock we saw the Germans massing for a counter-attack. They were coming over the ridge on the other side of the valley and two of our companies went forward to help meet this counter-attack. The forward British troops sent up red Verey Lights as a signal that the enemy were about to attack. Then our artillery and sections of machine guns opened fire: trees were uprooted; fountains of water and mud rose into the air as the enemy began to retire after suffering heavy losses.[72]

Signaller Gerald Dennis, 21st Battalion, King's Royal Rifle Corps

On the Westhoek Ridge, however, the situation was little short of desperate. The 8th Division's support brigade had been consumed in the fight to take the Green Line objectives and the same battalions that had made the initial assault were consequently required to hold their gains at all costs against vigorous counter-attacks.

We were stuck on the Ridge with very thin forces to hold it. After the attack was over the First Battalion had lost 600 killed or wounded out of a 1,000 men. Going back over the same ground I had covered earlier in the attack it seemed to me it had one of our dead laid out every few yards. There seemed to be very few men indeed in that part of the line and in the afternoon the Captain and I were the only ones in sight, both very thirsty. We tried numerous water bottles, both British and German, but they were all empty and we had to be satisfied with drinking from puddles.[73]

Private Alfred Warsop, 1st Battalion, Sherwood Foresters

Warsop and his officer were in a captured German trench and the built-up parapet was therefore behind them.

The shout went up, 'They're coming. The Jerries are coming!' There was only one thing to do – if we stayed in the trench we should be have been shot from above like rats in a trap, so I shouted, 'All out and on the back!' Two stayed in and five of us were on the back, one with a machine gun on the extreme left. He had only fired five rounds when he was shot and killed, then the next, then the one on my left. In theory it would be my turn next, but I thought I saw two men behind some bushes 25 yards in front. By now I was thoroughly frightened but I did draw my rifle, check my sights to 25 yards and very carefully squeezed the trigger at first one and then the other indistinct figure. By this time the man on my right was hit and how I escaped I shall never know unless I got them before they got me. A whistle blew on the German side and the men, quite a lot of them, made their way back to their own lines. A voice at the back said, 'Come down, Warsop, you can't do any more!' It was the Captain and a few more that had come up from the right. We couldn't understand why they had called off the counter-attack since they had taken the strongpoint on the right and worked round the back of us. They couldn't have realised how thin our line was there.[74]

Private Alfred Warsop, 1st Battalion, Sherwood Foresters

Eventually remnants of the 8th Division could hold on no longer and they retired from the German Second Line situated on the reverse slope, back up onto the crest of the Westhoek Ridge, and in the process also relinquished Westhoek village itself.

To the left, in the salient held by the 55th and 15th Divisions, nightfall brought no relief from the torments of the day.

An inky-black, wet night closed in on us and we were a tired, hopeless, wet through lot of miserable soldiers. The pillbox was crowded to almost suffocation with wounded, stretcher bearers, signallers, etc. and the resulting humid body heat made excursions out into a cold night a very distasteful business, quite apart from the danger. About midnight Rifleman Peet, an officer's servant, stumbled into the pillbox badly wounded and saying that Lieutenant Burton was 'out there' also wounded, but trying to get shelter. I ordered two stretcher bearers to come with me. They objected so I threatened them with my pistol and out we went on what I feared was a hopeless quest. The only illumination was from exploding shells and rocket lights. Eventually we saw him, a crouching figure, silhouetted by a shell burst. 'Thank God, Sergeant Major!' he said, as I got hold of his arm, but he groaned and said, 'The other one'. On getting him into the pillbox, I found his left shoulder blade blown away revealing a bloody mess that looked like his lung. He died on his way to the first aid station. This officer was acting as 'Liaison Officer' – keeping touch between our companies and the regiments on either side of us. He carried with him as much rum as he could, which he shared out to the men he met on his rounds, in his sympathy for them in their terrible conditions. This 'errand of mercy' he had just performed at the trench full of water in front of my pillbox. It was his last good deed in this world.[75]

Company Sergeant Major John Handley, 1/6th Battalion, King's Liverpool Regiment

All along the precarious front line miserable men skulked in shell holes and pillboxes, cursing the omnipresent rain that soaked them to the skin.

What a night it was. Did I get any sleep? I do not remember. The bed and the pillows were soft enough – and very watery – as I tried to find comfort in a shell hole. Luckier ones managed to find a piece of trench to rest in. I used my spade frequently to throw water out of the bottom. I had become accustomed to manage on a few hours' sleep and no doubt had a few naps. Like the others I had eaten sparingly, a little bread and a thin slice of bully. Water was precious and I drank but a little. The crawl out to an unoccupied shell hole to use a latrine was a frightening effort, not to be made unless absolutely necessary.[76]

Signaller Gerald Dennis, 21st Battalion, King's Royal Rifle Corps

Where possible reserves were moved up to help bolster the new line but in the rapidly deteriorating weather conditions, and given the problems of a mud and shell-hole wilderness, that in itself was a major operation of war. Late in the day the 10th Battalion, Cheshire Regiment received orders to move forward in case German counter-attacks drove out the 2nd Northamptons holding the Westhoek and Bellewaarde Ridges. The

Cheshires were ordered to take up a position on the reverse slope and not to occupy the trenches on the ridge unless they were required for a counter-attack.

> The Battalion would be lying out in the open, under an intense barrage from which they would have no protection. However, it had got to be, and my Battalion was 'for it'. It was now 11.30 p.m., pitch dark, the whole country was a mass of slimy mud and obstacles. No-one else in the Battalion except myself and one other had ever seen the ground before. I went on ahead with an orderly in the pouring rain, and although I knew every inch of the ground, was unencumbered with equipment, and had a stick to help me along, I found some difficulty in finding my way. Owing to the mud, it took me over two hours to get there, a distance of only a mile. When I got there, the 24th Brigade did not want us. However, the order had to be carried out. Waiting for the Battalion to arrive, and wet to the skin, I slithered about looking for any old German dugout to shelter in, but without success. Tried several times to shelter in a hurdle lean-to in the wood near the lake, but was always getting shelled, and eventually had to content myself with walking up and down in mud up to my knees in a vain effort to keep warm, with my clothes soaked, and with the water trickling down my neck. The worst night I have ever known. The Battalion began to arrive about 3.30 a.m. The men were fearfully done up, having been slithering about in the dark all night, wet to the skin, and carrying a lot of extra weight. I felt very bad at having to line them up out in the swamp, and put them in little ground in crump holes, most of them were deep in water. There was a little shelling, and being out in the open, we began at once to have casualties. About 7 a.m, to my great relief, I was told I could relieve the 2nd Northampton's right away. But it was not going to help us much, as they were holding new, half dug trenches, which the rain was fast filling, or making them crumble to nothing. The relief was quickly over, and I made my HQ in a German concrete machine gun emplacement on the Bellewaarde Ridge. The rain continued to pour, and there was a good deal of shelling. About mid-day the Germans started to bombard us heavily, and kept it up for the rest of the day. We had an awful time. There was no cover for the men. Trenches were soon non-existent, or became wet ditches in which men often sank up to their waists, and it often took six men to pull one man out of the mud. The Germans had got the range to an inch, had direct observation of us from our right and plastered the area

incessantly with crumps, whizz-bangs and 4.2's. Our casualties mounted rapidly. There was no cover, all one could do was to spread the men out in crump holes to minimise casualties. In the circumstances the men are apt to crowd together. It was only when I was about shaking them out that I got hit, although only slightly. First I was knocked off my feet by a bit of shrapnel, which fortunately only went through my boot and sock, and badly bruised my ankle. About 20 minutes later, I got a small piece of shell in the left hand which the doctor extracted. My poor fellows had an awful time, and many wounded sank in the mud, and were drowned in it before assistance could reach them. One officer, who had practically sunk in the mud out of sight, was found only half an hour after I had been speaking to him. We had about 200 casualties in the day, and besides this, there were men dropping from cold and exhaustion. The stretcher bearers could not compete with the number of casualties, and, in many cases, it required about 6 men to carry a stretcher, as each man sank in the mud at least up to his knees, and most men were too done up to be able to carry the weight. As it got dark, the shelling gradually subsided, but not so the rain, which fell incessantly. We got rations up with difficulty, but cooking was out of the question. The men just had to make the best of things, and spent the night in the mud, often up to their waists. Fortunately, we managed to get some rum which warmed them up a bit.[77]

Lieutenant Colonel A. C. Johnston, 10th Battalion, Cheshire Regiment

The line held. Although the 'icing on the cake' that marked the advances of the 55th and 15th Divisions had been lost, the Fifth Army had still made a considerable step forward by the prevailing standards of the Western Front. On the left two full German defensive lines had been taken and the Germans had been deprived of their uninhibited observation of the whole Ypres Salient from the Pilckem and Bellewaarde Ridges. Even on the Gheluvelt Plateau some progress had been made, with the German first line overrun and key observation points captured. Nine German divisions had been badly damaged and, although precise German casualties are hard to establish, most seem to agree that they suffered losses of around 30,000, of which 6,000 were prisoners of war, and 25 guns were captured.

When compared to the first day of the Battle of the Somme, the attack on 31 July 1917, subsequently termed the Battle of Pilckem Ridge, was undoubtedly a great success. But as the opening of the Somme had been an unparalleled military disaster, such a comparison will only ever be a bitter consolation. The success of a military operation ought really to be assessed with regard to the tactical and strategic objectives it was intended to achieve. The objectives of the Blue and Black Lines may have been achieved on the opening day of Third Ypres but the Green and Red Lines remained in German hands. In retrospect the day's events showed that Brigadier General Davidson had been right in his note urging caution and the restriction of advances only as far as the Black Line. Gough, backed by those such as Maxse and reluctantly endorsed by Haig, had aimed higher and pursued his dream of spectacular first-day gains right up to and including the elusive Red Line. In an overly ambitious attempt to reach these targets, his troops had been rendered vulnerable to strong German counter-attacks made by divisions that had been protected from the British bombardment. Gough had thus fallen right into the German trap. The failure to concentrate sufficient resources for the attack on the fearsome Gheluvelt Plateau had meant that there not even the Black Line had been taken, leaving the considerable successes on the left and in the centre exposed in an uncomfortable salient. By 1 August only half the job expected and required had been completed. But in achieving this the assaulting divisions had already suffered severe casualties that considerably reduced their military effectiveness, especially in the short term. Ahead of them the Passchendaele–Staden Ridge remained inviolate and any idea of entering Roulers in the near future had been reduced to a distant dream. The sheer strength of the German defences made it inevitable that any further progress would be slow and painful. Strategically the battle had failed to precipitate the beginning of a breakthrough to the Belgian coast to relieve the pressure, real or imagined, on the Royal Navy. This part of the plan already seemed fantastical. But the beginning of the long-drawn-out process of chewing up and spitting out German divisions had begun and would soon develop a grim momentum of its own. Even by the end of the opening day the strategic success or otherwise of the Ypres offensive looked likely to be measured by the results of a grim battle of attrition designed to run down the German forces in terms of numbers and morale.

The human cost of this limited achievement had been staggering. The Fifth Army had suffered 27,000 casualties killed, wounded and missing and the Second Army some 4,500, whilst the relatively fortunate French had lost under 2,000. Battalions full of strong fit men, forged by their training and previous battle experiences, had been reduced to husks. Even the strongest could not help but be moved by the scale of the losses and the suffering etched on the faces of those who had survived.

> On marching back behind Ypres, Brigadier Duncan, that hard stern soldier whom we feared, stood by the roadside taking the salute. 'March to attention!' rang out the order; then 'Eyes right!' and as we turned our heads we saw him standing erect, his right arm raised in the 'salute' and tears streaming down his face. It was indeed a sorry brigade he saluted that day – the remnants of battle – for barely a quarter of his men returned.[78]
>
> Company Sergeant Major John Handley, 1/6th Battalion, King's Liverpool Regiment

CHAPTER FIVE

AUGUST DESPAIR

I am still alive though at present I am more likely to die from drowning than from hostile fire. It has rained solidly for three days and the place is knee deep in mud. It is extraordinary weather for August.[1]

Major Roderick Macleod, 241st Brigade, Royal Field Artillery

Sir Douglas Haig had originally intended that the attack launched on 31 July should be resumed as soon as the British artillery had been moved forward in the wake of the infantry advance and their superiority re-established. Sir Hubert Gough responded by ordering the II Corps to attack on 2 August the original Black Line objectives that they had failed to capture on the Gheluvelt Plateau. Once this had been achieved, an attempt would be made all along the line to seize the Green Line that had been the original third objective on 31 July. However, despite this intention to maintain the momentum of the offensive, it was soon apparent to Haig's operational staff that although there were advantages in attacking as soon as possible, there were obvious difficulties as well.

We know from experience, however, that in these subsidiary operations, hurried preparations and the use of part-worn troops are generally the cause of failure, and that failure involves waste of valuable time and personnel. In this particular case we want to make absolutely certain of the artillery preparation, which will require very careful control and accurate shooting and two or more days of good flying weather prior to the attack. To ensure success, which is all-important at this stage, the corps ought really to attack with three fresh divisions and not put the 30th and 24th in again.[2]

Brigadier General John Davidson, Operations Section, GHQ

Good weather was important to allow the Royal Flying Corps to operate properly, probing behind the German lines to locate and to guide the artillery onto potential targets in the shape of German batteries, machine-gun posts and pillboxes. Good visibility was also required to make the best use of the newly captured observation points along the Pilckem and Bellewaarde Ridges.

Yet the weather was unremittingly awful and Gough had little choice but to cancel his planned follow-up operations on the Gheluvelt Plateau. The rain that had started on 31 July continued unabated for the next 72 hours. For the rest of August it rained on all but three days. This deluge had an immediate effect on the drainage of the battlefield and provoked a 'flood' of almost biblical proportions. Three years of shelling, culminating in the opening bombardment, had severely disrupted the network of streams, such as the Steenbeek, which flowed between the low ridges. Swollen by the rain and with their banks destroyed by the shells, the water flooded out of the stream beds across the low-lying areas to create an almost impassable marshland. Millions of shell holes filled with water and mud. Still the rain poured down. Even on the occasional days when the rainfall was minimal, a light drizzle continued to fall. Consequently, throughout the month there was no sustained period of 'drying weather' with sun and light breezes which might allow the battlefield some chance of recovering. It was a catastrophe for the conduct of the new offensive.

The troops at the front found it difficult to believe that those in high command understood their suffering. Stories, occasionally doubtless apocryphal, have multiplied illustrating the supposed ignorance of generals and staff officers of the awful conditions that the men in the front line were facing. As aerial photographs clearly show the state of the battleground, all senior officers would undoubtedly have had a theoretical grasp of the conditions in the front-line areas. Some, however, appear to have been surprised by the reality of the misery their men had to endure.

> One afternoon I was sitting in the Battery Commander's post talking to the captain over a cup of tea and he said, 'I can hear voices outside, "Goldie", there's somebody out there, go and have a look!' So I went outside and just as I turned round the end of the shelter to look – there was a General sitting there. Whether he was a Major General or Lieutenant General I couldn't say – one or the other. He sat there with his hands on his head, his elbows on his knees and he was crying like a baby. He really was crying and I heard him say, 'My God, and I've been

sending my men into that!' Evidently, that was the first time they'd been up the line and he really couldn't believe what he'd seen. The two staff officers with him, they were looking very, very depressed, very depressed indeed. I asked the General if he would like a mug of tea. He couldn't speak, he just shook his head and the senior of the staff officers shook his head as much as to tell me not to worry any more. I went back into my dugout and shortly after we heard them leave.[3]

Lieutenant Sydney Goldsmith, Royal Artillery

It is possible for almost anything to become controversial and the question of the rainfall figure for August 1917 in comparison to other years is now a 'hot potato' much debated in print. Essentially one side, led originally by David Lloyd George, firmly contended that all this could easily have been predicted by anyone with half an eye to previous rainfall statistics.

The August failures were put down to the wet weather. As if it had never rained before in that dripping climate! There is a well-known legend of the sun standing still to enable a battle to be won in the Vale of Ajalon, but there is no legendary precedent which would justify our modern Joshuas in expecting that it would dispel the clouds over the low lands of Flanders . . . Figures show what a reckless gamble it was to risk the life of the British Army on the chance of a rainless autumn on the Flemish coast.[4]

David Lloyd George, Prime Minister

Such views were given credence by a strange remark made by the Head of the Intelligence Section at GHQ in his post-war biography of Haig.

Careful investigation of the records of more than eighty years showed that in Flanders the weather broke early each August with the regularity of the Indian monsoon.[5]

Brigadier General John Charteris, Intelligence Section, GHQ

Unfortunately this statement had no foundation in fact. But it has regrettably been repeated *ad nauseam* by Haig's many enemies as proof positive that his whole campaign was nothing but an ill-conceived 'reckless gamble'. In 1958, after years of putting up with this nonsense, the wartime BEF's meteorological expert finally cracked after yet another fatuous repetition of this calumny.

It is quite contrary to the evidence of the actual records which show that the weather in August, 1917, in and around the battle area, was

> exceptionally bad. The rainfall directly affecting the first month of the offensive was more than double the average; it was over five times the amount for the same period in 1915 and 1916. The period is July 29 to August 28. The rainfall at Vlamertinghe was 157mm (6.18 inches) in 1917 and 29mm in 1916. At St Omer it was 30mm in 1915 (there was then no rain gauge at Vlamertinghe). The quite exceptional heavy rain from July 29 to August 4, 1917, was followed by muggy, stagnant weather which prevented the drying by evaporation, normal in the intervals of fair weather at that time of year.[6]
>
> Lieutenant Colonel Ernest Gold, Meteorological Section, Royal Engineers, GHQ

Although methods of weather prediction were not as sophisticated in the early twentieth century as they now are, rainfall records were accurately recorded and a recent analysis of the weather patterns has confirmed Gold's statement.[7] In addition Charteris flatly contradicted himself in another, later book based on his notes taken at the time.

> My one fear is the weather. We have had most carefully prepared statistics of previous years – there are records of 80 years to refer to – and I do not think that we can hope for more than a fortnight, or at the best three weeks of really fine weather.[8]
>
> Brigadier General John Charteris, Intelligence Section, GHQ

Two or three weeks of really fine weather is not a monsoon! The vision of an alien climate full of deadly swamps and totally unsuitable for prolonged military operations is dented by the realization that Flanders is situated less than 200 miles from London and has many of the characteristics of the English fenlands. Haig had not expected or required a veritable drought, but he was entitled to expect, as he did, a reasonably dry August with intervals of good drying weather to offset the effects on the ground of any rain that did fall. Generals need luck to be successful and in this case Haig and the men he commanded were conspicuously denied this essential requirement.

For the troops on the ground the early days of August were ones of utter misery as the rain poured down on them. Many who had had the good fortune to survive the opening day unscathed fell victim as the Germans poured shells onto the new British front line.

> I was sitting in a trench, soaked to the skin. I had to change my position as the side of the trench was slowly sinking being only made of wet mud.

> There was a flash in the sky. I realised with a shock that I had been badly hit. My right arm jumped up on its own and flopped down. It felt as if my left arm and part of my chest had been blown clear away. My first thought was, 'Blow me, I never thought I should get killed!' A feeling of nothing but surprise. Then I thought of home before losing consciousness.[9]
>
> Private Alfred Warsop, 1st Battalion, Sherwood Foresters

Warsop came round in a nearby pillbox that was being used as a makeshift first aid post.

> A doctor was just finishing bandaging me up and he said, 'Get a stretcher for this man as soon as you can'. I had been hit by a shrapnel shell full of steel balls the size of marbles that scatter from the height of 25 yards or so. One ball had blown an inch of bone out of my upper arm, one had taken a clean 'bite' out of my jawbone without breaking it and one had gone deep into the left of my chest, breaking the collar bone on the way in.[10]
>
> Private Alfred Warsop, 1st Battalion, Sherwood Foresters

Despite the severity of his wounds, Warsop was determined to walk out. He recognized that it was unlikely in the prevailing conditions that there would be sufficient stretcher bearers to carry him through the wasteland of mud.

> I persuaded a first aid man to put his hand in the middle of my back and hoist me on my feet. I tottered out determined to get down to the Menin Road or die in the attempt – on this occasion no idle phrase. It was all slippery mud, shell holes and trenches. I soon found that I had lost nearly all sense of balance with both arms useless. No doubt I was able to make that journey because I was suffering from shock and not feeling things as you normally would.[11]
>
> Private Alfred Warsop, 1st Battalion, Sherwood Foresters

Exhausted, he finally made it to safety.

The thunder of the guns continued unabated as the two sides sought to wrest primacy of control over the battlefield and impose their will on events. When the Germans did identify a British battery position the consequences were sudden and dreadful indeed for the gunners.

> I can hardly write this. At 2.30 p.m., without any warning, our gun position fairly caught it. Almost the first two shells scored direct hits

on our frail little sandbag shelters. The shelters were both full of men and were blown to pieces. For two hours the position was pounded with five-nines and some heavier stuff. I was with Major Sumpter and Lieutenant Nurcombe, resting in our mess, in the basement of a ruined house close by. We twice tried to get to the guns with stretchers, but the Hun had put down a box barrage and it was suicide to move about. We could not see the gun position for the smoke of the shells. For over two hours the whole area was flying and humming with shell splinters. We waited in agony of mind – but could do nothing – absolutely nothing. Then suddenly the shelling stopped and we went out there with stretchers. The place was a shambles, indescribable, a ploughed field of reeking craters with the guns pointing in all directions. A few men crawled from their little shelters, bleeding and staggering about and were led away. A doctor came running from the dressing station with an orderly and worked on the badly wounded. Men from adjoining batteries helped with the stretchers. When everyone alive had been taken away, we collected what fragments remained of the dead in blankets and sandbags – a ghastly harvest – and laid them in a dugout to await burial.[12]

Lieutenant Huntly Gordon, 112th Brigade, Royal Field Artillery

Of the forty-six men at the gun position, only eleven badly traumatized men remained – unhurt in body at least. Twelve were killed, thirteen wounded and ten were so badly shell-shocked they had to be evacuated. By some fluke, only one gun was put out of action and so the battery fought on.

Gough had his eye on the resumption of a general advance to the Green Line objectives right along the line and thus he did not concentrate his artillery resources but spread them right across the front of the Fifth Army. The Germans had a much clearer understanding of the importance of the Gheluvelt Plateau and their artillery, massed on the reverse slopes, pounded the front and rear of the II and XIX Corps areas leaving the rest of the line in relative peace. This sensible concentration of the inferior German artillery resources allowed them to gain local superiority in the crucial sector – a superiority that would prove vital when the British offensive resumed. The weakened divisions of the II Corps who had made the initial assault and who had been left holding the line were put under tremendous strain by this ceaseless barrage and as a direct result had to be relieved by 4 August. This meant that the divisions that replaced them, which should have been preserved intact for the next assault, were themselves subject in the front line to a battering from the German artillery for nearly a week before they were actually required to attack. Inevitably they too suffered casualties and became physically and mentally tired. On 10 August the rain eased slightly to allow Gough his chance. He planned an assault by the 25th Division to secure both Westhoek village and the German Second Line, which lay on the reverse of the Westhoek Ridge which had been lost to the German counter-attack on 31 July. Meanwhile the 18th Division would assault the heart of the Gheluvelt Plateau in an effort to capture Glencourse Wood and Inverness Copse on either side of the Menin Road.

When the infantry finally attacked, despite the heavy German shellfire they managed to make some initial progress thanks to the poor performance of the exhausted and demoralized German troops holding their front-line defence zone. An advance of some 800 yards was made, Westhoek village was finally taken and troops succeeded in entering Glencourse Wood and Inverness Copse.

> Never have the Bedfordshire Regiment been in better form. Held up by the wire of the first trench, it was an inspiring sight to see the leading wave firing at the Bosche in the 'standing' position while others cleared gaps in the wire, and then to see them rush the trench with a cheer, although machine gun bullets were flying all around. The Bedfordshire Regiment literally surged through the morass inside the wood, the trees of which had been rendered naked and mutilated by shell fire, but at the highest part of the wood and in other suitable spots the Bosche was holding fortified pill boxes . . . Without a halt the Bedfordshires fought their way through using bomb and bayonet, to their final objective and beyond it.[13]
>
> Captain Harry Driver, 7th Battalion, Bedfordshire Regiment

But then, as on the opening day, their real problems began. An uninhibited German box barrage crashed out to isolate the forward battalions and leave them vulnerable to the inevitable counter-attack as they tried to consolidate their positions.

> It was not very long before the Bedfordshire found themselves in a very exposed position. The Cheshire Regiment on the left were not quite up in line and on the right the Fusiliers had encountered a withering fire from

> machine guns, with the consequence that they had lost practically all their officers, they had to be content with small progress.[14]
>
> Captain Harry Driver, 7th Battalion, Bedfordshire Regiment

The gains on the Westhoek Ridge itself were protected from direct assault by the boggy morass formed by the overflowing waters of the Hannebeek stream in front of them. But elsewhere the Germans threw the British right back to their start lines at a total cost of some 2,200 British casualties. The consequences of launching an attack with tired troops and without artillery superiority were just as Brigadier General Davidson had predicted in his memorandum before the offensive began.

Gough appeared to be losing control of the situation and he seemed unable to respond rationally to the tragic press of events. His next full-scale attack, planned for 14 August, was predicated on the anticipated success of the 'catch-up' attack by the 18th Division on the Gheluvelt Plateau on 10 August. Therefore, when this second attempt also failed, the next attack should have been cancelled. It was clear that the situation could not be resolved until a further attack on the Gheluvelt Plateau had been successful in removing the German positions that continued to threaten the vulnerable flank of any troops advancing further from the Pilckem Ridge towards the Passchendaele Ridge. Yet Gough, apparently not recognizing the logic of this necessity, only allowed a couple of days' postponement due to the further heavy rain and ordered that the attack should press on regardless. Thus the Battle of Langemarck was launched along the length of the Ypres Salient at 04.45 on 16 August 1917. It was an ill-conceived attempt that, from the very start, was almost bound to fail. Artillery superiority had not been established, nor had there been any concentration of resources opposite the Gheluvelt Plateau. Finally, the unspeakably muddy conditions overwhelmed the efforts of the infantry and rendered tanks useless. Gough must bear much of the responsibility for the débâcle that ensued. But Haig could, and should, have stopped him.

In many ways the events of 16 August mirrored the events of 31 July. On the left the French I Corps attacked in some style supported by their superior concentration of artillery power. They achieved their objectives, advancing from Bixschoote to gain the line of the St Jansbeek stream which was a continuation of the Steenbeek. Next along the line, the 29th and 20th Divisions of the British XIV Corps attacked from their positions astride the Ypres–Staden railway and along the Steenbeek. Their objective was the intensely fortified village of Langemarck and the German defences concentrated along the Langemarck–Weidendreft road. The infantry were slowly learning how to overcome the pillbox threat but it remained a desperate undertaking.

> The three blockhouses were spitting out a terrific fire and we were obliged to take cover and move forward gradually by squads in quick rushes. At this period, Company Sergeant Major Skinner and I crawled as near to the blockhouses as possible and succeeded in disabling two of their guns by rifle fire. CSM Skinner, after we had got within about 70 yards of the blockhouses, crawled forward on his own initiative, while I covered his advance with my rifle. After ten minutes he succeeded in reaching that on the extreme left, and going round the back of it bombed the team of gunners with Mills bombs and compelled the garrison to surrender. The second blockhouse he put out of action by inserting bombs in the loopholes where the guns were mounted. By this time I had passed for the company to advance, and we succeeded in reaching the third blockhouse. CSM Skinner's haul was six machine guns, about 60 prisoners and a few trench mortars.[15]
>
> Captain A. H. Currie, 1st Battalion, King's Own Scottish Borderers

Not all such deeds ended in success and in recognition of his valour Skinner was awarded the VC. CSM John Skinner was a terrific character who had been wounded eight times in the war and was reputed to be engaged in a mad competition with one Quartermaster Sergeant Ross for the honour of being wounded for the ninth time. Skinner posthumously won his bet when he was shot in the head attempting to bring in wounded from No Man's Land in early 1918. In the end both divisions of the XIV Corps were successful and, although the swollen Steenbeek was a severe obstacle, the 20th Division did extraordinarily well to capture Langemarck, where they capitalized on the confusion amongst the exhausted German garrison who were not only worn down by the ceaseless shelling but then unlucky enough to be attacked just as they were finally being relieved by fresh troops.

The 11th and 48th Divisions of the XVIII Corps attacked with one brigade each across the Steenbeek towards the Langemarck–Winnepeg road and included among their objectives the village of St Julien. However, the artillery preparations there had not been successful in either destroying the German pillboxes or suppressing the German artillery. On the left, the 11th Division made progress alongside the 20th Division to reach Pheasant Trench, but the 48th Division managed only a meagre advance, although this did include the capture of St Julien. Casualties were heavy and then rendered appalling by an ill-fated attempt to advance out of the village up the slopes towards Springfield Farm.

The 36th and 16th Divisions of XIX Corps attacked towards the Zonnebeke Ridge which ran out as a spur from the village of Zonnebeke towards St Julien. The artillery preparations had been totally inadequate and scores of cleverly sited machine gun posts in solid pillboxes were waiting almost unscathed on the slopes of the ridge. The two Irish divisions were already exhausted before they went into action. After an extensive period providing working and carrying parties during the preparations for the initial assault in July, they had then been moved into the line on 4 August and spent almost two weeks under heavy artillery and machine-gun fire. This had resulted in the loss of half their battle strength before they even left their trenches.

> *July 31* to *Aug 12*: In and out of line on Frezenberg sector. Hell all the time! Mud awful, no trenches, no shelters, no landmarks. All movement by night, shellfire all the time and everywhere casualties enormous! Several killed every day and wounded every hour. *Aug 13*: Rotten time in bivouacs near Vlamertinghe. Bombing every night, rain every day and shelling all the time. Iron rations. *Aug 14*: Move up line to our fates. *Aug 15*: Day of misery for all and anxiety for officers who do not know what time attack starts until late at night. Impossible to get into position in dark under hellish shelling. *Aug 16*: Attack at dawn – given away by Sergeant Phillips. Boche puts up terrible barrage before zero as we are moving into position.[16]
>
> Captain Arthur Glanville, 2nd Battalion, Royal Dublin Fusiliers

The enigmatic reference to Sergeant Phillips was occasioned by the belief that spread throughout the army that treachery had given the Germans advanced warning of the attack.

> I was shown a report captured from a German dugout in the front line which had been translated and circulated by our GHQ. The night before, (August 15th) a sergeant of the Welsh Fusiliers who had been employed as a clerk at GHQ and had been returned to the line for disciplinary purposes had treacherously deserted to the enemy taking with him not

only information of tomorrow's attack, but also a copy of a map on which was indicated the position of every battery on that section of the British front.[17]

G. E. Mackenzie, 153rd Brigade, Royal Horse Artillery

In these circumstances the Irish had little chance of success, and they made a pitiably weak sight as the thin lines struggled forward lashed by machine-gun bullets and scything fragments of shell.

A and B Companies in front wave completely wiped out. I get order from Battalion to reinforce in full daylight over shell holes full of water. Under hellish fire I collect as many of the Company as possible and give the signal to advance but one after the other is shot down. I was nearly buried by shellfire but remained untouched. We reach front wave – mostly dead about 50 yards from Boche front line of pillboxes. There is one other officer, completely exhausted I place myself and about 10 men who have survived in his hands. We remain all day and night and next day in shell holes. It is death to move – to raise oneself an inch out of the mud.[18]

Captain Arthur Glanville, 2nd Battalion, Royal Dublin Fusiliers

Groups of the most determined men did manage to make some small gains but for the most part their sacrifice was entirely in vain as the German counter-attacks easily flung the two divisions back to their start lines.

The thankless task of attacking the German stronghold on the Gheluvelt Plateau fell to the 8th and 56th Divisions of the battered II Corps. The 8th Division had been returned to the line after a mere fourteen days' rest, despite having lost over 3,000 casualties in the attack on the Westhoek Ridge on 31 July. They were to attack across the Hannebeek stream towards the German Third Line defensive positions on the low ridge facing them. Meanwhile the unfortunate 56th Division were to fling themselves at Nonne Boschen, Glencourse Wood and Inverness Copse. The tension before the assault affected everyone no matter how senior in rank.

We were going to attack at 5 o'clock in the morning. I found myself sitting next to a young boy, just out, he was an officer. He started making every joke that I'd heard of for the last three years, repeated all these jolly jokes! I tried to control my temper because my nerves were fairly taut at the time. Then the boy suddenly realised I was the Lieutenant Colonel and he was full of apologies. He was the Divisional Artillery Liaison Officer.[19]

Lieutenant Colonel Alan Hanbury-Sparrow, 2nd Battalion, Royal Berkshire Regiment

Despite all the odds, at first the 8th Division made considerable progress breaking through Hannebeek Wood to capture the Zonnebeke Redoubt on the ridge. Hanbury-Sparrow waited with battalion headquarters as his men went into action.

> Well, the attack started punctually. Our men advanced and presently the German prisoners were coming back, some bleeding like pigs from wounds. As it got lighter I realised we must be on our objective, if anywhere. I went forward and I took this boy with me. About half way we got sniped at by a machine gun. First of all I laughed at the danger, then the boy got hit and he fell over. I tumbled into a shell hole just as two shots went straight over me. I lay doggo, pretended to be dead for a few minutes. When I thought it was safe, I got up again and there was that boy and he turned the most ghastly reproachful eyes upon me. However, I had to leave him there and I went forward. Suddenly I heard a shout, 'Get down, Sir, get down!' and I was amongst my own men in the shell holes. I realised we had hardly an officer left at all and they were beginning to run short of ammunition.[20]
>
> Lieutenant Colonel Alan Hanbury-Sparrow, 2nd Battalion, Royal Berkshire Regiment

Unfortunately, alongside them the attack of the 56th Division was an almost complete failure as the events of 31 July and 10 August repeated themselves. But this repetition was no farce; it was utter tragedy as men lost their lives to no effect and with no realistic chance of success. The 1/5th Battalion, London Regiment, known as the London Rifle Brigade, faced the awesome responsibility of taking the splintered remnants of Glencourse Wood.

> We were off at a slow walk, picking our way over the churned up earth. The ground made it impossible to continue in line and soon we were filing our way over obstacles and flooded shell holes. I remember jumping over a narrow trench filled to the brim with dead Germans and thinking just at that moment that they were tidier than us as they collected theirs. Today the barrage seems to lift quite slowly which was just as well because it was impossible to move quickly and hawky bits seemed to be sploshing into the marshy ground all around, but none hit me. Into the shattered wood we went with no Germans visible and came upon a sunken farm road or track in the side of which there were entrances to a dugout. Sergeant Carter and his runner were first at the entrance and were immediately killed from shots from the dugout. There

> were some bombs thrown at the entrance and I got on the other bank of the sunken track and fired bursts from the Lewis gun straight down the dugout steps using most of the precious magazine. They soon came up and the first one up in this situation is a very brave man as he has little chance of survival. What a crowd – probably 40 or 50 and of course they had had to take refuge as no man could have lived through that barrage in the open above ground. They had their hands up and appeared to have no weapons. Then some of our men started shooting at them – good old propaganda – hadn't they been told that the only good German was a dead one? We, the old soldiers stopped them as soon as possible.[21]
>
> Private W. H. A. Groom, 1/5th Battalion, London Regiment (London Rifle Brigade)

By now Groom and his comrades had lost contact with the creeping barrage and he had also become separated from the Number 2 of his Lewis gun team who carried the spare magazines and loading handle.

> On we walked through the truncated wood, but the machine gun fire rose to a crescendo and we seemed to be walking through a curtain of bullets. It was really devastating and chaps were dropping all over the place. There must, however, be no stopping even to look at anyone wounded, Captain Harper came rushing by with his arm smashed up and he shouted something to the effect about going back, it was hopeless and that we were being surrounded. Somehow, however, we just went on walking.[22]
>
> Private W. H. A. Groom, 1/5th Battalion, London Regiment (London Rifle Brigade)

The troops were cut down by a torrent of shells from the untouched German batteries; slaughtered by concealed machine-gun posts and found the going underfoot so bad that the creeping barrage was completely lost. The timetable of failure was quickly apparent to the toiling gunners behind them.

> When the barrage ended, an interval followed when there was nothing doing, except the eternal strafing by the Heavies. After that came the order: 'Re-bombardment of the 30 minutes line,' meaning a shortening of the range of 1,500 yards, and later still, 'Fire on the five minutes line.' Then we had another long period of waiting, during which we rebuilt the pits, previously taken down for the advance, with the despondent feeling that the whole weary show would have to be done again. As the day wore on we got the signal, 'SOS on old SOS Line,' meaning that

the Hun was counter-attacking and must be stopped, but the whole of these barrages of course fell on the top of our wounded, who had fallen during the advance.[23]

Major Neil Fraser-Tytler, 150th Brigade, Royal Field Artillery

Isolated parties had managed to penetrate through Glencourse Wood and the confused survivors desperately tried to consolidate their tenuous positions.

Suddenly I was alone; there was now no one near me. What had happened? Now the panic really started – this was it – and I changed direction to make for a shallow shell hole. As I did so, a bullet ripped through the case of the Lewis gun and it nearly swung me over but I made it. The nearest men visible to me appeared to be another Lewis gun team, at least I thought I saw a Lewis gun and they were possibly some 300 yards or so away and I saw them disappear into a hole. I could see no one else. With my entrenching tool I tried to throw up more cover but all I dug into was the grey uniform of a dead German and maggots. The Lewis gun was useless, in any case I had no ammunition so I took off the feed arm, put it in my pocket and smashed up the gun mechanism with my entrenching tool. It was difficult to look round as bullets were flopping into the earth at the back of the shell hole and the machine gun fire pouring into the wood was the heaviest I had ever experienced. I thought well this must be the end.[24]

Private W. H. A. Groom, 1/5th Battalion, London Regiment (London Rifle Brigade)

Gradually these vulnerable pockets of resistance were mopped up by German counter-attacks and for the most part simply ceased to exist.

There were Germans coming though the southeast corner of the wood in short rushes, as though they were on parade. They had reached the Lewis gun team and standing round the shell hole appeared to be shooting them. Partly paralysed with fear I wondered what the hell to do and suddenly I was out like a flash and dashed towards a group of shattered tree trunks.[25]

Private W. H. A. Groom, 1/5th Battalion, London Regiment (London Rifle Brigade)

Groom encountered other survivors as he fell back through the wood.

A group with an officer firing at the distant advancing Germans over tree trunks, the officer was waving his revolver and saying in the old heroic tradition that he would shoot the next men who fell back. We took no

> notice – it was damned silly – there wasn't a hope in hell of holding an isolated position in that wood with an attack on our right and no support on our left. I carried on walking back, picked up a rifle and eventually reached almost the exact spot on Westhoek Ridge where I started.[26]
>
> Private W. H. A. Groom, 1/5th Battalion, London Regiment (London Rifle Brigade)

The withdrawal of the 56th Division left the 8th Division in a familiar position, enfiladed on both flanks because of the failure of the divisions on either side of them.

> The crucial attack of the division on the right had completely failed. We were in a rather precarious position. The Brigadier came up and whilst he was there, there was a sudden stampede of our men, they were driven off the hill and they fell back. We fell back from where my temporary headquarters were and we took refuge behind an old parapet that I should think had been built in 1914, it was not thick enough really to be bullet proof. It was facing the right direction providentially and there about 50 of us took refuge. An attack started forming up out of Polygon Wood against us. At the same time there was a gun ranging on this particular trench. It had obviously seen us go there and I imagine it was one of four guns in a battery. I knew that once that battery got the range and opened fire – we were done. At the same time a machine gun, which seemed very much closer than I liked, swept the top of our parapet and killed three men in that process. They'd got the position exactly. I knew we were in a very parlous situation.[27]
>
> Lieutenant Colonel Alan Hanbury-Sparrow, 2nd Battalion, Royal Berkshire Regiment

In such dire circumstances an officer had one advantage over his men in that his responsibilities could distract him from his own personal fear. Colonel Hanbury-Sparrow was expected to show a good example of courage under fire to his men. Courage is not necessarily demonstrated by an act of incredible daring; this could after all intimidate men who had an all too shrewd idea that they might also be expected to do or die. More often it is conveyed by a simple display of insouciant disdain for danger or an incongruous act of normality. Both are likely to be more effective at reassuring men on the point of buckling under the strain.

> Well, I sat down of course, nothing to be done and I did what I generally did on those occasions – I played chess with my adjutant. I always had a little chessboard with pegs! We played on, rather aimlessly it's true, but it steadied the men. Then suddenly a shell fell into the trench. I thought to

myself, 'Now our time has come, you've had a long run for your money and I wonder what it will be like to be dead?' At that moment I realised that whatever happened I wasn't going to be killed. Now it's impossible to describe this consciousness. It's not like ordinary consciousness at all. It's something like a prophet of old when the Lord spoke, something quite overwhelmingly clear and convincing. I wasn't very proud of myself, because I didn't care what happened to the others – I was going to survive. I took a rifle and I began shooting. I hit two Germans at 600 yards and made a third skip for his life. The extraordinary part was this. That machine gun never fired again, that was the last shell that that gun fired, there was no reason why it should stop and the attack on our front, but not on the flanks, petered out and never came near us. It was as though for a moment I got a glimpse of time coming towards me. That was a great and strange feeling that I had.[28]

Lieutenant Colonel Alan Hanbury-Sparrow, 2nd Battalion, Royal Berkshire Regiment

Given how many men died that day confident that they, at least, were going to survive, Hanbury-Sparrow was a lucky man.

The situation in front of the 56th Division was desperate, even after the troops had fallen back to their jumping-off positions. The 13th Battalion, London Regiment (Kensingtons) had been in reserve at Halfway House and at 10.00 they were ordered forward to take up positions in Chateau Wood. Even the very trenches they occupied seemed to sum up the overall position they were in – named as they were Ignorance Trail, Ignorance Row and Ignorance Reserve.

In the early evening I was given the task of taking a dozen men from my platoon to find and bring back the Company's rations. This was not normally a job for a Platoon Sergeant, particularly without a Platoon officer but the situation was tricky to say the least. All around was water and shell holes; a meeting point had been arranged but how to find it? I was told that on the way to the rear I would, with luck, find a broken down tank of ours and, if I turned right for about 500 yards from there, I should meet up with the ration party. Shelling had quietened down when we set off. I followed a rough track between the shell holes and after a time came upon the dead tank. I turned right here as instructed and, without this useful landmark, I doubt if I could have located the Quarter-Master Sergeant which I did in a further 15 minutes. It was astonishing to see him so near the front; needless to say he was anxious to hand over to me and be gone. I would have liked to have gone back with him! Not to say that anywhere was particularly safe, but some places were safer than others. I was prepared to stay for a few minutes for a rest and a chat and tried to keep him in conversation, but he would have none of it and was away. With my party humping the sandbags containing the Company's rations, I turned about and made for the tank in the drizzling, murky gloom. Just about as we reached the tank, all hell broke loose – 20 minutes of hate from concentrated enemy guns. We ran individually to any shell holes we could find which were not yet completely filled with water – a completely spontaneous activity. The din ceased as abruptly as it had begun so that the stillness appeared uncanny. I gathered my party together and enquired if anyone had been hit. One had been unlucky (or lucky?) enough to have had the tip of his nose taken off; I applied a field dressing and sent him back to Headquarters, hoping he would be able to find his way. I could not spare a man to accompany him, but the further he got away from the line, the safer he would be. Then with much stumbling and cursing in the mud and rain we arrived back in the support trench and the men dropped their ration sacks. I reported my arrival and casualty to the Company Commander in his rough shelter in the trench. After hearing me he asked me where I was now going. 'Back to the rest of my platoon', I said. 'No need to', he replied, 'You have no platoon except those with you. A heavy shell landed in the middle of the rest, half an hour ago. There are none left.' [29]

Sergeant Sam Lane, 13th Battalion, London Regiment (Kensingtons)

The name accorded to the battle on 16 August, Langemarck, commemorates one of the few positive outcomes of that dreadful day. It was only on the left of the attack around the village itself that any progress was made, with an advance varying between 1,000 and 1,500 yards. Yet the tally for Gough's persistence totalled some 15,000 casualties, rendering yet more British divisions useless for combat without extensive reorganization and rebuilding. It was not only the German divisions that were being degraded by these incompetent, attritional attacks.

The recent operations entailed very heavy losses. It is pathetic. Over and over again one meets a man in our mess who is just moving up to the trenches. He is jolly, pleasant and full of spirits, and you wish him goodbye, good luck, and God speed. A few hours afterwards the news comes

> that he has gone west or has been mortally wounded. This forces one to think of the great lesson of life and death, and of the necessity for trying to frame one's life and conduct as if each day were the last.[30]
>
> Brigadier General W. R. Ludlow, Area Commandant, Ypres

Despite this high cost and very limited gain, Haig did not rein in his 'thrusting' general. At a corps commanders' conference held at Fifth Army Headquarters on 17 August Gough announced his plan for a series of local attacks to establish a suitable starting line for a resumed attempt to take the objectives intended for 16 August. Once this had been attained, he intended a major new offensive that would drive the British up onto the Passchendaele Ridge itself. In his subsequent memoirs Gough claimed that this continued persistence was not of his doing; he realized the difficulties his men were facing, but Haig was forcing him on for valid strategic reasons.

> The state of the ground was by this time frightful. The labour of bringing up supplies and ammunition, of moving or firing the guns, which had often sunk up to their axles, was a fearful strain on the officers and men, even during the daily task of maintaining the battle front. When it came to the advance of infantry for an attack, across the waterlogged shell holes, movement was so slow and so fatiguing that only the shortest advances could be contemplated. In consequence I informed the Commander-in-Chief that tactical success was not possible, or would be too costly, under such conditions, and advised that the attack should now be abandoned. I had many talks with Haig during these days and repeated this opinion frequently, but he told me that the attack must be continued.[31]
>
> General Sir Hubert Gough, Headquarters, Fifth Army

However, it is now widely felt that Gough was at best being disingenuous in these post-war remarks in an attempt to deflect the responsibility for this disastrous phase in the operations.

Perversely, these minor operations began with a veritable triumph of infantry-tank co-operation on 19 August. Sir Ivor Maxse's XVIII Corps was ordered to take a troublesome nest of fortified farms beyond St Julien. The original scheme was for a conventional infantry attack, but it was decided to try a surprise tank attack with infantry support.

> The line of pillboxes, which had held up the infantry, in spite of most

determined and gallant attacks and which were apparently impervious to shell fire, lay on the far side of the Steenbeek, with the St Julien–Poelcappelle Road running parallel behind them. If it were possible to move tanks along this road, they would be able to attack the pillboxes from the rear, and the solid foundations of the road itself would allow the tanks to approach their objectives from a comparatively short distance. I explained that surprise was the essence of the attack.[32]

Brigadier General C. D. Baker-Carr, Headquarters, 1st Brigade, Tank Corps

Maxse decided it was worth a try and so the preparations began. The tanks were formed into a Composite Company, under the command of Major R. H. Broome. The plan was for the tanks to advance at the highest possible speed along the remnants of the St Julien–Poelcappelle road under the cover of a smoke and shrapnel barrage onto all the high ground from which the road could be observed.

I was ordered to support them by observed fire from my OP and decided to put down a smoke screen on the rising ground to blind possible enemy artillery OPs and mortar detachments whilst the tanks were crossing the Steenbeek by the bridge at St Julien and during the advance eastwards. The attack began at 04.45 and the screen was good.[33]

Major Roderick Macleod, 241st Brigade, Royal Field Artillery

Machine-gun fire and a low-flying aircraft were arranged to try and conceal the telltale noise of the tanks getting into their starting position. The supporting infantry were ordered not to move until a pre-arranged signal was given from the tanks that they could rush forward and occupy the strongpoints.

Of the eleven tanks that started from St Julien at 04.45, four broke down or got ditched and only seven emerged onto what remained of the St Julien–Poelcappelle road. The covering barrage was successful and there was little effective directed German shellfire during the whole operation. At 06.00 the tanks arrived at Hillock Farm which they found unoccupied and a platoon of infantry came forward to occupy and consolidate the position. At 06.15 the male G29 and female G32 tanks approached the Maison de Hibou pillbox but could not get close owing to the state of the ground after leaving the security of the road. The laconic style of the tank commanders' reports cannot hide the success of the action.

Left St Julien at Zero and proceeded up the Poelcappelle Road and owing

> to road running west from Point C.6.a.7.1 being obliterated, missed it and went on, engaging the concrete emplacement at Maison de Hibou from the road at C.6.c.8.3 and fired about 40 rounds 6-pounder into the two back entrances of the strong points and about 60 of the enemy started running out, 30 of whom were captured by the Warwicks. Then got hopelessly ditched and continued using right hand 6-pounder – about 20 rounds – against enemy defensive line at about C.6.d.8.8. until Tank sank so deep could not elevate gun. Then evacuated Tank and took 3 remaining working Lewis guns and hammers of 6-pounders and helped Infantry to consolidate on the road and left of Hibou about Zero plus 6½ hours and handed over guns and ammunition to Infantry.[34]
>
> Second Lieutenant A. G. Barker, Tank G29, G Battalion, Tank Corps

The value of the 6-pounder gun firing from the rear against the pillbox proved to be a great factor in undermining the German morale. G29 was supported by concentrated machine-gun fire from the 'female' G31 tank commanded by Second Lieutenant Morgan.

> Left St Julien at Zero and proceeded up Poelcappelle close behind G.29. Used Lewis guns on both sides of the road and engaged the back entrances of Maison du Hibou in conjunction with G.29, and drove out about 30 of the enemy who were followed up by No. 5 Platoon 1/8th Warwick Regt. and captured. Then passed G.29 ditched and engaged 3 machine guns at C.6.b.3.2 on his right, for about 1½ hours, silenced one, the other being in a concrete dugout. Then turned back and owing to engine trouble halted near G.29 while crew put engine right. Went to see Infantry who had consolidated Maison du Hibou. Then returned home in Tank.[35]
>
> Second Lieutenant E .T. Morgan, Tank G32, G Battalion, Tank Corps

As soon as Maison de Hibou had been captured the reserve platoon of the Warwicks was brought up and the buildings were consolidated. Triangle Farm was found to be almost entirely in ruins, but the occupying Germans put up a strong resistance until a successful bayonet charge supported by fire from an accompanying tank.

Another two of the tanks were ordered to overrun the large Cockcroft pillbox. The male tank developed severe engine problems whilst in action. Six of the crew were rendered unconscious by engine fumes and their officer was wounded when he clambered out to try and get some fresh air into the tank. The driver then dragged in the officer and they managed to get back to St Julien before ditching. The other tank, G43, was more successful.

> Met with heavy machine gun fire from North, East and South, replied vigorously, and after ¼ hour between 30 and 50 of the enemy ran out from the buildings of the Cockcroft; killed a good many, got badly ditched on side of the road just South of Cockcroft. Got out of Tank with Lewis Guns, into shell holes close by. Seeing no sign of our infantry, released pigeon and sent 2 men back to tell our Infantry to come and consolidate Cockcroft. The men came back and reported Infantry would not come on. I then went back and saw the C.O. of the Regiment and got about 60 men, took them out to his Lewis gun line, and dug in. When the Infantry had consolidated the Lewis gun line I camouflaged the Tank and left 3 rifle bombers inside to hold Tank as strong point. Left infantry about 5.25p.m. Z day.[36]
>
> Second Lieutenant H. Coutts, G43, G Battalion, Tank Corps

Again the infantry were successful in consolidating the position. All of the objectives were captured and five of the seven tanks returned safely. The other two were only abandoned after Lewis guns and ammunition had been removed and added to the infantry garrisons. The total infantry casualties were just fifteen wounded, while the tanks lost two killed and eleven wounded. Approximately 100 casualties were inflicted on the Germans in addition to ten prisoners captured. The heavy casualties anticipated for a conventional infantry attack had been avoided.

Many of the young officers of the Tank Corps were the 'vanguardists' of their time and, like all revolutionary idealists, they confused the future possibilities for the employment of tanks with the contemporary reality. They kicked against what they perceived to be old reactionaries in high command wedded to outmoded forms of warfare. That they were wrong did not really matter to them; they were entranced with their own vision of how war could be – if only they had their way. The successful attack down the Poelcappelle road was a significant signpost to them that the conduct of warfare would soon move in their direction.

> It is important, because at this time there was a very strong anti-tank lobby at headquarters. Haig and the cavalry generals were all terrified that they would lose their horses and they were trying at home and at GHQ to have the tanks abolished. Now this just turned the tide and

> using that little battle as a lever our tank headquarters were able to persuade GHQ to try a bigger attack on exactly the same principles – that is to say sticking to the hard going where it hasn't been knocked about by shellfire, going in without any artillery preparation to get surprise and to have close co-operation with the infantry. And that was what led to the Battle of Cambrai.[37]
>
> Lieutenant Mark Dillon, G Battalion, Tank Corps

On 22 August the 15th and 61st Divisions of XIX Corps took part in a further attack designed to straighten the line. They were launched against the evocatively named, but deadly, pillboxes known as Potsdam, Vampir, Borry and Iberian Farms on the slopes of the St Julien Spur. Captain Philip Christison was initially in reserve. This in itself was hard enough to bear.

> At 01.00 hours we left and marched round the south side of Ypres, crossed the notorious Menin Road and up 'C' track to Cambridge Trench. We had to don respirators from then on as we struggled, heavy laden, along greasy, slippery duckboards or knee deep in glutinous mud, trying to avoid falling into shell craters filled with water. It was pitch dark that night and, what with wearing respirators and being under continuous shell fire of all kinds, it was one of the worst reliefs remembered. I made each man hold onto the haversack worn on the back of the man in front. As we progressed slowly along some shells fell in our trench causing casualties and confusion. The dead were heaved into shell holes and the wounded lifted out of the trench and left lying on the surface to await the stretcher bearers. One leading NCO slipped off the track into a huge shell crater full of water. He just disappeared and could not be got out as the sides of the crater were just glutinous mud.[38]
>
> Captain Philip Christison, 6th Battalion, Cameron Highlanders

As the attack began to break down the reserves were moved forward and attacked through the survivors of the first wave. Having gained their original objective they prepared for the inevitable counter-attacks.

> There was no immediate counter attack, but towards dusk one came in – headed by flame-throwers to add to our misery. This was a new one. Our rifles and light machine guns were now useless, being gummed up with mud, and we had to hurl grenades and then use pick handles in close combat. One had no time to feel frightened it all happened so quickly. I saw a large Hun about to aim his flame-thrower in my direction and

> Company Sergeant Major Adams with great presence of mind fired his Verey pistol at the man. The round hit the flame-thrower and with a scream the man collapsed in a sheet of flame. We beat off this counter-attack and formed a line of section posts, under heavy shellfire on any dry areas we could find. We had our tails right up as we had succeeded against all the odds.[39]
>
> Captain Philip Christison, 6th Battalion, Cameron Highlanders

After the attack the British line was indeed a little straighter, but this 'success' had been achieved at great cost in human life. Further to the right, on the Gheluvelt Plateau, the 14th Division of the II Corps launched another forlorn attempt to capture Inverness Copse. But, true to form, it failed. These piecemeal but ruinously expensive attacks could clearly not go on; something had to be done.

The politicians in London, the self-styled 'trustees for the fine fellows that constitute our army',[40] were clearly in a strong position to intervene in this whole ghastly affair. At the Cabinet War Policy Committee meeting of 20 June they had expressly demanded the right to suspend operations if they believed they were not proceeding satisfactorily. Whatever the debatable merits of the advances made on 31 July, there was no way of presenting the August attacks as anything other than a failure in comparison to Haig's earlier, optimistic predictions. However, although the politicians had marked their territory, they promptly relinquished it through neglect as the Cabinet War Policy Committee failed to meet again throughout the summer from June until late September. This might not have been of great significance if the Cabinet itself had kept an unblinking eye on the progress of events during its regular August meetings. Yet these Cabinet meetings were examples of politicians at their least inspiring. The operations on the Western Front just did not seem to attract their interest. The CIGS, Sir William Robertson, made regular reports charting the dreadfully slow progress at Ypres throughout August, but there was no real debate about the merits or otherwise of suspending the operations. Lloyd George regularly criticized the Flanders offensive and continued to press for a switch of artillery resources to support an Italian offensive that would *de facto* end Haig's efforts. But he took no action to ensure that such a course of action took place. No real investigation was launched into Haig's failure to reach his promised gains; Robertson and Haig were not ordered to curtail their operations and no positive contact was made with the Italian Government and generals to discover whether they were actually willing to take centre stage for the Allies' main offensive action in what remained of 1917.

As Prime Minister, Lloyd George had the constitutional authority to order his generals to conform to his wishes, but to do so he had to be certain that he could carry his coalition War Cabinet with him. The political divisions of the past were by no means buried and thus, though he blustered against Haig, he did not dare either directly dismiss him or provoke his resignation. In this, responsibility for the later stages of the Ypres offensive rests as squarely with him as it does with Haig whose commitment never wavered for a moment. He expected a hard struggle and was not surprised when he got one. Consequently through the dark, depressing month of August in Flanders in the absence of any alternative orders or firm guidance either from Haig or the politicians in London, Gough's stance was all too depressingly clear, based as it seemingly was on a simple faith in the playground maxim, 'If at first you don't succeed: try, try and try again.'

CHAPTER SIX

FOOTSLOGGERS

Tatham smoked away at his pipe and at last, as we were plunging through mud and filth, he said, 'This is what you might call the abomination of desolation, Padre!'[1]

Reverend Maurice Murray, 12th & 13th Battalions, Royal Sussex Regiment

More so, perhaps, even than the Somme, Passchendaele has become synonymous with the very worst conditions experienced during the First World War. Whereas in Picardy it was the hopes of the wartime volunteers, be they Territorials or New Army, that were massacred in the relentless struggle, by the middle of 1917 in Flanders, such finer feelings had largely vanished. The nature of the war had changed. Throughout the BEF the men knew that for all concerned it was a grim struggle for survival. They remained determined to prevail, but few any longer maintained the zealotry of a crusade against the 'Hun' demonized by the propagandists earlier in the war. The war had developed its own unstoppable momentum and a sense of impotence was beginning to take hold. Without doubt conditions in the Ypres Salient prior to the opening of the great 1917 offensive were bad enough. It already had an evil reputation. But amazingly things continued to worsen and, through a combination of dreadful weather and murderously intensive fighting, degenerated to such a level that the word Passchendaele has become almost a curse in the English language.

Amidst a landscape literally laid waste, and inconceivable to anyone who did not experience it at first hand, the soldiers lived in a state of unmitigated purgatory.

> Rain, mud, gas shelling and constant bombardment. I had never seen such a scene nor thought it possible. The whole country was water-logged, small spits of muddy land joined shell holes great and small, full of water; many with dead men and animals, the stench of which made us retch. In

the blinding rain in the dark, heavily weighted men would slip into a shell crater and drown in gas contaminated mud often unheeded by their comrades. I found I lost three in this way when we reached the front line.[2]

Captain Philip Christison, 6th Battalion, Cameron Highlanders

The only feasible way of crossing this wasteland, bereft of landmarks and seemingly dissolved into liquid, was by specially constructed tracks.

It was one mass of mud and water. In fact one shell hole ran into another. The only method of getting back and forwards was on a duckboard track. They were laid right from behind right up to the front line and I understand that one track, 'B Track' they used to call it, was nearly two miles long. They were about six foot long and about two foot six or a yard wide, slats across and laid on the mud. In some places where there was a lot of traffic they used to make them wider – double. They were steady underfoot unless sometime Jerry in his shelling would hit one and then you had to get across as best you could.[3]

Gunner George Cole, 250th Brigade, Royal Field Artillery

The tracks were laid under the supervision of the Royal Engineers assisted by working parties drawn from the long-suffering infantry.

We used to have to go up on working parties carrying sawn tree trunks, about two inches thick, to lay a road through the mud for the Royal Engineers. These logs were coming up with GS (General Service) wagons and they were dumping them down. We were carrying them up, two men to a log and the REs were putting them down. We laid about 100 yards or so. Jerry waited till we got that done, then he started to blow it all up again – and he reduced it to splinters. The next day we went up again, we got a bit further. When we went next morning that was all in splinters.[4]

Private Alfred Griffin, 9th Battalion, King's Royal Rifle Corps

As the German shells searched the rear areas, smashing tracks and roadways to pieces, the Royal Engineers used anything that came to hand to construct the foundations of the tracks.

Our job was to make roads or footpaths for the troops to walk on in and out. There was always plenty of bully beef and there was about 144 tins of bully beef in a box, a strong hardwood box. We used to put them down, they sank down about a couple of foot, it gave a good hard footpath to walk on.[5]

Sapper George Clayton, 175th Tunnelling Company, Royal Engineers

Such tracks were the cardiovascular system of the front line. Everything moving either up or down had to pass along them carried by working parties of tired troops.

> Our work for a fortnight was to conduct nightly two parties of infantry, 150 in each, up a track; to pick up one duckboard per man halfway up, carry them to the end of the track and lay them in position. It was a most unpleasant operation and one which we were not envied by anybody, as it involved being above ground and unable to take shelter, in a heavily shelled area, for from six to twelve hours every night. A duckboard is heavy and cumbersome to carry, especially for a man already loaded with rifle and ammunition, and the rate of progress was dreadfully slow; one to one-and-a-half miles per hour was a good average speed to maintain. It is an incomprehensible fact, but a fact it is, that if a considerable body of men are marching in file or single file the men at the head of the column may be marching at regulation speed only, but those at the tail will find it necessary to march much faster, or even to double in order to keep up. On this duckboard track a carrying party strung out until it was half a mile long. The last men of it could never keep pace with the front men, and were constantly passing word up the line to 'step short in front' or 'halt in front', while those in front, dawdling along with shells dropping round, would growl back 'close up in rear' or 'hurry up there'.[6]
>
> Major C. L. Fox, 502nd Field Company, Royal Engineers

For the infantry, fatigue parties filled their nights and many survived the murderous battles in the front line only to be killed whilst ostensibly on rest, having been commandeered for the ubiquitous working or carrying parties.

> A great deal of your time was occupied in fatigue parties carrying up rations, wire, duckboards, one thing or another. You usually carried those up tracks, fascines sunk in the mud. Now if you got off that, or if your load fell off it, then you had to fish it out and if you went to get it you perhaps fell in. Now the mud at Passchendaele was very viscous indeed, very tenacious, it stuck to you. Your puttees were solid mud anyway. When you took your puttees off you scraped them and hoped for the best; you couldn't put them on again. But it stuck to you all over, it slowed you down. It got into the bottom of your trousers, you were covered with mud. The mud there wasn't liquid, it wasn't porridge, it was

> a curious kind of sucking kind of mud. When you got off this track with your load, it 'drew' at you, not like a quicksand, but a real monster that sucked at you.[7]
>
> Lewis Gunner Jack Dillon, BEF (Unit not known)

The exhaustion of the troops and their young officers was intensified by the inevitable confusions of organizing complicated administrative arrangements in the worst possible conditions.

> Back here we are cursing someone pretty loudly for mismanaging all the fatigues. No-one minds very much if they feel they are helping their side in the fight but when they have to march half way through the night in driving rain to the rendezvous and then find no-one there and no work to be done they have every reason to curse.[8]
>
> Captain Charles Dudley Ward, 1st Battalion, Welsh Guards

Throughout the campaign, new battalions of men were marched forward along these continually renewed tracks into the very maw of the German guns.

> Each man and officer carried a rifle and bayonet; greatcoats were worn, small haversack with mess-tins on back, full pouches of ammunition 170 rounds and an extra bandolier of 50 rounds per man; three sandbags tied on the back of the belt, a full water bottle, two grenades, and a pick or shovel on the back as well as the entrenching tool and gas respirator at the alert (i.e. worn on the chest) and a spare P.H. helmet (anti-gas and made of flannel with eye and mouthpieces) across the body. Every soldier carried sewn inside the front of his tunic, on the right hand side a first aid dressing consisting of a bandage, an ampoule of iodine and a safety pin all inside a cotton envelope. My signallers carried, instead of picks, the D.3 telephone and rolls of telephone cable. The rule of the road was that down traffic had precedence, that is, wounded men and runners (men with messages and orders) as well as troops relieved after duty in the front line kept to the track while carrying parties going forward and relieving troops got off the track to enable those downward bound free passage.[9]
>
> Second Lieutenant Robert Johnston, 16th Battalion, Royal Scots

Every night the German shells claimed new victims from the thousands of men who passed up and down the tracks. It was not directly aimed fire but rather random shots fired speculatively, and a man's survival was purely dependent on good fortune. Those victims whose luck deserted them just lay where they had fallen.

> Every morning we used to go up this duck boardtrack from below Boesinghe right up to Langemarck. We were stepping over a couple of dead men laid across the track because they couldn't be moved into the side, they'd have been sucked into the mud. They were collected by the Pioneer Party and buried. It was a nightmare because all you had was a couple of duckboards side by side and either side of it was about ten feet of mud. With the top of a tank sticking out of it here and there. If you fell off it would take a traction engine almost to pull you out. It was that deep – sucking mud – there's a memorial on the Menin Gate to 60,000 men whose bodies were never recovered in that small Ypres salient. They were all sucked into the mud. The track stopped at Langemarck. The place had been flattened to the ground and there was a board at the side of the road, propped up and on it was stencilled, 'This was Langemarck'. That was the only evidence there was that a town ever stood there. You couldn't see a building or a tree as far as the eye could see.[10]
>
> Private William Collins, Royal Army Medical Corps

The presence of countless corpses in various stages of putrefaction littered across the battlefield gave the whole Salient a lingering stench of death.

> Ooohh, a horrible smell. There's nothing like a dead body's smell. It's a putrid, decaying smell, makes you stop breathing, you think of disease. It's a smell you can't describe unless you've smelt rotten meat. You've got the smell right under your nose all the time and if there's one at the bottom of the trench and you keep walking over it the black slime comes out – and that's not pleasant![11]
>
> Private Alfred Griffin, 9th Battalion, King's Royal Rifle Corps

The corpses seemed beyond enumeration in the places where the conflict had flared most brightly. When things had quietened down the grim task of mass burials began.

> I had been detailed for burial work. Our first task was to link up shell holes until we had a ditch about 4 feet deep and some 40 to 50 feet long and sufficiently wide to allow us to get the bodies in. Orders were that we were to take from the pockets of the corpses the pay books and personal effects such as money, watch, photos and so on. One identification disk

had also to be detached and the other left on the body; the boots were to be removed, if possible, as salvage was the order of the day. A small white sandbag was provided for each man's effects the neck of which was tied and the identification disc attached thereto. It was a very gruesome job. Corpses, corpses everywhere in various stages of mutilation. The many bodies lying around the pillbox bore mute testimony to the stern struggle that had taken place. Most of them were British troops and included some kilted Scots. We did not go about our work with a very good grace. Hamlet's gravedigger had a humour all of his own but on this corpse strewn field men could hardly joke in the presence of so many mangled bodies, bodies of comrades who, but a few days back, had known 'Slumber and waking; loved . . . . Seen dawn and sunset', and now here they were to lie for ever in a filthy muddy grave far, far from home and kindred. Our stomachs revolted but at the end of two days we had laid to rest about three dozen mutilated bodies. Before we heaped the cold dank earth over the bodies I was able to read the greater part of the Burial Service over them. It was a strange scene. I felt constrained to ask if anyone had a 'Book of Common Prayer' for it seemed scarcely decent to cover those 'Bleeding pieces of earth' with filthy mud without giving them some sort of Christian burial, although nothing we could do could 'back to those mansions call the fleeting breath'. At least we, their comrades, could show some measure of love and respect for those who had irrevocably lost the greatest thing they had possessed – life itself. My helper gathered round as I stood by the burial trench and reverently played the parson.[12]

Lieutenant Harold Knee, 1/1st Battalion Hertfordshire Regiment

Real padres at least knew the words of the burial service but, as guardians of the army's conscience, they also tried to keep some kind of order and record the last resting place of the men who had died.

I then said the Committal words of the Prayer Book Burial Service and these additional words for the benefit of the Corporal and for my own or anyone who might be present, 'Lord, we thank Thee for the example of this brave man who gave his life for his country. Grant him eternal rest and teach us to number our days that we may apply our hearts unto wisdom. Amen.' Then I and the Corporal each placed 12 spades full of earth, only it was always mud up there, on the body, and beckoning to the next two men who would be hidden in a shell hole 25 yards away, went on to the next body. The men behind shovelled 24 spades full

> between them and so it went on. The place was marked and correct map references made afterwards in reserve. The manner of marking such graves is either to place the man's tin hat on a reversed rifle or to put a rifle alone in the ground – there are always heaps of rifles about, or to put his name on a piece of paper in an empty bottle and corked with something. Sometimes a rough cross can be made if there is time and opportunity. I did this once, either of one of the various pieces of revetting timber or two pieces of iron tied together with telegraph wire.[13]
>
> Reverend Maurice Murray, 12th & 13th Battalions, Royal Sussex Regiment

In keeping with the barbaric nature of the battlefield, even in death the corpses were not at peace. Almost inevitably these pathetically inadequate graves were all too rudely hewn open again by further German high-explosive shells. A steady barrage of gas shells also deluged the rear areas and the ghastly odour of corpses mixed seamlessly with the diluted poisonous gas drifting across the low ridges and valleys.

> Over that, like a chord of C E G, this was the E of the chord, you got the smell of chlorine gas – which as pear drops, the same kind of pear drops you had known as a child, you could not describe it better. The stronger and more attractive the pear drop smell got, the more gas there was and the more danger there was. These were a prevailing thing. But if you were walking up L track, usually carrying something, a shell dropping into the mud, very deep mud, stirring it up, would release a great burst of these smells.[14]
>
> Lewis Gunner Jack Dillon, BEF (Unit not known)

Driven by necessity, wherever possible the British troops pressed the former German pillboxes into use as relatively secure headquarters.

> Battalion Headquarters and Signallers were in a concrete dugout or pillbox with a roof about four foot thick. This pillbox was oblong in shape, divided into two compartments. It had wooden doors and shutters over the windows, both doors and shutters being covered with sheet steel. On the interior walls, floor and roof were marks made by Mills bombs, no doubt made when the pillbox was captured. A large crack ran around the walls just under the ceiling, as if the roof had been 'lifted' by the explosions of the bombs, but the structure was otherwise intact, in spite of the shelling it had been subjected to.[15]
>
> Signaller Sydney Fuller, 8th Battalion, Suffolk Regiment

Such pillboxes, despite the evidence that others had died there, still offered a welcome degree of security and the sense of a relative safe haven from the storms of the battlefield.

> I lay down and lit up my pipe. The feeling of security which I always felt when in a good pillbox, was great after the hazardous life in an open trench; and I don't think I have ever enjoyed a pipe more than I did that night, feeling warm and secure after the nervy journey.[16]
>
> Second Lieutenant Douglas McMurtrie, 7th Battalion, Somerset Light Infantry

Yet not all of the pillboxes did in fact offer the security that the soldiers craved. In some cases the Germans had thought ahead in constructing their defences.

> It had a wonderful field of fire looking over where our people attacked from. But I noticed one thing – the Germans are clever as cats! The back of the pillbox facing the German line was paper thin, all the rest of the pillbox was two feet thick. So that if we attempted to use it they could put a shell right through into the box – if they were accurate enough.[17]
>
> Private William Collins, Royal Army Medical Corps

Nevertheless, despite the consequences of such an eventuality, most pillboxes still provided at least some degree of protection from the relentless German shellfire raining down upon them.

> The Headquarters at one time were in an old Boche strong point. Unfortunately, as it was the only place protected, some of the men in the trench round about it would rush to it for shelter, whenever heavy shelling started. As many as possible squeezed inside, but it seldom contained all, and it was no doubt the enemy's target – we had several casualties in the trench outside. It was little use telling the men not to come, for each hoped to be fortunate enough to find room inside, and the desire for security overmastered all else. The floor of the dugout was a foot deep in water, which kept getting slowly deeper as the water in the trench increased, and its smell was horrible, as it was partly mixed with the blood of the men killed outside.[18]
>
> Lieutenant Colonel Norman Macleod, 7th Battalion, Cameron Highlanders

A direct hit on a pillbox was a traumatic experience but, in contrast to a shell arriving in an occupied shell hole, it was survivable.

> About 8 o'clock in the evening Fritz commenced a terrific bombardment along our front and everyone immediately withdrew to the shelter of the

concrete pilboxes which became very overcrowded. The bombardment lasted for about two hours and was so intense that no living thing could have escaped being hit out in the open. Scores of hits were made on the pillboxes which shook with the terrific concussion and it was impossible to keep a light lit, consequently we were all crowded together in the darkness. As there was no door to the structure it was possible to see the firework display which was taking place. For some reason the enemy had suddenly got the wind up for there were lights of every colour being sent up into the sky and these, with the flashes of the bursting shells, made a very impressive spectacle, but still not one which anybody wished to step outside to enjoy! One or two men stood nearest the doorway were wounded owing to a shell bursting just outside the entrance. When the bombardment was about at its height, someone shouted, 'GAS!' with the result that all was confusion. Most of us, contrary to orders, had laid aside our gas helmets and now when they were wanted it was impossible in the darkness to lay hands on them. The panic caused by the alarm gave rise to a free fight in the darkness for possession of gas masks. The alarm, however, proved to be false as the gas was not the dangerous sort but tear gas shells and very soon we were all crying with tears running down our cheeks and eyes smarting.[19]

Signaller Stanley Bradbury, 1/5th Battalion, Seaforth Highlanders

Even a near miss from one of the heavy-calibre shells could have dramatic effects.

The pillbox was tilted over by a 9 inch shell which exploded just outside. It would have fallen 'door down' and drowned us all, but it righted itself again before it lost its balance. All night the enemy made a shambles of this place and gradually the pillbox filled with water until we had about 2 feet depth over which we lived, ate and slept. It smelt of gas and dead bodies and turned one's stomach over. However we escaped being casualties and remained sane.[20]

Signaller Guy Buckeridge, 37th Divisional Signal Company, Royal Engineers

Every night ration parties went back to local supply dumps in the rear areas to collect food for the men at the front. The Germans knew exactly what routes they had to follow and shelled them at random throughout the night. It was largely a matter of good fortune whether they caught the ration party or not. One party, led by Lieutenant George Horridge, ran out of luck.

> The ration party consisted of two parties and we'd arrived at this trench. At the side of the trench was a steel plate about nine feet long by three feet wide which somebody had put up. The first party were dumping the rations against this steel plate. I was on one end of it, another officer was in the middle and another at the left. We were watching the rations being dumped. I happened to look up to the right and I could see shadowy forms coming. I said, 'Hello, here's the second ration party, I'll just give them a shout, tell them where we are!' I took two steps – not more – and a big shell fell on the plate I'd been leaning against. A tremendous flash and I was blown down against the side of the trench. I picked myself up, realising that, as far as I knew, that nothing had hit me. There was a dead silence. I said, 'Are Mr Mast and Mr Hudson here?' They were the two officers who'd been with me – no reply. Then a sort of hubbub broke out. This shell had not only killed the two officers, it had killed four of the ration party, one of whom had both legs blown off, and wounded eight others. The whole thing was a terrible shock. We had to get the wounded away, in the dark, and we knew the gun was pointing at the same place and might fire another shot at any time. I think I had a certain amount of shell shock because when we got them away and everything had gone quiet again I went and found an old pillbox and lay down in a corner. I stayed there for 24 hours more or less asleep or out. I don't remember very much about it – it was a terrible shock.[21]
>
> Lieutenant George Horridge, 1/5th Battalion, Lancashire Fusiliers

The food that the ration parties risked their lives to fetch was basic indeed. It was almost impossible to get hot food up to the front line and tinned food was the staple diet with endless supplies of bully beef and Machonachies meat and vegetable stew. Bread was a rarity and the troops made do with hard, unyielding biscuits that were not unlike dog biscuits. Cheese and tins of jam completed their diet all washed down with sweetened tea. With nothing but such uninspiring fare on offer, the arrival of parcels from home offered the chance to taste the luxuries of civilian life. They were much anticipated and greatly cherished on arrival, but occasionally the sense of disappointment could be almost tragic to behold.

> One fellow got a parcel from his wife sent out from home. He opened up this parcel, we were all sitting opening our parcels and mail. Sid Baker says, 'Oh boys, look boys!' He held up a tin of plum and apple jam. A

parcel from home and this tin of plum and apple was in it. We were building dugout walls with it! He laughed like to kill himself! His own wife had sent him a tin of jam! [22]

Private Stewart Sibbald, 238th Machine Gun Company, Machine Gun Corps

Given the surrounding decrepitude and ready availability of raw corpse flesh it was inevitable that some sectors of the battlefield were infested with rats.

There were a hell of a lot of rats and they were very tame. The first night I was there, I felt a bump on my stomach. I'd hung up my water bottle and tied to it was my iron rations – a tin of bully beef, some tea and some very, very thick dog biscuits – and that was hanging over my bed. At one time I thought a rat had gone on to the bed and jumped up! But I think really what happened was the rat came down the cord of my water bottle, ripped open the bag and the bully beef had dropped on me! If you got anywhere near them and pushed them, they didn't move any more than was necessary to get rid of the push and keep on eating whatever they were eating. They always found bits of food about. They were big rats and very tame. I don't know whether I liked them but you got used to this particular variety, they didn't seem to attempt to bite, least I never got bitten anyway! Once I saw some rats in a hole and I'd got a field gun cartridge and it had got some of the cordite in it. I put a match to it and shot it into the hole, there was far more in it than I expected and I had to run because of the threatened explosion! [23]

Corporal Harry Hopthrow, Signal Service, Royal Engineers

Even more irritating than the rats were much smaller pests. The ubiquitous lice crawled across the soldiers' bodies in droves.

When a new draft came out they would say they didn't intend to have any lice. We just used to laugh and say, 'All right, we'll wait and see!' Shortly after, we'd find them rubbing their shoulders up against the trench and ask them what was the matter. They said, 'Oh, my skin isn't feeling so good!' But they had them all right. When you were out of the line everybody used to strip off and go down all the seams of your jacket with a candle or a needle. You were nearly walking sometimes but you couldn't do anything about them, your blankets were all infested. Very odd times we got a bath. If you were lucky and the engineers were there they would set some baths up. As you went in you dropped all you had, left them outside as you went in. There were old wine casks cut in two, maybe there was hot water in, maybe there wasn't. I stepped into a one that was cold! Cor strewth! Mind, it was a good job I was young and healthy! Then you had a bath and when you came out they'd give you a new set of underclothes. By the time you'd marched back to your billet you were lousy again. You couldn't kill them![24]

Private Joseph Pickard, 1/4th Battalion, Northumberland Fusiliers

It was not only the men's bodies that suffered during tours of duty in the front line. Their minds were under ceaseless attack as they tried to prevent themselves from betraying the inner anxieties and sheer naked fear that constantly plagued them. The ability to survive relatively mentally unscathed depended largely on personal character. Some men were naturally imbued with greater reserves than others and were able to continue with less apparent difficulty. They found a variety of methods of distracting themselves from the horrors that surrounded them and could even achieve an enviable sense of detachment towards their surroundings.

One or two signallers and I had to walk in the open straight in front of the Germans who were perhaps two or three miles off, but they could see us all right – and they had a 'Bang'! They made some beautiful shooting, made rings round us and one of the lads, a tall handsome youth, said, 'Never did see such shelling!' It was exactly like applauding a conjuring trick in the halls or a piece of fast bowling in a test match. It struck me, 'Well, what self-control!' But he was really looking at a remarkable feat of skill on behalf of some other human being and I thought a lot of that.[25]

Lieutenant Edmund Blunden, 11th Battalion, Royal Sussex Regiment

The calmest were usually those who felt least and were able to transcend the immediacy of their situation. Uncowed by a sense of the awful possibilities all around them and apparently unmoved by the sudden randomness of the terror that could strike at any moment, they were able to retain greater control over their actions. One such remarkable character was Lieutenant Hugh Colvin who was to win the VC in the September fighting at Ypres.

Colvin came into my concrete dugout and there were various odd shells round about while he was in there. A small shell hit the corner outside of the concrete which didn't do a great deal of damage. The place was lit by candles stuck in bottles and of course all the candles went out and there was a general air of fumes and so forth – that's all that really happened.

> But the place was pretty hot inside and the ceiling was covered with flies. When I lit the candles again Hugh Colvin was sitting in a chair opposite and he just looked up at the ceiling and said, 'You know, that didn't even shake the flies off the ceiling!' He was a very calm character with no nerves, no imagination at all. A marvellous bloke, marvellous, very capable and a very brave type too.[26]
>
> Lieutenant John Mallalieu, 9th Battalion, Cheshire Regiment

Not blessed, or cursed, with such courage, some men desperate to escape adopted various subterfuges and deceptions to make themselves appear unfit for action. Those in charge had to be alert to what was going on around them.

> I used to take my platoon up the line to do a lot of repair work. It was a bright morning and we'd left the Menin Road and were marching up this plank road to go further up towards the Salient. The sun was shining right in your face and all of a sudden one of the chaps fell. I went to him, had a good look at him and when he came round I said, 'Are you all right?' He said, 'No, I'm not all right!' I said, 'You can find your way back, can't you?' 'Yes, yes!' 'Right-ho, get back . . .' I thought that was funny. So I thought, 'I think this fellow's swinging it!' The next morning we got on the way again and I was walking just behind him – he didn't know I was behind him! He had his eyes on the sun, staring at the sun till it sent him dizzy! When he'd been staring a good minute or so I gave him such a push on the back! He turned round as if to say, 'What's that for!' I said, 'Keep your eyes on the bloody floor! Don't keep looking at that fellow up there!' He didn't do it again! You see what they do – they think of all sorts of little things! It just depends on the individual.[27]
>
> Sergeant Joe Fitzpatrick, 2/6th Battalion, Manchester Regiment

Fitzpatrick may have appeared harsh, but such malingerers directly exposed their comrades to correspondingly heightened risks and hardships and it is not surprising that many men had little sympathy for them. However, when men did crack under the strain, there could occasionally be real understanding from officers and NCOs who shared their trials. Captain Graham Greenwell was leading his men up to the front ready for an attack when one of his men broke down.

> We had to attack a line of German blockhouses which were situated around Passchendaele in seas of mud. There was a newly joined youngster in my company. We were in single file because you didn't dare

get off what was left of the duckboards because you could find yourself up to the neck in muddy sump holes. A newly joined youngster in my company, he was younger than me, he suddenly collapsed and said that he couldn't go on. He simply couldn't face it any more. So I said sternly to him, 'You get up and go on, if you go on, you may well not be shot, but if you lie here or go back, you'll be shot for a certainty!' He pulled himself together, and he got through. When we got back I told the Company Sergeant Major that I wanted this boy to have accelerated leave because I thought he was in such a bad state, that he really required it. As a result, my CSM arranged it so that he should go on leave without it appearing too great a favour. That was possible for an officer to do. I never saw that boy again, but I reckon I saved his life that day![28]

Captain Graham Greenwell, 4th Battalion, Oxfordshire and Buckinghamshire Light Infantry

The bedrock of courage required to carry on day in and day out, running precariously up to the edge of oblivion or worse, underlines the strength of character shown by the majority of men in these circumstances. A soldier was stuck in the line with his battalion living in nightmarish conditions until his division was withdrawn on rest. Unless they were wounded there was little chance of an early escape with honour from the grim freemasonry of terror that existed amidst the shell holes. Given the nature of the fighting, casualties could occur all over the battlefield at any time of the day and night. Stretcher bearers were constantly on call but in many cases, particularly during major attacks, isolated wounded could wait for long periods of time before help arrived – and when it did it was often too late.

At some stage of the fighting in the last few days, a line of 'rifle pits' had been dug by our men. From one of these, a few yards short of my platoon's post, I thought I heard groans and I went out with a stretcher bearer to see what could be done. We found in one of these pits four men sitting, their legs all tangled in the middle. One began to talk deliriously, one could talk sense and stated that the other two were dead. Any attempt to move them (the live or the dead) only raised cries of pain, as the living were both wounded in the leg as well as elsewhere and had been there helpless for two days. We had to give up the job for the moment, but later I got up another stretcher bearer from Company Headquarters and they got them out at last in time to get them away before morning. The delirious man died on the way, the other reached the Battalion aid post at least in safety, so he may have survived.[29]

Lieutenant Gilbert Fleming, 7th Battalion, Rifle Brigade

The pain suffered by the severely wounded could be indescribable and occasionally threw up a terrible moral dilemma.

Before we got to the front line a shell dropped amongst our lads and one got very, very badly wounded. He was screaming out, 'Shoot me, Sergeant, shoot me! The pain, shoot me!' Well, I would have done, I'd have helped him out, he was in that much pain. I'd have pulled my revolver out and shot him, but I didn't want any witnesses. You don't know how far it would have gone. Myself, personally I would have done, definitely! And if I'd been badly wounded I'd have shot myself to save any time and trouble.[30]

Sergeant Joe Fitzpatrick, 2/6th Battalion, Manchester Regiment

The failure to help their comrades in circumstances such as these, where each man knew it could easily be him and might very soon be so, created a long-lasting sense of guilt.

I tried to assist a lad in this copse about 100 yards from our jumping-off trench, I called to him, 'Are you hit, son?' He said, 'Yes, I am – a little!' There was no hope of getting to him; he was in the middle of this huge sea of mud, struggling. I saw a small sapling in this bit of a copse we were supposed to be using as a front line after our attack. We tried to bend it over to this boy. The look on the lad's face, it was really pathetic. We were by then seasoned soldiers, but he was only a mere boy and it seemed to prick my conscience that I should try and do something for him. But I couldn't do a thing, had I bent a little more I should have gone in with him, had any of us gone anywhere near this sea of mud we should have gone in with him as so many did.[31]

Private Cyril Lee, BEF (Unit not known)

No one knew when the blow would fall and although the thought of being hit haunted most men's thoughts, it was always a terrible physical and mental shock when the time came. Many were in a daze as they were helped back via the Regimental Aid Post to the Casualty Clearing Station and safety.

We had to take turns sitting near the narrow doorway and it was my turn to sit between the window and the door. We were trying to get a little rest

TOP Field Marshal Sir Douglas Haig with General Joseph Joffre and David Lloyd George

ABOVE General Sir Herbert Plumer

RIGHT General Sir Hubert Gough

The 11th Battalion, Durham Light Infantry move up into the line, 31 July 1917

A carrying party crossing the Yser Canal, 31 July 1917

Troops occupying the new support line, 31 July 1917

German prisoners carrying a wounded British soldier on Pilckem Ridge, 31 July 1917

Attempting to pull a field gun out of the mud, 2 August 1917

Stretcher bearers struggling through the mud, 1 August 1917

A sapper sleeping by the road near Hooge, 9 August 1917

German prisoners captured at Ypres

RIGHT A German shell bursting near a camouflaged 8″ howitzer battery at Boesinghe, 17 August 1917

BELOW British soldiers watching the British bombardment with a 6″ howitzer in the foreground, 16 August 1917

OPPOSITE TOP A battery of 18-pounders in action

OPPOSITE BELOW Loading a 15″ howitzer

LEFT Sydney Fuller in October 1914, shortly after his enlistment

ABOVE Major Neil Fraser-Tytler

BELOW LEFT Cecil Barton, photographed as a Subaltern in 1915

BELOW RIGHT The Reverend Maurice Murray

Australian Lewis gunners occupying the front line on Broodseinde Ridge, 5 October 1917

Men of the 4th Battalion, Coldstream Guards outside a captured German pillbox borderinį the Houlthulst Forest, 9 October 1917

A derelict Mark IV Tank on the battlefield

Mules struggling in the worsening mud

A line of GS wagons caught by German shellfire crossing Bellewaarde Ridge

All that remained of a British aircraft which crashed in flames in Chateau Wood

Men of the Highland Light Infantry resting on their way up to the line

A British doctor and padre ministering to the wounded of both sides

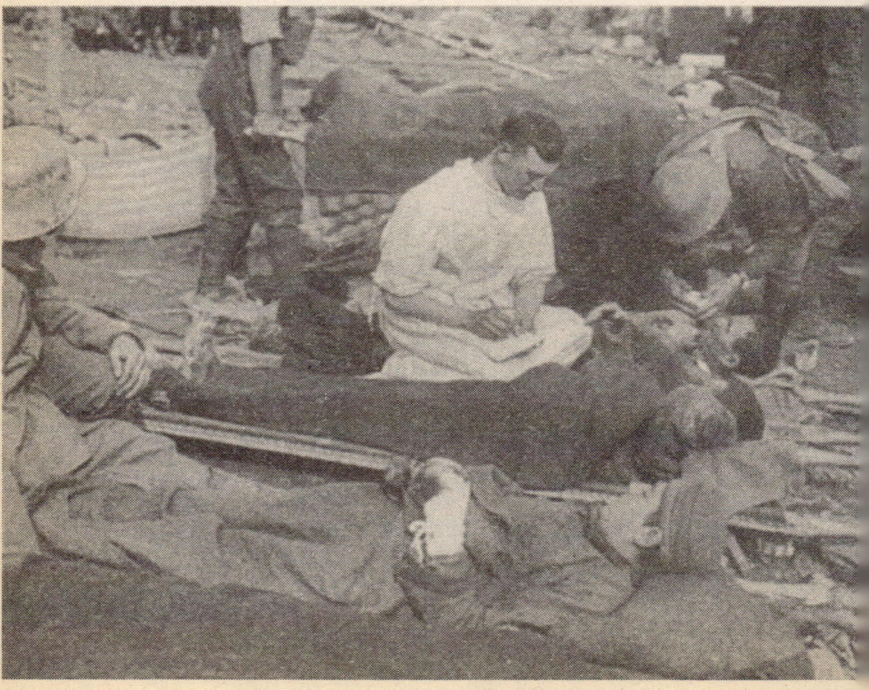

A German concrete gun emplacement smashed by British shellfire near Zonnebeke

Just one of nameless thousands – a battlefield corpse in the mud

A Canadian working party carrying duckboards passing stretcher bearers

BELOW and BELOW RIGHT Canadian stretcher bearers bringing in the wounded

ABOVE A panorama of the Passchendaele battleground

BELOW Aerial photograph of Passchendaele village

BOTTOM Aerial photograph of Passchendaele village – after the battle

and I daresay may have been half-asleep. I am sure I was. Suddenly a most terrific noise and explosion took place and we were all knocked over and I felt a violent singing on a very high note in each ear but especially the left, all other sounds being very, very far away. We got out or were got out somehow but I collapsed as soon as I stood up, but I remember that I saw the faces of all the dressers who were alive. One had a cut on his forehead and another on his face. I noticed that my left legging had been ripped off by a piece of shell, as clean as if it had been done by a razor. From top to bottom. It fell off my leg when I attempted to walk. Two of the dressers took me to Battalion Headquarters where Gatchell was and he ticketted me as 'Wounded. Concussion'. I remember resisting and being silly about wanting to stay on. Eventually the Adjutant sent me down with his own servant. I tore my ticket off my shoulder strap and told the Adjutant's servant that I must go back to the line and generally behaved like a baby. I expect it was lack of food as well as the shell shock. How we got down I do not know but that man was awfully good and gentle as well as strong. It was a nightmare walk. I remember the awful, awful mud more than anything.[32]

Reverend Maurice Murray, 12th & 13th Battalions, Royal Sussex Regiment

If they were not wounded or killed then eventually the endless days passed and the unit would be moved out of line on rest. The men were relieved in the front line at night and moved down the tracks to safety. In these circumstances minor discomforts were tolerated cheerfully.

About noon we were ordered to prepare for a move at 2.30 p.m., when the buses would be ready for us. We were ready on time (not 'arf) but the 'buses' were late and we had to wait two hours. The 'buses' turned out to be ordinary lorries and there was quite a crush. I was unable to get a seat and had to stand on a tail-board, hoping the chains would not break. Started at 4.40 p.m. The enemy was shelling one of our balloons near Dickebusch and when we were halfway through that village one of the shells burst near us. We heard the bullets whizz all around us but no-one was hit. Rather an uncomfortable ride for me, standing all the way and getting covered with dust, but under the circumstances I did not mind that.[33]

Signaller Sydney Fuller, 8th Battalion, Suffolk Regiment

They moved back into billets in the villages to the west of Ypres.

It was a typical billet for the neighbourhood; it was a very large farm, and two companies of us, officers and men, were accommodated there. We officers had a big downstairs room for a mess and slept up in the loft; the men were in the barns and stables and a small number in tents out in the meadow. We were warned not to expect a long rest and had plenty to do in the way of baths, re-clothing, re-equipping etc. However, I found time to visit Bailleul one afternoon.[34]

Lieutenant Gilbert Fleming, 7th Battalion, Rifle Brigade

Away at last from snipers, machine guns and shells the men relaxed, seeking solace and comfort in the familiarity of old routines.

I got the men into the farm nearby, saw that they got tea and their rum rations and then went to find my own tent. My servant had got a canvas bed already and had put out my things. There was a pile of letters and a parcel of kit. The first night after being in the line, getting into pyjamas and a warm valise was very much appreciated.[35]

Second Lieutenant Douglas McMurtrie, 7th Battalion, Somerset Light Infantry

Tranquillity was much prized, but although they had left the front line they carried with them the mental stigmata of their experiences.

Never before had any battle affected our nerves so badly. Practically all the day there was the noise of shells, swish, swish, rumble, rumble in the ears. This had never happened before so we must have been suffering from severe mental shock. Quite a number of us survivors mentioned this. Neuralgia was so common there was a queue at the medical tent for sedatives. I was going along a field path to the medical tent for tablets with another man when there was a sudden burst of machine gun fire from a nearby practice firing range. We immediately dropped flat on the range and how foolish we felt at this reaction miles behind the front line. It was another proof that most of us were suffering from a type of shell shock.[36]

Private W. H. A. Groom, 1/5th Battalion, London Regiment (London Rifle Brigade)

Yet even at rest the troops were not safe. By 1917 aerial warfare had progressed significantly from the primitive state of its evolution on the outbreak of war in 1914. The latest generation of aircraft could carry substantial payloads of bombs, whilst the problems of night flying and navigation had been successfully overcome. Consequently the threat of air raids had greatly extended the reach of war and indeed the German Gothas had range enough to strike at London itself. Just as the formerly invulnerable civilians had been drawn into the maw, so the exhausted soldier resting in billets far behind the lines and out of artillery range found that there was no respite.

> About an hour before lights out as we stood in groups round the field we heard the unmistakable throbbing of enemy planes; the drone of Boche aero-engines was quite different from ours. I leaned my back against a large tree that grew a few yards from my tent and looked towards the sound of the aircraft. Our anti-aircraft guns were busy when suddenly I heard a CRASH! As a bomb burst some five fields away. Crash! Crash! Crash! As other bombs exploded nearer and nearer to our field. Before the last crash some of the men had flung themselves into their tents and lay flat, whilst I remained standing against the tree so that it stood between me and the bombs.[37]
>
> Signaller Gerald Dennis, 21st Battalion, King's Royal Rifle Corps

Night after night the German bombers droned across the rear areas dropping their bombs.

> The night after we arrived in Siege Camp, we were heavily bombed and suffered one killed and 14 wounded in casualties, besides horses and mules killed and transport destroyed. It was amusing to see the aircraft picket continually answering the aircraft call, viz three blasts on a whistle. They would come doubling out of their tents and extend into open order and remain with loaded rifles ready to fire at the low flying aeroplanes – but immediately the bombs began to drop not one of the picket was to be seen! The German airmen were not satisfied with dropping bombs but continually poured a hail of bullets on to the Camp from their machine guns and it is remarkable that there were not many more casualties in these constant raids from this particular source of destruction. It really is a beautiful sight to see an aeroplane caught in the searchlights and unable to get out of them. As many as 20 powerful lights would search the sky until they found the hostile planes which they invariably did and, once found, it was very difficult for the pilot to get out of the beam. Immediately one searchlight found its victim, it would remain steady on to it and the other lights would then switch on to it and keep the aeroplane in the cross formed by the numerous searchlights. Then there would immediately burst out a tremendous rattle of machine and Lewis gun fire from the men below which would be answered by those in the aeroplane and by the hasty dropping of bombs so as to lighten the weight carried and enable the plane to fly higher and so out of the reach of the

searchlights. These duels were at all times very exciting to watch as it was possible to see the bullets of both sides make their way to their targets owing to the use of what were known as 'tracer bullets' which had the appearance of sparks flying through the air at great speed.[38]

Signaller Stanley Bradbury, 1/5th Battalion, Seaforth Highlanders

In these circumstances air raids were infuriating and strangely disturbing for men already familiar with hell on earth.

German aeroplanes were continually coming over night and day and dropping bombs all around us, killing horses and men. Somehow it was much worse for the nerves to have a good chance of being bombed when out at rest, than having the same chance in the line – where one expected such unpleasant things.[39]

Second Lieutenant Douglas McMurtrie, 7th Battalion, Somerset Light Infantry

Despite it all, a rest period was still much to be treasured. It offered a chance to live, to experience the lesser and greater pleasures that life had to offer for perhaps the last time.

I am living at a Chateau and yesterday Higgins (my great chum) and self took the two daughters of the place for a walk into a neighbouring town – we hardly saw a soul and yet last night I guarantee that every French farm within miles had the news. Jingo it is funny – wherever the boys went they were told about two officers promenading with the two Mademoiselles from the Chateau. My fancy, the smaller of the two, is called Marguerite – Mother she is just glorious – not exceptionally beautiful, perhaps, except her eyes, but with a daintiness and charm of manner the like of which one could never find in an English girl – as timid as a gazelle and as perfect in her simplicity as the flower whose name she bears, and talk about snuggle – she's the finest snuggler that I have ever met. How would you like a French daughter in law – but there, don't worry I would never summon up enough courage to ask her.[40]

Lieutenant Cyril Lawrence, 1st Field Company, Engineers, Australian Imperial Force

Not all the men were content with such delicate sipping from the jug of life. Some of them took great quaffs and spilt it wherever they pleased!

Before we left there occurred something which I must note because of its humour, though it is the humour of Rabelaïs or the Decameron. My part in it was nil and beyond hearing a squeal and much screaming of angry women I know nothing beyond what Percy Battye told me. It appears he was wakened by an old man, who lives in the farm, and the two women I have referred to as strumpets – the latter in their night dresses. The old man could speak no English and was too frightened and excited to attempt French, so the women translated his Flemish into bad English and French. He was going round the farm locking up and had reached the pig stall in the stable, where he said he heard the pig grunting. He was about to lock up when the door burst open and a man dressed only in a shirt ran out and disappeared into the night. He was sure it was one of our men. And then both women, shouting at once, accused one of our men of behaving indecently with the pig! Battye turned out the guard, the servants and some corporals and hunted high and low for the beast – but found no-one. All he discovered was that a wild figure had run past the sentry. He put out extra sentries to watch for the man and went to bed. This morning the mother of the two women – a fearfully evil old hag – triumphantly produced a slipper which, she said, had been found in the pig house. Again she urged Battye to find the wretch, who had sunk to such depths as to have an affair with a pig. To cut the story short they discovered that the only man who possessed such slippers was the canteen man – of another regiment. This man was brought before him and then in an agony of nervousness the man confessed that though appearances were dead against him it was the girls he was concerned with in the pig house and not the pig! Then Percy, with true Sherlock Holmes perspicacity, remembered the night dresses he had seen these two creatures in and that they bore traces of the farm yard!!! [41]

Captain Charles Dudley Ward, 1st Battalion, Welsh Guards

CHAPTER SEVEN

GUNNERS

Passchendaele was the final horror, in fact I think it was really the only battle of the First War in which I can remember nothing but evil.[1]

Lieutenant Richard Talbot-Kelly, 52nd Brigade, Royal Field Artillery

Guns were the key element in any military calculation of the Great War and throughout the Third Battle of Ypres they remained the true masters of the battlefield. Almost nothing in an attack could be achieved without the artillery first smashing down the enemy's defences, killing or concussing the garrison whilst simultaneously deluging the defending batteries with shells to prevent them from firing into the attacking infantry struggling across No Man's Land. Although only infantry could actually occupy the ground, they were chaperoned everywhere by their artillery. When a position had been captured, it was supporting gunfire that brought the infantry sufficient time to consolidate their gains by disrupting and finally smashing the approaching counter-attack forces. At the same time, the gunners had to win the next round of the never-ending battle to suppress the opposing artillery. Guns had to be moved forward into new positions while new hostile battery positions had to be pinpointed and eliminated. There was no time for rest; even a short period of weakness would allow the enemy's artillery to seize control of the battlefield, rendering the hard-won gains vulnerable to recapture.

For the Royal Artillery the offensive in Flanders was both one of the most crucial and frustrating episodes of the war. The intensely muddy conditions that immediately took hold following the onset of heavy rain made moving the guns an alarming prospect, with men and horses condemned to struggle desperately against an omnipotent, glutinous enemy.

One shell pitted, vast, mud swamp stretching for miles and miles, where it always seemed to be raining, and from which the villages once dotting its fertile fields had long been obliterated, muddy mounds of broken bricks hardly distinguishable from the filthy desert around, the Salient was indeed a waking nightmare which one had to live, not dream.[2]

Lieutenant R. G. Dixon, 14th Battery, Royal Garrison Artillery

Once the guns were under way the chances of finding a flat field, as recommended in the field service regulations, in a battlefield deluged with shells of all calibres, were remote.

One day I suddenly received orders from a staff officer to meet him at a certain map reference in order to tell us where to fix up a new battery position. When I looked up this reference on the map I found it was the village of Westhoek – but when I got there, there was no village to be seen at all. There wasn't a wall standing, you couldn't see any buildings and even the roads had been obliterated. I met the staff officer and he pointed to a place about 40 yards away from this corduroy road and he said, 'You will put your guns there!' He went away and I was left to figure out what at first seemed to be an absolutely impossible position. Immediately off the corduroy road there were huge shell holes full of water and anything that had fallen into them. In the particular place where we would have to go there was a mule in the first huge crater. It seemed at first absolutely impossible to get there at all. However, we had to carry out our orders and when I was able to bring up some men we started to fill in the first of these craters full of water. We threw in a lot of boxes – of stores and ammunition – we didn't know what was inside them, but we found a lot of boxes about and we threw those in. We found a lot of bricks, we threw those in on top. Then more of anything we could possibly find, until eventually, we were able to lay planks over the top. We brought up one gun with great difficulty – because these were heavy six-inch howitzers – we got it off the road on to the first part. Then we had to get it from there past other shell holes which we had to fill in and it took us a very long time, but we did eventually get one of our guns about 30 yards from the road.[3]

Major W. Stoneham, Royal Field Artillery

Once in position, the nature of the long-contested battlefield meant that exposed corpses were an omnipresent symbol of death not long deferred.

In front of our guns ran a little gully and as the weather worsened the overflow from the shell holes turned this gully into a little stream with the result that a number of old corpses became exposed showing all their bones as white as snow as this rain water had been flowing through for almost three years. There was one body that lay exposed right in front of my gun and the rains had washed the skeleton's bones like ivory. As a matter of fact, his ribs formed a kind of trap which filtered the brushwood that flowed down the gully and left a clear space in the middle of clean rain water into which I used to dip my 'enamel mug' for a clean drop of water for a shave.[4]

Gunner A. J. Heraty, 241st Brigade, Royal Field Artillery

Guns were difficult to camouflage even in terrain blessed with woods, vegetation and buildings. But, bereft of almost all natural features, the Salient offered virtually no cover and everything was washed a drab uniform colour of 'mud'.

In the Ypres salient, the ground was so devastated that the camouflage netting might give you away. What we did was to 'untidy' the position. We used to throw about bits of old sackcloth, packing, sandbags and half a rum jar. Instead of putting the battery handspikes and levers and things in neat order, we used to throw them about. We were told to do this by the planes that used to help. They said, 'For God's sake don't have any kind of order! Have your battery positions as untidy as you can make it and that will do more to defeat the German than anything else. Never allow men to approach the guns the same way all the time or they will make track and that will be visible from the air.[5]

Lieutenant Cyril Denys, 212th Siege Battery, Royal Garrison Artillery

Following the advances in July and August, the captured pillboxes offered the promise of a suitable berth for the officers at the gun positions and their signallers. But living in accommodation with such a brutal history not only had a heavy emotional cost, there were practical difficulties as well with the past occupants making their presence felt long after their deaths.

I could have heaved my heart out, we had to scrape the dead Germans off the walls and the stench was terrible. Our infantry were not taking chances and just threw one, or maybe two, Mills bombs into each 'blockhouse'. These were the holes we had got to sleep in that night. There were duckboards on the floor of the pillboxes but the water had risen above them owing to the heavy rains. After we had scraped them off the walls we had to clear the water out before we could get down for a bit of rest. In the weeks we used the pillboxes for cover we had 'nuisances' to contend with, apart from the lice and rats – namely maggots. Although we had washed the walls down with raw creosote they still persisted in crawling all over us.[6]

Gunner A. J. Heraty, 241st Brigade, Royal Field Artillery

The degree of protection offered was frequently deceptive and, as the infantry had found, even the pillboxes did not guard against all the consequences of a direct hit. A heavy shell did not actually have to penetrate the inner fastness to have fearsome effects on the flesh and blood of the cowering occupants.

The whole place was shaken by a colossal thump and explosion, and the thick concrete roof of the corridor just outside the doorway of our little room came in in a shower of smashed material of all shapes and sizes. Underneath it, under the pile of rubble on which the rain now dripped through the great hole above, lay one of the cooks on his stomach. I was momentarily stunned by the explosion, as was everyone, but only for a few seconds. Our two friends leapt out and dragged the unfortunate man from under and into the room with us, laying him on his back on the floor. His head was a bloody mess of brains and bits of cement and even as we looked at him, his heels began a devil's tattoo on the cement floor as he died. 'It's Jenkins', said the Lieutenant. 'The poor bloody fool! I gave strict orders that they were to wear their tin hats even in here!' But Jenkins hadn't worn his tin hat and the poor fellow was dead, his brains pulverised by smashed concrete driving downwards from that shell hole in the roof. His steel helmet would have saved him.[7]

Lieutenant R. G. Dixon, 14th Battery, Royal Garrison Artillery

Although, for legitimate reasons, command posts such as brigade headquarters were located as safely as possible, they too endured miserable conditions as Colonel Rettie found on his arrival at Wieltje where an old mineshaft and workings had been pressed into use.

Enter that hole in this trench and 'mind the step'. There are about thirty of them, covered with wet slime continually drip, drip, dripping. There is a repulsive looking rope on one side. At first you decline to touch it; but a warning slip and you seize it readily in spite of the dirt. Mind that wireless operator at the landing half way down; don't step on him in the murky gloom. At last you reach the bottom and stand in a black and slimy river, slowly moving onward and disappearing in the darkness, revealed by some weary looking electric lights. Is it the Styx, you ask? Anyway it stinks. Is it the portal of the infernal regions? Is it always as hot as this? These are the next questions that rise to your mind. As you have descended you have been gripped by the throat by a sultry atmosphere, which grows worse as you descend and which at the bottom makes you sweat and wonder how long you will be able to stick it. We now ask a dirty individual, clad in shirt and slacks, where Brigade Headquarters is. He asks, 'Which Brigade? There are two Infantry and three Artillery Brigade Headquarters here.' We tell him the number and then he says he does not know, but thinks it is round the corner to the right, pointing to another passage at right angles. We reach it and find that the stream we have been wading down is not the main one; the one we have now come to is much broader and deeper. Efforts have been made to put planks along it; but they are unstable and greasy, so mind you don't take a toss. I feel like a rat crawling along a drain, but without its agility. We pass several doorways opening into what look like cells, where evidently the spirits of the damned sit working. On enquiring at some of them for our destination we are always told, 'further on'. At last we reach a cell where a cheery voice greets us with, 'Oh, there you are!' On these occasions, you can always tell by their voices the fellow who is handing over and the fellow who is taking over. 'Here are your maps, here's your zone, etc., etc.' We know the front only too well, so there is, little delay in taking over. We ask if they won't stop to lunch (our mess by this time is descending one of the cataracts) but they say they are engaged to lunch at the club in Poperinghe. They seem in a deuce of a hurry to get off; I don't blame them.[8]

Colonel W. J. K. Rettie, 175th Brgade, Royal Field Artillery

Further forward the gun crews and their officers lived in a nightmare combination of tension and death with German shells raining down on observed or likely gun positions behind the British lines. If a British battery was registered as a German target, it might not necessarily precipitate a sudden onslaught but simply the start of a slow, steady, nerve-jangling trickle of shells. Having survived the explosive arrival of each one the predictable pattern of fire would cause anticipation and anxiety to rise across the gun position.

Once we were sitting in a dugout where we were being shelled and we learnt from our telephonist that a German aeroplane was observing for a German battery and directing its fire on to us. After a few shells had fallen we found that when our telephonist received the signal from the German aeroplane it took 17 seconds for the shell to reach us. After that we knew exactly when the shells were coming. As soon as you got the buzz from the telephonist you counted up to 17 seconds and then - CRUMP – the shell fell outside. Fortunately we were in a pretty good dugout. It had a curious effect on us and as I counted up towards 17 each time, as I got nearer the figure 17, it was just as if a hand had been thrust right inside me and twisted me round.[9]

Major W. Stoneham, Royal Field Artillery

Artillery batteries suffered awful casualties, not just from the cumulative effects of shells bursting near the gun positions, but also from a range of other potentially lethal assaults.

We have been barraging since 5 o'clock this morning without stopping, even though at a slow rate of fire. We have been shelled off and on the whole time. In addition one of our own 6-in batteries has been dropping its shells on our heads; fortunately they have not exploded. To complete the day several German aeroplanes have just been over us and dropped a dozen large bombs. They just missed the battery, falling a hundred yards in rear. I hate bombs, they make such a nasty sort of noise and the pieces fly very low. Now, as I am writing, he has just begun to give us gas shells. I must put my gas helmet on at once. What a life![10]

Major Ralph Hamilton, 106th Brigade, Royal Field Artillery

The conditions under which the gunners eked out their miserable existence simply made matters worse as their physical and mental health began to give way under the impossible strain.

To begin with, I was the only officer left at the guns. The other subaltern at the Battery and my Major had been knocked out before we moved up to our advanced positions to support the first infantry assault. My Battery Captain, who had got partially blinded by mustard gas, was back at the horse transport lines looking after our supplies. Half the men in my Battery at the guns were suffering from the ague. I had only one sergeant standing on his feet. Almost immediately, the weather broke and the conditions in which we lived were extremely ghastly. I think the weather more than anything else got one down. It rained so continuously that when one woke up in the morning in the little scrape that you had scratched out of the ground to get out of the way of the worst of the splinters, you felt the water bubbling and oozing in the small of your back. One was as afraid of getting drowned as one was of getting hit by a shell and actually of course the extraordinary quagmire masked and blinded a lot of the effect of the shells which sank so deeply in the mud that the splinter and blast effect was to a large effect nullified. By this time in the war over 80 per cent of the German heavy artillery spent its time plastering our gun areas, just as ours did the same to theirs. So day and night one lived in a permanent hail of shellfire. We had a gun knocked out almost the moment we moved into our battle positions. Later on we tried to send a damaged gun of ours back to ordnance – it vanished into the mud of an unseen shell hole and for all I know it is still there.[11]

Lieutenant Richard Talbot-Kelly, 52nd Brigade, Royal Field Artillery

In the crowded rear area of the Salient, no battery was ever likely to find a safe, secluded position. Even when camouflage was possible or a site found which was out of direct German observation, the guns could come under heavy fire as a result of being located near a prime target likely to attract German shells.

The new Monmouth Road was largely responsible for all the hostile fire directed at us. Large numbers of horses and mules were daily killed on the road and we spent much of our spare time burying these. After a while, the place became a kind of cemetery and the stench of decaying flesh appalling. Burying horses is never a pleasant occupation; but as we had to do it on a large scale, it became all the more distasteful, and we grew careless about it. Here and there, a hoof sticking out of the ground added to the repulsive aspect of our surroundings.[12]

Captain Maurice Walker, 154th Siege Battery, Royal Garrison Artillery

The unforgiving, relentless stream of shells meant that men at all levels were put to the test by constant close escapes from death which seemed almost miraculous to those lucky enough to survive.

At 2 o'clock we were very heavily shelled with 5.9s right into the battery. Selwyn and I, who sleep in the mess, put up with it for the first dozen rounds but when we had four running within 20 yards, we decided to clear out and ran across to the No. 1 Gun. We had just got there when a shell landed practically on us. I really think it was about the closest shave I have ever had. We had just time to lie down in the mud, right in the open, when the horrid thing burst, certainly not more than 10 yards off. I thought the debris would never stop falling; a huge clod of earth, twice as big as my head, fell on my back from heaven only knows what height. It knocked all the wind out of me and this morning I am so stiff I can hardly move; my back and side are black and blue.[13]

Major Ralph Hamilton, 106th Brigade, Royal Field Artillery

Much of the shelling was speculative counter-battery work. But occasionally the Germans were confident in the exact position of a target and sought to obliterate a battery.

I arrived in the morning at the battery position at the Admiral's Road site where we had the old German trench running quite close to us. We had made a bit of the old German trench into our own battery dugout which was a little safer than mere sandbags would have been. I arrived in the morning with my batman and a colleague who was slightly older, he ought to have been senior but he wasn't. We found the Major in command of the battery who had been stopping at the battery. He looked out, it was a filthy day, raining more than usual, and he said, 'I don't think there's a chance of German air observation today, they just won't be able to do it in this weather, I think I'll get the motorcycle and go into Poperinghe to get my hair cut!' Poperinghe was our sort of 'wicked city'! So off he went and Vernon, the other subaltern and I sat down and did a little odd firing. We had the usual harassing programme, we used to fire on what was thought to be awkward places for the Germans, cross-roads and things like that. About lunch-time, I heard a noise which I recognised as a German 5.9 howitzer shell on the way. There was the usual shock and explosion and it was in front of the battery position – rather too close. Shortly afterwards I heard the noise again and a similar German shell landed rather too close for comfort the other side of the battery. But still it was perfectly possible that these were only casual German rounds fired as part of a programme to harass the area in which we were – and not directly at us. So we had to wait and see. There followed two more rounds, one short and one plus. I said to Vernon, 'I think that's it!' He said, 'So do I!' He blew a whistle, which was the signal and the men rapidly got off the guns and came back to the old German front-line trench where their heads were down, there was concrete and it was away to a flank. I was very relieved that they'd all got to safety because the fire increased and very soon we were getting rounds every few seconds, falling in and round the battery position. It was getting to look very nasty indeed. The thing that was frightening me particularly was that I knew that, if at this point the infantry was attacked and put up

SOS rockets, it would be absolutely essential that we should get all the men back on the guns whether they were under fire or not. God knows what we would have lost – this had happened to another battery not very distant from us and they'd lost a great many of personnel because they couldn't leave the guns. The rule was quite simple, if the infantry were out of the trenches – either because they were in an offensive or because the Germans were attacking them – the gunners were to stay on the guns. Well, we got no SOS rocket! We simply stopped and watched detonation after detonation in the battery position. At intervals, either Vernon or I would make our way along the old German front line trench to see if we'd got a stray round and any men had been hurt. Nobody had, not a single man was touched. The afternoon wore on and we tried to estimate from the speed of the detonations how many batteries were firing on us and we came to the conclusion that it was probably three, two 5.9-inch howitzer batteries and conceivably an 8-inch howitzer battery. It was that sort of fire, what was described as a 'shoot to destruction', their idea being they would shoot until we were quite out. It got dark after a bit and fire slackened. The Germans were reckoned to have a trick of stopping fire of this kind and waiting until the gunners got back and then starting again very suddenly. I remembered this story and I said to Vernon, 'I think you and I had better have a look first!' We went out and we found that all the guns had been hit. One in spite of its five tons of weight was blown completely on its back. Obviously it was finished. Another gun was very badly damaged and then splinters had made a bit of a mess of the other two. Then we went back to our dugout and I was right – they did start again but they didn't go on very long. I didn't think they'd do it twice so the second time they stopped we sent the men back to the gunpits to do what they could to clear up – though it wasn't much. After dark my commanding officer, the Major, arrived back from Poperinghe and he came into the battery position from the far side from where we were. He was horrified to find there wasn't a gun in action. He thought to himself that he would find half his men casualties on the ground, he thought we must have been caught. But to his relief nobody was there and then he found us and we explained what had happened. Next day the ordnance came round, all our guns were taken, two were patched up quickly and the other two we had to wait for some days before new ones arrived.[14]

Lieutenant Cyril Denys, 212th Siege Battery, Royal Garrison Artillery

In such circumstances, with shells randomly spattering around, sleep was difficult. Lieutenant Huntly Gordon found himself a convenient berth in an old bread oven for his first night under fire.

> Then arose a problem. Should I sleep with my feet at the open end to protect my head from flying shell-splinters and whiffs of gas, or my head at the open end to minimise the chance of being buried alive by a direct hit? I chose the latter alternative, lay down with my gas mask on, said a prayer that I might be preserved from 'things that go bump in the night' – and shut my eyes. But sleep was slow to come. Every now and then, a shell burst some distance off. I could hear others, like lost souls, whimpering their way overhead for some remoter destination. And I realised that at that very moment a German gun might have fired the shell that in half a minute would crash through my oven roof and mangle me . . . The thought was so appalling that for the sake of sanity I shut it out from my mind. This would be my lot in the days to come, to live under sentence of sudden death, yet somehow to ignore it. Men of older years and longer war experience would be looking to me, their officer, for an example; and in that I simply dare not fail. No allowances could be made; there could be no excuse for showing fear in front of them. Regardless of inner turmoil, I simply must appear calm. There seemed only one way to achieve this: to clamp down an iron control on one's natural feelings and to distract one's mind by positive action of some sort.[15]
>
> Lieutenant Huntly Gordon, 112th Brigade, Royal Field Artillery

As the weeks passed, Gordon gained in experience; but if anything these experiences merely exacerbated his fears. He now knew the rending power of German shells.

> Some of the shells came down with a peculiar scream and a thump that made the whole building wobble; they were said to be armour-piercing, or delay action fuses. In our brick cells after a time the merriment became rather forced. Through one's mind the unspoken question ran – 'Am I imagining it, or is that another one on the way? Yes, here it comes. Keep talking at all costs' – Whoop! CRASH! After a while we gave up the pretence and looking at each other with a wan smile, consented to suspend the conversation as the climax came. I started reading *Pickwick*; that is, I held the book in my hand, every now and then turning over a page, but the words which I read and re-read meant nothing. If there had

been something urgent to do, distraction might have been possible. But there wasn't. Every nerve was tuned in to the terrifying crescendo of each shell – as they came one after another, remorselessly, jolting the brain as hammer blows.[16]

Lieutenant Huntly Gordon, 112th Brigade, Royal Field Artillery

Few men possessed a bottomless well of courage. Whereas the infantry, at least theoretically, had the prospect of leaving the front on rest, the artillery stayed in the line week after week, pelted with shells night and day. It was not surprising that some gunners were eventually ground down and found wanting by others still fortunate enough to have retained some mental reserves.

This afternoon 5.9s and 4.2s are falling fast all over this part of the valley. Another man has gone off his head, but I have refused to allow him to leave the guns. It is simply a matter of everyone having to control their nerves. I am very sorry for the man, but if the idea once gets about that a man can get out of this hell by letting go of his nerves, heaven help us.[17]

Major Ralph Hamilton, 106th Brigade, Royal Field Artillery

It was not only the men that suffered, their unfortunate horses and mules shared the dangers and miseries of Ypres. Strangely, the plight of these animals often caused even greater anguish than the sight of human casualties.

Heaving about in the filthy mud of the road was an unfortunate mule with both its forelegs shot away. The poor brute, suffering God knows what untold agonies and terrors, was trying desperately to get to its feet which weren't there. Writhing and heaving, tossing its head about in its wild attempts, not knowing that it no longer had any front legs. I had my revolver with me, but we couldn't get near the animal, which lashed out at us with its hind legs and tossed its head about unceasingly. Jerry's shells were arriving pretty fast – we made some desperate attempts to get at the mule so that I could put a bullet behind its ear into the brain, but to no avail. By lingering there, trying to put the suffering creature out of its pain I was risking not only my life but my companion's. The shelling got more intense – perhaps one would hit the poor thing and put it out of its misery.[18]

Lieutenant R. G. Dixon, 14th Battery, Royal Garrison Artillery

The suffering of the horses and mules inspired a sense of guilt in the men, who perhaps felt instinctively that their animal friends had not asked to become involved in the murderous affairs of man.

> The mules used to scream when they got wounded, they were worse than the men in a way. If they were too bad, you used to put a revolver bullet through their brain. You hear very little about the horses but my God, that used to trouble me more than the men in some respects. We knew what we were there for; them poor devils didn't, did they?[19]
>
> Signaller Jim Crow, 110th Brigade, Royal Field Artillery

Some men coped reasonably well with the death of their animal pals; others could be almost unhinged by the death or maiming of a favourite horse.

> Our ammunition wagon had got up and it had only been there a second or two when a shell killed his horse under the driver. We went over to him, tried to unharness the horse and cut the traces away. He just kneeled and watched this horse . . . A Brigadier came along, a brass hat, he tapped this boy on the shoulder and said, 'Never mind, sonny!' This driver looked up at him, just for a second or two and all of a sudden he said, 'Bloody Germans!' Then he pointed his finger and he stood there as though he was transfixed, stood there like stone. The Brass Hat said to his captain, 'All right, take the boy down the line and see that he has two or three days' rest.' He turned to our captain and he said, 'If everyone was like that who loved animals we would be all right.' [20]
>
> Gunner H.V. Doggett, Royal Artillery

The Germans were particularly skilful in deploying gas to neutralize British batteries. Thousands of gas shells rained down to poison and debilitate the sweating gun teams. If gas masks were worn, not only were they uncomfortable, but they restricted the operational efficiency of the gun teams. Everything was more difficult wearing a mask.

> There's no great noise about it because there's only sufficient explosive in the shell to open it up. The shell itself is filled with liquid gas. The nose is spigoted into the cylinder part and held on with either lead rivets or wooden pegs, then in the bottom there's a bursting charge which compresses it enough to sheer those rivets and allow the gas to come out as liquid and it evaporates. There wasn't any great danger from splinters or explosives or anything like that. All that happens is that around you, you hear these thuds and plops and there are clouds of vapour rolling about.[21]
>
> Signaller Leonard Ounsworth, 144th Heavy Battery, Royal Garrison Artillery

One ludicrous tale of how best to ward off the effects of gas set in train a habit likely to have serious consequences for the post-war health of one gallant young officer.

> I always gave my cigarette ration to my batman, I used to have 100 cigarettes coming out every month from Philip Morris, Turkish, and 100 also Turkish, from Bartlett in Piccadilly. I never smoked more than about 50 in a month until my batman came to me and he said, 'You know, sir, that a Major in one of the other batteries, he never wears a gas mask.' So I said, 'Well, he must be a bloody fool!' He said, 'Not at all, if he smokes cigarettes – they must be "gaspers" – continuously, he doesn't have to wear a mask!' So I, like a fool, thought, 'I'll start this!' I did wear a gas mask always when things were bad but I thought, 'Well, I'll try this business of smoking!' And instead of 50 a month, I was smoking 40 a day! It was many years before I could give it up![22]
>
> Lieutenant Murray Rymer-Jones, 74th Brigade, Royal Field Artillery

Despite all these obstacles and hindrances, the British guns never seemed to be silent. Constant readiness was regarded as an obligation, so the work was incessant. Registration, concentrated barrages, SOS calls from the infantry, attacking fleeting targets of opportunity, harassing fire, counter-battery work – on and on they thundered.

> We never had six guns in action all at once. There was always one or more down at St Omer having a new liner put in. The nominal life of a 60-pounder was supposed to be 3,000 rounds and we were going up to 5,000 and over. As we were firing 1,000 rounds a night average out of the four guns you can imagine it wasn't long before a gun had fired its 3 or 4,000 rounds – within about a fortnight or three weeks they wanted relining, so that we were always one or two guns short.[23]
>
> Signaller Leonard Ounsworth, 144th Heavy Battery, Royal Garrison Artillery

Maintaining the rate of fire was exhausting for the men but it also quickly used up the available supply of shells. New stocks constantly had to be moved up to the forward battery positions.

> Every night, we collected our 18-pounder shells and used our horses with packs over their saddles. Each pack had eight pockets, four each side. We sat straddle-leg over the riding horse with shells between our legs and led the off-horse. The Engineers or someone else had laid heavy planks in an attempt to form a road. As soon as we left the planks we tried to pick our

way between shell holes, the whole vista resembling nothing more than a pepper pot. The off-horse would hold back or make a leap forward, often dragging us off our rider-horses, both horse and rider were stuck in the shell hole, with the flash of guns forming our only light. This became impossible. Each rider took 16 shells on his two horses but was lucky to land with half that amount. It was soon discovered that no man could manage two horses and in future it was one man to one horse. Very often we made two journeys each, taking the whole night. The guns must be fed.[24]

Driver Rowland Luther, 92nd Brigade, Royal Field Artillery

Delivering sufficient quantities of ammunition in this way was a laborious business and whenever it was possible, the gunners used the mechanical contrivance of a Decauville light railway to feed the insatiable guns.

The Decauville light railway, when it had been laid up to the battery was a great saving to the wagon lines. The ammunition, rations, drinking water in petrol cans and stores being put on trucks and driven up by petrol engine at night. Each truck could carry 900 rounds of ammunition, sufficient for a night's firing and a little over. The track was laid up our shallow valley which was subject to heavy German fire. The driver of the engine did not always like this, and uncoupled his engine and went back. I had to send down parties from the sections not engaged in night firing to push up the trucks by hand.[25]

Major Roderick Macleod, 241st Brigade, Royal Field Artillery

The removal of the spent shell cases was a moot point in such conditions. The mounds of discarded cases littered gun positions all across the Salient.

We heard we had once more changed our Divisional Royal Artillery Commander and that the new arrival, whose name is General 'B', was coming to inspect the Brigade in action. He is an individual well known for having a 106 fuse temper and 'non-delay' language far in advance of any other general in the regiment, and worst of all it was reported that his pet mania was the immediate clearance of all empty cartridge cases from gun positions. The careful return of empty shell cases is no doubt very necessary, but on some positions it must pay the tax payer best to let them lie until the next advance. Casualties to horses and men, while performing the slow job of loading them up into the wagons, may thus be avoided. But this was no excuse in the General's eyes and he slated two batteries of Brigade unmercifully on account of them. It was to be our turn next day. Just behind our guns were two huge craters filled to the brim with shell cases, at least 10,000 of them. All seemed lost; however, that night came Inspiration. At dawn I arose, found an old notice-board and swiftly the battery painter covered its face with the following legend: –

C. 28. C. 53. Dump.

All 18-pdr. and 4.5 cases to be dumped here.

Result, much kudos for our very neat position and a broad smile on the face of our Colonel, standing behind the General.[26]

Major Neil Fraser-Tytler, 150th Brigade, Royal Field Artillery

The inanimate guns also suffered as the ceaseless firing tested their manufacturers' specifications to the limit and beyond. The results were inevitable. Lieutenant Dixon was giving an infantry officer a familiarization tour of local batteries, when he approached the battery commanded by Major Lloyd George, the son of the Prime Minister, behind Admiral's Road.

We were about 20 yards away from these six-inchers when there was suddenly a most unusual roar from No. 3 gun, and a huge flash and a cloud of smoke. When the ear splitting noise had died in its own echoes and the smoke had drifted away, we beheld only the stump of the barrel, with the elongated length of it lying grotesquely in front of the sand-bagged wall, and coils and coils of wire wriggling fantastically above the emplacement. A shell had burst inside the barrel; it was what was known as a premature. The gun had broken in half. The place was a shambles in the correct sense of the word, which is a slaughterhouse. Two men were dead, and the rest of the gun's crew were wounded with the exception of one. One unfortunate fellow was lying unconscious with a bit of his thigh as large as a dinner plate scooped out of the flesh, with the blood bubbling and sending up steam into the bitter air. We left their comrades to get on with the job of first aid and getting the wounded to the Casualty Clearing Station. My companion looked a bit white under his open-air tan. Casualties he was used to, but ripped, torn and mangled men all mixed up with fantastic coils of springy wire tape from the broken barrel was a pretty ghastly sight indeed. 'My God!' said he, 'I'm glad I'm in the footsloggers!'[27]

Lieutenant R. G. Dixon, 14th Battery, Royal Garrison Artillery

Except in the most desperate of circumstances the gun positions had no direct view of their targets. To achieve observation of their firing each battery therefore sent forward an observation officer accompanied by signallers to maintain a telephone link between them and the gun positions. Reaching the observation post, or OP, was invariably a nightmare journey.

I made that journey many times. Each time I feared it, and most times we were spotted by the German artillery observers and fired upon. Their field guns had every yard of our roads and tracks 'taped' to a nicety and he was wont to loose off two or three rounds if he saw any movement upon them. I can still remember the swift, high pitched shriek of those small shells as they plugged into the mud near us, exploding harmlessly, luckily for us, in the depths of the morass. We were never hit, by the grace of God, for the deep mud was our salvation, that mud which we cursed and in which we stuck and staggered, slipped and slid, tugging our boots out of it each time we made a fresh step. Jerry's shells showered us with filth, they disturbed the riddled and broken corpses, they re-shredded the putrid flesh into scraps. It was easy to go 'missing'; if you got hit, the chances were you slipped into some yawning shell hole full of greyly opaque water concealing unmentionable things and you drowned there. Wherever you went in this nightmare country you saw obscene things protruding from the mud. All around us lay the dead, both friend and foe, half in, half out of the water-logged shell holes. Their hands and boots stuck out at us from the mud. Their rotting faces stared blindly at us from coverlets of mud; their decaying buttocks heaved themselves obscenely from the filth with which the shell bursts had smothered them. Skulls grinned at us. These corpses were never buried, for it was impossible for us to retrieve them. They had lain, many of them, for weeks and months; they would lie and rot and disintegrate foully into the muck until they were an inescapable part of it to manure the harvests of a future peace-time Belgium. Horror was everywhere. One grew accustomed to these things but I never grew accustomed to the all-pervading stench of decayed and decaying flesh, mingled with that of high explosive fumes, that hung over miles and miles of what had been sweet countryside and now was one vast muck heap of murder.[28]

Lieutenant R.G. Dixon, 14th Battery, Royal Garrison Artillery

Early on in the campaign, observation posts were often located in the battered remains of former farmhouses.

We used to observe from Hussar Farm, go in the upper floor. The boards were all gone, we used to get up a staircase which was hanging on by a wall and walk round the edge where the floor was still to some extent attached to the wall to get round to the window. In the middle there was a heap of boards and brickwork, slates and tiles from above – completely open up above – it was just a wreck. We didn't learn until later there was a couple of dead mules underneath until the horse flies started getting busy. The stink was terrible.[29]

Signaller Leonard Ounsworth, 144th Heavy Battery, Royal Garrison Artillery

Later, as the guns moved forward in the wake of the advancing infantry, the observation officers took up residence in former German pillboxes. Ounsworth moved forward to Jasper Farm, which had been captured by Company Sergeant Major Handley and his men on 31 July.

The observation post at that point was at Jasper Farm, that was a Jerry pillbox. There had been a farm there some day no doubt, but all we had was a Jerry pillbox with the entrance of course facing the enemy. First time I saw it I didn't like it one little bit. There were two or three dead Jerries in the approach trench outside and we found out later there was another couple under water inside it and the stink was abominable.[30]

Signaller Leonard Ounsworth, 144th Heavy Battery, Royal Garrison Artillery

In the intensity of the battle the pillboxes had become charnel houses, and their proximity to the front line meant that there was little or no opportunity to clear them out properly.

The rooms are more than half full of stagnant water and we had to crouch down on planks supported at water level on a heap of corpses underneath. The stench really was awful and we all had to smoke continuously to keep it down. It must have been full of Bosches when our chaps lobbed some bombs in a few days ago. Now frequent bubbles break the surface of the oily scum. We were careful not to stir it up. Thank God, we didn't have to be in there for very long or I would have tried my luck in the open.[31]

Lieutenant Huntly Gordon, 112th Brigade, Royal Field Artillery

In places where no such edifices existed, the officers and their signallers were forced to crouch with the infantry in whatever pitiful shelter they could find.

> The forward observation post would be an enlarged shell hole, probably with some sandbags round it and duckboards to keep you a little bit out of the wet. You'd get your head below the level of the sandbags, you couldn't build them up far or you'd be spotted, but you could get a little shelter from them. You used your binoculars to look though the gaps. Sometimes you couldn't do that and there was nothing for it but to look over the edge. That wouldn't last long if the Germans were near! You couldn't get much range of vision because we never really had the dominating ground, but I could see 400–500 yards inside the German line from one of our posts. I could see two ruined farms from one post I was in, they must have been 300 yards in. I very rarely saw the Germans, they were no chaps for exposing themselves. I used to think sometimes our people were a bit careless like that. But the Germans were pretty careful. Once, I saw some Germans labouring along behind the line, evidently carrying a latrine bucket. The temptation was too strong for me and I let go two howitzer shells. I'm glad to say I missed them but it seemed to me afterwards that it was a shit's trick! It was totally irrational – they were enemies; they'd have shot me as soon as they possibly could. But they were engaged on this humble task and I had a feeling that I shouldn't have done it.[32]
>
> Lieutenant Cyril Denys, 212th Siege Battery, Royal Garrison Artillery

Gazing out from these awkward, inhospitable positions, across a uniformly desolate landscape into the German lines, made the role of the observation officer uncommonly difficult. It was often very hard to see anything with certainty.

> Owing to the flat nature of the country, it was very difficult definitely to pin-point batteries at a long distance, and we used to have many arguments on this subject at the OP. As a result of this, the officers in the battery became divided into three schools of opinion. One party said they could see Bosche batteries firing and locate them accurately. Another said they could see batteries firing but couldn't locate them. The third party said the others were all talking nonsense, and what they thought were guns firing, were in reality shells from British guns bursting a long distance away. Each of the officers firmly believed his own opinion to be correct,

and acted up to it, with the result that on some days reports came from the OP that batteries were very active at several places, while on other days the Bosche was evidently taking a holiday. This subject caused us endless amusement in the officers' mess, where feeling ran very high about it.[33]

Captain Maurice Walker, 154th Siege Battery, Royal Garrison Artillery

One of the key roles of the OP was to identify potential targets for the future and register the guns on them. Registration was a process whereby the co-ordinates required to land a shell accurately on the particular target were worked out and then recorded for future use.

Registration invariably had to take place when a battery moved from one position to another in order that the battery commander would know exactly where he stood in relation to the enemy positions, his trenches and so on. To give him his ranges and deflections. In other words to definitely register and calibrate his guns so that the figures were known there immediately if any SOS was put up by the infantry or if there was a call for a barrage. He would know exactly where to put that down because he had pre-registered it all. His calibrations were all there in his battery office. He knew to get to a certain barrage line or trench line he had to correct his guns to that firm deflection, elevation to range and so on.[34]

Wireless Operator Leslie Briggs, Royal Flying Corps

Once a likely future target had been identified, the process of establishing the exact range began.

The forward observation officer picks out shall we say a ruined farm inside the German line and identifies it on his map. He rings up the battery and says, 'I think we could register on "A42 B5 C8"' They'd look it up and work out what elevation and line was required for the guns to get this square. Then I would be told, 'Number One gun ready!' And so I'd say, 'Fire, Number One gun!' Then I'd presently hear a 'RRRRRRRR' like this going overhead and up would go a spout of earth. Well over the farmhouse and perhaps 60 yards to the left. In our howitzers we didn't go in yardage because of the high angle fire, you went by degrees and minutes in elevation and right and left. So I'd look at this round and I'd say, 'Correction, drop 3 minutes, left 1 minute!' Or something like that. 'Number Two gun ready, Sir!' 'Fire Number Two!' Then you'd see another round go up. This one short! So you'd say, 'Up 1 degree!' And so on till you'd got them all and it was Number One's turn with the corrected range and line. It was most exasperating how often you had to do this. You'd correct and the next round would be all wrong! The reason was of course that these howitzers were turned out very quickly so the gun error was considerable and we all thought the ammunition, which we very often bought from America, we used to think it wasn't as good as our ammunition. But that would be patriotic prejudice! Registering was to find what each gun was doing wrong so that you could correct it. Number 4 might be persistently firing short; well, if you knew how short she was firing you could add it on. If you had your guns properly registered you could confidently open fire on somewhere. You never knew with artillery whether you would hit it but you would know your rounds would be grouped round it.[35]

Lieutenant Cyril Denys, 212th Siege Battery, Royal Garrison Artillery

Being in effective control of where the shells landed, the observation post officers did at least occasionally have the professional satisfaction of dealing out death and destruction to their enemies. In one such case Major Hamilton was on his regular liaison visit to the Colonel of the 12th Battalion, Royal Fusiliers. Here he was given the news that a junior officer had actually managed to locate a viewpoint from which a German battery could be seen. After a journey, which tested his gunner nerves, to the Lone Star Post only 20 yards from the putative German front line, Hamilton reached the vantage point.

My guide, by name Mears-Devenish, pointed out the place where he had seen the German guns firing this morning. For some time I could make nothing out, but after examining the place for some time through my Zeiss glasses, I saw one gun. It was right in the edge of a wood, covered over by branches. I could clearly see the shield of the gun and one wheel; later I picked out two more guns. There used to be a German battery there in very large concrete pits, but our heavies have smashed these up and the guns at present are in the intervals between the old pits. I fired my salvo of smoke shells as I had arranged with Rentell. There was no doubt about them. They sent up a vast column of smoke like an 8-in shell bursting. I at once gave a correction by guess, switching onto the hostile battery. After some time I got the guns definitely onto the gun that I could see. It was such a wonderful sight to see Huns walking about in the open. I next put a salvo of high explosive close to my target and having located the place I at once gave them five rounds of gunfire from all guns. The range was exact and so was the height of the bursts. My 25 shells arrived almost simultaneously and simply plastered the Huns who were moving in the trees. After that I ranged a single gun with high explosive non-delay onto one of the German guns; the range was 4,800 yards; all the same the shooting and laying were excellent, round after round falling within a few yards of the target. One shell hit a wheel and brought the gun down on its axle; shortly afterwards another shell fell right into the German ammunition dump beside the gun. It blew up with a tremendous explosion and wrecked the whole place. When the smoke cleared away I could see the gun lying on its side pointing the opposite way to what it had before. I then tackled a second gun and got two hits into its emplacement, but the camouflage of branches was so thick round it that I could not see the result. Before I could finish it off my wire went and I had reluctantly to stop firing.[36]

Major Ralph Hamilton, 106th Brigade, Royal Field Artillery

After completing a tour of duty at the observation post, which was usually only of short duration, the journey back to the gun positions had to be done at night. If not, the difficulties and dangers encountered along the way multiplied rapidly.

One night we'd been there and we should have been relieved before dawn. This other mob never turned up and it got to daylight. We found out then, they'd arrived and they'd been at another pillbox nearby, Uhlan Farm, only about 200–300 yards away. You'd only got map codings to go by, there was no landmarks left at all. That meant we had got to get away and it was no longer darkness. We crawled as best we could till we got to the road. Well, of course, Jerry had us under observation and it took us about three hours to get back to the battery because every time we moved we had field guns on us. By then we were thoroughly fed up. I had one man, Boiling, nicknamed 'Bubbler' who was a Londoner, a well-educated man, he played for Blackheath rugby team. When we got back to our battery they were in action. He just walked up to a gun that was ready to fire and pushed them out, got onto the lanyard and gave it a jerk – fired the gun! The No. 2 on the gun looked at him a bit amazed and 'Bubbler' said, 'I hope I hit some bugger in the back of the neck!'[37]

Signaller Leonard Ounsworth, 144th Heavy Battery, Royal Garrison Artillery

Observation posts were only part of the answer. Many of the German defensive positions and gun batteries lay concealed on the reverse slopes of the Gheluvelt Plateau. No gunner would ever be in a position to see them from within the British lines and so aerial observation was absolutely essential. Observers in the air carried out much the same role as their counterparts on the ground, first locating their targets and then inexorably directing the guns onto their target. The Royal Artillery and the Royal Flying Corps therefore developed a close, symbiotic relationship.

> About 03.00 hours a plane from No. 6 Squadron would leave the aerodrome and fly over the lines. The observer then kept his eyes on the Hun territory until he saw a battery firing. He then would pin-point the location of the battery on his map and fly back to our battery, sending us down by wireless the information required for us to lay the guns on it. As soon as our wireless operator got the messages from the plane, he telephoned them to the Battery Commander's post. At this hour of the morning the Battery Commander, or the officer acting for him, was usually asleep, so the telephonist on duty would wake him. This was always a very painful proceeding. The Battery Commander then measured the range to the target and, by means of telephone, sent the information required for laying the guns to the Section Commander, who awaited the messages alongside the guns. The guns were loaded and laid on the target as quickly as possible. When they were ready the plane was notified by means of ground strips. From the time the plane called up until the guns were ready, was usually about four minutes. If we took longer, owing to somebody's stupidity or errors, the Battery Commander cursed us all soundly. When the observer saw that we were ready, he would order us to fire.[38]
>
> Captain Maurice Walker, 154th Siege Battery, Royal Garrison Artillery

The observation aircraft were two-seaters – often RE8s – with the pilot in front, and the wireless operator/gunner behind to spot the fall of the battery's shells.

> We start flying at dawn and go on till dark, each pilot having to do at least three hours a day. Our particular job is to range the artillery on certain positions which they wish to wipe out and in the three hours we are given four different targets to register. In addition to this, we always carry two bombs which we drop over the Hun line. On a clear day we are able to do our ranging from behind our own lines quite easily; but it's usually misty and cloudy and then we have to sit on top of the Hun position at a fairly low altitude. Meanwhile we are getting 'Archied' and

machine gunned fairly persistently. I always have an observer with me and while he ranges the artillery I steer clear of our machines, at the same time dodge 'Archie' and look out for Hun machines.[39]

Lieutenant Jack Walthew, 4 Squadron, Royal Flying Corps

His observer would transmit by wireless the co-ordinates of a target to a signaller at the battery's gun positions. Corrections for the fire of the guns were given using what was known as the 'Clock Code' introduced in early 1915.

The short-wave tuner enabled you to receive with headphones messages which were being sent in Morse from the air by pilots and observers. The tuners were quite intricate because you had to tune what was an open circuit and when you'd got a perfect tuning you put a switch over and tune it again on a closed circuit, the object being to cut out as much as possible of interference and jamming. By the time you'd got your machine tuned to that right wavelength then you were ready to go. The object was to make sure that we got the messages from the observers absolutely correct otherwise the corrections on the guns would be all haywire. You opened up your station when the machine came up from the squadron and called you at the battery. You had your own specific call signs which you recognised immediately. It gave the squadron sign and the battery sign. From then on the observer would ask you to stand by. He had already been told the target on which he'd got to range. The shoot would commence by your signalling to the observer by means of an American white strip about two feet wide, weighted at each end and put out in the forms of letters such as 'K' or 'L' or 'N' or 'D' as the case may be in accordance with a code. When you were ready to engage a target he should have been flying from the battery position to the target. As he was approaching the target he would give you what was called a 'G' signal which meant 'Fire!' You would pass that signal immediately to your battery commander who would then give the order for one of his guns to fire. Your observer was still proceeding towards the target hoping to arrive over the target at practically the same time as the shell which was due to burst on or near the target. He would then turn and come back towards the battery having worked out the correction. As he came back he would signal that correction to you and you would again report that to your battery commander. The way he was able to correct where that shell had fallen was by means of a device called the 'clock code'. It was comprised of a circular disc of transparent material which had twelve radial lines coming out from the centre of a pin and eight concentric circles. The observer would fix that device onto his map on his dashboard in the cockpit. He would register where that round had fallen by giving the correction on direction based on one or other of those twelve lines corresponding from one to twelve on a clock. Then the rings would be varying distances from the target and they were lettered 'Y' 'Z' 'A' 'B' 'C' 'D' 'E' 'F' with the inner ring being 10 yards from the target, the next one 25, the next one which would be 'A', 50 yards, 'B' 100 yards and so on. If you got a correction coming back 'A9' it would mean that the round had fallen within 50 yards of the target at nine o'clock on the clock. The battery commander was in a position to correct his gun or guns for subsequent round, so that eventually with any luck at all he would be able to register an 'OK' on his particular target. When a point was reached that the observer felt that he could not get any more accuracy he would come back to you in the air and give you a signal which meant 'Go on firing' or 'Gun fire'. You would pass it on to your battery commander and he would know then that he could let fly because he was registered on his target and he could do as much damage as possible.[40]

Wireless Operator Leslie Briggs, Royal Flying Corps

Retrospectively described, this sounds like quite a straightforward procedure. But it is important to remember that the artillery observation aircraft were flying through air liberally laced with British shells.

While we were shooting one day with our usual observer, Lieutenant McCullagh, a shell from the guns struck the aeroplane from which he was observing. The plane immediately burst into flames and disappeared from view. Both Lieutenant McCullagh and the pilot, Second Lieutenant Middleton, were killed; not a trace of their remains was ever found. This accident was quite unavoidable, as the aeroplane was evidently flying directly in the line of fire.[41]

Captain Maurice Walker, 154th Siege Battery, Royal Garrison Artillery

Such incidents were perhaps inevitable given the density of the artillery traffic passing both ways. But the consequences, nevertheless, were tragic.

What the devil is this coming down? The air is full of little bits of white stuff and chips of wood. Pick that bit up. Good God! Aeroplane fabric. The machine that disappeared. Hit by one of our passing big shells. Someone says, 'Poor beggar,' the others collect souvenirs.[42]

Lieutenant Cyril Lawrence, 1st Field Company, Engineers, Australian Imperial Force

Pinned above a specific location for a considerable length of time, the RE8s became extremely vulnerable whilst flying backwards and forwards. The prime aim of the German single-seater scouts was to shoot down these troublesome 'birds'. Conversely, the British scouts existed primarily to protect their weaker brethren in the RE8s by driving off, or preferably destroying, the German predators. Attacking and destroying the equivalent German observation and reconnaissance aircraft was an important complementary role, but one that was always secondary to defending the operations of the British reconnaissance machines. The best way for the British scouts to fulfil both purposes was to dominate the skies above the front lines and the RFC therefore adopted an aggressive policy of forward patrolling throughout the war. By the summer of 1917, with the latest British scouts, the SE5s, Sopwith Camels and Bristol Fighters, they had at last been equipped with the aircraft that could seek to match the German scouts in aerial combat. Every day, when the weather permitted, the scout pilots set off on their patrols to seek out and destroy any German aircraft that they came across.

> We used to take off on these big squadron offensive patrols usually in the afternoon. Kitted up in our long sheepskin thigh boots, leather coats, helmets and goggles. By the time you got all that in the cockpit there wasn't much room and we were wedged in. We ran our engines up for two or three minutes, time to get them warm and then took off. At about 500 feet we would begin to get in formation and head slowly out towards the lines. We were about 20 miles behind the lines so we had time to climb up on our way over to get height this side of the lines. We usually got up to 15,000 or 16,000 feet before we actually crossed the lines into enemy territory looking for trouble. Our eyes were continually focusing, looking, craning our heads round, moving all the time looking for those black specks which would mean enemy aircraft at a great distance. Between clouds we would not be able to see the ground or only parts of it which would sort of slide into view like a magic lantern screen far, far beneath. Clinging close together about 20 or 30 yards between each machine, swaying, looking at our neighbours, setting ourselves just right so that we were all in position. Sooner or later, we would spot the enemy. If we were lucky, it would be below us, but we were always under the enemy. Our machines, good as they were, were still not up to the Huns' who usually had a 1,000 to 2,000 feet ceiling clear above us. Even at

16,000 feet we were liable to be jumped from on top. That didn't have to worry us. We were usually outnumbered two or three to one. We used to engage irrespective if there was anybody above or not – just chance it. Usually the top flight of enemy aircraft who were above us would come down and jump us as we went down. It's not really possible to describe the action of a fight like that. Having no communication with each other we simply had to go in and take our man and chance our arm – keep our eyes in the backs of our heads to see if anybody was trying to get us as we went down. But there was always the point where you had to go down anyway whether there was anybody on your tail or not. The fight would begin – engage and disengage with bursts of 30 or 40 rounds, three in one tracer, so there was always some idea of where you were firing because your sights were really no good in these dogfights. There wasn't time to focus; it was just snap shooting. The whole squadron would enter the fight in good formation but within half a minute the whole formation had gone to hell. Just chaps wheeling and zooming and diving. On each others' tails – perhaps four in a row even – a German going down, one of our chaps on his tail, another German on his tail, another Hun behind that – extraordinary glimpses. People approaching head-on, firing at each other as they came and then, just at the last moment, turning and slipping away. The fight would last perhaps altogether ten minutes or a quarter of an hour and would come down from 15,000 feet right down almost to ground level. By that time probably ammunition exhausted or guns jammed and then there would be nothing left but to come back home again.[43]

Lieutenant Cecil Lewis, 56 Squadron, Royal Flying Corps

These huge swirling dogfights, replete with the dazzling energy and colour denied to the landlocked soldiers who struggled on stoically beneath them, have come to epitomize the First World War in the air in the public imagination. Yet it is important to remember that even by 1917 the RFC had developed only a minor independent role. The lion's share of its work was to support the troops on the ground and through the crucial importance of maintaining the accuracy of the guns it was to the Royal Artillery that the RFC was truly beholden.

And what was it all for? To smash the enemy, destroy his defensive works, kill his troops. When the guns opened up together it could be a truly awe-inspiring sight.

> It was a terrifying spectacle. Up to that moment, there had been but sporadic gunfire from both sides. Now, at one shattering second of time, synchronised perfectly, five thousand guns and howitzers opened their iron jaws and belched flame and smoke. All hell raced across the grey firmament above us as thousands of shells screamed their way towards the Germans. The whole of the horizon behind us danced with flame, the gun flashes lit up the outline of the low ridges and the lowering clouds above. Overhead the express trains screamed and bellowed and roared and away ahead of us on the slopes of Passchendaele Ridge the fire of hell erupted as our barrage fell upon the German lines. Stunned as we were by the colossal assault on our minds and bodies, we still had time to feel sorry for the enemy. 'My God' shouted my Sergeant – you had to shout to be heard at all in that gigantic tumult – 'The poor buggers!'[44]
>
> Lieutenant R. G. Dixon, 14th Battery, Royal Garrison Artillery

It is hard for anyone who has not witnessed a full-scale bombardment to understand the all-encompassing, universal power that it generated.

> The concussion is simply awful. No one could ever imagine it unless they actually experienced it. Nothing but great spurts of flame, screaming and sizzling of shells, and banging and crashing of big guns. At times it becomes so terrific that you cannot distinguish any one crash (even of the biggest gun), it is simply one great throbbing pulsating jolting roaring inferno.[45]
>
> Lieutenant Cyril Lawrence, 1st Field Company, Engineers, Australian Imperial Force

But the power lay evenly distributed between both sides. It was a heavy-weight contest of equals. Ultimately the prolonged gunnery duel of Third Ypres raged on at a level that neither men nor machines could sustain in the long term.

> We are trying to make the pace too hot for the Germans. They seem to realise it and are retaliating fairly heavily. They seem to have plenty of stuff to throw about at any rate. I don't think the intensity of this fighting can be kept up for very long and one side or the other will have to give in sooner or later. This is only what I imagine is happening. The Bosche, at present at any rate, shows no sign of cracking. He is still fighting very stubbornly and his artillery is still active. If we could only smash up all his guns we would have a walk-over, as his infantry are no great shakes; what stops us more than anything else is his artillery and machine guns.[46]
>
> Major Roderick Macleod, 241st Brigade, Royal Field Artillery

The gunners knew and understood their importance. They accepted their heavy responsibility and recognized that, come what may, they must stick it out at their posts. The infantry, after all, depended on them for their very existence.

> We were sustained by the thoughts of our duty to the men at the front. I remember on one occasion standing to the guns in readiness for the SOS as the Germans were expected to counter-attack. We got the call to action and no sooner had we commenced to fire than the enemy guns began to shell our position. Not a man flinched. In fact, we were so eager to serve the guns that we had no time to think of danger. We came through the ordeal with a few minor casualties.[47]
>
> Bombardier Charles Smith, 152nd Brigade, Royal Field Artillery

And so the men of the Royal Artillery, who have unjustly since been eclipsed in the popular memory of the war, fought on in the greatest artillery battle the world had ever seen.

> This was war, and we were fighting a war, and further than that most of us did not think. We didn't like it, and we would have preferred to be out of it, and indeed, when chance invalided us home to Blighty, we were thankful to be out of it. Yet, once home, there was a lurking sense of 'letting the side down', of being safe while one's friends out there were sticking it out and one was not with them, sharing their life and toil, their hardships and dangers. One hated it, but wanted to be back in it, because it was shirking to be elsewhere. One was so much less of a man if one was not at the front; for us it was the one reality[48]
>
> Lieutenant R. G. Dixon, 14th Battery, Royal Garrison Artillery

CHAPTER EIGHT

BITE AND HOLD

When I got to the top of Broodseinde Ridge it was really surprising to see before you the green fields of Belgium. Actual trees! Grass and fields of course churned up a good deal by barrage shells – but as far as we were concerned it was open country! Then to look back, from where we came, back to Ypres . . . . There was devastation. Then I could see why our own gunners had had such a gruesome time. You could see the flashes of all the guns, from Broodseinde right back to the very Menin Gate.[1]

Captain W. Bunning, 24th Australian Battalion

As Sir Hubert Gough increasingly lost his way in the swamps surrounding Ypres, the deeply humiliating failure of the attacks launched on 22 August finally forced Sir Douglas Haig to reassess the overall progress of the offensive. It was obvious that the momentum of the attacks had stalled and could not progress until the Gheluvelt Plateau had been captured. After considering the situation Haig tacitly acknowledged that Gough had failed, and decided on a complete change of tack. At the Battle of Messines Sir Herbert Plumer had clearly demonstrated his mastery of the exhaustively prepared 'bite and hold' type of operation that left as little as was possible to chance and minimized casualties. Earlier in the year Haig had decided to place his wager on the thrusting Gough as having the best form for the modified 'steeplechase' he had envisaged on 31 July. But on reflection, although he remained true to the concept of 'horses for courses', he chose Plumer for the new challenging 'point to point' that he recognized was facing them if they were to get across the Gheluvelt Plateau up onto the Broodseinde Ridge beyond. On 23 August, Haig briefed Plumer at his Second Army Headquarters at Cassel prior to a full-scale conference at GHQ that would be attended by

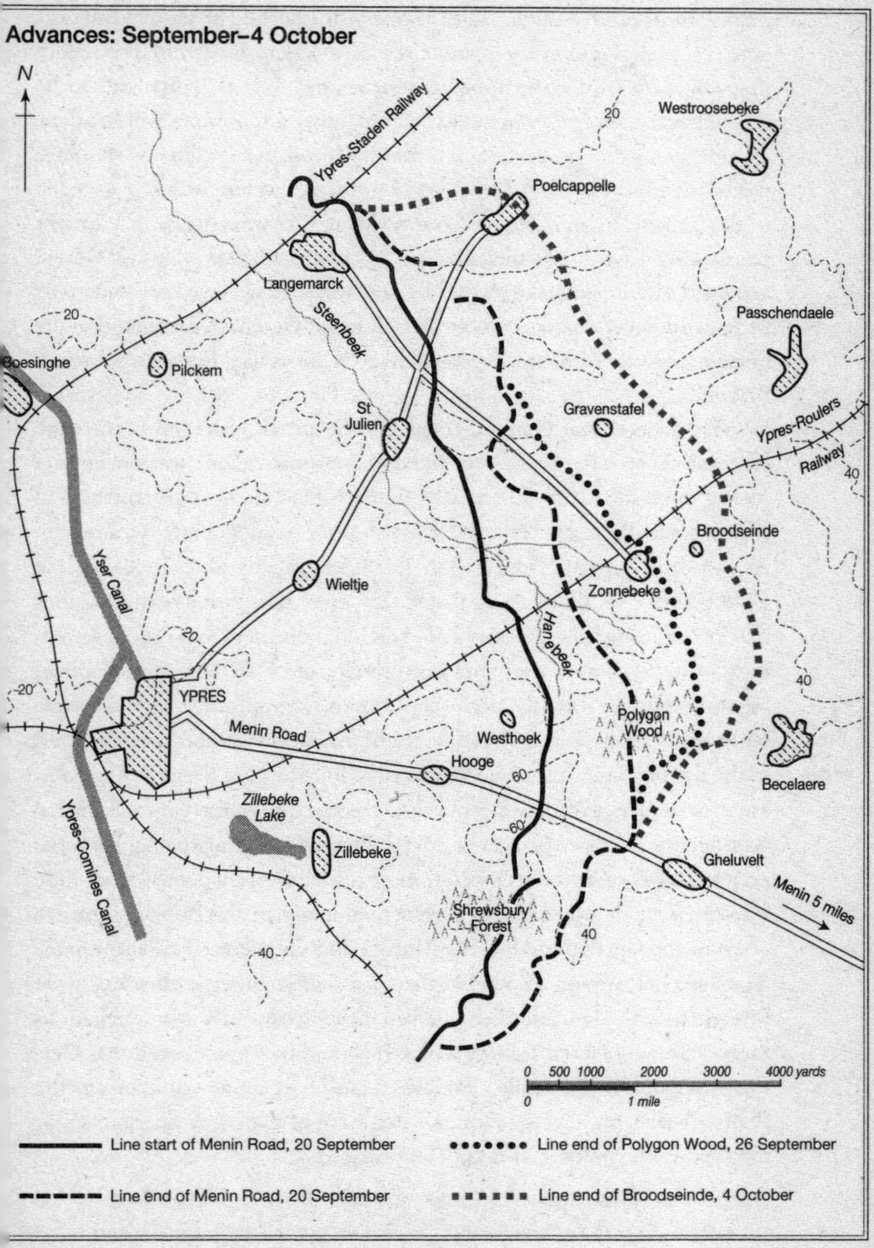

Advances: September–4 October
N
Ypres-Staden Railway
Westroosebeke
Poelcappelle
Langemarck
Steenbeek
Passchendaele
Boesinghe
Pilckem
St
Julien
Gravenstafel
Ypres-Roulers
Railway
Broodseinde
Yser Canal
Wieltje
Zonnebeke
Hanebeek
YPRES
Menin Road
Westhoek
Polygon
Wood
Becelaere
Hooge
Zillebeke
Lake
Zillebeke
Gheluvelt
Menin 5 miles
Ypres-Comines Canal
Shrewsbury
Forest
0 500 1000 2000 3000 4000 yards
0 1 mile
Line start of Menin Road, 20 September
Line end of Menin Road, 20 September
Line end of Polygon Wood, 26 September
Line end of Broodseinde, 4 October

both Plumer and Gough. The primacy of the Gheluvelt Plateau was explicitly stated and every possible resource was to be diverted to secure that objective with no extraneous distractions. The II Corps was to be transferred to Second Army in early September and Plumer would attack as soon as success could be guaranteed. Plumer was willing to shoulder the burden but asked for three weeks to prepare. Haig willingly acceded to this proviso in an ironic reversal of his earlier impatience at Plumer's painstaking ways during the initial planning of the Ypres offensive. Gough accepted and indeed controversially later claimed to have had some part in instigating the changes. Tragically, Haig left Gough in command in the interim period, with drastic consequences for many households across Britain.

What indeed had Gough achieved? The mixed successes of the first day had been effectively overshadowed by his failure to concentrate resources on the tactically crucial Gheluvelt Plateau, the consequences of which were then exacerbated by the poor campaigning weather in August. In the month from 31 July to 28 August, casualties totalled some 68,000 killed, wounded and missing. No fewer than twenty-two divisions had been through the mill and could no longer be held to be effective military formations until they could be rebuilt out of the line. Overshadowing this was the rapidly declining state of morale, not only in these battered divisions, but in the other eight divisions that had been involved in the fighting and were still considered fit for front-line service. The combination of the excruciating physical discomforts caused by the dismal weather, the routine dangers of trench life and the heartbreakingly futile attacks launched without hope of success had severely dented what little was left of the happy-go-lucky stereotyped image of the British 'Tommy'.

From the German side of No Man's Land the picture was also mixed. They too had rapidly expended their fighting strength as divisions were brought into the line and then relieved through necessity just days later as mere shadows of their former selves. It should be remembered that German divisions had a smaller establishment of just nine battalions to the British twelve, but, nevertheless, twenty-three of the thirty divisions so far involved in the battle had had to be replaced.

> The 10th August was a success for us, but on the 16th we sustained another great blow. The English pressed on beyond Poelcappelle and, even with an extreme exertion of strength on our part, could only

> be pushed back a short distance! During the following days fighting continued with diminished intensity. The 22nd was another day of heavy fighting. The 25th August concluded the second phase of the Flanders Battle. It had cost us heavily.[2]
>
> General Erich Ludendorff, German GHQ

The Germans had invested enormous effort in their defensive systems around the Ypres Salient. From their perspective, although they had retained control over much of the Gheluvelt Plateau, despite all their efforts they had still lost the tactically valuable high ground on the Pilckem and Westhoek Ridges. It was becoming all too apparent that if the Allies undertook limited offensives after thorough preparations, as at Vimy and Messines, then they could not be stopped from making tactically significant advances, even by the strongest German defences.

> The costly August battles in Flanders and at Verdun imposed a heavy strain on the western troops. In spite of all the concrete protection they seemed more or less powerless under the enormous weight of the enemy's artillery. At some points they no longer displayed that firmness which I, in common with the local commanders, had hoped for. The enemy managed to adapt himself to our method of employing counter-attack divisions. There were no more attacks with unlimited objectives, such as General Nivelle had made in the Aisne–Champagne Battle. He was ready for our counter-attacks and prepared for them by exercising restraint in exploitation of success. In other directions, of course, this suited us very well. I myself was being put to a terrible strain. The state of affairs in the West appeared to prevent the execution of our plans elsewhere. Our wastage had been so high as to cause grave misgivings, and had exceeded all expectation.[3]
>
> General Erich Ludendorff, German GHQ

Bearing Ludendorff's conclusions in mind, it is not unreasonable to conclude that the opening month of the offensive was typically attritional – damaging to both sides, but offering some consolations that beckoned the British to fight the battle to its conclusion.

In September, despite his replacement at the battle's helm by Plumer, Gough seemed unwilling to concede his failure by remaining quiescent while Plumer prepared for the next major assault on the Gheluvelt Plateau. The Fifth Army launched a series of utterly pointless small-scale attacks and 'raids' along the rest of the line. The human consequences of these actions are typified by two actions that took place on 6 September. At 07.30 the 1/5th and 1/6th Battalions, Lancashire Fusiliers attacked German pillboxes on St Julien Spur. Lieutenant George Horridge, who from his service at Gallipoli was no stranger to doomed attacks, was in support as they went over the top.

> Our objective was a German pillbox called Borry Farm. My Company was detailed to stop in the front line and our headquarters were in a pillbox. The Company Commander whose job it was to go over the top was called Captain William Tickler, famous for 'Tickler's Jam'. When the time came, Captain Tickler's Company got out of their trenches and advanced at a walk. Nothing happened until they'd gone about 100 yards – then all hell was let loose. We were getting crossfire from both sides as well as the pillboxes in front. Well, Tickler's Company advanced and I'm afraid he lost a lot of people. They never took Borry Farm and Tickler himself got behind a bit of high ground. He sent a message back to send stretcher bearers to an officer who had a leg blown off and was very badly wounded. There were two stretcher bearers in the pillbox with me and I knew that the machine guns were playing on the entrance. I thought that to order these stretcher bearers out was tantamount to ordering them to death, so I escaped this by saying, 'Captain Tickler is signalling for stretcher bearers!' One of them, Holt, immediately said, 'All right, I'll go!' The other, Renshaw, said, 'I'll go too!' Holt crept out through the hole in the pillbox, put the stretcher on his shoulder, which was promptly knocked off by a machine gun bullet – he himself wasn't hit. He picked it up again and went off and Renshaw followed him. Neither of them were killed and I later managed to get Holt the Military Medal. A very fair couple. During the afternoon, Tickler sent a signal message, 'Germans massing for counter-attack, SOS!' So I got hold of an SOS rifle grenade and put it in the rifle. The only entrance to the pillbox was a small hole like a fireplace, level with the ground. I put my head and shoulders through this and let off the SOS which burst into two red balls and two green balls – that was the SOS signal for the artillery to fire – they had no choice. If the SOS was sent up from the front line the artillery was forced to open fire, they didn't have to wait for any commands from their own commanders. It seemed a long time to me – it was probably about five seconds – and nothing happened. I wondered if they'd seen it so I let another one off. Then sure enough the barrage came down and it was a remarkable sight. Just a curtain of fire

coming down and it was pretty accurate because it got beyond our people onto the German support lines. If Captain Tickler was right in thinking they were massing for a counter-attack it never came. Towards the evening, Tickler withdrew his troops, what was left, it was quite hopeless. Then, strangely enough, the Germans and ourselves seemed, by instinct, to stop fighting and our and their stretcher bearers could go out in No Man's Land. We could see each other and nobody fired a shot, nobody took any notice, we just went collecting the wounded. That's how the battle ended.[4]

Lieutenant George Horridge, 1/5th Battalion, Lancashire Fusiliers

Of the 140 men of Tickler's Company who went forward only forty came back.

To the left of the Lancashire Fusiliers, a company of the 1/5th Battalion, Seaforth Highlanders attempted a raid on Pheasant Trench in the Poelcappelle sector. None of them reached the German lines and the raid was a complete failure, leaving the survivors trapped in shell holes in No Man's Land. In these circumstances it was almost impossible for battalion headquarters to keep control of their men as the moment the raid started all means of communication were lost. Without information little could be done to help, as any artillery support depended on a firm grasp of exactly where the British troops were. In these circumstances the signallers had an awesome responsibility that many shouldered without complaint.

No sooner had the barrage opened than the enemy retaliated with a very heavy and perfectly accurate barrage, breaking our wires and cutting off communications in the first five minutes. Something had to be done to restore communication as this was the only means of obtaining news of the attack; owing to it being daylight and the absence of trenches, runners could not be employed. Consequently, it was 'up' to the signallers. I had a whispered conversation with one of my pals, Tommy Lodge, and we informed the signalling officer that we would go out and try to repair the breaks in the line. Bent double, we crept out of the pillbox, expecting at every minute to be blown to pieces, and by quick rushes gained a low hedge which fringed a ditch called Letterbokker Beek along which the wire ran for a short distance. We were now in full view of the enemy's trenches who were not long in letting us know it. After about 20 yards the wire left the ditch and stretched over the open straight to D

Company trench about a further 30 yards away. The air was full of bullets from machine guns and snipers and all around great clouds of earth and mud flew into the air as the shells burst. Consequently, after leaving the ditch, we were obliged to wriggle the remainder of the distance flat on our stomachs. Within 10 yards of the ditch we discovered a break in the line and set to work to repair it, then we carried on for about another 10 yards when 'whizz-phut!' a bullet buried itself in the mud within half a yard of my face covering me with dirt. We remained perfectly still with our heads buried in the mud whilst a few more bullets dug themselves in besides us. This was too exciting, so after a lapse of many minutes we wriggled to the edge of a large shell hole and very slowly with the least possible movement rolled over the edge into a pool of water at the bottom. Here we remained for quite a time asking each other how we were to get back. When I attempted to leave our place of refuge, as soon as I got over the edge another bullet came whistling over my head and so back into the shell hole I rolled without any ceremony whatever. This was a rum go, but there was worse to follow. An aeroplane not more than 50 yards up came flying along the Company's front, sprinkling the ground with bullets from its machine gun. Our only hope was to pretend we were dead so we stretched ourselves flat in the hole and remained so for about half an hour until the gentleman in charge of his machine had ceased his antics and I must say there never were two better dead men living than we two. When things had quietened down a little we peeped over the edge of the shell hole and tugged at the wire which ran along to D Company. This resisted our pull and we concluded it was intact – not that it would have made much difference if our conclusion had been otherwise as we had had enough! So returning to the opposite side of the shell hole, we wriggled over the top and very slowly crawled back to the ditch. After what seemed like an eternity, we reached our Headquarters fully determined not to volunteer for any more similar jobs. We discovered that communication was restored very soon after we set out – this would be when we repaired the first break – but immediately after it was destroyed again, so all our efforts had been in vain.[5]

Signaller Stanley Bradbury, 1/5th Battalion, Seaforth Highlanders

Despite the frustrating lack of progress made in such attacks, attempts at innovation in the attacking tactics employed were under constant consideration by the much maligned staff officers and senior commanders.

New techniques and practices that might just reap some small advantage were tried whenever possible in the hope that they would tip the balance, making the difference between success and failure. The best form of infantry tactics to counter the German defensive methods was a matter for keen debate amongst the new battalions training for the next attack.

> Attacks on strong posts by platoons and companies figured prominently in our training, and the general formations for attack by a battalion were the subject of continual study. Unfortunately, which is the best form of attack was (and probably still is) a matter of warm dispute on the part of the Higher Command. Some advocated two companies in front and two in support; others three in front and one behind. Others, again, supported 'blobs' and another school 'worms'; while a third body of opinion pronounced 'leap-frogging' the only feasible scheme. The training in the attack, therefore, if lacking in continuity, was certainly not lacking in variety. Sheets of instructions poured in upon us in the most bewildering fashion, till even the most careful student was muddled beyond hope of recovery. Eventually all officers more or less abandoned any hope that they may have cherished of solving the higher mysteries of the attack and devoted their whole attention to musketry, bayonet fighting, bombing and so forth, trusting to the general efficiency obtained to solve the final problem as set by the enemy.[6]
>
> Captain C. E. Wurtzburg, 2/6th Battalion, King's Liverpool Regiment

One stratagem designed to confuse, distract or expose the Germans consisted of 'Chinese attacks'. These used silhouette figures or dummies operated by wires to create the illusion of troops advancing across No Man's Land accompanied by a creeping barrage. The German sentries would raise the alarm and the front-line positions would be manned to repel the imaginary British attack, only for the barrage to return and cause considerable casualties among the defenders before they could take shelter again. The dummies were also designed to attract German fire and, in some cases, distract them from the true target further along the line. As the German machine-gun posts and artillery batteries opened up in response to the perceived British attack, they would immediately reveal their concealed positions to the waiting British artillery observers who were all too willing to ensure that retribution would be swift. Once this had been done a couple of times, the Germans became not unnaturally hesitant in taking up their firing positions immediately and were hence vulnerable to the real attack when it finally came. At the forefront of these experiments were Sir Ivor Maxse's XVIII Corps, who employed their Cyclist Battalion on this life-threatening task.

> Presently a number of motor lorries came up the track from the main road and stopped opposite the camp. Their arrival was the signal for a sudden shouting of orders. Fatigue parties were soon busy taking tarpaulins from off a 'dump' in one corner of the camp. On these being removed they revealed a huge number of silhouette figures of men in khaki, all in fighting order. These were hurriedly loaded into the lorries until they were full of their strange cargo.[7]
>
> Private V. R. Magill, Cyclist Battalion, XVIII Corps

Mounting the lorries, the 'Cyclists' drove as far forward as humanly possible into the Salient. Then carrying two dummies, one under each arm, they stumbled up the slippery tracks to the front line.

> We got to work straight away on fixing the dummy figures in position ready for the morning. Protecting parties crawled out over the top and disappeared silently into No Man's Land to deal with any prowling enemy patrols which might disturb us in our work. The remainder of us were split up into sections, each under an NCO who was responsible for seeing that his dummies were correctly in position according to instructions.[8]
>
> Private V. R. Magill, Cyclist Battalion, XVIII Corps

Tentatively they moved into No Man's Land.

> What a crawl that was, it seemed miles. With our rifles slung across our backs and the dummies under our arms we were naturally handicapped in our movements. Around shell holes and craters, pausing when those rockets burst with their flood of light overhead, lying full length when those cursed machine gun bullets came singing past our ears. After going about close on a hundred yards we stopped and commenced to get the dummies in position. Our chief difficulty was the ground which had been churned up by constant shellfire, it was practically impossible to find a level spot.[9]
>
> Private V. R. Magill, Cyclist Battalion, XVIII Corps

Tormented by German star shells and the intermittent passing scythe of machine-gun bursts they hurried as best they could to complete their task.

> When that was finished, one man out of every three had to remain in a

shell hole a few yards in the rear of the figures with the wire of each leading from them to him. When dawn came and our barrage fire opened up on the enemy lines he was to slowly pull each wire thereby bringing the dummies in view of the enemy.[10]

Private V. R. Magill, Cyclist Battalion, XVIII Corps

Magill and his friend Noaks took up their positions in a shell hole and in fear and trembling awaited the dawn when they would deliberately trigger a holocaust of shells all around them.

All of a sudden, there was a whistle and a crash! Followed by another, and yet another, all practically simultaneous until we were enveloped in one cascade of falling shells. It was the barrage! Yes, we were for it now. Up with the dummies! Pulling those wires one at a time with our heads as low as possible we kept the 'figures' on the move. Shells falling like rain were howling and shrieking as they passed over our heads and burst in front of the enemies' first line. Some were dropping perilously short showering us with dust and dirt. The enemy by this time had apparently recovered from the suddenness of our bombardment for he now began to reply to our fire. It very soon was a hard job to tell which were our shells and those of our enemies. Shell splinters were humming and droning, hitting the top of our hole with a thud. This was not all, machine guns on both sides opened up adding to the tumult. Any minute I was expecting to be the last, nothing I thought could survive this hell of a shelling . . . 'Those dummies are having a rough time!' said Noaks. I could hardly catch what he said owing to the hell of a row around us. I did not answer. I was not much concerned how the dummies were getting on; they were there to be shot at – and they were getting it too. I was certainly not anxious to rob them of what was theirs![11]

Private V. R. Magill, Cyclist Battalion, XVIII Corps

The Germans were forced to man their front lines by the sight of the 'attacking troops'. Consequently they were completely exposed as the British shells rained down.

The enemy I thought must be having a hell of a time in that inferno. In my mind's eye I could see him 'standing to' waiting for our 'attack' to develop. He'll have to wait a damn long time, I thought to myself. At the same time I could not help smiling at the way he was being taken in. 'Rat-tat-tat-tat!' 'Rat-tat-tat-tat!' His machine guns were sweeping round above our heads in a murderous way. Those dummies must be riddled by now,' muttered Noaks. 'Yes, and probably blown to hell in the bargain!' I replied. Some of the ones I was working I knew were out of action by the feeling when operating the wires.[12]

Private V. R. Magill, Cyclist Battalion, XVIII Corps

Blasted by the German barrage as it swept back and forth across No Man's Land, and with the dummies all eventually blown to bits, the 'Cyclists' just had to endure until the furore died down. Eventually a relative calm descended.

The reaction of those tense moments left us feeling somewhat dazed, personally my senses seemed numbed, my throat had a horrible burning sensation, my mouth was parched with thirst and I could hardly see out of my eyes for dust and dirt.[13]

Private V. R. Magill, Cyclist Battalion, XVIII Corps

But they had survived, Magill had lived to tell his tale.

By the end of August, Plumer had completed his plans for a step-by-step advance and on 29 August he was able to submit them to Haig at a GHQ Conference. His intentions were crystal clear; his objectives strictly limited. The Second Army was to devote all its efforts to an advance right across the Gheluvelt Plateau divided into four distinct steps, each of which would be separated by six days. Meanwhile on their left flank Gough's Fifth Army would advance alongside, in an exactly corresponding manner, to capture St Julien Spur and the London Ridge. Only when the Gheluvelt Plateau was under the complete control of the Second Army would the Fifth Army then advance onto the main Passchendaele–Staden Ridge. At this point, *if the opportunity offered itself*, Gough would be given the chance to thrust for the Belgian coast in accordance with the original plans of those seemingly distant July days. Despite this acceptance of the necessity for a more cautious and methodical approach, the German defences remained strong; their defensive principles clearly unchanged.

It seems to me the Bosch are not using as many star shells as they used to. I don't think this is because they are short but they don't want to give away their positions which are – as regards the front line – shell holes and strong patrols at night waiting to catch our patrols. I believe from what I hear their real line is a good bit further back, but their forward positions are still very strong on account of numerous blockhouses of concrete, the shell hole parties and patrols merely connecting them up at night.[14]

Captain Charles Dudley Ward, 1st Battalion, Welsh Guards

The real German line was indeed stronger than it appeared and behind it, out of artillery range, lay the deadly counter-attack divisions ready to pounce on the tiring British divisions before they had a chance to consolidate and whilst their artillery support was still fragmented in trying to move forward.

It seems apparent that Plumer had learned from his experiences at Messines where he had allowed Haig to talk him into extending his objectives from the original plan of just 1,500 yards to up to 3,000 yards. As will be recalled it was during the attempts to secure the further objectives that most of the British casualties were incurred. This time an initial advance of between 1,000 and 1,500 yards was all that Plumer intended in the first step. Once that had been achieved, consolidation was the key. No matter what supposed tactical opportunities might flaunt themselves before the attacking formations, this would remain the overriding priority. Plumer and his staff had identified a crucial weakness in the German defensive plan. The British would seize only the forward zone and no more. This limited advance would then allow the artillery to continue to cover the new front line from their existing gun positions and thus avoid the inevitable disruption caused by an advance. Meanwhile, the German counter-attack divisions would have further to move forward to reach the new British front line which would leave more time for the British infantry to consolidate their captured positions. When the Germans finally got into a position from which they could counter-attack, they would be met by a concentrated artillery barrage supplemented by the massed machine guns of the infantry.

The first step was to maximize the concentration of artillery behind the Second Army. Previous operations had demonstrated that field guns were almost useless against the reinforced concrete pillboxes and blockhouses that littered the battlefield. The limited range of these guns also reduced their effectiveness when engaged on counter-battery work. Medium and heavy artillery were the only means of smashing these vipers' nests. Plumer's Second Army was allotted a total of 1,295 guns and howitzers, but the startling statistic is that no fewer than 575 of these were classed as medium or heavy pieces. In total there was just over one gun or howitzer for every 5 yards of the front. Consequently, given the shortened frontage of the attack and the reduced distance to the final objective, there was an almost fourfold increase in the number of shells raining down on the Gheluvelt Plateau. Plumer's meticulous chief of staff laid down the principles of exactly what the preliminary bombardment was to achieve and how it was to be conducted.

General Principles on which the Artillery Plan will be drawn

PRELIMINARY BOMBARDMENT

1. To break down obstacles which are impassable for infantry, but in doing so to create as few new obstacles as possible. To bombard strongpoints.

2. To isolate from the rear the enemy's batteries and front systems so that he cannot bring up ammunition or replace guns and cannot bring up food or stores without suffering serious loss. To keep him short of food. To reduce his morale.

3. To teach the enemy to lie at the bottom of his shell holes or dugouts whenever any barrages are going on. After one barrage has passed over him he must always expect others. In doing this, cause as many casualties as possible to reduce his morale. This will be effected by working a succession of dense creeping barrages of every available nature of gun and howitzer over the whole area to a depth of 2,000 yards beyond the last objective.

4. To carry out observed destructive shoots on hostile batteries from now on. As soon as batteries are isolated, see 2 above, to begin intense counter-battery work.

ATTACK

5. The attack will be made behind 5 barrages which will cover a depth of about 1,000 yards.

6. Immediately prior to and during the attack all known hostile battery positions will be neutralised.

PROTECTIVE MEASURES AFTER GAINING THE OBJECTIVE

7. Barrages to a depth of about 800 yards will be prepared beforehand which can be put down when the enemy counter-attacks, and arrangements will be made for all or any portions of these barrages to creep forward so as to embrace the whole of the enemy reserves.[15]

Major General Charles Harington, Headquarters, Second Army

To sustain a series of bombardments of this degree of intensity millions of shells would be required. This was a major logistical problem that could not be solved by a few mules, sweating drivers and General Service wagons alone. One advantage of the reduced opportunities for German artillery observation was the correspondingly greater scope for the employment of light railways.

> The ammunition supply was now very regular and various spurs were built by the Light Railway authorities to enable ammunition to be brought direct to the guns. We built a small platform for shells near the guns and a large placard labelled, 'Villain Junction', showed train drivers where to stop when coming up at night with loads. Second Lieutenant W. White was appointed stationmaster and he used to superintend and check the unloading of the trucks. His chief duty was to entice the engine driver away from his engine with the promise of a tot of rum, while a party of men detailed for the purpose, used to load coal into sand bags from the tender. Coal was a great luxury and we employed many ruses to get hold of it![16]
>
> Captain Maurice Walker, 154th Siege Battery, Royal Garrison Artillery

Plumer and Harington also made adjustments to the tactical methods used in deploying their assaulting infantry. They sought to replace any remaining vestige of advancing in rigid lines with a flexibility of approach intended to overcome individual problems as and when they were identified.

> The waves of attack, which have been hitherto used, do not give sufficient elasticity, nor are the platoons and sections sufficiently under the control of their leaders to deal with sudden opposition likely to be encountered under the new conditions. The leading wave, in one or two lines, should be extended to force the enemy to disclose his positions, the remainder in small groups or in files ready to deal with unexpected machine guns or parties of the enemy. It must be impressed on all subordinate leaders that rapidity of action is of paramount importance, and that any delay in assaulting these points adds to the seriousness of the situation and increases the difficulties of dealing with it. Known machine gun emplacements and defended points are dealt with by parties previously told off for the duty. Careful study of the ground and aeroplane photographs will go a long way towards increasing the 'known' and giving all leaders a clear idea

of the points from which opposition may be expected. The rear waves must keep closed up until across No Man's Land, and gradually gain their distance after this. Officers must be trained to ensure this is done.[17]

Major General Charles Harington, Headquarters, Second Army

The importance of consolidation was also unequivocally emphasized.

It should always be assumed by every formation that they will have to meet a counter-attack, and the steps to be taken to defeat it should always be included in every plan, and all ranks should thoroughly understand that this is their real opportunity for inflicting loss on the enemy, who will expect them to be disorganised to some extent and an easy prey.[18]

Major General Charles Harington, Headquarters, Second Army

Even though the Second Army had moved to centre stage, Gough's Fifth Army still deployed a formidable force of artillery and together the two armies had a comfortable numerical superiority. The Germans had amassed some 750 guns, of which 550 were concentrated behind the Gheluvelt Plateau directly facing Plumer. These guns simply had to be overwhelmed, or at the very least hampered to the point of distraction, if Plumer's plan was to work. One welcome boon for the gunners was that for the most part the first three weeks of September were dry and sunny. At long last the battlefield began to dry out. It became easier to bring up the shells and site the new batteries; the guns were more accurate with a firm platform beneath them and above all artillery observation both in the air and on the ground was vastly more efficient. As a result the pace of the preliminary bombardment gradually quickened throughout September. It was not an easy task, as the Germans had built multiple gun pits that made it extraordinarily difficult to pinpoint the exact location of their guns at any one time. The German gunners fought hard to keep the superiority they had gained in the August battles.

Once again, it is 'Der Tag' and again we are nibbling at the Bosche line. Our Battery is busy closing up the Hun guns and during the day in addition to carrying out our programme during the attack, we received many calls from aeroplanes who saw Hun guns active. The Hun strafed the Battery area just before zero hour and broke all the communications to the guns, but we got these put right just in time. He did little damage though he hit No. 2 gun pit twice. During the day too, he endeavoured to neutralise the Batteries about our area with shrapnel and high velocity guns, but we got off with no damage.[19]

Lieutenant Robert Blackadder, 152nd Siege Battery, Royal Garrison Artillery

Unsurprisingly, the German guns were not completely suppressed. But in the final analysis, although the counter-battery work did not entirely eliminate them, it did achieve enough to allow the plan to proceed.

To prepare for its central role the Second Army was reorganized and the Australians and New Zealanders of I Anzac Corps were added to its strength. The Anzacs, together with the rebuilt X Corps, would bear the brunt of the new assault on the literally blasted woods and copses of the Gheluvelt Plateau. The date for the attack was set for 20 September.

The night before the battle I spent in a concrete pillbox, Ferdinand Farm. It had very, very thick concrete walls but it was a curious sort of place to have a headquarters. It had been built by the Germans and so the entrance faced the German lines. It had enormously thick concrete walls, but inside it was only about five foot high. At the bottom of the pillbox there was about two foot of water. The water was simply horrid, it had refuse in it, old tins and indeed excreta. Whenever shells burst near it the smell was perfectly overpowering. Luckily, there was a sort of concrete shelf the Bosche had made which was about two foot six off ground level. On this four officers and six other ranks spent the night. There wasn't room to lie down, there was hardly room to sit upright and we more or less crouched there. At the outside of the pillbox there was an enormous shell hole – I should think a 9.2-inch – across this was a plank because there was about six foot of water in the shell hole. The only way you could get into the pill box was over the plank and inside the shell hole was the dead body of a Bosche who had been there a very long time and who floated or sank on alternate days according to the atmosphere. It was also lousy. It was not a place I would enter now for a great deal of money, but we were extremely glad to be in it that night.[20]

Lieutenant Douglas Wimberley, 232nd Machine Gun Company, Machine Gun Corps

As Zero Hour approached, the line was wreathed in a woodland mist and light drizzle which made visibility poor.

I walked down the road in a thick fog and just enough light to make out that both banks were crowded with our men who had been there since midnight waiting for the attack. I sat down and chatted with some of them, but it was too dark to recognise anyone. After my tea we all came out about 5.35 and waited five minutes till quite suddenly our barrage began. It was of course simply tremendous falling just in front of us. As it went forward, we all crept forward too, through the fog amongst the trees, which were quite bare by the time we reached them. The light was perfect, just light enough to see our way (of course by compass) and to recognise one another, while the thick mist hid us from view.[21]

Reverend John Bloxam, 16th Battalion, Sherwood Foresters

At 05.40, the destructive force of the guns was unleashed with a truly deafening and awe-inspiring roar. The Battle of the Menin Road had begun.

Just look at our artillery. Just look at it, at all those countless flashes. See how they stab at the darkness from their hiding places, not in dozens but in hundreds, and yet these are only the heavies, the lighter guns are well up and we cannot see them. See the red glares that light up the country for miles where a Hun shell has landed amongst some cordite. The whole place seems ablaze as far as the eye can see: flash after flash, some singly, some in groups when a battery fires together, but isn't it all beyond description, beyond belief, even beyond imagination. Feel the terrific vibration and the jolting and hear the ear splitting, nerve-racking noise of it all. It is not a bit of use trying to talk, or even shout because bellow as you like no one can hear you.[22]

Lieutenant Cyril Lawrence, 1st Field Company, Australian Engineers

In addition to the rain of shells, concentrated machine-gun fire was an integral part of the final barrage.

Our shells were firing over our heads onto the Germans, our machine guns raining lead into them. I've never experienced anything like it in my life and I don't want to experience it again. It was terrible. Solid metal going through the air. Our Company had a machine gun posted every 30 yards – we were the advanced section of the light artillery you might call it. The artillery behind us and the infantry in front of us. We had to cover the infantry while they went forward and we followed them forward.[23]

Private Stewart Sibbald, 238th Machine Gun Company, Machine Gun Corps

The barrage seemed to eclipse even the memories of that of 31 July.

The bombardment next morning when it started, was the heaviest bombardment I'd ever seen in that war. There was such a din from the

> swish of the shells going over our heads and the bursting shells in front of us that we felt no fear, because we couldn't hear the explosions of the German shells fairly near us.[24]
>
> Lieutenant Douglas Wimberley, 232nd Machine Gun Company, Machine Gun Corps

Covered by this ritualized expression of a nation's hatred and determination to prevail, all along the line the infantry surged forward.

> Over we went. At first all seemed confusion, the strongholds were holding out, fighting for dear life and our waves of men were getting collected into masses, men were falling fast. But soon the individuality of the British Tommy asserted itself and the strongholds were surrounded and bombed out, the occupants paying the extreme penalty. Explosive bullets and phosphorous bombs were being fired at us, one bullet sang past my head, striking the edge of a man's helmet next to me and cut my face with the pieces. A phosphorous bomb hit one of my men, setting him on fire, which started off the ammunition he was carrying and the poor fellow was in a bad way till some of his comrades put him out of his misery. My company, however, soon reached its objective and we started consolidating. While standing on the top with my rifle by the side of my leg I felt something hit the stock but took little notice and did not find till later that the bullet had struck the trigger guard, breaking it and tearing off the magazine. Had it hit the magazine, it would have gone through my shinbone. We hurriedly consolidated ourselves, digging a deep narrow trench, which was as well, as we were subjected to pretty heavy bombardment for the two days we were to hold the line. We were, however, extremely fortunate as the heavy shells went everywhere but just on top of us. The enemy massed for counter-attacks several times but could not make headway against our barrage.[25]
>
> Signaller Maurice Gower, 16th Battalion, Rifle Brigade

In all the confusion and noise the troops of the Second Army advanced into the maelstrom. Although the fighting was hard the new tactics seemed to be working. The 2nd and 1st Australian Divisions of the I Anzac Corps, alongside the 23rd, 41st and 39th Divisions of the X Corps, managed to smash the planned 1,500 yards through the line of woods on the Gheluvelt Plateau, the names of which for the previous month had been a roll call of failure: Nonne Boschen, Glencourse Wood, Inverness Copse. At the end of the day the new line stretched from the splintered remnants of the western edge of Polygon Wood to just in front of the mass of German pillboxes on Tower Hamlets Spur.

Simultaneously the Fifth Army went over the top alongside them, deploying the 20th Division of the XIV Corps, the 51st and 58th Divisions of the XVIII Corps and the 55th and 9th Divisions of the V Corps. They collectively hurled themselves forward once again to try to seize the Gheluvelt–Langemarck Line which crossed the low slopes of the Zonnebeke Spur and Gravenstafel Ridge. This time, despite strong resistance, they were largely successful in advancing the line. Pillboxes that had dealt out death for so long were overrun and it can be assumed that few of the garrisons were taken prisoner. Borry Farm, Potsdam House, Iberian Farm and Gallipoli Farm all fell to the increasingly effective tactics of the British infantry.

> It was decided that as soon as a small body of troops were fired at from a pillbox that they should lie down while other troops on their flanks worked round – this being quite possible as the arc of fire of a machine gun is only very limited. The troops were trained specially not to permit just one machine gun to hold up the entire advance and so allow the creeping barrage to run away from them.[26]
>
> Major Stanley Gordon, 1/6th Battalion, King's Liverpool Regiment

In accordance with their standard tactics the German counter-attack divisions moved forward. But this time with the British line advanced only a short distance and with the men alert to the need for rapid consolidation, they found a cohesive and determined resistance.

> On the 20th September, the great attack of the Highland Division met our own regiment. It was a drumfire of several hours and this lasted on even after the Highlanders had stormed our front line and were trying to get onwards through all these shell holes. We were started by our Battalion Commander and I had a platoon of Grenadiers. We sprang from shell hole to shell hole. The drumfire was so heavy that I didn't notice the singular shells. We advanced and drove the Highlanders a bit back, but we couldn't reach the front line where our third battalion had been vanquished. They were all gone, partly dead, partly taken prisoner, we didn't see any of them again. We happened to catch some of the Highlanders, it was a funny view for us to see soldiers with kilts and naked knees. Our soldiers laughed a good deal about that.[27]
>
> Hartwig Pohlmann, 36th Prussian Division

However much the British regimental proclivities amused some German soldiers, for the vast majority it was no laughing matter. This time they faced well dug-in British troops covered by a wall of bursting shells and chattering machine guns.

> The 51st Highland Division took their objectives and all seemed to be going well – we had various counter-attacks that were beaten off. At about three in the afternoon some wounded began to pass, saying that the counter-attack was beginning to succeed. Then some more passed by and one man said, 'You'd better be quick because the Bosche will be here in a few minutes.' At that, I and the other Company Commander naturally moved forward, because we wanted to get some of our guns to form a defensive flank. Going forward to a place called Haanixsbeek Farm we had to go through the German barrage. We were literally covered with water and mud every few yards that we went. Both I and my runner were blown off our feet once or twice. But we got there all right; unfortunately when we got there the runner was hit and he died soon afterwards. I'm glad to say that the Jocks beat off the attack and that was the end of that. In that particular battle my 16 machine guns fired 160,000 rounds.[28]
>
> Lieutenant Douglas Wimberley, 232nd Machine Gun Company, Machine Gun Corps

Despite the tenacity with which the British troops clung to their new line, the Germans threw themselves forward time and time again.

> The three counter-attacks were preceded by the most intense bombardment I have ever experienced from the Hun in my now fairly long knowledge of this war. First they came on down the road crowded in close mass, and we scattered them by machine gun fire. Then they tried again in more open order, supported by flammenwerfer, which fortunately never came into action. Finally in the twilight they made the most determined effort of all, after a terrific bombardment: this drove in the outpost line which another regiment, passing through us, had formed in front of us, but our men held fast, used their rifles, and the attack collapsed.[29]
>
> Captain Harry Yoxall, 18th Battalion, King's Royal Rifle Corps

As casualties proliferated, the medical services were stretched to the limit and continually harassed by German artillery fire.

> We could just see the sun beginning to show through the thick cloud of smoke rising out of the valley, beyond where our barrage was falling. We

> could see some men in places advancing over the crest of the ridge and our shrapnel bursting all along the line. Aeroplanes were flying very low, up and down the line and blazing away at the Hun with their machine guns. We saw a red flare go up indicating that the first objective had been taken. Wounded now began to come in very fast, and we were kept going all the time. Our shelter had been knocked down and we had to do the dressings in a muddy trench or in the open, behind the pillbox. Later on in the afternoon we got our shelter fixed up again and did our dressings there. During the afternoon the Hun shelling along Bellewaarde and Westhoek Ridges got pretty hot and several came pretty close. One large one landed about 10 yards from the pillbox whilst I was trying to tie a radial artery and covered us with mud and dirt. My fingers became all thumbs and I wasn't much use for a minute or so from fright.[30]
>
> Captain Donald Coutts, 24th Australian Battalion

The medical personnel needed all the assistance they could get. Much of this came from the more conscientious padres who went out to scour the wilderness for the wounded.

> We had many adventures, some tragic, some humorous, though there was an element of tragedy in all that was humorous. The really funny thing was when I slipped into a shell hole and got stuck in the mud. It was only up to my knees but it took three men to pull me out, partly because we were laughing so much, even a poor boy with a broken thigh lying beside us could not help laughing and I really think it cheered him up for a bit.[31]
>
> Reverend John Bloxam, 16th Battalion, Sherwood Foresters

Bloxam's activities in rescuing the wounded were in fact deadly serious and his selfless compassion was later recognized by the award of the Military Cross.

Despite the scope of the preparations, the attack did not succeed along the complete length of the front and problems were experienced on both flanks. In the north the 20th Division suffered heavy casualties in attacking from Langemarck towards the strongly fortified Eagle Trench, having placed too great a reliance on burning oil drums launched by Livens projectors rather than conventional artillery.

> I got wounded and for about 12 hours was stuck in a hole with mud and water, shells falling all over the place and surrounded by dead and wounded men. When night came on, I came away with an officer and some other wounded. Although wounded we could walk slowly. Then we

lost our way. We had also with us a badly wounded man on a stretcher, which two of us had to carry. We wandered about for hours over fields full of shell holes, old trenches, ditches and ponds of water, trying to find our way, but could not. After about three hours of this wandering about we came upon a sergeant with some men who knew the way, but when we left them, we again lost ourselves. After another hour or so, we fortunately found this sergeant again. This time we got on the right road. After another two hours walk we came to a Red Cross Station. During all this wandering about the Germans must have seen us, as wherever we went their shells kept on falling almost on us. At the Red Cross place they only took the man on the stretcher. The rest of us wounded had to go on to the next, another two hours walk. When we got a certain distance the Huns' shells came on again – falling about us. The other men ran and left me behind as I could not run as my wounds were in my leg and on my back. Then for about an hour I struggled along, I finally arrived about 2 o'clock in the morning at the other Red Cross station in a wretched state of exhaustion, my clothes in rags and covered in mud – in fact I felt more dead than alive. From there I was put in a motor and sent to hospital.[32]

Private Archie Jackson, 10th Battalion, Rifle Brigade

However, even in the areas where resistance was strongest the assaulting troops succeeded in making progress and above all they remembered their training. When the German counter-attack came they were ready and able to take their revenge for casualties suffered.

Although the troops were very tired I got them to clean all the German rifles that were there because if we ran short of ammunition we'd have German rifles and ammunition to use. Which as it turned out was exactly what happened. The next morning the Germans did counter-attack. We weren't expecting it because a counter-attack is usually preceded by a bombardment. They just got up out of their trenches and came at us. The sentries spotted them, then the shout went up, 'FIRE!' That was all – you hadn't got much time to do anything else. They came over absolutely shoulder to shoulder. We had our rifles, we had the German rifles, we used both and we just fired and fired and fired. We had mud to help us which slowed them up, they could only plod. I picked targets, they were never more than 70–80 yards away so it wasn't difficult to take a man and fire at that man. I am sure that I must have personally killed four, or five or six Germans that morning. It was really the closest I ever came to looking eye to eye with a German. It was very exciting – it was them or us –

> they got to within 20 yards of us. I was told afterwards that we left 166 dead Germans on our company front. I know we took 23 prisoners.[33]
>
> Lieutenant Charles Austin, 12th Battalion, Rifle Brigade

Almost for the first time, the German counter-attacks were an unmitigated failure. The British artillery still dominated the battlefield and turned it into a preview of hell for the German infantry.

> Daylight has fully broken now and we can see around us. On our left the shattered remains of Polygon Wood – gone – absolutely wiped out – simply a mass of huge splintered trunks and matchwood lying everywhere. In front two or three pillboxes stand up like warts – further beyond, another ridge covered with a mass of wreckage resembling Polygon Wood. Along the summit of this ridge pillboxes stand out against the rising sun. On our right Inverness Copse and everywhere, everywhere the sea of great shell holes, lip to lip – not a trace of grass – of the farms or the hedges or the fields remains – just one heaved-up mass of turned-up earth. Away over upon our half left is the mound in Polygon Wood . . . At about 1 o'clock in the afternoon there is a furious fusillade of machine guns from the Tommies' position in Inverness Copse. What is happening? Look away over on the opposite ridge and see – little figures in fours and fives come hopping across – ducking and diving into shell holes. In the wood itself great shells are bursting – a man can be seen standing on a pillbox – a shell burst near and he flies fully 20 feet into the air and comes down like a stone. The figures continue to bob up and down in the holes but always getting nearer – they seem to be getting more numerous. Suddenly right in their midst there comes a huge cloud of earth flying heavenwards – then another and another and in less time than it takes to write dozens of huge shells are tearing the whole face of the ridge to pieces – the air is full of yellow spurts of smoke that burst about 30 feet up and shoot towards the earth – just ahead of each of these yellow puffs the earth rises in a lashed-up cloud – shrapnel – and how beautifully placed – long sweeps of it fly along that slope lashing up a good 200 yards of earth at each burst. The breeze is blowing fairly strong towards the Hun and the seeing is good. Nothing is happening on our front and we can watch it all. First of all those little groups stagger on through the great bursts – then they seem to lose direction and travel in diagonal lines – then their number ever growing less they break up into individuals. Now only a very few can be seen, the rest being lost in the awful cloud of smoke and dust – these few seem to cease going ahead and in two minutes

> more they are crawling, running and jumping everywhere like beings possessed of a Devil – the cloud closes upon them. Fifteen minutes afterwards it has blown over and not a trace of any living thing remains.[34]
>
> Lieutenant Cyril Lawrence, 1st Field Company, Australian Engineers

The bitter fighting swirled round the key points up and down the line, but overall the British held firm.

The first of Plumer's 'bite and hold' operations stands as a conspicuous contrast to the operations carried out in August. Limited in ambition and predicated on the idea that what was won must be capable of being defended, it signalled a clear-cut change in approach. But that is not to say the price of success was any less than the price of failure. During the battle casualties totalled approximately 21,000 amongst the Second and Fifth Armies. It has been suggested that these casualty numbers were high, but unfortunately they were only to be expected. The troops were attacking a series of semi-permanent defence works occupied by determined defenders who had withstood numerous assaults and were confident of withstanding more. Plumer had no magic wand; he could not remove the Germans from the battlefield or reduce their skills and experience, no matter how hard his artillery might try. But what he could offer was a gradual, painstaking approach to what had seemed an intractable problem. His methods at least gave his men the best possible chance of success in capturing and retaining their objectives. In this, aided fortuitously by drier weather and better ground conditions, he was remarkably successful. For a short period at least, he changed the overall character of the Ypres offensive.

HAIG WAS greatly encouraged by the successes achieved during the Battle of the Menin Road. He considered that just four more similar steps would suffice to capture the whole of the Passchendaele–Staden Ridge and this in turn would facilitate the long-delayed advance towards Roulers and the Belgian coast. Consequently he warned the naval authorities and Sir Henry Rawlinson of the Fourth Army adjoining the Belgian Coast that amphibious landing operations were once more a possibility. Furthermore, he moved the cavalry forward just in case the whole German front collapsed under the pressure of Plumer's hammer blows. Haig's optimism has since been the object of criticism but, however much in retrospect these decisions seem absurd, it is easy to imagine the derision that would have been heaped upon him had he not taken the requisite measures to ensure that his army was ready to exploit any opportunities if they had suddenly arisen. The Germans, after all, were certainly worried by the turn of events.

> The enemy's onslaught on the 20th was successful, which proved the superiority of the attack over the defence. Its strength did not consist in the tanks; we found them inconvenient, but put them out of action all the same. The power of the attack lay in the artillery, and in the fact that ours did not do enough damage to the hostile infantry as they were assembling, and above all, at the actual time of the assault. . . . We might be able to stand the loss of ground, but the reduction of our fighting strength was again all the heavier. Once more we were involved in a terrific struggle in the West.[35]
>
> General Erich Ludendorff, German GHQ

With the improvements in the weather and greater emphasis on meticulous preparation, throughout September the battle for the control of the skies above Ypres grew ever more vicious. The vital work of the artillery observation, reconnaissance and contact aircraft continued unabated. In consequence the role of the single-seater scouts grew in importance as they sought to drive away the predatory German scouts. Day after day the scouts clashed thousands of feet above the infantry and gunners that they indirectly served. The pace grew ever more frenetic as the handful of leading 'aces' prospered and their unlucky, unskilled, or inexperienced foes fell to earth. Occasionally these leading figures themselves clashed and one battle to the death in the heavens above Flanders has attained a mythic quality. On 23 September Captain James McCudden and B Flight of the élite 56 Squadron, RFC were patrolling in their SE5s in the early evening above the Ypres battlefield. Banks of clouds obstructed any clear overall view but it was soon apparent that the heavens were full of aircraft.

> We went north, climbing at about 6,000 feet. A heavy layer of grey clouds hung at 9,000 feet, and although the visibility was poor for observation, the atmosphere was fairly clear in a horizontal direction. Away to the east one could see clusters of little black specks, all moving swiftly, first in one direction and then another. Farther north, we could see formations of our own machines, Camels, Pups, SE5s, Spads and Bristols, and lower down in the haze our artillery RE8s.[36]
>
> Captain James McCudden, 56 Squadron, Royal Flying Corps

As his flight passed over Poelcappelle the experienced McCudden spotted an SE5 of 60 Squadron in distress being pursued by a silver-blue German Fokker Triplane and led his flight to the rescue. Their intervention allowed the SE5 to escape, but, to their surprise, although outnumbered six to one the German pilot turned to fight. The first passes made it obvious that this was no ordinary adversary.

> The Hun triplane was practically underneath our formation now, and so down we dived at a colossal speed. I went to the right, Rhys Davids to the left, and we got behind the triplane together. The German pilot saw us and turned in a most disconcertingly quick manner, not a climbing nor Immelmann turn, but a sort of flat half spin. By now the German triplane was in the middle of our formation and its handling was wonderful to behold. The pilot seemed to be firing at all of us simultaneously, and although I got behind him a second time, I could hardly stay there for a second. His movements were so quick and uncertain that none of us could hold him in sight at all for any decisive time.[37]
>
> Captain James McCudden, 56 Squadron, Royal Flying Corps

The mystery pilot was Leutnant Werner Voss who, having shot down forty-nine aircraft, was second only to Freiherr Manfred von Richthofen in the list of German air aces. Voss was soon handing out punishment to those who strayed into his sights.

> I attempted to follow the example of the others in so much as to zoom away so as to get a better position and await my turn to dive a second time. As happened in my last dive, my pressure had gone 'fut'; in consequence my zoom was but a feeble climb. I take my hat off to that Hun, as he was a most skilful pilot, but he did give me a rough passage. On seeing my feeble attempt, he whipped round in an extraordinary way, using no bank at all, but just throwing his tail behind him. He attacked me from the side and I had the opportunity of observing that he was one of the very latest design, being a triplane. He was at very close quarters and could hardly miss me. The bullets ripped all around me. I did not stick my machine down in an attempt to run, trusting to my dodging ability, as I certainly would have done two months ago; but dived just enough to give me speed to turn under him to prevent his getting on my tail. The others were above, and I knew sooner or later they would drive him away, and the longer I stayed the better their opportunity to nail him. Of course, I did not think all this out; it all came naturally, and

> at the same time came more bullets, while I worked away in the 'office' trying to rectify my pressure. I do not know how many times I turned under him. I did not stop to count, but it seemed an eternity. He finally got too close for me and I resorted in desperation to the old method of shaking a pursuing machine. On the completion of my second revolution of my spin, I flattened out, and to my intense relief the Hun was no longer following me.[38]
>
> Lieutenant Verschoyle Cronyn, 56 Squadron, Royal Flying Corps

As Cronyn nursed his crippled aircraft to safety, Voss also succeeded in forcing a second SE5 flown by Lieutenant Muspratt to abandon the fight. A red-nosed Albatross joined Voss in the dogfight but, like stewards round a prize-fight ring, other formations of British aircraft held further reinforcements at bay in the crowded sky. Every time the SE5 pilots thought they had finally got him in their sights, Voss eluded them.

> I dropped my nose, got him well in my sight, and pressed both triggers. As soon as I fired up came his nose at me, and I heard clack-clack-clack-clack, as his bullets passed close to me and through my wings. I distinctly noticed the red-yellow flashes from his parallel Spandau guns.[39]
>
> Captain James McCudden, 56 Squadron, Royal Flying Corps

After fighting bravely the red-nosed Albatross disappeared, but Voss fought on as the circling, swirling aircraft gradually lost altitude.

> At that altitude he had a better rate of climb, or rather zoom, than we had and frequently he was the highest machine of the seven and could have turned east and got away had he wished to, but he was not that type and always came down on us again.[40]
>
> Lieutenant G. H. Bowman, 56 Squadron, Royal Flying Corps

It could not go on. Voss may have been brilliant, but B Flight contained some of the best scout pilots in the RFC. They could not be held off for ever.

> I, myself, had only one crack at him: he was about to pass broadside on across my bows and slightly lower. I put my nose down to give him a burst and opened fire, perhaps too soon. To my amazement he kicked on full rudder, without bank, pulled his nose up slightly, gave me burst while he was skidding sideways and then kicked on opposite rudder before the results of this amazing stunt appeared to have any effect on the controllability of his machine. Rhys Davids was then on his tail. Whether or not, to have a

> crack at me, this flat turn of Voss' enabled Rhys Davids to get there I cannot say, but I should like to think so, as I doubt any SE5 could have got on the tail of the triplane if Voss had not had his attention distracted; but Rhys Davids was there, with his prop boss almost on Voss' rudder.[41]
>
> Lieutenant G. H. Bowman, 56 Squadron, Royal Flying Corps

Rhys Davids made no mistake. Voss, who had gratuitously defied death and the odds stacked against him in a manner that epitomized the romantic view of aerial warfare, was doomed.

> I got east and slightly above the triplane and made for it, getting in a whole Lewis drum and a corresponding number of Vickers into him. He made no attempt to turn, until I was so close to him I was certain we would collide. He passed my right-hand wing by inches and went down. I zoomed. I saw him next with his engine apparently off, gliding west. I dived again and got one shot out of my Vickers; however, I reloaded and kept in the dive. I got in another good burst and the triplane did a slight right-hand turn, still going down. I had now overshot him (this was at 1,000 feet), zoomed, but never saw him again.[42]
>
> Second Lieutenant Arthur Rhys Davids, 56 Squadron, Royal Flying Corps

Close by, McCudden saw the final moments.

> I noticed that the triplane's movements were very erratic and then I saw him go into a fairly steep dive and so I continued to watch, and then saw the triplane hit the ground and disappear into a thousand fragments.[43]
>
> Captain James McCudden, 56 Squadron, Royal Flying Corps

However exciting a spectacle, in reality this unequal contest was just one of thousands of small battles that made up the campaign to control the air above the Ypres battlefield. Werner Voss was dead; Arthur Rhys Davids died just a month later on 27 October and James McCudden died in an aircraft crash in July 1918 – an old man well before his time, a decorated veteran who had been awarded the VC, DSO and Bar, MC and Bar and MM, and just 23 years of age.

Far below the personal battles of the 'aces', the anonymous preparations for the next bite and hold attack on 26 September went on apace. The guns began their barrages; the infantry were reorganized and new divisions moved into the line to make the assault. However, the reduction in preparation time allowed to the artillery from three weeks to one, coupled with the complications of moving guns forward across the torn ground, meant the British gunners once again faced a gruelling private battle of attrition with the German guns. Both sides suffered heavy casualties as the shells rained down on the gun positions but still they continued to thunder out their message of destruction.

> We are having a very hard time, we are now in the VIII Corps and preparations are being made for a further advance on our left, so we are kept busy neutralising the many Batteries, which the Hun has brought up against us. We fire at intervals from dawn till about midnight and have as many as 20 or 30 targets a day. The Hun shells us too but we have had few casualties. It is a difficult task arranging the Battery work and carrying out all these shoots, the ammunition question is the worst as the men are so done up.[44]
>
> Lieutenant Robert Blackadder, 152nd Siege Battery, Royal Garrison Artillery

In a desperate effort to disrupt the evident British preparations the Germans launched a spoiling attack in the Polygon Wood sector. They were fortunate for they struck just in the middle of a period of natural confusion. The 23rd Division was in the process of being relieved by the 33rd Division. In the fighting that followed Private Donald Price was acting as a company runner as his unit moved into the line. It was apparent that the Salient had not been completely transformed by the recent British advance and a period of half-decent weather. It was still an evil place, which could exhaust, demoralize and finally destroy or maim a man in just a few short hours.

> We'd got through a place called Sanctuary Wood and we were making our way up to the front line. And it was hell. There was not a soul about, not a tree, not nothing. All these Verey lights up, the whole place looked dreadful, it looked evil. Pieces of equipment, pieces of mules, pieces of men. You had to go up on duckboards and if you fell off a duckboard, if you weren't pulled out you were for it. You got sucked down by all this mud. It was that thick. We were going over and I'd got to take another message. The Sergeant Major said, 'Take this back to the officers' dugout!' Jock Mayle was with me and we had to run along one of these duckboards on top, because there was no path, no nothing. More often than not the shelling had tipped them up and you had to find where the next one was to scramble to it. We were running down this in the dark and he started. Poor old Jock, a shell came and knocked him out, killed him behind me. I dashed on with this message to the dugout.

> I slid down this dugout and I was absolutely knackered and poor old Jock had gone west behind me. This bloody officer, I gave him this message and this officer said, 'Right, get back as quick as you can!' I could have shot him, I was bloody exhausted and he'd got his whisky and his candle down there and he says, 'Get back as quick as you can!' I scrambled up from the dugout and found my way back to the trench. The Sergeant Major was there and he says, 'What's the matter with you?' I said, 'I'm tired! Absolutely knackered!' All of a sudden, 'BOOM!' they started again. I got a real beauty, shrapnel burst above and I got a real smack above the left knee. Then a mustard gas shell burst on the back of the trench and it plastered my back with mustard gas. The Sergeant Major said, 'Off you go!'[45]
>
> Private Donald Price, 20th Battalion, Royal Fusiliers

It was a brief but salutary introduction to the horrors of life in the Ypres Salient. Although the German attack was only relatively successful, it did completely disrupt the offensive preparations of the 33rd Division.

The plan for 26 September was for an almost uniform advance by the Second and Fifth Armies of between 1,000 and 1,250 yards on a reduced front some 8,500 yards wide. The main tactical objectives along the line were the village of Zonnebeke, the remainder of Polygon Wood and the venomous nest of pillboxes known as Tower Hamlets. On the northern flank, in the 3rd Division sector, the 2nd Battalion, Suffolk Regiment were given the responsibility of crossing the Hannebeek stream to capture Zonnebeke. They moved up into their assembly positions near Hannebeek Wood and readied themselves for action.

> About midnight we split up into 'section diamonds' and lay all around the assembly positions in shell holes, huddled up to keep as warm as possible. Overhead the sky was cloudy but the guns had eased up and an ominous silence fell over all. Mysterious figures moved about giving final instructions and cheering up the men. Even so, not till 3 a.m. was I told that we were to 'go over' at 5.50 a.m. A heavy mist was rolling up and between one and three the cold was intense. At 3.45 was the quietest time of all and instinctively we knew the guns were preparing. Then at 3.50, with two hours to go, every gun in Ypres, and behind, started in our direction, and it seemed as if the Heavens had been wrenched open. You could have read a paper by the gun flashes, five miles away on average. It was truly majestic and far eclipsed the Ancre or Arras. The screeching,

tearing and 'wobbling' overhead was unparalleled and caused us to forget the weary chilly night of suspense. Occasionally looking over the shell hole to pierce the mist I could see absolutely no-one, and yet in our immediate vicinity were scores of thousands of men – all waiting for zero at 5.50.[46]

Lieutenant C. J. Huffield, 2nd Battalion, Suffolk Regiment

The German guns were stung into immediate retaliation and shells crashed down in the vicinity of Hannebeek Wood. But even this physical rending of the air was unable to arrest the momentum of the psychological tension. As the hour approached only the prospect of the coming assault had any reality.

5.45 came, 5.46, 5.47, and at 5.48, with my heart beating almost audibly, it seemed, I got up from my cramped attitude and started fetching up the men. A dark misty dawn was approaching but we had a half hour start of it, and with other figures in the mist all around us we moved off at 5.50, yet in five minutes we were all over the place as regards formation, in spite of all the text books! Thirty yards was all the visibility I could command, and soon we got to the Hannebeek which we forded over knee-deep. By then the 'Institute' pillbox was emptying belt after belt into us and some of my men were down. We were keeping close to our barrage in spite of the fearful morass we were in, and the star-shells indicating 'barrage lift' were a Godsend. It was impossible to hear one's own shouting, and sheer exhilaration kept us going, marvellous to relate, in exactly the right direction.[47]

Lieutenant C. J. Huffield, 2nd Battalion, Suffolk Regiment

As they advanced, the Suffolks began to run into isolated parties of Germans. The wider context of the battle was lost in a mass of individual actions.

I was fired at from about 15 yards range and missed. Careful and quick examination revealed a bunch of about six of the hated round tin hats in a shell hole. I fired back and challenged them to surrender. Two came out 'hands up' and pointed to several others wounded and bleeding in the hole. Eventually they jog-trotted back Ypres-ward. Next we were fired at by a light machine gun and on replying with our Lewis gun we killed the German officer responsible – I can see him now, 20 yards away, on his back, breathing his last in the mist.[48]

Lieutenant C. J. Huffield, 2nd Battalion, Suffolk Regiment

With day slowly breaking through the mist and the German outposts overrun, the men at last approached the remains of Zonnebeke itself.

> The brickworks suddenly confronted us, together with the village, our visibility being now about 100 yards, and I pointed it out to my men to their great excitement. We had kept marvellously to our direction. A few snipers amongst the heaps of brick rubbish had to be dislodged . . . We had arrived about half strength and it had taken us over two hours to do that one mile. Suddenly the Australians, who had taken Polygon Wood on our right, joined up with us and our happiness was complete. In all directions the enemy was running away up Broodseinde Ridge.[49]
>
> Lieutenant C. J. Huffield, 2nd Battalion, Suffolk Regiment

Along the whole length of the attack the murderously intense fighting raged, but overall the Germans still had no answer to Plumer's tactical acumen. Repeatedly their counter-attack divisions were consumed in fruitless attempts to retake ground already securely consolidated by the British and Australian infantry protected by their devastating curtain of shells.

Once again British and Imperial casualties were high, totalling some 15,500 men, but the German losses were no less serious and probably greater. For the second time in a week the battle had been decidedly in favour of the British and it appeared as if the whole character of the offensive operations was swinging their way. After two severe tactical defeats in a week, it was obvious to the German High Command that their much-vaunted system of flexible defensive zones was no longer working and in fact was being rather subtly used against them.

> The depth of the penetration was limited so as to secure immunity from our counter-attacks, and the latter were then broken up by the massed fire of artillery. After each attack I discussed the tactical experiences with General von Kuhl and Colonel von Loszberg, sometimes at the front, sometimes on the telephone. This time I again went to the front in order to talk over the same questions with officers who had taken part in the fighting. Our defensive tactics had to be developed further, somehow or other. We were all agreed on that. The only thing was, it was so infinitely difficult to hit on the right remedy.[50]
>
> General Erich Ludendorff, German GHQ

The solution that the Germans devised was to reinforce the front line with extra machine guns and troops in an attempt to increase the difficulty the

British would face in overwhelming the forward defensive zone. Furthermore, the counter-attack divisions were not to attack in a disorganized fashion as they reached the point of contact, but were to wait until the next day when the situation had properly clarified and proper artillery support could be arranged. This partial return to the tactics of 1916 showed that the Germans were floundering.

Haig was delighted with the results of what was to become known as the Battle of Polygon Wood on 26 September. At GHQ he remained unwavering in his conviction that the Germans were about to collapse under the enormous strain of the fighting in Flanders. The two successful attacks had, GHQ believed, significantly weakened the Germans.

> Our position is improved and there is no reasonable doubt but that we can secure the whole ridge next month. That is the minimum. If the weather holds fine we may do much more. But the weather is now the dominant factor. As the sun loses power, it necessarily takes much longer to counteract each fall of rain. The general situation as regards the battle is strangely like the Somme. Now, as then, we had worn down the German resistance to very near breaking point; then as now the weather went against us. It is a race with time and a fight with the weather.[51]
>
> Brigadier General John Charteris, Intelligence Section, GHQ

However, despite the sanguine outlook at GHQ, like Sisyphus consigned to the infernal torment of straining each day to push his boulder up the hill only to have it crash down to the bottom at sunset leaving the whole task ahead of him to do again the following morning, the British seemed doomed almost to reach the top only to run out of time. Buoyed by his natural optimism and determined not to miss any flickering chance that might present itself to decide the matter, Haig continued to look beyond the 'bite and hold' operations and ordered Plumer and Gough to designate reserve formations to allow the immediate exploitation of any apparent opportunities that might occur as of 10 October. His subordinates were not quite as hopeful but both agreed that a German collapse was a distinct possibility in late October.

The next round of the battle was scheduled for 4 October. The I and II Anzac Corps of the Second Army were to lead an assault on the Broodseinde Ridge, Zonnebeke Spur and Gravenstafel Ridge, whilst the XVIII Corps of Fifth Army attacked towards Poelcappelle. These main attacks were to be supported by operations undertaken by the XIV and X Corps designed to secure both defensive flanks. Once again only a limited advance of around 1,500 yards was to be made. The preliminary artillery bombardment would initially concentrate solely on identified strongpoints and counter-battery work, leaving a hurricane bombardment to be unleashed at zero hour itself, intended to surprise and stupefy the Germans. Once again, the fresh infantry divisions trudged into the line in preparation for the assault.

> We arrived at Brigade Headquarters after a very nerve wracking journey through our guns which were all firing hard. There was scarcely a yard of ground which did not contain either a gun or an ammunition dump. Sanctuary Wood we found uncomfortable for the Bosche strafed it freely as we passed through. While waiting at Brigade an aeroplane fight took place and a German plane with both wings shot off on one side and the engine still roaring came rushing down and burst into a vivid sheet of orange flame as it struck the ground where it continued to burn for the next half hour. The two detached wings floated down some five minutes after the machine itself had crashed. Battalion Headquarters was eventually reached and proved to be a concrete structure just below the ground. While waiting for the CO to arrive the Bosche scored no fewer than seven direct hits on it with fairly heavy shells – but the place was so admirably constructed that beyond blowing out the candles and causing the roof to 'cushion' no damage was done.[52]
>
> Second Lieutenant Frank Glover, 1st Battalion, East Surrey Regiment

Although the Germans had lost many of their observation posts on the ground, the relatively low level of the ridges meant that their kite balloons could still peer behind the British lines and select any particularly tempting targets for special attention from their artillery.

> We'd had our breakfast and were clearing up and our signaller came down. We said, 'What you down for?' He says, 'A Battery's got slaughtered during the night and we're to go up during the day . . .' I said, 'What, we're to go during day?' He says, 'Yes, I've just come down with orders.' I said to Jock, 'Thank God we won't be going, we're on picket so we can't go!' But by God this corporal came and he says, 'You, you, you, you . . .' We had to try and get some ammunition up to the guns. It was just horses, about 20–30, each driver had two horses with this pack thing you put round the horse with eight shells – four either side. There was a ring of German observation balloons connected to

batteries and they were watching for anybody that came through. Every time we tried to go through they started strafing. Of course we turned round and galloped back, then we re-formed and Sergeant Emsley said to me, 'Look, Towers, I want you at the front about five or six yards behind me, and when I give the signal to gallop, we gallop and they'll follow you!' The Sergeant went off, he says, 'Follow me, give me five yards.' He had just his own horse; he hadn't a lead horse. He gave me the signal and I shouted, 'GALLOP!' and we set off. They dropped a shell right between the two of us and that was it. I remember going up in the air and landing on the floor. My leg was stiff out. I never saw the horses, I never looked for the horses! There was a shell hole and I rolled down that. When I looked up over the shell hole top there was not a soul about, 'Oh God, I'm going to be left here . . .' My leg was stiff, the shrapnel had gone right into the knee cap. I was looking to see if there was anybody to help me. All of a sudden these two RAMC men appeared from nowhere. One said, 'Now what's up?' I showed him. He got a bottle of iodine and he put it in the hole . . . Ohhh . . . The pain was terrific, I had more pain then than ever. They ran some bandaging round and put me on a stretcher. But what they did was lift me up on their shoulder – and I was covering them. I said, 'Oooh, for God's sake put me down!' 'No, you're all right, you'll be all right!' So off we went. But I couldn't see where they were going, it was open barren land. All of a sudden, they stopped and put the stretcher down. I said, 'What's up, aren't you going on?' They said, 'You're all right, don't worry!' They cleared some stuff away and there was a trap door. They lifted it up and there was a slide, they put the stretcher on, fastened a rope and lowered it down, it was a proper hospital underneath – it had been a German hospital underground. They took me down into a theatre and I always remember them giving me anaesthetic, it was terrible . . . They had a white mask that fitted on your face and this sister had a bottle. They pressed it on and when that drop went on you fought. They held you down, 'You're all right, stop it . . .' Next news, I woke up and I was on the train. They took us to a place called Etaples, their base where there was a hospital. There were two big marquees made into one, and there were all duckboards. They put me in a bed and it turned out it was a Canadian Hospital. I had a Thomas splint which was a round wooden ring with iron bars down and a foot-rest. You were all strapped in that but it was uncomfortable and the pain from my knee was getting terrible. I was looking down this marquee and there was an officer coming up with two sisters. He had his arm round them and he was laughing and talking. I never smelt a man smell more like a distillery in my life! He stank of whisky; they'd been drinking. I thought, 'Well, if that's an inspection, he isn't inspecting much!' He came past me and I said, 'Excuse me, Sir, could you have a look at my knee, it's driving me crazy, the pain!' 'Right!' So they took the bandages off and he said, 'Oh, there's a fluid there – we'll tap that tonight.' So they came for me to go to the theatre and I thought, 'Thank God for that!' I woke up in the early hours of the morning and I said, 'What's the matter here . . .' My hand dropped off – I said, 'Oh, my God! My leg's gone!' They'd taken it off, guillotined it off and never said a word. I thought, 'Oh my God, what am I going to do now!' Because the only thing I knew was the men on crutches with a tin can begging . . . And I was a footballer – my football career was finished! I'll never forget that day – I prayed to die! What a shock, I'd never given it the first thought. There was nobody there. They'd guillotined it. They just cut all the flesh round, then saw through the bone, put some gauze on, then leave it. Then a nurse came up and she took the blanket off and started to take the gauze off. Tearing this gauze off, it was dried on and she was pulling it. It was like pulling a toe out. I was in agony. I think I called her every name I knew. I said, 'You're inhuman, woman!' She wouldn't take any notice – I'm damn sure she was deaf. She just pulled them off, she could have wet it and it wouldn't have been as bad, but she wouldn't. When I'd got wounded, I'd thought, 'Thank God for that, I shall be out of it now!' It was a joy. We thought that a nice little wound would get you to Blighty – but I'd never expected this. I'd rather have stopped out than lose my leg, I'd rather have been killed.[53]

Driver William Towers, 245th Brigade, Royal Field Artillery

No respecter of personal tragedy, the callous machinery of battle ground on as all across the Salient the artillery duel continued as unremittingly fierce and unforgiving as ever. The constant firing meant that the guns themselves were suffering more and more from the effects of severe wear and tear. One artillery officer's diary recorded the daily grind.

26–28 September: The attack has passed off successfully but still our guns are kept very busy. Twice we have run out of ammunition so they send us 1,000 rounds at a time now. One gun is out of action, the carriage having cracked – we blame the heavy firing for this accident. I reported to Headquarters that our guns were becoming dangerously hot with the amount of firing we were doing and that slackened things off a bit. *1–3 October*: The continual firing has at last damaged our guns, the platforms are breaking again and recuperator troubles are putting the guns out of action.[54]

Lieutenant Robert Blackadder, 152nd Siege Battery, Royal Garrison Artillery

Whatever GHQ might think about the overall situation of the Germans, in the face of continual pressure their gunners showed no slackening of resolve and they were a formidable enemy.

We were working up for an attack the following morning on Broodseinde supporting the Australians. We were in a gun position in the triangle between road and railway at Zonnebeke. We'd been counter-batteried quite a lot during the course of the day and in the evening we decided, as we hadn't got anything else to do until the battle began next morning, we would withdraw the detachments to some dugouts in the railway embankment about 3–400 yards away to a flank. So about 8 o'clock we did. It was one of the noisiest nights I've ever had but we were in rather good dugouts so we were comparatively safe. About 4 o'clock in the morning we said, 'Come, we must go back and get ready for the battle!' To our amazement two 4.5-inch howitzers had completely disappeared. Two guns in the middle of the battery, there were six in line, had entirely disappeared and there was the largest shell hole I had ever seen. It must have been about 20 yards across because the guns were normally spaced 20 yards apart. There was no sign of these two guns at all and yet no very large shell had been fired at us. We tried to work out what had happened and we ultimately came to the conclusion that there must have been a direct hit by a German shell on one of the gun pit dumps alongside one gun and that must have set off a simultaneous explosion in the next door gun because these two guns were quite heavy things and there was literally nothing left of them – there were no pieces to be found anywhere. The other four guns in the battery were all covered up and buried in mud. I think that when the battle started we managed to get one into action. My friends in 29 Battery who were immediately behind us were in the same boat, they'd got six guns out of action. Between us the two batteries should have had 12 guns. Fortunately, the attack went well and nobody said anything. But nobody ever believed us – they said, 'Where are your two guns?' We said, 'Well, come and look at the hole that they left – we can't find anything of them.'[55]

Lieutenant Kenneth Page, 40th Brigade, Royal Field Artillery

The spearhead of the attack was to be formed by the I and II Anzac Corps. The Anzacs moved up to their jumping-off positions overnight. The assault was timed to begin at 06.00, but shortly before this the troops were unexpectedly subjected to an intense German bombardment.

> We were the leading wave for the attack on the ridge and beyond. We moved out into position at midnight; Zero Hour was 06.00 a.m., that was over the top. My left flank covered us on a big lake that we had to go around, on the left and on the right. At 05.30 it rained a little but it was not uncomfortable. We were in position and everything was quiet, many waves no doubt forming up behind us and to our right. At 05.30 up went not the usual white flares from the Germans – but yellow flares. We didn't know what it meant but in a few seconds we knew – down came a very heavy barrage, right on our line, most of us eased forward a bit because we found they were dropping just on our position.[56]
>
> Captain W. Bunning, 24th Australian Battalion

In some sectors the British assault battalions suffered dreadful casualties as the shells rained down on them.

> Oh, it was a lovely 'baptism of fire' that night. We had to dig ourselves in, and early in the morning, Fritz started strafing. Oh Lord, if ever a fellow was afraid, absolutely frightened to death, it was this child. Then one of my section took shell shock when a big 'un dropped a couple of yards off the parapet and then the instinct of the leader, or one whose place it is to lead, came to the top and I became as cool and steady as a rock. I had twelve men when we went in, I came out with three. Oh it was ghastly . . . Our Battalion lost so heavily from shellfire whilst lying in reserve preparatory to going over on the following morning that we could not attempt our job and consequently we remained in support till the attack was over.[57]
>
> Corporal Laurie Rowlands, 15th Battalion, Durham Light Infantry

After 30 minutes of tense waiting the British barrage finally crashed out with a savage ferocity that dwarfed the effects of the German shellfire that had preceded it.

> We waited there till 6 o'clock and then at that moment, the Germans' barrage lifted and ours came down. As we always tried to keep up very close to our own creeping barrage – so away we went. To our surprise, as we went down the slope we could see Germans running about in our

barrage. There was not much fighting as far as that was concerned, they were soon devastated by our barrage. We went on, past the big pillbox near the lake, that sort of mopping up was done by the waves behind us. We went on and took what was called the Red Line. It was just 40 yards below the actual top of Broodseinde Ridge. There we dug in and consolidated. The barrage waited for us and the battalions behind waited there for half an hour or so whilst we consolidated our position. Then at the psychological moment, smoke shells came over which indicated to them that the barrage was about to creep forward. The 24th Battalion went through on to their objective which was the Blue Line. My casualties in my Company were not really heavy, not as heavy as one expected from the early shelling. After we'd consolidated one moved forward just to check up and see the fields of fire suitable for your men, siting your positions. When I got to the top of Broodseinde Ridge it was really surprising to see before you the green fields of Belgium. Actual trees! Grass and fields of course churned up a good deal by barrage shells – but as far as we were concerned it was open country! Then to look back, from where we came, back to Ypres . . . There was devastation. Then I could see why our own gunners had had such a gruesome time. You could see the flashes of all the guns, from Broodseinde right back to the very Menin Gate.[58]

Captain W. Bunning, 24th Australian Battalion

The explanation for the confusion and German activity was simple. They too had been planning a dawn attack on 4 October but had been overwhelmed by the power of the British hurricane bombardment at Zero Hour.

The joke about this last attack is that Fritz had planned a large attack to take place precisely at the same minute as ours . . . However, we blew first and gave him the shock of his life. His having massed troops for an attack like this only made our victory all the greater as they were caught in our artillery barrage and cut to pieces to say nothing of the huge number of prisoners we got. Well, when I went up after the attack had succeeded, and went over the ground where Fritz had been formed up ready to attack, I saw one of the 'best' sights I have seen in the war. Where the Huns had been massed and formed up for the attack they lay there dead in thousands – it was grand to see them – good dead Huns absolutely in piles. I have never seen so many 'stiffuns' before, and it is only when you see sights like this that one realises what a hiding Fritz is getting. Every other shell hole in this area had a dead Hun or part of one in it and some had as many as five in them. How the Kaiser would have liked them for 'fat'.[59]

Captain Edwin Trundle, 26th Australian Battalion

For the Germans the coincidence of the attacks had terrible results. The increased concentration of German troops in the front line did nothing to increase their power to resist a British attack based on the power of artillery. The bombardment flayed the forward zone and merely killed vastly more Germans than would otherwise have been the case. Human bodies could not blunt the effect of high explosive and shrapnel shells by mere numbers alone.

Although the central attack on Broodseinde Ridge was a great success, problems were encountered on the flanks. As the 7th Division attack went in south of the Australians alongside Polygon Wood, Private Ernie Rhodes found the time for a private moment of contemplation and prayer, motivated entirely by the simple but heartfelt desire to live a little while longer.

Good God, yes, you were nervous, because you expected at any moment one would be for you. You knew it was quite possible. In a heavy barrage you could hear them coming. I've been on a heavy barrage when there were that many going over that you couldn't speak to your pal – the noise of the whistle of the shells – Ooooh! it was shocking. Well, you prayed to God, definitely! If a man tells you he hasn't then I think he tells lies. I did! I was always a little bit religious but that was the time when you really prayed hard to your 'Maker' to save you. When you got in a real bad barrage. Normally you never bothered, once it had lifted you were back to your old self again. That fear didn't stay with you.[60]

Private Ernie Rhodes, 21st Battalion, Manchester Regiment

Setting aside his inner reservations, Rhodes went across No Man's Land.

We went over in extended order and this lad in front of me he got a lot of shrapnel down his face. I naturally dropped to him right away but Corporal Foster said, 'Come on, leave him, he'll get attended to, come on, get off!' Which I did. You just had to get through the best way you could. It was terrible; the conditions were shocking. Everywhere was nothing but water and holes. We got so far along, past Jerry's first line, the trenches were gone. We got held up there and I had to get down

> because there was a machine gun, bullets were whizzing past. I dropped and there was some chaps there. They said they couldn't go on because of this machine gunner. So I said, 'Oooh, right!' I got my rifle, got my rifle grenade, got it set – and it went straight in amongst them. I don't know whether I killed them all or not. I got up and we went on. I felt nothing, just a job I had done. We went on and took the Germans' second line. There was a dugout there and an officer and two Germans came up. This chap, he was the Company Runner, Green, he shot one of these Germans and he shouldn't have done. This poor German had a watch and his purse in his hand. He started firing at these other two and I knocked his rifle out of his hand because our fellows were coming up after us and he could have killed some of our own. But apart from that, it wasn't my line. I didn't believe in that, so I knocked his rifle away. I called these two Germans back, motioned to them and they came back and got this wounded lad.[61]
>
> Private Ernie Rhodes, 21st Battalion, Manchester Regiment

The demoralized German survivors were killed, or made prisoner according to the circumstances of their capture and the inclination of their captors. Even then they had to pass through their own artillery barrage before they made it safely back to captivity.

> Two Huns carrying down one of our men on a stretcher were knocked out by a shell which killed the man just outside Battalion Headquarters. The Bosche, both of whom were mortally wounded, we carried to shell holes and they were both dead next morning.[62]
>
> Second Lieutenant Frank Glover, 1st Battalion, East Surrey Regiment

On the northern flank opposite Poelcappelle, as part of the 48th Division attack, the 1/5th Battalion Warwickshire Regiment were successful in their attack on the Winchester pillbox, but for them as they consolidated their position the horror was just beginning. One intelligent young officer subsequently analysed his personal traumas and fears over the next three days as the German shells searched the ground for prey.

> We settled down on our objective in a group of shell holes and there we sat for three days. On the second day it began to rain and rained continuously so that the bog of Passchendaele spread out into a lake. All day long one had nothing to do but sit in the mud, shivering, wet and cold, with no hot food, very short of sleep and having been rather mentally shattered by the fighting of the previous day. The Germans did

not in fact counter-attack us, however they shelled us very scientifically mostly from their 150mm guns which we called 5.9s. You could hear these shells coming – they took five or six seconds perhaps to come – and in five or six seconds you can pass through quite a number of psychological changes. Your mind can get through various phases. You'd hear in the distance, quite a mild 'pop' as the gun fired 5 miles away. Then a 'humming' sound as it approached you through the air with a noise rather like an aeroplane, growing louder and louder. As it grew nearer you began to calculate with yourself whether this one had got your name on it or not.[63]

Lieutenant Charles Carrington, 1/5th Battalion, Warwickshire Regiment

Each shell was a shrieking banshee that wrenched and pulled at the nerves of men who were absolutely powerless to influence the predestined trajectory imparted by the minute adjustments of some impersonal gun layer far behind the German lines. Instead, in increasing uncertainty and eventually horror, they just had to sit it out.

You listened, calculated, hoped or despaired, making imaginary bargains with fate, laying odds with yourself on the chances of these various horrors. One particular gun would seem to be firing more directly on you than the others. You would wait for its turn so intently as to forget other perhaps more real dangers. At last it comes. You hold frenziedly on to the conversation; you talk a little too fast; your nerves grow tense and while you continue to look and talk like a man, your involuntary muscles get a little out of hand. Are your knees quivering a little? Are you blinking? Is your face contorted with fear? You wonder and cannot know. Force yourself to do something, say something, think something, or you will lose control. Get yourself in hand with some voluntary action. Drum out a tune with your finger-tips upon your knee. Don't hurry – keep time – get it finished, and you will be safe this once. Here superstition and neurasthenia step in. Like the child who will not walk on the lines in the pavement and finds real safety in putting each foot on a square stone you feel that your ritual protects you. As the roar of in approaching shell rises nearer and louder you listen in inward frenzy to the shell, an outward calm to the conversation. Steady with those nervous drum-taps on your knee; don't break time or the charm is broken and the augury vain. The shell roars near.[64]

Lieutenant Charles Carrington, 1/5th Battalion, Warwickshire Regiment

In such circumstances seconds seemed like unending tortuous hours. Each shell carried the individual threat of instant dissolution. Briefly dissipated by the crash of detonation and scream of shell fragments, the terror then began all over again. It was a trial of biblical proportions.

> The noise would grow into a great crescendo and at a certain point your nerve would break – in this flash of time, in a fifth of a second – you'd decide that this was the one, throw yourself down into the mud and cringe in the bottom of the shell hole. All the other people around would do the same. Well, you may save your life by doing that. Sometimes you miscalculate and this is a shell which isn't for you at all but it goes sailing busily on and plunks down on somebody else 300–400 yards away. When a shell arrived it would plump into the mud and burst with a shattering shock. The splinters of the shell flew off, killing splinters, which might fly 50 yards away from the point of impact, you might find a fragment of jagged iron, nearly red hot and weighing half a pound arriving in your shell hole. They would take another second or two before they would all settle down in the mud. Then you get up and roar with laughter and the others laugh at you for having been the first one to throw yourself down. This of course is hysterics! It becomes a kind of game in which you cling on and try not to let the tension break. The first person in a group who shows the sign of fear by giving way and taking cover, he'd lost a point and it counts against him. The one who holds out longest has gained a point – but in what game? What is this for? After 18 months in France I was still trying to pretend to be brave and not succeeding very well and so were we all. All the time one was saying to oneself, 'If they can take it – I can take it!' The awful thing being that this is not an isolated experience but it goes on continuously minute after minute and even hour after hour.[65]
>
> Lieutenant Charles Carrington, 1/5th Battalion, Warwickshire Regiment

Carrington had to endure this mental and physical torment for some thirty-six hours. All along the line, other men were undergoing similar personal trials. It was not surprising that even a teetotaller might turn to drink to dull the mental and physical anguish.

> They came round with this rum ration in the morning. I told them, I says, 'I don't drink!' Whoooh! The language he used – he didn't half give it to me. He said, 'I'll pour it down your bloody throat!' Anyway, I got it! I coughed and spluttered and my eyes ran – but I never refused it again

> though because I was lovely and warm and I'd been perished because I was wet through, it had been raining. It put you right, I never refused a rum ration again – never.[66]
>
> Private Ernie Rhodes, 21st Battalion, Manchester Regiment

The Battle of Broodseinde had once again been a tremendous success, although certainly not without cost. British and Anzac casualties for the period totalled around 20,600. Yet the consequences of the Germans' tactical errors were self-evident, not only in their far more plentiful dead who lay across the battlefield and the 5,000 prisoners taken, but also in the numerous intelligence reports that clearly indicated their overall morale *was* suffering. For a moment, launching a further attack to exploit the situation was considered. But in the end Plumer wisely decided that the Germans still possessed adequate infantry reserves and almost undiminished artillery strength. In such circumstances a further attack without the customary artillery preparations might lead to a wholly unnecessary disaster.

Plumer had been brought in by Haig specifically to solve the problem of securing the Gheluvelt Plateau that had defeated Gough. In this, he was undoubtedly successful. Nevertheless, serious drawbacks associated with his approach of limited step-by-step advances were also becoming apparent. The bite and hold advances took a great deal of time and effort to organize, but only moved the front forward very small distances. Such limited advances of 1,000–1,500 yards meant there would never be any chance of a breakthrough; no lines of German guns would ever be captured and consequently their artillery strength would remain relatively unimpaired. In a battlefield entirely dominated by artillery this was crucial and made it imperative that the whole process be repeated before each step could be undertaken. This might have been acceptable in June or July; but October was upon them and very little of the already truncated traditional campaigning season remained. The autumn rains waited in the wings. Tactically significant advances on the borders of the Ypres Salient had little or no strategic impact on the war; yet the Ypres offensive was meant to deliver a strategically significant advance to clear the Germans from the Belgian North Sea coastline. Haig may have been optimistic that the Germans were about to collapse, but there was surely an element of wish-fulfilment in his optimism. Given the nature of the British tactics there was no other way that the offensive could succeed other than by a sudden German disintegration.

In London, the British Government throughout September and early October seemed unaffected by the series of successes achieved by Plumer. Their eyes remained fixed on alternative strategic visions, made all the more tantalizing by the negligible possibilities of their being brought to fruition. As ever, the option of switching resources to Italy was seen as a means of achieving great things without massive loss of British lives. A concrete proposal to lend 100 guns to the Italians for use in an offensive in the Isonzo valley was put forward and eventually agreed by Haig. The loan was made only on the condition that they should be returned when he needed them in Flanders. Any triumphant feelings harboured by Lloyd George at forcing this concession were soon dashed. The Italian generals proved as unmalleable as his own when, having received the guns, they promptly announced their decision not to launch any further offensives in 1917 as they sensed the Austro-Hungarians were building up their forces on the Italian front. This provoked the War Cabinet to call a special meeting of the Cabinet War Policy Committee on 24 September to discuss the whole strategic situation. Yet during the meeting there was no rational discussion of the relative worth of the Flanders offensive. Instead they debated the merits or otherwise of reinforced and renewed operations against Turkey. This emerged as Lloyd George's new preferred option, now the perfidious Italians had let him down. Various fantastic and phantasmagorical schemes to knock Turkey out of the war were put forward to be rightly smashed on the rocks of the Government's professional military advisers.

On 3 October the Committee reconvened, and by then Lloyd George had sharpened his attacks on Haig by comparing his previous promises earlier in the year with the relatively limited progress that had been achieved. However, Lloyd George failed to use this piquant criticism in an attempt to suspend the Flanders offensive, but instead sought to use it to compel a proper military consideration of an offensive against Turkey, probably in Palestine. By veering erratically during 1917 from supporting the Nivelle offensive to vehemently promoting the cause of Italy, and then with equal enthusiasm calling for an attack on Turkey, Lloyd George undermined his own position. His vacillation, disappointments and consequent frequent changes in mind meant that he was unable to develop a proper alternative global strategy to replace the existing concentration of resources on the Western Front. Those who opposed him saw each new proposal as a desperate attempt to identify any course of action, however unsuitable, other than British offensives on the Western Front. Given the unbending 'Westernism' of his professional military advisers and his reliance on controlling a coalition cabinet, Lloyd George needed to have a rock-solid case if his fellow politicians were ever to support him and risk the public outcry that would befall them if the War Cabinet were to dismiss the Commander-in-Chief in the middle of a war. His mercurial behaviour meant that he signally failed this test of credibility.

At the rate of progress Plumer was achieving, even granted unseasonably fine weather, it was obvious that months of fighting lay ahead before any strategic goals could be achieved. As sunny weather had been conspicuously absent in August, what were the chances of a dry October and November? Slowly the focus of the battle was changing. Although tactically improved, the British line was still poorly sited and to a certain extent overlooked by the Germans on the Passchendaele Ridge that extended north-east of the Gheluvelt Plateau. Increasingly the focus of the British tactical aims centred on the capture and control of the Passchendaele Ridge to allow them to halt over the winter in relative security. Meanwhile, the lofty strategic aims which had formed the basis of the offensive had slowly mutated into those which could be applied to any major offensive on the Western Front: the continued degrading of Germany's reserves of manpower through naked attrition and the raw necessity of distracting them from capitalizing on any weaknesses that might be perceived in Britain's French, Italian and Russian Allies.

> The wastage in the big actions of the Fourth Battle of Flanders was extraordinarily high. In the West we began to be short of troops. The two divisions that had been held in readiness in the East, and were already on the way to Italy, were diverted to Flanders.[67]
>
> General Erich Ludendorff, German GHQ

From the German side of the fence, the Battle of Broodseinde made it clear that a more considered tactical approach would be required if they were to stop Plumer's relentless advance.

> It was extraordinarily severe, and again we only came through it with enormous loss. It was evident that the idea of holding the front line more densely . . . was not the remedy.[68]
>
> General Erich Ludendorff, German GHQ

Following his own instincts, Ludendorff ordered the creation of an advanced zone between the British front line and the line that the Germans actually intended to hold. In an attempt to prevent or disrupt the attacking British troops crossing this zone, they planned to rely upon the power of their concentrated artillery and massively increased barbed-wire entanglements. In one sense this revised assessment of German defensive tactics was unnecessary as a far more powerful force was about to intervene on the German side. On the afternoon of 4 October the fine weather that had prevailed since the start of September finally broke as a miserable drizzle began to fall across the Ypres battleground. For the British the tragedy was about to resume.

CHAPTER NINE

JOURNEY'S END

The confusion and fog of war was never more marked due to the conditions of ground and weather. There was a complete absence of landmarks and communications while neither the Battalion Commander nor the Brigadier were able to control the battle. Just junior leaders, young officers and NCOs and men sticking it out without hope of survival.[1]

Second Lieutenant Robert Johnston, 16th Battalion, Royal Scots

Following the successful battles of the Menin Road, Polygon Wood and Broodseinde, the preparations for the next stage of the attack were almost completely undermined by the catastrophic return of atrocious weather conditions. As a result the shallow valley formed by the Steenbeek river and its various feeder streams became an absolute quagmire which severely hampered the artillery preparations. It was almost impossible to move the guns forward which meant that instead they were forced to operate at their extreme range just to hit the German front-line defences. In these circumstances counter-battery work was impossible, leaving the German artillery massed behind the Passchendaele Ridge largely untouched. Even when guns were left *in situ* at the sites they had occupied before the Broodseinde advance, the batteries had great difficulty in maintaining an adequate supply of shells across the liquid wasteland that quickly evolved behind them. Observation was difficult or impossible because of the bad visibility conditions and even if they could see their targets there were numerous technical gunnery problems. Firing the guns was fraught with difficulty, as they could not be firmly anchored to provide the secure platform that was essential for precise shelling.

4–7 October: The pushes on our left continue and all goes well, but the poor guns are having many troubles as a result of the continuous firing. Still we have been able to keep three of the four going without

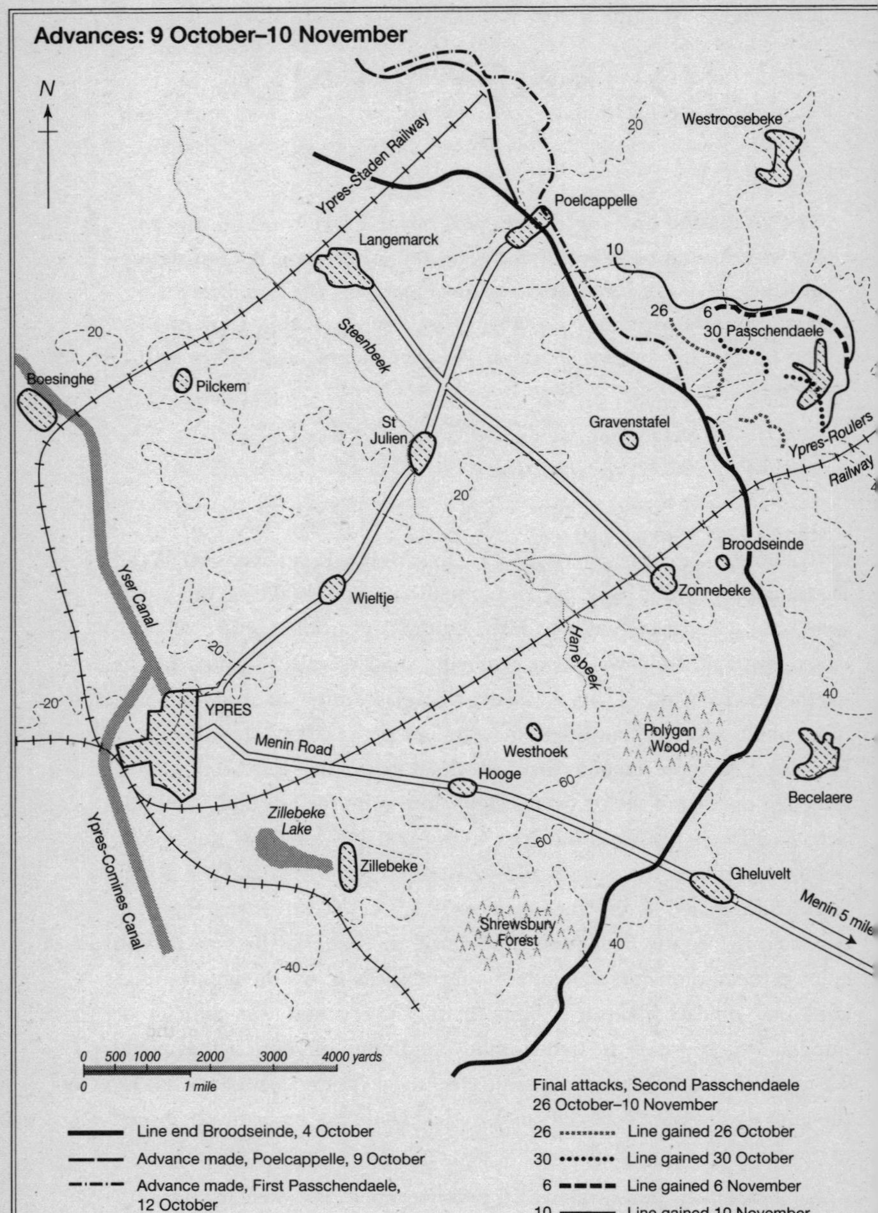

Advances: 9 October–10 November
N
Ypres-Staden Railway
Westroosebeke
20
Poelcappelle
Langemarck
10
26
6
30 Passchendaele
Steenbeek
20
Boesinghe
Pilckem
Gravenstafel
St Julien
Ypres-Roulers Railway
20
Broodseinde
Yser Canal
Wieltje
Zonnebeke
Hanebeek
20
40
-20
YPRES
Polygon Wood
Menin Road
Westhoek
Hooge
60
Becelaere
Zillebeke Lake
60
Zillebeke
Gheluvelt
Ypres-Comines Canal
Shrewsbury Forest
40
-40
0 500 1000 2000 3000 4000 yards
0 1 mile
Line end Broodseinde, 4 October
Advance made, Poelcappelle, 9 October
Advance made, First Passchendaele, 12 October
Final attacks, Second Passchendaele 26 October–10 November
26 Line gained 26 October
30 Line gained 30 October
6 Line gained 6 November
10 Line gained 10 November

interruption. The long spell of fine weather has at last broken and we are now in a sea of Flanders mud and find it hard to get the ammunition to the guns from the railway some 300 or 400 yards away. We have had some heavy shelling from the Hun, but our luck holds despite the 12 inch shells he gave us one night. The damage done is insignificant and the casualties nil.[2]

Lieutenant Robert Blackadder, 152nd Siege Battery, Royal Garrison Artillery

Rain they had suffered before in August. This time not only did it pour down, it was also desperately, miserably cold.

There was no ground to walk on; the earth had been ploughed up by shells not once only, but over and over again, and so thoroughly that nothing solid remained to step on; there was just loose, disintegrated, far-flung earth, merging into slimy, treacherous mud and water round shell holes so interlaced that the circular form of only the largest and most recently made could be distinguished. The Infantry in the outposts moved hourly from shell hole to shell hole, occupying those that had just been made and which had not, in consequence, yet filled with water. All honour to them and the way they 'stuck' it. Covered with mud, wet to the skin, bitterly cold, stiff and benumbed with exposure, cowed and deadened by the monotony of 48 hours in extreme danger and by the constant casualties among their mates, they hung on to existence by a thin thread of discipline rather than by any spark of life. Some of the feebler and more highly strung deliberately ended their own lives.[3]

Major C. L. Fox, 502nd Field Company, Royal Engineers

It was true that many men who had served in the Salient for a long time finally reached the end of their tether. They felt they just could not go on.

It was mud, mud, everywhere: mud in the trenches, mud in front of the trenches, mud behind the trenches. Every shell hole was a sea of filthy oozing mud. I suppose there is a limit to everything but the mud of Passchendaele – to see men keep on sinking into the slime, dying in the slime – I think it absolutely finished me off. I 'knew' for three months before I was wounded that I was going to get it, I knew jolly well. The only thing was I thought I was going to get killed. Every time I went out to mend the wire I think I was the biggest coward on God's earth. Nobody knew when a wire would go but we knew that it had to be mended, the infantrymens' lives depended on these wires working. It didn't matter whether we'd had sleep, we just had to keep those wires

> through. There were many days when I don't remember what happened because I was so damned tired. The fatigue in that mud was something terrible. You reached a point where there was no beyond, you just could not go any further. This night I reached my lowest ebb, I'd been out on the wires all day, all night. I hadn't had any sleep, it seemed for weeks, and no rest. It was very, very difficult to mend a telephone wire in this mud. You'd find one end and then you'd try and trudge through the mud to find the other end. As you got one foot out the other one would go down. It was somewhere near midnight. The Germans were sending over quite a barrage and I crouched down in one of these dirty shell holes. I began to think of those poor devils who had been punished for self-inflicted wounds, some had even been shot. I began to wonder how I could get out of it. I sat there and kept thinking, it's very lonely when you're on your own. Then in the distance I heard the rattle of harness, I didn't hear much of the wheels but I knew there were ammunition wagons coming up. I thought, 'Well, here's a way out – when they get level with me I'll ease out and put my leg under the wheel and I can plead it was an accident.' I waited and the sound of the harness got nearer and nearer. Eventually I saw the leading horses' heads in front of me and I thought, 'This is it!' I began to ease my way out and the first wagon reached me . . . You know, I never even had the guts to do that, I just couldn't do it . . . I think I was broken in spirit and mind.[4]
>
> Bombardier J. W. Palmer, 26th Brigade, Royal Field Artillery

Fate intervened the very next night, when Palmer and a friend were out repairing the battery telephone lines.

> The next night my pal came out with me. We heard one of their big ones coming over. Normally, within reason, you could tell if one was going to land anywhere near or not. If it was, the normal procedure was to throw yourself down and avoid the shell fragments. This one we knew was going to drop near. My pal shouted and threw himself down. I was too damned tired even to fall down. I stood there. Next I had a terrific pain in the back and the chest and I found myself face down in the mud. My pal came to me, he tried to lift me up. I said to him, 'Don't touch me, leave me. I've had enough, just leave me.' The next thing I found myself sinking down in the mud and I didn't worry about the mud. I didn't hate it any more – it seemed like a protective blanket covering me. I thought, 'Well, if this is death, it's not so bad!' Then I found myself being bumped about and I realised I was on a stretcher. I thought, 'Poor devils these

> stretcher bearers – I wouldn't be a stretcher bearer for anything.' I suddenly realised I wasn't dead! I realised I was alive! I realised that if these wounds didn't prove fatal that I should get back to my parents, to my sister, to the girl that I was going to marry. The girl that had sent me a letter every day from the beginning of the war. I thought, 'Thank God for that!' Then the dressing station, morphia and the sleep that I so badly needed. I didn't recollect any more till I found myself in a bed with white sheets and I heard the lovely wonderful voices of our nurses, English, Scots and Irish. Then I completely broke down.[5]
>
> Bombardier J. W. Palmer, 26th Brigade, Royal Field Artillery

Given the deteriorating conditions that plagued their troops, the sheer level of optimism maintained at the Headquarters of Sir Herbert Plumer and Sir Douglas Haig at the prospect of further operations in October is perhaps surprising. Blinded by the success achieved at Broodseinde they seem to have acted as though the battle was all over bar the shouting. In this approach they were greatly encouraged by a series of intelligence reports received at that time which indicated that the Germans were having difficulty in keeping up with the pace at which the battle was consuming their divisions. Thus, overlooking their manifest problems in securing an adequate artillery preparation, the date of the next attack was actually brought forward by one day to 9 October. Behind the British lines, all the usual confident preparations for a breakthrough were made. The exploitation reserves concentrated by the Second and Fifth Armies were readied; the cavalry were present and correct in their eternal role as 'bridesmaids never the bride' in the twisted marriage of artillery and infantry which marked the front line; the whole of the Canadian Corps, which was soon to be transferred to the Second Army, was earmarked for the next phase of attacks once the Passchendaele Ridge had been captured. All was made ready for when the German front collapsed. Unfortunately there was to be a salutary lesson in the difference between what the Germans found merely difficult and what was impossible. Their battered front-line divisions were replaced, new counter-attack divisions arrived and their artillery was further strengthened. Although this huge effort drew deep on the German reserves and militated against their deployment against the French and Italians, it was small comfort for Haig's armies as they struggled through the godforsaken mire on the approaches to Passchendaele. As the day drew near and the rain still poured down, the question of cancelling the offensive was considered. But Haig was desperate to seize the moment; they would attack regardless.

The plan was for the XIV and XVIII Corps of the Fifth Army to push forward on the front between the Houthulst Forest and Poelcappelle, whilst the II and I Anzac Corps of the Second Army made the main assault on the Passchendaele Ridge itself. Young officers studied their part in the plans, and the ground over which they were to attack, with their customary zeal. The Guards Division, as part of XIV Corps, were to attack alongside the French First Army on the British left flank, pushing strongly towards the Houthulst Forest.

> This Division is for it with the 3rd Brigade in reserve, so we shall have a nasty, sticky time with big shells. It is not to be for some days but I have possessed myself with maps and have been studying the country. Aeroplane photographs show a stretch of millions of shell holes with nothing resembling an enemy trench till you get about two miles back, on the edge of a forest. In one or two places they show wee square looking points which are blockhouses of concrete and shell holes which have been dug out probably for machine guns. Otherwise nothing is visible except those patches where villages once stood and which are always suspicious points. Everyone is of course talking 'attack' and there is a great eagerness for the latest news of plans and also to look at maps – the whole thing gives a weird feeling of unrest.[6]
>
> Captain Charles Dudley Ward, 1st Battalion, Welsh Guards

The changing mood of the fighting was apparent even to the men of the Royal Flying Corps from the relative comfort provided by their tents and huts at airfields well behind the lines.

> The guns are already busy on a wide front. Even back here the night is horrible with the vivid flashes of the guns all along the front and the continual thudding and thundering. I shudder to think of the poor infantry spending a night in such an inferno. The pouring rain and bitter cold is enough to dampen anyone's spirits, let alone the horror of gunfire at night. The weird fantasy of the bursts of light and the booming music play upon the nerves.[7]
>
> Lieutenant Frederick Ortweiler, 29 Squadron, Royal Flying Corps

Many men assumed that the pouring rain meant the offensive would be finally wound up for the winter. One Australian officer wrote on 8 October:

> I believe that if the weather had only held over another two or three weeks we would have had Fritz well on the run in Flanders, and would have had numerous opportunities of following him up and further knocking him about with our cavalry. Now I fear that it must be a wash-out for the year – tough luck, but we have to take things as they are and keep plugging away.[8]
>
> Lieutenant C. F. Sharland, 40th Australian Battalion

Unfortunately for Sharland, he kept plugging away and was killed in action just four days later on 12 October.

As the men prepared for their ordeal the pillboxes which had proved remarkably versatile over the past four months as fortresses, observation posts, safe havens in a storm of shells, headquarters and hospitals, found yet another unexpected function. Bizarrely, almost blasphemously after all the horrors that had marred their grim portals, one at least was pressed into service as a makeshift church.

> In one of these small pillboxes, as they were well named, our Catholic boys assembled. The building was so low that we could not stand upright. By the light of a solitary candle, all crouching down, we sang, 'Faith of Our Fathers', 'Sweet Sacrament Divine' and 'Soul of My Saviour', and then after Benediction all the boys received Holy Communion. Shorn of every outward sign of solemnity, yet I scarcely remember a service more impressive than this, in that cramped underground vault, with the voices of the singers within punctuated with the crash of shells without.[9]
>
> Father Benedict Williamson, 49th Division

Under the prevailing conditions the infantry had extreme difficulty moving forward ready to attack.

> At 3 o'clock in the morning we were to move forward to take up our final positions before the attack, which was to be at dawn, started. While making this move, I had the misfortune to fall into a shell hole which was practically full of water. I was up to my waist. Every man was intent on looking after himself and the platoon filed past and I began to think that I was going to be drowned. I managed to hold the gun above my head. Fortunately, my platoon officer, who was bringing up the rear, saw me and shouted to the fellows to come back and pull our gunner out of the shell hole, as we could not do without him! It was hard work for three of them to pull me out and I was plastered with mud, my revolver holster being filled with mud and my revolver rendered useless.

When we reached our final positions I endeavoured to scrape as much mud off as possible, but I'd got nothing really to remove it and I had to go over plastered.[10]

Private T. A. Bickerton, 2nd Battalion, Essex Regiment

The artillery sent officers forward to liaise with individual assault battalions in an attempt to try and maximize the effectiveness of their support during the battle. Thus Lieutenant Murray Rymer-Jones was attached to the 1st Battalion, Irish Guards whose commanding officer was a future Field Marshal and one of the outstanding military commanders of the Second World War.

We were going down to the battalion that we were supposed to be attached to for this forward observation work. It was Colonel Alexander [later Field Marshal Earl Alexander of Tunis] who was then at the age of 25, commanding the 1st Irish. I went down to report at his headquarters. What I was doing up there was to go with battalion headquarters when they started the attack. I had rather different ideas in this case. The whole thing in my mind was that you must get right forward in order to see what your shells, the wretched shrapnel, is doing. This was the creeping barrage that they always did. Well, if the troops didn't get on, the creeping barrage went on and it was absolutely useless, this is what happened in so many cases. We arrived at battalion headquarters which was practically on this sluggish dirty river. There Alexander said, 'Oh, fine, come in!' I said, 'Well, I'm afraid I don't want to because I want to go further forward.' He said, 'Captain Redmond is commanding the forward company so you can go up there if you like!' So, I went forward again. We saw Redmond, he had a face like a prize fighter, but he was a very charming man. On this occasion, he'd got a balaclava over his head and he looked like something from a pretty rough picture. I said, 'I'd like to be with you, if you will, because I want to see when the barrage starts in the morning. I'm particularly keen on seeing if it's effective or not.' This was much lower than where the guns were and when they put on the meteorological corrections for the day they may not have accounted for this drop. He said, 'Well, I'm afraid there's no room in here!' It was a tiny pillbox. It was drizzling with rain. So I and the gallant signallers had to prop ourselves against the wall outside. We were there for some four hours. Then of course it was approaching five o'clock and the Guardsmen were getting out on the tapes they'd put out about 40 yards ahead of us. So we got in touch with their forward people and waited for the Zero hour.[11]

Lieutenant Murray Rymer-Jones, 74th Brigade, Royal Field Artillery

When the barrage finally opened up it was found to be extremely patchy in its effectiveness along the line, depending on local circumstances. On the left the Guards Division were fortunate when they went over the top at 05.20 on 9 October.

Battalion Headquarters sent down a message that the Brigade of Guards were going to attack at dawn that morning and that a creeping barrage would open at the same time. I woke up about 5.30 a.m. having had a short sleep to hear a tremendous noise. I got out of my little hole and found that both we and the Germans were carrying out a heavy bombardment, machine guns were being fired and the noise was deafening. This was the first bombardment I had been in and I shall never forget it. The din was awful, shells were exploding everywhere with a great many too close to be pleasant. An aeroplane was flying about 100 yards above us and was firing down into our trench and the sky was full of red flashes.[12]

Second Lieutenant Douglas McMurtrie, 7th Battalion, Somerset Light Infantry

From their positions in reserve the Welsh Guards watched through the breaking light of day as the bombardment wrought its havoc on the German lines.

At the appointed hour, the more or less steady firing broke into a perfect hurricane and we got out of our pillbox to look at it. It was just dawn and the whole horizon was alight with bursting shells and coloured lights from the Bosch. But though there was a cold fresh wind it was too misty to see much. I stood on top of the pillbox and watched while it grew lighter. There was very bitter enemy firing behind our jumping off line. The French were using smoke signals which did not make it easier to see but finally, about 8.15 I was rewarded by seeing through my telescope, the French and English lines advancing – a slowly moving line of light blue and brown men and in front of them the smoke and flash of bursting shells. It really was exciting.[13]

Captain Charles Dudley Ward, 1st Battalion, Welsh Guards

From the other side of the looking glass it was indeed exciting, but not the sort of experience that anyone in their right mind would choose to repeat.

> The approach to the ridge was a desolate swamp, over which brooded an evil menacing atmosphere that seemed to defy encroachment. Far more treacherous than the visible surface defences with which we were familiar, such as barbed wire; deep devouring mud spread deadly traps in all directions. We splashed and slithered, and dragged our feet from the pull of an invisible enemy determined to suck us into its depths. Every few steps someone would slide and stumble and, weighed down by rifle and equipment, rapidly sink into the squelching mess. Those nearest grabbed his arms, struggled against being themselves engulfed and, if humanly possible, dragged him out. When helpers floundered in as well and doubled the task, it became hopeless. All the straining efforts failed and the swamp swallowed its screaming victims, and we had to be ordered to plod on dejectedly and fight this relentless enemy as stubbornly as we did those we could see. It happened that one of those leading us was Lieutenant Chamberlain, and so distraught did he become at the spectacle of men drowning in mud, and the desperate attempts to rescue them that suddenly he began hysterically belabouring the shoulders of a sinking man with his swagger stick. We were horror-struck to see this most compassionate officer so unstrung as to resort to brutality, and our loud protests forced him to desist. The man was rescued, but some could not be and they sank shrieking with fear and agony. To be ordered to go ahead and leave a comrade to such a fate was the hardest experience one could be asked to endure, but the objective had to be reached, and we plunged on, bitter anger against the evil forces prevailing piled on to our exasperation. This was as near to Hell as I ever want to be.[14]
>
> Private Norman Cliff, 1st Battalion, Grenadier Guards

Nearby, Rymer-Jones had been granted his request and moved forward with the leading waves of the Irish Guards.

> There was a very large pillbox with the Germans in, about 30 people in it and of course their machine guns opened out straight away. We crossed the Broombeek, which was another very minor little stream, it doesn't appear on the maps at all. I left a signaller there in case the wires were broken. The one line, and I must say that it never failed, a most astonishing thing really because the barrage the Germans put up was pretty heavy. We crossed there and came then under rather heavy fire from the pillbox. An Irish sergeant came over to me, he'd just got a hole in his face, scarlet, pleading with his arms, he couldn't see, one of his fellows followed him and I said, 'No, you must get back! If he can walk,

so much the better. If he can't, make him sit and the stretcher bearers will pick him up and take him away.' I'll never know whether he lived or not. Meanwhile an Irish sergeant got round behind the pillbox, climbed over the top and dropped Mills bombs through the opening. Well that discouraged the people inside and they came pouring out – those that weren't wounded. The war picture makers in the glossy magazines would have loved that. I was walking on and the French came up on my left, great big men, with their greatcoats looped back, and they were shooting these people as if it was a grouse shoot. The Germans soon gave up and came in as prisoners. Meanwhile we managed to get back to the battery and they made a correction which was all right. We pootled on and eventually came to another line of the German defence, and I found a pillbox that I could put my signallers in. So they were in touch, under cover. I went back and saw the battalion commander, another battalion had come in then to replace the Guards. Then my Colonel got through to me and we were able to give him all the latest line where our troops had got to. Then it was more or less finished until the evening. After we'd been there some time – night had fallen – a very nice looking tall subaltern officer came in to report that his troops were lying out between there and Houthulst Forest which was where the Germans had their strength. He said, 'If they get in the shell holes, they drown. We've had two drowned already in this nauseating gas and filth.' While he was saying this, I've never seen anything like it, this huge boy, he gradually collapsed in himself and was asleep on the floor until we picked him up and put him on a wire bed in the corner. I was able to get through and say that the Germans were massing in front of Houthulst Forest. Having corrected the shrapnel they were able to open out on the target I gave them and afterwards the Germans were lying about dead in masses. Not a pretty sight but it was very effective – we were able to break up their counter-attack.[15]

Lieutenant Murray Rymer-Jones, 74th Brigade, Royal Field Artillery

Despite the difficult conditions, overall the French and the Guards Division had been successful.

However, further along the line the attack largely floundered deep in the liquid mud as the creeping barrage moving ahead of the troops proved ragged or almost non-existent. For the first time since August the artillery had completely failed to establish any kind of dominance over the battlefield. In consequence the unsubdued German batteries were able to pour shells into the stumbling troops, machine guns rattled from undisturbed pillboxes and thick belts of barbed wire were left uncleared. The accumulated tactical skills and initiative of junior officers and NCOs could count for little against such odds. The 4th Division attacked just to the left of Poelcappelle village itself.

> Only three of us out of my machine gun section of eight, actually arrived. Fortunately Number 2, with a bag of spares and Number 3 with magazines. We had stopped just inside the corner of a ruined house at the side of the road and here we had another miraculous escape – one of our own shells falling right amongst us, but for some reason or another although we were blown all over the place, none of us were hurt. I decided that if the Germans counter-attacked we weren't in a very good position to use the gun, so we had a consultation and made up our minds to move forward, into a shell hole about 20 yards immediately in front of us. We got up and ran and unfortunately my Number 2 got a bullet wound through his leg. This was only a flesh wound, but it was all that he wanted! It was a 'Blighty' one and he soon made his way crawling off to the rear. We had some difficulty in setting up the gun owing to the ground being so soft. It had rained all the night before and my Number 3 just eased himself up a little to adjust the bipod at the front of the gun a little, when he also got a 'Blighty' one. This left me on my own. I decided I would do much better to stay up and if the Germans did counter-attack I would try to do what I could with the gun on my own. Fortunately, no counter-attack developed, but nobody dared to move because the German snipers were so active. I watched a heavy machine gun team try to come up from the rear and all of them were either wounded or killed.[16]
>
> Private T. A. Bickerton, 2nd Battalion, Essex Regiment

Above the fully realized hell that has become associated in our collective 'folk memory' with Passchendaele flew the Royal Flying Corps. Skimming just above the waves of mud they sought to disrupt the German infantry by directly attacking them from the air. The highly trained scouts of the Royal Flying Corps were exposed to terrific dangers in their desperate efforts to assist the infantry in their advance.

> Our task was to fly into that tunnel below the flight of the field gun shells, look for any target we could see – any Germans in trenches, enemy machine gun posts – anything at all – shoot it up, fly through the 'tunnel'

> and come out at the other end. We were warned that we must not try to fly out sideways, if we did we would almost certainly meet our own shells in flight and be brought down by them. Once we entered the 'tunnel' there was nothing for it but to carry on and go through to the very end. We flew in pairs. I led, being flight commander. I and my companion flew to the south of the tunnel, turned left and entered it. Instantly we were in an inferno. The air was boiling with the turmoil of the shells flying through it. We were thrown about in the aircraft, rocking from side to side, being thrown up and down. Below was mud, filth, smashed trenches, broken wire, limbers, rubbish, wreckage of aeroplanes, bits of men – and then in the midst of it all when we were flying at 400 feet I spotted a German machine gun post and went down. My companion came behind me and as we dived, we fired four machine guns straight into the post. We saw the Germans throw themselves on the ground. We dived at them and sprayed them – whether we hit them, we didn't know. There was no time to see – only time to dive and fire, climb and zoom on to the next target. We saw a number of the grey-green German troops lying in holes, battered trenches that had been trenches and were now shell holes. We dived on them, fired and again we were firing at a target which we could not assess. We were being thrown about. A third time we dived on another target and then our ammunition was finished. We flew on rocking out of that inferno, out of the 'tunnel' and escaped. I felt that never at any time had I passed through such an extraordinary experience when we ourselves were shut in by a cloud of shells above real damnation on the ground.[17]
>
> Captain Norman Macmillan, 46 Squadron, Royal Flying Corps

The tanks were launched along the Poelcappelle road as the mud made anything else unthinkable. This type of approach had worked well on 19 August but there were obvious disadvantages to advancing along a narrow road under artillery fire with no opportunity whatsoever for any kind of evasive manoeuvre. It proved difficult enough just to stay on the narrow road.

> We moved up to the lying up area by St Julien farmhouse in the middle of the night and then we had a brew-up. Unsheeted, did our pre-battle maintenance, loaded our guns, saw that everything was shipshape and then took our camouflage nets off. Then we warmed our engines up and started to get ready to go off – hoping that nothing was going to happen.

Nothing did happen, it was a dead quiet night, there was hardly any machine gun fire, no shelling at all. It gradually got light and we moved off at 6 o'clock for a 6.15 zero. There were ten tanks there, only one failed to start and he never lived it down of course. But, poor chap, it wasn't his fault, it was the engine. We went off line ahead and my own tank was the fourth. We moved off at 100 yards interval. It then turned into a really cold beastly drizzle which made these pave sets frightfully slippy – they were like ice – and as our tracks very nearly spanned the causeway we had to go very, very, very carefully. I was so windy that we went too cautiously and we lost the three in front. We went jogging along and after a bit, we came round a corner and there I saw two of them stuck. Whether it was shellfire or the Germans, I don't know, but there was an enormous tree across the road. It was some tree. The only way was to climb over it. The first tank had got away with it and he'd gone on ahead, the second tank had slid off, possibly on account of the mud left on the tracks of the first tank. He was sideways off the pave, quite out of action, stuck half across. That presented a problem because he was obstructing a road and couldn't get on. We got out and had a talk. It was still perfectly quiet, no noise at all. He agreed to really sacrifice himself, he drove his tank off into the mud. That cleared the road for me. I had a first class driver and with consummate skill he got over the log, drove up it and then swung slightly right so he was directly at right angles to it, then dropped down with a frightful crash on the pave on the other side – and we were off! That delayed us about twenty minutes and we'd only got about another ten minutes along the road when I thought the world had come to an end. We ran straight into the counter-barrage of the Boche. He'd evidently seen our leading tank which was some way ahead and we caught it. I've never been so frightened in my life. I think everybody was. The blues and reds and yellows, all the pyrotechnic colours in the world. Then there was a most almighty crash and a sheet of flame came up from the starboard side – we'd had a direct hit. We got out our extinguisher and put the fire out and then we had a look around. Of course the engine was completely broken up, we were immobile in the middle of the road. The shelling was still going on, if anything more intense, and we were being machine gunned. I had three men wounded. One had got his leg blown off and he died later on that night. We got the whole lot out with the tank between us and the Germans and then sat down to take stock, because we didn't know what to do exactly. Then looming out of this murk came the tank behind me. It was commanded by a great friend of mine. I stopped him, we crawled up and told him what had happened. He didn't stand a hope of getting on, if he'd have gone off the pave he would have stuck too. No communication at all – one can only shout to each other. We decided the best thing to do was to go back and warn the others to avoid a complete débâcle. I got my crew inside the second tank – there were sixteen of us in the tank then! The driver of that tank was again a very skilful man, he eased that tank round on the 10 foot causeway. It was a most extraordinary feat, got it round and away we went back. We'd gone on for a few hundred yards and there we saw why there was no other tank coming. The whole lot was stuck on this tree trunk. They'd all gone round, they were all ditched, one had had a direct hit and there was the company! Then we had to make up our minds what we were going to do. We put on the unditching beam. Well, of course we got stuck and the only thing to do then was to call it a day. I got my crew out, we walked back and found a duckboard track to a dressing station. We were very lucky in finding a very gallant team of RAMC stretcher bearers, who had no right to be up there at all, but they took on this poor chap with the leg off, took charge of him. We went back to the lying up area where I expected to get an almighty rocket from my company commander, instead of which he was delighted to see me, thought we'd all been written off. The interesting thing about the front tank was it only got around the corner from me when it was also hit, broke a track and they had to evacuate too. So that meant that nine tanks were written off, none were recovered and nothing was achieved at all. That was the last tank attack in the Passchendaele battle in October.[18]

Lieutenant Horace Birks, D Battalion, Tank Corps

Their company commander recorded the impression made as one wounded officer staggered back into St Julien.

The weary night had passed with its fears and standing in front of the ruin we looked down the road. It was bitterly cold and tragedy hung over the stricken grey country like a mist. First a bunch of wounded came and then in the distance we saw a tank officer with his orderly. His head was bandaged and he walked in little jerks, as if he were a puppet on a string. When he came near he ran a few steps and waved his arms. It was 'X' who had never been in action before. We took him inside, made him sit down and gave him a drink of tea. He was badly shaken, almost hysterical, but pulling himself together and speaking with a laboured clearness, he told us what had happened. His eyes were full of horror at the scene on the road. He kept apologising – his experience might lead him to exaggerate – perhaps he ought not to have come back, but they sent him back because he was wounded; of course, if he had been used to such things he would not have minded so much – he was sorry he could not make a better report. We heard him out and tried to cheer him by saying that, of course, these things must happen in war.[19]

Major W. H. L. Watson, D Battalion, Tank Corps

Later the Tank Corps Brigade Engineer and his team were sent up to salvage what they could and to try to clear the road.

I waded up the road, which was swimming in a foot or two of slush; frequently I would stumble into a shell hole hidden by the mud. The road was a complete shambles and strewn with debris, broken vehicles, dead and dying horses and men . . . As I neared the derelict tanks, the scene became truly appalling. Wounded men lay drowned in the mud, others were stumbling and falling through exhaustion, others crawled and rested themselves up against the dead to raise themselves a little above the mud. On reaching the tanks, I found them surrounded by the dead and dying; men had crawled to them for what shelter they could afford. The nearest tank was a female. Her left sponson doors were open. Out of these protruded four pairs of legs; exhausted and wounded men had sought refuge in this machine and dead and dying lay in a jumbled heap inside.[20]

Anon. officer, Headquarters, 1st Tank Brigade

The main attack on the Passchendaele Ridge was made by the 2nd Australian and the British 49th and 66th Divisions which were all part of the II Anzac Corps. It was hopelessly smashed and valuable reserve battalions were fruitlessly expended in the lost cause of trying to improve a situation that was beyond rescue.

We moved out in artillery diamond formation of Platoons . . . There were some horrible sights of wounded men which we passed on the way up which might easily have un-nerved the men. As we got over the ridge beyond the ruins (which the Germans had made into pillboxes of Neautleer) we started going under machine gun fire from across the valley at Bellevue. The mud was so dreadful, that it was impossible to move in any line formation because it was only possible to walk on the ridges between the shell holes. So I gave the order to open into formation of sections. We then crossed under some tall trees on top of Ravebeek. We

> were now going under tremendous machine gun fire and we had to go forward in short rushes and then lie flat in the shell holes mostly covered by water, many bullets dropping round you, within a few inches, splashing mud into your face. We naturally lost a number of men there. There are no landmarks at all, and to get our way I had to go entirely by the contours on the map.[21]
>
> Captain Godfrey Buxton, 1/6th Battalion, Duke of Wellington's Regiment

Without doubt the Battle of Poelcappelle had been a dreadful failure. The few minor advances made towards Passchendaele were soon isolated and the exhausted troops forced back by a combination of raking enfilade fire and the usual counter-attacks which this time the artillery had been unable to smash. In reality even the impressive-looking gains on the left had not in any way weakened the German position as they had merely moved the British line closer to the awesome defensive works already prepared by the Germans in the Houthulst Forest.

Unfortunately the full extent of this failure was not immediately apparent to those who most counted in overall command. Communications with the front-line units were disrupted or broken by the constant German shellfire and Plumer was fooled by optimistic early reports into believing that his divisions had made some progress towards the Passchendaele Ridge. News of their subsequent precipitate retreat unfortunately took longer to get through. Thus when the 42nd Australian Battalion moved up into line to relieve the troops of the British 66th Division they found that the local situation was completely confused. Positions that had been reported captured were clearly still in German hands and the actual location of the front line was unknown. One junior officer went forward into the Ravebeek Valley to see for himself.

> The slope was littered with dead, both theirs and ours. I got to one pillbox to find it was just a mass of dead, and so I passed on carefully to the one ahead. Here I found about 50 men alive, of the Manchesters. Never have I seen men so broken or demoralised. They were huddled up close behind the box in the last stages of exhaustion and fear. Fritz had been sniping them off all day, and had accounted for 57 that day – the dead and dying lay in piles. The wounded were numerous – unattended and weak, they groaned and moaned all over the place . . . Finally, the company came up – the men done after a fearful struggle through the mud and shell holes, not to speak of the barrage which the Hun put

> down and which caught numbers. The position was obscure – a dark night – no line – demoralised Tommies – and no sign of the enemy.[22]
>
> Lieutenant W. G. Fisher, 42nd Australian Battalion

The failure to appreciate the true nature of the situation was to have fatal consequences as Haig, not unnaturally given his overall optimistic perspective, ordered yet another push for the summit of the ridge.

Meanwhile in London, on 11 October, the War Policy Committee met for the last time. Despite the discouraging military advice they had been given as to the feasibility of a Palestinian offensive designed to knock Turkey out of the war quickly, this scheme remained at the forefront of their collective attention. Lloyd George found considerable support for his trenchant views on the predicted failure of further operations in Flanders, but in the end the politicians were unable to bring themselves to make a decision to suspend them. Wherever they looked for military advice from their existing professional advisers they always seemed to get back the same message of the absolute primacy of the Western Front. The only remaining course open to the War Policy Committee was to back Lloyd George in his wish to consult alternative military advisers in the desperate search to find anyone with real military credibility who was willing to tell them what they wanted to hear; to find a senior general who would back the 'Easterners' and give them the chance to take political action to crush the 'Westerners'.

In Flanders, with the rain tumbling down and the squalid quagmires growing ever deeper, the next attack became the first to take the name by which the entire Ypres offensive has since become popularly known. The First Battle of Passchendaele should really have been called the Second Battle of Poelcappelle; but that would have been a recognition that the starting point and objectives of the attack were largely the same. Hitherto Plumer had won success through a series of carefully prepared attacks resolutely centred on the principle of first establishing artillery supremacy. Now, driven on by Haig, he announced a renewal of the attack just three days later on 12 October. His principles had finally been overtaken by a combination of events: the pressure from Haig who remained convinced that German collapse was imminent and the ever worsening weather. The result was that in effect, if not intention, Plumer acted exactly as Gough had done during the reverses of the August battles. It was no longer a methodical step-by-step advance; he too was reduced just to battering his men against the German 'brick wall' in the hope that it would collapse. It is sadly symbolic of this loss of rhyme or reason that his poor battered Second Army divisions were expected to make an advance of up to 2,500 yards in places – far more than had been expected of them under the greatly more propitious circumstances in September.

The problem of getting the assault battalions into their jumping-off positions grew greater with every day of unremitting rainfall. Once again the infantry were physically exhausted before they even reached the front line.

> We left the pillbox about 11.45 p.m. and moved forward towards our position for the attack, following a duckboard track all the way, the only possible way of getting over the ground, which was a waste of shell holes many of which were nearly full of water. Even on the duckboards progress was slow and difficult. Many boards had been broken by the enemy's shells and in some cases had been destroyed or broken away. Now and again somebody would step on a duckboard which was balanced like a see-saw with the result that he fell in the mud and water. It was impossible to see in front of one's feet and a light would only have brought a worse evil – shelling.[23]
>
> Signaller Sydney Fuller, 8th Battalion, Suffolk Regiment

The German shellfire, flaying the duckboard tracks behind the line, often caused serious casualties and provoked an all-pervasive mental fatigue which fast eroded their reserves of courage.

> A rain of shells falling on both sides caused some panic, and the men began to trot after having settled their steel helmets a little to that side on which the iron rain was falling most. The stretcher bearers were cursed for their slow pace by those in the rear who could not rudely pass by – the track being so very narrow with shell holes full of water waiting to receive their carcasses should they happen to slip. 'Mind the hole' or 'Wire overhead' or 'Duckboard gone' – these warnings, pitched in a low key, were passed down the line as the men almost tripped and cursed their way along. There were mutterings, groans and something akin to gasping sobs, as we shuffled our way along in the inky blackness punctuated by the flashing of gunfire and aerial flares. The whole area had been turned into a huge sea of mud and water which was continually being churned up by shells large and small; shell holes almost lipped one another and some were deep enough for a man, or indeed a mule, to drown. It was a

> particularly sticky squelching kind of mud which could not have been negotiated without the aid of duckboards which had to be frequently replaced. The nerves of even the strongest of men were known to give way under the strain of helping, or being helped, out of this slough of despond and some had to be brutally kicked, tugged and lugged to their feet as they lay nerve-shattered in the mud asking only to be left there to die.[24]
>
> Lieutenant Harold Knee, 1/1st Battalion Hertfordshire Regiment

Fully conscious of their obligations the Royal Artillery tried their absolute best. They knew that the lives of their comrades in the infantry depended on them. But even the strongest will in the world could not overcome the dark forces of nature that made the guns almost uncontrollable.

> At 05.00 very dark, raining and blowing, we went up to the gun, about 400 yards away. And what a job it was getting there through the mud and sometimes falling into the water-logged shell holes. The gun was just on the muddy, open ground, no shelter at all. The previous evening we had scoured the vicinity for some timber to put the gun wheels on and also a log for the gun trail. The ammunition was dirty and had to be cleaned. All this in the rain and cold. So the eventful hour came, 05.25 a.m., 12th October 1917. We commenced firing and after every shot the gun dug into the mud as also did the trail. It was a case of making adjustments after every shot and this was very hard work. Numbers of our boys who had been wounded were coming back – walking wounded – and we being the first they encountered stopped at our gun for assistance. At one stage our gun resembled a small Dressing Station. They all had the same story to tell, of trenches filled with water, of men bogged down in mud, of the wire not being cut because our full artillery fire was not available, and also of shells simply ploughing into the mud without exploding. There was little we could do other than say a word of cheer and comfort and send them on.[25]
>
> Bombardier Bertram Stokes, 3rd Brigade, New Zealand Field Artillery

In front of the guns the infantry responded as best they could to their officers, but it was thoroughly hopeless. The underlying faults of the failure two days earlier had not been rectified or even addressed. The weather was still unremittingly awful and consequently ground conditions were appalling. The artillery still could not operate effectively, leaving the German artillery, machine guns and barbed wire all largely intact, and the heroism of the assaulting troops was again consumed in an entirely lost cause. The result of this cavalier squandering of lives was utterly predictable and the yardage gained was minimal. The trivial advances that were achieved were of no tactical value, indeed in some sectors ground was actually lost. Even the natural ebullience of the Australians had been eroded. A party of the 42nd Australian Battalion was ordered to re-establish the line next day.

> Our units sank to the lowest pitch of which I have ever been cognisant. It looked hopeless – the men were so utterly done. However, the attempt had to be made, and accordingly we moved up that night – a battalion 90 strong. I had A Company with 23 men. We got up to our position somehow or other – and the fellows were dropping out unconscious along the road – they have guts, my word! That's the way to express it. We found the line instead of being advanced, some 30 yards behind where we had left it – and the shell stricken and trodden ground thick with dead and wounded – some of the Manchesters were there yet, seven days wounded and not looked to. But men walked over them – no heed was paid to anything but the job. Our men gave all their food and water away, but that was all they could do.[26]
>
> Lieutenant W. G. Fisher, 42nd Australian Battalion

Over 13,000 casualties were suffered and morale plummeted in the Second and Fifth Armies. The Quartermaster of the 1st Battalion, Royal Welsh Fusiliers expressed his bitter feelings in a letter sent to one of his old battalion officers, Siegfried Sassoon, who was at that time back in Britain after his controversial anti-war protest earlier in the year.

> What a useless slaughter of innocent lives. Yet it goes on and will do indefinitely till one or the other side has had enough. It wouldn't matter so much if everybody paid an equal share in the sacrifice. Yet, it is the same men all the time. If you don't get killed on Monday, you can go over the top again on Tuesday and so on till you get outed. The same men all the time. The only people in the army who yell about the war being proceeded with till 'Germany is brought to her knees' – etc. etc. – are the people in nice safe cushy jobs miles behind the line. They are the people who pack the leave boats every 3 months regular as clockwork... What a game – oh my masters – what a game![27]
>
> Lieutenant Joe Cottrell, 1st Battalion, Royal Welsh Fusiliers

Exhausted by the desperate and hopeless nature of their lives, individual soldiers became afflicted by a general despondency. This was perhaps illustrated by a growing unwillingness of some ordinary soldiers to put themselves in greater personal danger just to assist their fellows.

> Bombardier Marshall brought up the rations and was returning along the duckboard track to the mess cart when he was blown to bits by a 15cm shell which landed very close to the track. Gunner Clarke who was walking down the track close to him got a large piece in the back . . . There was a bad show by some infantry soldiers who were the only witnesses. They didn't seem to want to stop in that unhealthy spot, so they did nothing for Clarke, but walked on to the battery and told some of the gunners that a man, probably one of ours, was wounded two or three hundred yards down the track, but they wouldn't go back and help as they 'had to be getting on'. Our own gunners also seemed rather slow on the uptake and one of them came across and told Rickard and me in the 'mess'. I was pretty annoyed that nothing had been done and Rickard and I set off with a stretcher. We both had gum boots on and the duckboards were very slippy and when we got Clarke on to the stretcher it was almost too much for us owing to the difficulty of keeping on our feet. The dressing station was over half a mile from the battery, but luckily we soon met with some assistance from some RAMC men. On our way back we collected most of Bombardier Marshall into one shell hole, and managed to find some papers, letters, etc. in what was left of his jacket.[28]
>
> Major F. J. Rice, 82nd Brigade, Royal Field Artillery

Despite the best efforts of his officers, Gunner Clarke died.

By now it was almost impossible to get supplies forward to the front line across the broken morass of the Steenbeek. One Signaller who formed part of a ration party was Sydney Fuller, a veteran of the opening day of the battle. Having picked up the food and water rations from the dump at the head of the light railway, he set off back across the wastelands.

> From Pheasant Farm onwards there was no duckboard track and we had to guess our direction. Several 8 inch shells were flying about and one dropped among us about 6 yards from me. I was well down in the mud by the time it struck the ground and was not hit although the mud flew around in a shower. My head rang like a bell for some time and felt as if someone had kicked it. One of the party, Crow, got a small bit

> through a boot heel. A little farther down we found one man who had been recently killed. Every few yards someone would get stuck fast in the mud and would have to be pulled out by one or more of the others. I pulled two out like that and it was no easy job. Once one was fairly in the mud, strength was of no use – the more one struggled, the tighter and deeper one got.[29]
>
> Signaller Sydney Fuller, 8th Battalion, Suffolk Regiment

In the pitch-dark featureless wilderness, lit only by the occasional flare or star shells, it was incredibly easy to get lost and ration parties frequently failed to arrive. Even when they did make it they had often been forced by their desperate exhaustion to dump the food they were carrying.

> The mules and packhorses had been told to get up as far as they could with water and other necessaries for the men and all our food. They had not been heard of and Bonnie Goetz only arrived about 9.00 dragging with him Martin Smith and announced that they had left the animals on some road and had lost themselves and though they had found us could never find the mules again. What must I do but suggest that I find them. And so I set off with eight men to bring up as much as they could carry and make a dump with the rest. We were still floundering about, falling into every shell hole and tripping over every bit of wire at 1 a.m. I knew roughly where I was but could not find those mules. The men were beat and could scarcely move and I decided to try and get back and hoped that the mule drivers would dump their stuff and we should find it in daylight. I pointed out their direction to Goetz and Martin Smith and left them to their fate. I with my eight men continued to flounder and nothing but an obstinate faith in the North Star, which I only saw occasionally, kept me going. The Bosch shelled like blazes and we were terrified and exhausted. But I got them back.[30]
>
> Captain Charles Dudley Ward, 1st Battalion, Welsh Guards

As a result of the intermittent arrival of supplies the troops were often forced to rely on the emergency rations they had carried into the front line themselves.

> During our spell in the front line, we had no hot food or drink. We had to resort to our emergency rations, as it wasn't possible for the ration parties to go beyond the Pilckem Ridge. They would have got lost in the morass: there were no landmarks, roads, houses or trees. The emergency rations consisted of a tin of bully beef, some hard 'dog' biscuits and small

> packets of tea and sugar, all in one cotton bag. Most of the men had some other items of food, just in case. But the strain and stress of battle left no time for hunger.[31]
>
> Second Lieutenant Robert Johnston, 16th Battalion, Royal Scots

German shells were still falling all over the Salient. Nowhere was safe and many men adopted an essentially fatalistic approach. The sad remnants of the 42nd Australian Battalion had been pulled back some 1,000 yards from the haphazard collection of shell holes that was acting as their front line.

> Here we stayed four days, and got shelled to hell, but no-one minds that – a shell drops alongside, and one merely calls it a bastard and curses the Hun, and wipes off the mud. Anyhow we are out now and I don't mind much. Only I'd like to have a talk with some war correspondents – liars they are. The reaction is still to come and I'm rather frightened of it – I feel about 80 years old now.[32]
>
> Lieutenant W. G. Fisher, 42nd Australian Battalion

After the catastrophe of the First Battle of Passchendaele the sense of urgency that had inveigled Plumer into betraying his own principles was no longer so keenly felt. The planning for the next stage of the offensive therefore brought a welcome touch of realism back to the proceedings. Nothing could ensure failure more than another attempt without proper preparations and it was agreed at the GHQ Conference held on 13 October that all future attacks would be postponed until the weather improved enough to allow an adequate concentration of artillery strength for the task in hand. The Second Army as it was constituted in mid-October had effectively been worn out by their actions. The I and II Anzac Corps had fought hard but desperately needed a period to rest and recuperate. As Haig had finally given up on the idea of a breakthrough he felt able to release the Canadian Corps from their protected position in reserve, where they had been waiting the elusive moment when they could pursue the retreating Germans, to relieve the II Anzac Corps on 18 October. The reduced scale and importance of the Ypres operations was demonstrated by the fact that it was to their Corps Commander, Lieutenant General Sir Arthur Currie, rather than Plumer, that Haig turned to take effective control of the operations directed against the capture of the village of Passchendaele high on its eponymous ridge. Currie was an unusual character, somewhat larger than life; he had initially commanded the 2nd Canadian Infantry Brigade in 1914 and his undoubted military talents had been rewarded with rapid promotion. On assuming the main responsibility for what remained of the Ypres offensive Currie behaved very much as Plumer had done on taking over from Gough back in August. He demanded time to move the Canadian Corps into the line; to move forward and register the guns; to engage in comprehensive counter-battery work; to identify and bombard the pillboxes and barbed wire. He proposed to take the ridge in three stages with at least four days between each attack to allow for reorganization and renewed artillery concentration. The lessons had been re-learnt and he was granted the time that he required to get ready for the first stage of his attack on 26 October.

While the preparations to support the planned Canadian Corps attack were under way the Fifth Army, in co-operation with their neighbours in the French First Army, were required to make an attack to keep up the overall pressure on the Germans. A fierce bombardment was opened up all along the Salient as if to indicate the beginning of a major new push but in fact only elements of the 18th, 34th and 35th Divisions attacked in the Poelcappelle sector at 05.35 on 22 October. In dreadful conditions the guns struggled as best they could to support the infantry as they attacked.

> It was a horrible morning of driving rain and mist, and it was a perfect miracle that our infantry ever advanced at all, but somehow they managed to, and captured the fringe of the forest, thus robbing the Hun of observation of our immediate area. Our task in the barrage was a simple one, assisting in the forming of a second creeping barrage in front of the main barrage. Luckily for once extreme accuracy of fire was not essential, as we had not been able to register the guns, which slid about everywhere on their impromptu platforms, and now and then kicked themselves off their perches, sinking immediately axle deep in the mud.[33]
>
> Major Neil Fraser-Tytler, 150th Brigade, Royal Field Artillery

In the wake of the attack Fraser-Tytler moved forward across the swamp to reconnoitre new positions for his battery.

> While we were trying to locate our new front lines a Hun machine gun gave us a burst and we went to ground in the lip of a large crater filled with the usual reddish coloured slimy water. The Hun was shelling all around and a shell, luckily a dud, landed plumb in the water beside us,

causing a great upheaval of slime. Then suddenly out of the depths there arose a hideous helmet-clad head – a dead Hun with features contorted in a ghastly grin and one arm outstretched, attempting as it were, to pull us into the mire also, and then slowly sank back into the loathsome depths from whence he came.[34]

Major Neil Fraser-Tytler, 150th Brigade, Royal Field Artillery

One of the battalions attacking that day was the 16th Battalion, Royal Scots who pushed forward astride the Ypres–Staden railway at Poelcappelle Stop. Their acting signal officer, Second Lieutenant Robert Johnston, initially remained back at the battalion headquarters as the troops went over the top. But the situation in front of them was soon totally confused as communications with the forward companies broke down.

Late that afternoon, just before dusk, the Adjutant, who had received only one message from the forward troops all day, told me to hand over to Sergeant Davies and find out what was happening in front. I went forward and came across Norman Honeyman who had been at Gailes with me and was the only one left with myself of the 12 officers who had joined the battalion in May 1917. He was commanding some 20 or 30 men – all who were left of Roger Owen's Company. He was quite out of touch and said he had been halted by the intensity of the barrages – both Bosche and British – which seemed to have fallen on our area. I continued my search to our left flank and found a dozen or so NCOs or men with a number of wounded. I took these men with me and combed the area finally sending Fox back with the wounded and an oral report to Battalion Headquarters. The fit men I led back to the embankment and when dawn came I found myself with some 25 men on the original tape line to the left of the railway, nearer which, but further forward, was Norman Honeyman's party. We could see bodies all over the place. Most shell holes held a body – dead, wounded or unhurt. The wounded were hoping to be able to pull out at darkness, but everyone remained out of a sense of duty and nothing else. All were soaking wet, cold, miserable, hungry and living for the minute. As soon as I located the area in which Norman Honeyman had his party I crawled and ran to him. He saw me and got up to meet me – and as he reached me he fell shot through the head. Throughout the whole time there was a constant crackling of rifle fire and the noise of exploding shells, mostly, I believe, random fire on the area around the station. Norman's batman who crawled over to us helped me to cover his face with sandbags and placed the body in a shell hole. His personal effects in his pack, and his cigarette case which had a bullet hole through it, were left with his runner. We placed an upright rifle and bayonet in the shell hole and hung Norman's steel helmet on it, taking off one of his identity discs to give to the Padre after the battle. I stayed with Norman's men for the rest of the day, sending a runner to Fox to tell him to report that I had taken over command of D Company as all their officers were casualties, that we were exhausted and must withdraw that night. An hour or so later we saw Bosche advancing along the railway line towards the station and opened fire on them. Fox's party used their Lewis gun too and the counter-attack faded away, but for 15 minutes it seemed possible that we would be cut off. The rest of the day was one of complete misery and at dusk I gathered the men with me and withdrew, collecting Fox's party en route, and deployed them in a perimeter around the station, getting the wounded back to Battalion Headquarters. Leaving Fox in command, I reported to the Adjutant in person, who told me that Major Bussell had been concussed when outside the pillbox and had gone down the line with the wounded. I never saw him again. A few stragglers, including an officer, joined me and I took command when the Adjutant became ill and had to be evacuated.[35]

Second Lieutenant Robert Johnston, 16th Battalion, Royal Scots

The remnants of the battalion were pulled out of the line and at Boesinghe railway station they awaited transportation to their transport lines at Reninghelst. It was a scene that had been repeated many times since 31 July.

In the station was a smart, clean and strong battalion of the Staffords who had just de-trained and formed up. Their Colonel looked at my wet, miserable, muddy, filthy, unshaven party, which included some wounded. Dick Fox had a rifle with fixed bayonet, no greatcoat, no equipment – only a cotton bandolier and his gas mask – he had a three days black growth of whisker and looked terrible. I had lost my greatcoat, but my solitary star on each shoulder of my Tommy's tunic, was clearly visible. The Colonel came over to me and asked where I had come from. I told him and discovered that he was going to that area that night. He said, 'Your platoon seems to have had a hard time and looks worn out – or is it your Company?' 'No, Sir!' I replied, 'It is the Battalion, Sir!' Just then Regimental Sergeant Major Rae arrived and seeing me said with tears in his eyes, 'Where's the Battalion, Sir?' 'This is it!' I said – and for the first time I felt like breaking down. When we got to Reninghelst the pipes and drums were there to play us to our billets. There were two officers and 27 men. Fortunately, two other officers and 130 men turned up within the next few days – all had become lost en route to the attack or lost during it. The confusion and fog of war was never more marked due to the conditions of ground and weather. There was a complete absence of landmarks and communications while neither the Battalion Commander nor the Brigadier were able to control the battle. Just junior leaders, young officers and NCOs and men sticking it out without hope of survival. We lost some 20 officers and 400 men in this shambles in conditions almost indescribable for their sheer misery and despair. The staff work was both inadequate and inept. We never saw a staff officer in the forward area. When the attack commenced we were all tired, dispirited and exhausted men without thought of victory. Our morale was very low, no jokes or singing in the ranks, a feeling of dumb despair, strangely enough accepting our position without thought or questions, dumbly obedient, but certainly lacking the inward fire required to enthuse the spirit for success in the attack. During the battle no-one had a hot meal nor were any rations brought forward. For four days we were never dry, our clothing down to our underclothes was soaking wet. I drank rum and water and strangely enough never felt really hungry – fear must have taken its place. The common denominator of infantry soldiers in this battle was misery. The Generals who ordered us forward for this attack should have been sacked. I look back in anger at those responsible. For once – and once only – we were unable to bury our dead and that in itself is proof of the impossible task we were ordered to carry out.[36]

Second Lieutenant Robert Johnston, 16th Battalion, Royal Scots

Epitomizing a wider experience along the length of the Fifth Army attack, the fate of Johnston and his men starkly highlights the disproportionate effort and sacrifice required for the most minimal advance across a featureless wasteland that was of no conceivable value to anyone.

Despite the sacrifice of the men of the Fifth Army, the preparations for the Canadian Corps attack on 26 October did not go smoothly. They were hampered by the inclement weather and the vigorous activities of the Germans who, for some reason, refused to remain quiescent whilst Currie readied his forces. Nevertheless, time and concentration of effort did in the end bring their own rewards and definite progress was made in reducing the German defences and targeting their batteries. But it was a crude fight that summed up the vicious inhumanity of attrition.

> All finesse has left the war now; it seems to have degenerated into slinging a given weight of shell on to a certain area in a detailed space of time. Many batteries apparently never attempt to observe their own fire and generally speaking things have got pretty slack among the bad ones. One sees heavy guns on the forward slope of Pilckem Ridge in full view of Hunland, and, in fact, guns and howitzers, slung down anywhere and anyhow, the only deciding factor being whether it was possible to get ammunition up to them.[37]
>
> Major Neil Fraser-Tytler, 150th Brigade, Royal Field Artillery

As the British and Imperial troops slogged up the Passchendaele Ridge the science of war had indeed been reduced to a contest of brute strength.

At last, at 05.40 on 26 October, the Second Battle of Passchendaele began. The Canadians launched a two-pronged attack designed to advance the line just 500 yards. The 4th Canadian Division moved forward along the narrow top of the ridge whilst the 3rd Canadian Division advanced up Bellevue Spur on the other side of the Ravebeek Valley. The fighting was hard but, assisted by a decent rather than overpowering bombardment, they winkled their way forward to achieve their objectives. Meanwhile to the left of the Canadians the benighted Fifth Army continued its attempt to advance across the lowland swamps bordered to the north by the grim Houthulst Forest, prior to moving up onto the ridge with the distant, and hence unlikely, objective of Westroosebeke. The enervated Fifth Army attack was simply ghastly to behold and worse to experience. The 50th, 57th, 58th and 63rd (Royal Naval) Divisions attempted to advance across the marshlands. The 1/5th Northumberland Fusiliers attacked the strong German positions close to the Houthulst Forest.

> You were just sitting on the edge of this shell hole with your feet in the water. When the whistle went and you went forward it was a toss up whether your legs would come or not! The ground was yellowy green, soft quicksand. I got one leg in there and two fellows got hold of my rifle and pulled me out. You were plunging forward – you couldn't walk – there was nothing to be seen, your mind and thoughts were on the ground you

were travelling on, avoiding quicksands. A whole roof of shells and God knows what on top of you. Machine guns whistling past your ear, whizz bangs – God there was everything! There was hardly anybody left when we got to the wire. You were no further forward – it was worse than a stone wall. There was no hope of getting through. We just thought, 'God, we've got here! How are we going to get back?' [38]

Private Joseph Pickard, 1/5th Battalion, Northumberland Fusiliers

No one could cope with the crude necessities of fighting in such conditions. It was simply physically impossible to overcome the effects of the mud.

There was no chance of getting wounded and getting a Blighty one at Passchendaele. You could either get through or die, because if you were wounded and you slipped off the duckboards you just sank into the mud. Each side was a sea of mud. You stumbled and slid along. If you slipped you went up to the waist, not only that but in every pool you fell in there were decomposed bodies of humans and mules. If you were wounded and slipped off, well then that was the end of you. These duckboards were taped by the Germans and he was shelling them the whole time. In most places, if shells start dropping you run to the right or the left and get some cover. But if you were on the duckboards, you couldn't run! There was mud to your right and mud to your left – you had to face it and go on. I've seen men coming out covered in mud – they just scraped the mud from their eyes. They had in their hands what looked like a muddy bough of a tree – it was their Lewis gun! One little party of men was trying to make their hole more comfortable, scooping it out and some hundreds of yards away the Germans were doing the same. In their miseries they didn't take any damn notice of each other.[39]

Warrant Officer Richard Tobin, Hood Battalion

The landscape had become a surreal panorama of primeval ooze but, even in the midst of this desolation, fleeting glimpses of incongruous beauty arose to highlight the nihilism that had taken hold of the world.

Suddenly the fury opened. Our barrage and theirs started simultaneously. We were only a few yards behind ours and I just had time to glance at lovely nature being made hideous by fiends. Behind in the West, a full moon setting, all the stars shining, just in front was a white mass of our fire, a hedge of explosions, and through the smoke a wonderful dawn coming – long streaks of gold and red and grey and all round us the German barrage (as strong as ours) and over all the vile stink of the explosions. I had just taken it in as we wormed slowly forward, when the shell for our little party arrived and we fell in the hole. One friend of mine had his leg off and I had to see him slowly die as I couldn't move. My actor friend I got back safely, wounded in both arms. Heavens! It was a business . . . Thank God, I'm alive to write to you. I don't know what to say as I am still half dazed and rather shaky in the legs, especially in my knees. Oh, it was horrible, horrible. And the hopeless folly of it all.[40]

Private Mark Yewdall, 1/28th Battalion, London Regiment (Artists' Rifles)

As with the attacks made by all the British divisions that of the 58th Division was a total failure, and it was a bitter commanding general who drew up a report summarizing his views of the action.

Out of 170 Field Guns covering the Division 50 guns were out of action . . . With ground in the condition which prevailed on the 26th October, all hope of men successfully rushing a hostile position the moment the barrage lifts is out of the question. Under the most favourable conditions advancing infantry are never much nearer than 40 yards the tail of the barrage. Men could move no quicker than 100 yards in a quarter of an hour, and the enemy had ample time to re-man his positions before our men could reach him. The creeping barrage on the 26th moved at the rate of 100 yards in 8 minutes, even if it had moved 100 yards in 18 minutes I doubt if troops could have kept up to it. . . . Zero hour at dawn is never varied and the enemy has become extremely alert at this period. I imagine though that the difficulty of varying it cannot be overcome owing to forming up difficulties. In addition to this, troops are launched into the attack half frozen with the wet and cold and on empty stomachs; this fact alone takes the starch out of the stoutest heart. I do not think the importance of a full stomach and a daylight attack in winter are sufficiently realised.[41]

Major General A. B. E. Cator, Headquarters, 58th Division

Cator's conclusions were echoed by the men who bore the brunt of the fighting that day.

All this warfare pleases the Germans. They mow us down and have hardly any men there themselves. One pill box only had 3 men who surrendered. What a wicked thing it is to order an advance at this time of the year. It is simply driving men to their death – to gain a few yards.

> What will happen when the Germans have settled the other fronts and come over here in force can easily be imagined by anyone who has been and seen.[42]
>
> Private Mark Yewdall, 1/28th Battalion, London Regiment (Artists' Rifles)

To the right of the Canadians the 5th and 7th Divisions of the Second Army undertook operations designed to improve the position on the edges of the Gheluvelt Plateau. These were also a total failure. Casualties on 26 October were high. The Canadian Corps lost approximately 3,400; the rest of the Second Army lost over 3,300 and the Fifth Army lost some 5,400. In total there were over 12,000 casualties, which once again represented a very small step forward at a very large cost.

After a further four days of preparations the second stage of the battle was launched at 05.50 on 30 October. It proved an almost exact replay of the first, as the 3rd and 4th Canadian Divisions attacked on both sides of the Ravebeek and advanced in dreadful conditions right up to the boundary of Passchendaele village. They suffered heavy casualties and at one point the whole issue hung in the balance as the men of Princess Patricia's Canadian Light Infantry faced a pillbox and machine gun nests placed squarely across the route along Meetcheele Spur. Two amazing acts of pure heroism then saved the day.

> For most conspicuous bravery and leadership when in charge of a section of four machine guns accompanying the infantry in an attack. Seeing all the officers and most of the non-commissioned officers of an infantry company had become casualties, and that the men were hesitating before a nest of enemy machine guns, which were on commanding ground and causing them severe casualties, he handed over command of his guns to an NCO, rallied the infantry, organised the attack, and captured the strong point. Finding that the position was swept by a machine gun from a pillbox which dominated all the ground over which the troops were advancing, Lieutenant Mackenzie made a reconnaissance and detailed flanking and frontal attacking parties, which captured the pillbox, he himself being killed whilst leading the attack.[43]
>
> *London Gazette* citation for Lieutenant Hugh Mackenzie VC,
> 7th Canadian Machine Gun Company, Canadian Machine Gun Corps

A sergeant showed no less incredible courage and devotion to duty in circumstances of almost certain death.

> For most conspicuous bravery in attack, when, single-handed, he captured a commanding pillbox which had withstood heavy bombardment and was causing heavy casualties to our forces and holding up the attack. He rushed a sniper's post in front, destroyed the garrison with bombs, and, crawling on the top of the pillbox, he shot the two machine gunners with his revolver. Sergeant Mullin then rushed to another entrance, and compelled the garrison to surrender. His gallantry and fearlessness were witnessed by many, and although rapid fire was directed upon him and his clothes were riddled with bullets, he never faltered in his purpose, and he not only helped to save the situation but also indirectly saved many lives.[44]
>
> *London Gazette* citation for Sergeant George Mullin VC,
> Princess Patricia's Canadian Light Infantry

So reduced in scale had the offensive become that the actions of individuals such as McKenzie and Mullin could have a significant impact on the results at the end of the day. The crest of the hill was gained but it was uncertain whether it could be held. The situation was chaotic, as few officers or NCOs had survived. Consolidation was essential as the Canadians were vulnerable to any sustained German counter-attack properly backed by their artillery. At 15.00 a situation report was sent back to battalion headquarters from the front line.

> There are about 100 men out in front of the pillbox. These are in the charge of three corporals and one lance corporal. They are supported on the right by a party sent up by the Royal Canadian Regiment. Position for fire is a good one. They have two Lewis guns. Another party of 75 rifles command the ridge and the valley below on the left and join up with the 49th. We have four Lewis guns and a limited supply of ammunition. A party of Germans approached our trench at about 1 p.m. The artillery replied to our SOS and had several direct hits dispersing the party. At present, they are moving around under cover of a white flag picking up their wounded.[45]
>
> Lieutenant J. E. Puley, Princess Patricia's Canadian Light Infantry

The men held out and the Germans proved unable to organize a concerted counter-attack, despite the weakness of the Canadians' sketchy positions. At midnight Major Sullivan moved forward to take over command from the exhausted Lieutenant Puley, and he too reported back to headquarters.

> I find our line consisting of shell holes running about level with the pillbox, well held in small separate posts. Captain Wood of the Royal Canadian Regiment brought up his company of 30 other ranks with me and has dug in 50 yards behind the pillbox. There are only 8 RCR left in the front line with two officers. We have six Lewis guns in working order and hold the crest of the ridge. The enemy have apparently dug themselves in 200 yards in front of us. One of their patrols has just come up to our line, but was beaten off. I figure I can hold this line against any counter-attack they put across.[46]
>
> Major Sullivan, Princess Patricia's Canadian Light Infantry

Just a few minutes after sending back his report Major Sullivan was mortally wounded by a German sniper. Despite everything, the advanced line survived the night and thus became the new status quo.

> Have been around all posts; sniping not good today; think shelling yesterday spoiled the Bosche nerve. Could see with glasses 4th Division on our right front about 500 yards away, but swamp between makes visiting difficult.[47]
>
> Major Niven, Princess Patricia's Canadian Light Infantry

To the left of the Canadians, many senior officers of the Fifth Army had expressed serious reservations about the wisdom of attempting another attack on their front. But these well-founded objections were overruled as it was considered essential that the Canadians receive some support on their left flank whilst attacking. Unsurprisingly the Fifth Army operations resulted in yet another dismal failure and Major General Cator was furious at the further useless sacrifice of some 1,361 men of his 58th Division. He deliberately threw caution to the winds to convey his displeasure in his post-mortem report. First he dealt with the dismal state of communications.

> More difficulty was experienced in maintaining communications on this occasion than I have hitherto experienced during the War. No information reached either Divisional or Brigade Headquarters till 1 p.m., the causes of failure being chiefly due to weather and condition of the ground. . . . Many messages sent back by runners who got bogged and were shot down. The majority of the company signallers were hit. The first runner to get back to Meunier House arrived utterly exhausted at 12.30 p.m. . . . Pigeons were saturated in mud and water and couldn't fly . . . No contact aeroplane went out although those belonging to the Canadians and the enemy aeroplanes were out.[48]
>
> Major General A. B. E. Cator, Headquarters, 58th Division

He then turned to the reasons for failure, gradually losing control of his temper until he culminated in a heartfelt denunciation of the stupidity of it all.

> The operations were a failure: A) The ground was impassable and so powerless were the troops to manoeuvre that they were shot down whilst stuck in the mud. B) The barrage was ineffective and troops were unable to keep up with it. C) Oblique hostile machine gun fire was very effective. D) The only Lewis gun succeeded in getting into action was useless in three minutes. E) All uncovered rifles were useless, all covered rifles ditto within ten minutes. F) Power of manoeuvre was nil. G) On this sort of ground men must be extended, where sections were in column the whole section was put out of action by machine gun fire. To sum up the situation, neither FIRE NOR MOVEMENT was possible, and any prospects of success under these conditions were nil.[49]
>
> Major General A. B. E. Cator, Headquarters, 58th Division

The doomed attempt to reach Westroosebeke was at last abandoned. The long agony of the Fifth Army was over. But it was too late for far too many of Cator's men. Every futile death had a hidden personal tragedy. Four days before the attack Private Jack Mudd had written back to his beloved wife:

> Out here dear we're all pals. What one hasn't got, the other has. We try to share each others troubles, get each other out of danger. You wouldn't believe the Humanity between men out here. Poor little Shorty, that's one of the fellows that came out with me, he used to tell me about his Hilda – that was his young lady's name – about his home he had already bought and when he got home he would get married and come over to see me and introduce her to you. He used to make me laugh with his talk, how he loved his Hilda. But unfortunately, he will never see her again, poor fellow. He would give me half of anything he had. I often think of him. Yet, poor fellow, I don't think he even had a grave but still lies there in the open. Still, dear, I don't want to make you sad but it just shows you how we seem to stick together in trouble. It's a lovely thing is friendship out here.[50]
>
> Private Jack Mudd, 2/4th Battalion, London Regiment

After the attack on 26 October Private Jack Mudd was reported missing in action. His body was never found.

The First and Second Battles of Passchendaele, which were fought in such utterly wretched conditions and resulted in heavy casualties, seemed to have little obvious tactical or strategic rationale. By the end of October few of the original strategic aims remained for the campaign. The goal of removing the German submarine bases from the Belgian coast was no longer credible and there seemed to most observers equally little chance of driving the Germans significantly back from Ypres to clear the lingering threat to the Channel Ports. Furthermore the parlous situation facing the French army had largely been stabilized and it is ironic that on 26 October the French launched a carefully planned operation in Champagne that was actually larger in scale than the British attacks then being carried out at Ypres. In these circumstances it is inevitable that, ever since and with varying degrees of vehemence, the question has been asked – why, following the failure at Poelcappelle, was the offensive continued at all? What purpose remained? The answer lies in a strange blend of lingering optimism and pragmatic necessity.

Some strategic rationale did remain in the diversion of widely stretched German resources from other areas of the war. It is claimed that the offensive was continued as an attempt to deflect German attention from the trials and tribulations that had recently befallen Britain's war-weary Allies. The overthrow of the moderate Russian Menshevik government by the Bolsheviks, who were intent on ending their part of the war, had caused great alarm amongst Western politicians. Closer to home the bolstering of the Austro-Hungarian forces in Italy by German divisions precipitated a successful joint offensive at Caporetto commencing on 25 October. The Italians quickly crumbled, resulting in a rapid retreat that threatened to get completely out of control. These two blows to the Allied cause were extremely dangerous but as ever the Westerners claimed the only real answer lay on the Western Front. It was Haig's contention that if the BEF maintained its constant pressure at Ypres, it would in effect act as a tourniquet and prevent these wounds to the Allied cause from becoming fatal.

Haig also remained convinced that the Germans in Flanders were on the verge of collapse and that just one more hammer blow might shatter their resistance. After all, their soldiers were being forced to endure the same dreadful conditions at Ypres as the British. Based on his own experiences in 1914, his belief was that the Germans had missed the opportunity of a great victory during the First Battle of Ypres when one more strike might have broken through the overstretched British lines and taken them to the Channel Ports. He was determined not to make the same mistake himself. If the Germans really were about to give way, and the final blow was never struck, then not only would he be held responsible for letting the opportunity slip through his fingers but all the sacrifices that his troops had made since 31 July would have been made in vain. Haig was not prepared to countenance either possibility and his own deep-rooted conviction that a great victory lay almost within his grasp remained one of the foremost reasons why he chose to continue.

Another important factor in prolonging the offensive was to help cover the preparations for a surprise attack that had been approved by Haig to be launched on 20 November in the Cambrai sector lying north-east of the old Somme battlefields. The Ypres offensive, fulfilling its attritional role, had effectively denuded the rest of the Western Front of adequate levels of German troops and this created propitious conditions for a great experiment. The ground conditions in the Cambrai sector, where no major offensive had ever taken place, were ideal for the mass deployment of tanks, which the new innovative plan intended to use to smash through the German barbed wire and break down the Hindenburg Line defences. The latest advances in artillery techniques of pre-registration were to be employed to the full to allow the bombardment to crash out with devastating force as the tanks and infantry surged forward. The absence of a preliminary bombardment blasting away for days before the attack would, it was hoped, both ensure surprise and leave the ground relatively uncratered for the easy passage of tanks. High hopes were entertained for the Cambrai attack and it was felt that if operations at Ypres were continued it would be of great value in pinning down German troops and reserves a significant distance away in Flanders.

Tactical priorities had also begun to loom large in the minds of the British generals. It has been said that, even today, if you stand where the British front line was in October 1917 it is obvious why they had to go on and wrest control of the Passchendaele Ridge. This, however, is only of relevance if the British front line remained where it was. There was another option. Viewed objectively, Haig would have done better to withdraw to the line of the Pilckem Ridge and then across the Gheluvelt Plateau. This position would have been far easier to defend from German attacks, as it would leave the devastated and flooded Steenbeek valley in front of rather than behind the British front line. Such a tactical withdrawal would also greatly have lessened the severity of the salient punched out from Ypres which was vulnerable to German fire from three sides. However, such a logical course of action was both emotionally and politically unacceptable. It would have been completely unthinkable at that time to give up the ground that so many had sacrificed their lives to win. There would have been a national outcry. Bearing this in mind, and recognizing the equal impossibility of remaining pinned down just below the crest of the Passchendaele Ridge throughout the winter, the only option was to continue the advance until the front line rested firmly on the top of the ridge and then echeloned back across the face of the Houthulst Forest on the left.

An analysis of all these factors makes it clear that in reality by the end of October the great Flanders offensive had already finished. Its strategic potential had been significantly reduced and all that really remained were a series of minor operations intended to secure an improved tactical position, even if, perversely, every step forward actually worsened the severity of the new salient jutting out from the British lines and centred round the Passchendaele Ridge.

Throughout the last dreadful phase of the doomed offensive the War Cabinet made its presence felt, but very much in the subsidiary role of 'noises off'. As October wore on they began to take a serious interest in casualty figures, with the aim of assessing the impact of the Ypres battles on British reserves of manpower. When the military authorities duly supplied the figures they revealed that between 31 July and 31 October approximately 250,000 men had been killed and wounded. Of these 110,000 had become casualties in October alone. Although the Ypres Salient had long been a drain on British manpower, the offensive was proving a positive torrent of lost and ruined lives. Optimistic estimates of German casualties were as high as 250,000. Having obtained this information the War Cabinet could have used it to direct an end to the slaughter. But nothing was done to halt this haemorrhaging of the lifeblood of the Empire. A further chance to intervene came when the French Army, despite its gradual recovery, asked Haig to take over a greater stretch of the overall Allied front. Haig threatened to suspend his offensive if this request was not rejected. Here was a golden opportunity for the politicians, but their reaction betrays the uncertainty and confusion at the heart of the War Cabinet. The suspension of the offensive was exactly what most of them wanted and the necessity of providing help for their brave French allies would provide an ample fig leaf to cover the real motives for their actions. Yet meekly they gave way and duly refused the French request.

One action that the War Cabinet did take was to seek a second military opinion as to the efficacy of operations conducted on the Western Front. Desperate to get the response he wanted, Lloyd George handpicked two officers known to be at odds with Haig and Robertson, namely Field Marshal Sir John French, the previous commander of the BEF, and General Sir Henry Wilson, a senior but disaffected Francophile staff officer. Their report was predictably full of venom directed against both Haig and Robertson, and it recommended the formation of a joint Allied staff to examine the conduct of the whole war and make recommendations as they saw fit. In the short term this report was to have little effect other than further poisoning the atmosphere between Haig and Lloyd George.

The increasing danger emanating from the possibility of the total collapse of the Italian Front under the pressure of the successful Austro-German offensive at Caporetto provoked an instant response from Lloyd George. Haig was ordered to send two of his divisions from the Western Front as soon as possible to Italy. As a result, on 28 October the 23rd and 41st Divisions began the move to the Italian Front. This showed that Lloyd George was prepared in certain circumstances to dictate to his military advisers. Yet still he could not summon the nerve to cross them directly and cancel the increasingly futile attacks involving ever decreasing forces in the narrow Passchendaele Salient. Consequently the offensive staggered on into its last two weeks.

THE ACTIVE frontage of operations had now declined to just a few hundred yards. Futile attacks by individual battalions to straighten the line or improve the jumping-off positions for the next major attack were a daily occurrence. Men died in actions so obscure that they did not even merit a name. On 3 November the 42nd Battalion, Royal Highlanders of Canada were ordered to capture the Graf House pillbox on Bellevue Spur. The fighting was chaotic and many of the men had no idea where the pillbox was located.

> The night was an uproar. We dove into the mud and saw the signal go up for the Stokes mortar support. The German Maxim stopped firing and we jumped and started running again. There was a flaming white-hot instant – and oblivion! When I recovered consciousness my head was splitting with pain and a terrible nausea had seized my stomach. The Stokes shell had dropped beside us, throwing me bodily across the road and knocking Brown down. He was rolled over on his back, feeling for wounds, as I saw him. All around us was a clamour of machine guns, bombs and rifles. I heard McIntyre shouting, 'Five rounds rapid!' Then his voice shut off abruptly. I discovered my nose had been bleeding and when I tried to get up I collapsed again with dizziness.[51]
>
> Private Will Bird, 42nd Canadian Battalion (Royal Highlanders of Canada)

The attack was a total failure. One party had reached Graf House but had come under heavy fire and the few survivors had been forced to withdraw. Once again piecemeal attacks with no real purpose were being allowed to eat away at the numbers, strength and morale of the attacking troops.

The guns were still operating under conditions of great difficulty, as even a brief interval in the rainfall at the start of November could do nothing to dry out the sodden battlefield.

> The conditions are awful, beyond description, nothing we've had yet has come up to it, the whole trouble is the weather which daily gets worse. One's admiration goes out to the infantry who attack and gain ground under these conditions. Had I a descriptive pen I could picture to you the squalor and wretchedness of it all and through it the wonder of the men who carry on. Figure to yourself a desolate wilderness of water filled with shell craters, and crater after crater whose lips form narrow peninsulas along which one can at best pick but a slow and precarious way. Here a shattered tree trunk, there a wrecked 'pill box', sole remaining evidence that this was once human and inhabited land. Dante would never have condemned lost souls to wander in so terrible a purgatory. Here a shattered wagon, there a gun mired to the muzzle in mud which grips like glue, even the birds and rats have forsaken so unnatural a spot. Mile after mile of the same unending dreariness, landmarks are gone, of whole villages hardly a pile of bricks amongst the mud marks the site. You see it best under a leaden sky with a chill drizzle falling, each hour an eternity, each dragging step a nightmare. How

weirdly it recalls some half formed horror of childish nightmare. One would flee, but whither? One would cry aloud, but there comes no blessed awakening. Surely the God of Battles has deserted a spot where only devils can reign.[52]

Major John Lyne, 64th Brigade, Royal Field Artillery

The guns were worn out by the constant firing that had been required of them for so long. Batteries found their nominal firepower slashed as the guns dropped out and replacement guns could not be got forward across the swamps.

1–5 November: We now have only 2 guns in action – broken platforms being the trouble. The long ranges we have to fire at require the full charge and the platforms cannot stand much of that.[53]

Lieutenant Robert Blackadder, 152nd Siege Battery, Royal Garrison Artillery

For many of the gun crews, stuck in the horrors of the Salient with minimal rests since the battle commenced five months before, it was the end.

Things were certainly pretty bad at the guns, the air still reeking of gas, the ground saturated with the mustard gas liquid and the men all half blind and covered with mustard gas blisters. Every order had to be given in writing, as neither I nor the NCOs could articulate a word, and to complete the humour of the situation everyone was sick at every possible opportunity.[54]

Major Neil Fraser-Tytler, 150th Brigade, Royal Field Artillery

Mustard gas remained an insidious enemy. The Germans doused the artillery lines with gas shells and the effects were usually worse than they immediately appeared.

We did not at first realise the full danger of this and just laughed because no-one had a voice, but when people began to blister and swell, and two men of my old Battery died horribly from eating bread which had been splashed with this stuff, we got the wind up thoroughly. The whole area was tainted; one could touch nothing with safety; even our own Doctor, who came to see us, slipped in the mud and was so badly blistered by it that we never saw him again. The gas casualties were bad enough, but oh! The shell casualties were pathetic. I lost many of my greatest friends in the Battery, horribly mutilated in the mud and towards the end was as near a raving lunatic as possible.[55]

Major Shiel, 250th Brigade, Royal Field Artillery

Having been moved up behind their infantry in October, the Canadian gunners suffered alongside their British counterparts in the final stages of the long-drawn-out agony.

> We had our usual six guns in action there. By the time we came out we had had 23 guns knocked out. They were not all destroyed and some of them were back in action again in a few days. We worked with skeleton gun crews. Our duties were limited pretty much to barrage work. A gun crew consisted of an NCO and two or three men instead of the usual six. Our average strength at the gun lines including officers, signallers and the cook was 36. From among these, we had 63 casualties of whom 15 were killed. I spent 31 months in France and Belgium and I would do all of the rest over again rather than those six weeks at Passchendaele.[56]
>
> Gunner Ernest Black, Canadian Field Artillery

Despite everything they stuck at it, braving it all.

> Sometimes the sun shone, pale and wintry in that November air; but most of the time rain came and the shells landed, now blowing up black spouts of mud, now white columns of water like ghosts that drifted and danced and vanished over the gloomy landscape. And every night there were one or two more casualties amongst the drivers; and few, indeed, were the days when some gunner did not fall. Yet there was nothing to do but 'stick it out'; and day after day, the men set their teeth, wondered, 'Who next?' and went about the business of war.[57]
>
> Gunner Wilfred Brenton Kerr, 67th Battery, Canadian Field Artillery

At 06.00 on 6 November the Second Battle of Passchendaele restarted in earnest, when the 1st Canadian Division continued the drive along Bellevue Ridge while the 2nd Canadian Division directly attacked the blasted remnants of Passchendaele village.

> The barrage started up at six in the morning. It was terrific, I remember turning round and looking back and everything seemed to be on fire. My platoon was supposed to have its left flank on the Passchendaele church. That was our landmark. We jumped off at six o'clock, it was noontime before we consolidated and we only went 2,000 yards, but you couldn't get any faster. You'd go up to your knees in mud and you couldn't get out. There was nothing left in the village, it was absolutely flat. When we got there the church had been hit several times. We got about 18 or 20 prisoners up out of the basement of the church, but that's as far as we

got. We couldn't dig a trench because if you dug a trench you had a brook, so all we could do was just man the lips of the shell holes.[58]

Lieutenant J. G. McKnight, 26th Canadian Battalion (New Brunswick)

At long last with one great heave the Canadians took the crest of the ridge and captured the village. But it was a symbolic triumph rather lost on many of the participants.

Once again we tried to advance, but were met by an artillery barrage from beyond the village. We managed to move ahead away from the shells, but ran into machine gun fire just as we were again bogged down. The utter hopelessness of our position was devastating. We lay there, in shell holes half-filled with water, and just waited for whatever would happen. For me, it came in a great crash and blackness as a shell burst only a few feet away. When I came to I was lying in a bed in a tent hospital somewhere near Mont des Cats. I seemed to be paralysed from the waist down.[59]

Private Magnus McIntyre Hood, 24th Canadian Battalion (Victoria Rifles)

Yet still the agony was not over. On 10 November the last official gasp of the campaign occurred as the 1st Canadian Division attacked again along the ridge.

On the evening of the 9th of November, the duckboards were crowded with files of infantry moving up, poor fellows, to the last assault, in no cheerful mood, yet grimly resolved to do their best even amid the appalling conditions with everything against them. Early in the morning, every gun in the Salient woke to concerted action for the last barrage.[60]

Gunner Wilfred Brenton Kerr, 67th Battery, Canadian Field Artillery

The Canadians won around 500 more yards of awful shell-blasted ground. Strangely, at this late stage in the offensive, the British II Corps returned to the fray, attacking to support the Canadians' left flank. The 1st Division had been originally earmarked for the combined assault landing on the Belgian coast that should have followed the triumphant break-out from the Salient in August. Now it was participating in the death throes of an entirely different campaign. The men went over the top at 06.05 in driving rain. No words could convey the futility and hopelessness of their task. Perhaps more effectively the commanding officer of the designated reserve battalion described this ineffable experience in the prosaically dull language of a situation report.

> On the right, the South Wales Borderers never reached their objectives; on the left, the Munsters got to theirs but were unable to hold it. The German barrage was very severe and from 09.30 until dark the shellfire was intense. This was partly accounted for by the fact that our counter-battery artillery was unable to move up within range owing to the state of the ground.[61]
>
> Lieutenant Colonel A. W. Pagan, 1st Battalion, Gloucestershire Regiment

Following the familiar pattern the attack failed, and indeed at one point the British front line was at risk from a German counter-attack. The infantry knew it was hopeless; the artillery had long suspected that it was. Nothing more could be done, the fighting would go on all winter but the offensive was officially over at last. Their duty done, the Canadian Corps began to move out on 12 November.

> And so we left the Salient, that Valley of the Shadow of Death. We stayed one night at the wagon lines in the shattered city; next morning we packed our belongings and equipment on the wagons; and about nine o'clock, in a pale sunlight, with the roar of the guns behind us, we turned our backs on Ypres and moved down the great road toward Poperinghe, to relief and security. And all the ways to the south were filled with men wearing the maple leaf.[62]
>
> Gunner Wilfred Brenton Kerr, 67th Battery, Canadian Field Artillery

For four months the finest fighting units of the British Empire had been shovelled into the raging inferno of the Third Battle of Ypres. The conflagration had consumed tens of thousands of lives and brought tragedy and suffering to countless 'survivors'. The offensive was over but the questions multiplied which have grown ever louder as the years passed. What was it all for? What, if anything, had been achieved? Who was to blame for its failure?

> The losses of the Canadian Corps at Passchendaele were in the neighbourhood of 16,500 men; all these in exchange for a few wretched heaps of bricks on a small rise in water-soaked Flanders. For some time the Corps was too stupefied to think; but gradually, in the months that followed, as the Corps regained its strength and reviewed in detail the action and the price, questions arose, doubts were implied which grew stronger with every passing week . . . Had we not been doing precisely the same as the Germans had done at Verdun, sending our best and

bravest against a well-prepared enemy, who knew for weeks in advance where we were going to attack and could almost guess the date? Was this not mass slaughter?[63]

Gunner Wilfred Brenton Kerr, 67th Battery, Canadian Field Artillery

---

ONE THING was certain, the Germans certainly knew they had been in a fight at Ypres and Ludendorff's retrospective conclusions fully supported the strategic basis claimed for the battle of attrition and even for the idea that the Germans had been pushed some considerable way towards their collective breaking point.

On the 26th and 30th October and 6th and 10th November the fighting was again of the severest description. The enemy charged like a wild bull against the iron wall which kept him from our submarine bases. He threw his weight against Houthulst Forest, Poelcappelle, Passchendaele, Becelaere, Gheluvelt and Zandvoorde. He dented it in many places, and it seemed as if he must knock it down. But it held, although a faint tremor ran through its foundations. The impressions I continuously received were very terrible. In a tactical sense, everything possible had been done. The advanced zone was good. The effectiveness of our artillery had considerably improved. Behind almost every division in the front line there was another in support; and we still had reserves in the third line. We knew that the enemy suffered heavily. But we also knew he was amazingly strong and, what was equally important, had an extraordinarily stubborn will. Lloyd George wanted victory. He held England in his hand. Only one thing we did not know; how long the battle would continue. The enemy must tire some time.[64]

General Erich Ludendorff, German GHQ

It is richly ironic that Lloyd George received the credit from Ludendorff for Haig's grim sense of purpose and the attritional mayhem that he had generated in Flanders. Right to the end the British Government continued to wring its hands at the dreadful state of affairs in the Ypres Salient, whilst actually doing very little of any consequence to secure change. They blustered at the incompetence and lack of perspicacity of others, particularly Haig and Robertson, but signally failed to provide a coherent strategic alternative themselves. Instead they fluttered like a butterfly from one ill-conceived scheme to another. Lloyd George's favoured alternatives were all either strategically flawed or desperate leaps into the dark. The proposed Italian offensive was always of questionable value and the Italians themselves wisely refused to accept the poisoned chalice of their projected role. The Italian generals doubted their ability to deliver success against an Austrian Army reinforced by German troops released by a decline in Allied pressure on the Western Front, and events at Caporetto proved they were right. The benighted Balkans offered little promise other than the dismal prospect of enlarging what many already saw as a giant 'internment camp' of Allied troops at Salonika. Further investment of resources in the Palestinian and Mesopotamian theatres of war was undermined by the fact that ultimately, there, the British were fighting the wrong enemy. The decaying Turkish Empire had been a long-term strategic bulwark for the British Empire against the Near East ambitions of France, Germany and Russia. Alliances are temporary but strategic imperatives are permanent, and although necessity forced Britain into war with the Turks the destruction of Turkey was not necessarily in the longer-term interests of the British Empire.

It is tempting to view the overall position adopted by David Lloyd George with a touch of scorn. There he was, the seemingly powerless Prime Minister of Great Britain, relentlessly bullied in his Cabinet playground by his cruel professional military advisers and his shifty Cabinet colleagues. But we should avoid this temptation to criticize his failure to take resolute steps to stop the offensive. He could have taken action, but in the end we must recognize the fact that, despite his own personal convictions, he felt unable to take the political risk of enforcing his will on his generals, his Cabinet and the British people. As a political operator of consummate skill Lloyd George, like his nemesis Haig, was at the peak of his profession. In all fairness, just as we accept that Haig was unable to impose his will on events, for reasons that were often outside his control, so we must exercise that same latitude for Lloyd George. As head of a coalition government he did not possess the bedrock of support on which he could rely from either political party or outside in the country at large. He could have taken a gamble, but he judged that the risks were too great and that his government would fall, thus immeasurably damaging the British war effort through a prolonged period of political uncertainty at the crucial stage of the war. He was probably right.

And what of Field Marshal Sir Douglas Haig himself? What are we to make of his Flanders offensive? Firstly, in the fundamental position he adopted he was unequivocally wrong. The Germans were not at the end of their tether and they did not break as he had predicted in 1917. That is not to say they were not threatened, stretched and deeply worried by the series of smashing blows that Haig launched at Ypres. But they did not collapse, their front was not broken and, despite all the successes and half-successes mixed in with the failures, Haig's armies had only reached as far by the middle of November as Gough's ludicrously optimistic 'Red Line' had planned for the first day. Meanwhile, behind the Germans' front their submarine bases continued to ply their deadly trade. Haig had chosen to believe wholeheartedly the Head of his Intelligence Section, Brigadier General John Charteris, rather than question his reports more deeply in the light of other less sanguine sources, and this confidence in Charteris proved misplaced. It was undoubtedly true that Imperial Germany was struggling to cope with the pressure of global war. There was evidence of declining morale in both its army and its navy, political agitation was rife at home and the economy was under a horrendous strain from the ruinous financial cost of the war coupled with the sapping effects of the unrelenting Allied naval blockade. But a powerful, highly motivated European nation state has enormous powers of resistance unless its armies are actually defeated in the field and in 1917 Germany's military strength remained extremely formidable. The problems were piling up, but they were not yet terminal; Germany was staggering, but not yet on the ropes.

Did Haig's Flanders offensive significantly weaken the military strength of Germany? The hammer blows undoubtedly caused severe damage, but quantifying the effects is much more difficult and the comparative analysis of casualty figures is an unrewarding minefield. In all it would seem that about 200,000 German soldiers were killed, wounded or taken prisoner during the Messines and Ypres operations. By any standards, for a single nation this was a crushing blow. Unfortunately, in achieving this, the British Empire itself suffered some 275,000 casualties and the French in the region of 8,500. Although the Allies, bolstered by the entry of the United States into the war, had greater long-term reserves of manpower than the Germans the impact of such heavy losses was severe. A further complication was that the whole situation was materially changed as the bulk of the German divisions released from their service on the Eastern Front following on the final collapse of Russia moved inexorably to reinforce the Western Front, arriving there before the slowly mobilizing Americans. In consequence, in the short term, the German position on the Western Front was probably marginally strengthened by the end of 1917. Yet the prospects for the Allies in 1918 would surely have been far poorer if Haig and the BEF had not so relentlessly attacked and harried the Germans at Ypres in 1917.

Haig's offensive did also successfully prevent the Germans from discovering or exploiting the mutinous weakness of the French Army following the disaster of the Nivelle offensive. It has been claimed by his critics that, after the war, Haig exaggerated his concerns over the state of the French Army to explain his more controversial decisions. The question is debatable, but either way it is undoubtedly true that he *was* aware of the seriousness of the French situation, and if he did subsequently exaggerate the urgency of his concern, it was nevertheless a very real concern. The idea that Haig was not genuinely influenced by the apparent imminent collapse of the French Army, the hitherto senior partner on the Western Front, is in itself unrealistic.

After the Third Battle of Ypres was over, Haig's own front-line divisions remained criminally under-strength on the Western Front. The morale of the British Army had been sorely tested and the nature of their morale had changed after their trials on the Somme and at Ypres.

> Perhaps you would like to know something of the spirit of the men out here now. Well, the truth is (and as I said before I'd be shot if anyone of importance collared this missive) every man Jack is fed up almost past bearing, and not a single one has an ounce of what we call patriotism left in him. No-one cares a rap whether Germany has Alsace, Belgium or France too for that matter. All that every man desires now is to get done with it and go home. . . . I may add that I too have lost pretty nearly all the patriotism that I had left, it's just that thought of you all over there, you who love me and trust me to do my share in the job that is necessary for your safety and freedom. It's just that that keeps me going and enables me to 'stick it'. . . . Aye girlie, it's ghastly, but thank God for those dear ones at home who love true and trust absolutely in the strength, the courage and the fidelity of those who are far away midst danger and death. These are my mainstays, and thoughts of them always come to stay me and buck me up when I feel like chucking it up and letting things slide. God bless you darling, and all those I love

and who love me, for without their love and trust I would faint and fall. But don't worry dear heart o' mine, for I shall carry on to the end be it bitter or sweet, with my loved ones ever my first thought and care, my guide, inspiration and spur.[65]

Corporal Laurie Rowlands, 15th Battalion, Durham Light Infantry

The degree of psychological exhaustion and consequent demoralization varied considerably from soldier to soldier, and it is worth noting that despite the sentiments expressed by Corporal Rowlands in February 1918, later that year he was awarded the Military Medal for gallantry in action. Although riven with a cynical fatalism and utterly without illusions as to their personal motivations, the determination of the men of the BEF to persist alongside their comrades was to endure despite all the horrors of Passchendaele.

The simmering distrust that had festered between Haig and Lloyd George throughout 1917 meant that Haig was effectively starved of reinforcements to rebuild his forces in early 1918. This was to have near disastrous consequences when the Germans launched the first of their last great series of offensives on 21 March 1918. This was the real climax of the war. It was then that the real tragedy of the last month of fighting on the Passchendaele Ridge was cruelly exposed. Plumer, who in November 1917 had briefly been sent to Italy to take command of the British forces there, had returned with his chief of staff, Charles Harington, to his old stamping ground in command of the Second Army in the Ypres area. Once the German March offensive had broken through Gough's Fifth Army in the Somme area, the situation became desperate and Haig appealed to Plumer for any divisions he could spare. Harington left a rather emotional account of their conference.

We knew what terrible responsibility was resting on Haig and what he must be feeling as we entered his room. He greeted us exactly as if nothing had happened. He was just calm, cheerful and courageous. I marvelled as he took us over to his big map and unfolded to us the latest situation. It was a heartrending story as one thought of our poor divisions fighting for their lives to stem the tide of overwhelming numbers of Germans. He told us the story in as calm and clear a manner as if he had been describing the situation at a war game. When he finished he said, 'Well, Plumer, what can you and your Second Army do for me?' I was now to witness to a scene between two great men in a crisis. First of

> all my Chief, with 14 divisions holding 33 miles of front including the Passchendaele Salient, without a moment's hesitation said, 'I'll give you eight divisions at once.' Haig then said, 'That means you must give up Passchendaele.' 'Not I!' answered the stout-hearted Commander of the Second Army in a tone I shall never forget.[66]
>
> Major General Charles Harington, Headquarters, Second Army

As promised, Plumer sent eight divisions straight away. In the end, of his fourteen divisions he sent all but two, replacing them at Ypres with the battle-weary divisions from the Third and Fifth Armies that had borne the brunt of the German attack.

On 9 April the second phase of the German offensive opened with an attack against the First Army which held the line immediately to the south of the Second Army in the Lys valley opposite Armentières. Once again the Germans broke through and advanced rapidly and the right flank of the Second Army became inexorably drawn into the battle. With his army now consisting mainly of tired and depleted divisions, and with no prospect of reserves, it was a desperate period for Plumer and Harington. The Messines Ridge and Kemmel Hill both fell as the Germans moved north to threaten directly all communications to the ridiculously exposed Passchendaele Salient.

> The hardest nut came over Passchendaele. By every form of combinations and permutations we tried to hold on to Passchendaele. We felt if we once brought in our fist the Salient would be over-run and our beloved Ypres, the defence of which had been the pride of the Second Army through all those years, would go. The prospect was too tragic. We had lost our Messines Ridge. Was our immortal Ypres to go? Think of the effect on the Germans with their eyes on the Channel Ports if they got Ypres. I think now of a conference in my room. I think of the stout and gallant troops holding on to Passchendaele at the risk of being cut off.[67]
>
> Major General Charles Harington, Headquarters, Second Army

The Passchendaele Ridge, far from being a tactical necessity, had become a veritable noose around the neck of the troops that occupied it.

> The Army Commander was with me standing at my desk examining the map. I knew what he was feeling about Passchendaele. We both knew that the limit had been reached. We should have to come out. The risk was too great. No more help could come from anywhere. Meteren was in

flames. Hazebrouck was threatened. At last I summoned up courage to say what I had feared for days. 'I think, Sir, you will have to come out of Passchendaele.' The effect was magic. My old Chief, always like a father to me, made one last bid. He turned on me and showed the most wonderful example of his bulldog tenacity that I have ever seen. I can hear it now – 'I won't!' It was indeed a plucky effort. The next moment I felt, and I have often felt it since, his hand on my shoulder – 'You are right, issue the orders.' He knew it all the time. He knew it was coming. We both did. We did not talk about it. He went off to his room.[68]

Major General Charles Harington, Headquarters, Second Army

The mental anguish of giving up without a fight the battered ridge that had cost so many lives can only be imagined. Yet the ever professional Plumer and Harington were not downcast for long and threw their efforts into ensuring that the next line of defence under the battered ramparts of Ypres itself did not fall. And in this they were successful. Although the Germans nearly broke through, they ultimately failed.

The morale of the BEF had been tested in the fiercest of battles and, although it had wavered, it had not been found wanting. Once the German effort had been spent, the time was right for the tide to turn again. Following the dramatic seizure of the initiative at the Battle of Amiens on 8 August, the British and Imperial troops at all levels from the highest commanders to the front-line soldiers were able to draw upon a series of new tactical skills and patterns, many of which had first been tried out and successfully developed in 1917: the capture and solid consolidation of limited objectives ('bite and hold'); the deployment of sophisticated, closely supporting artillery bombardments; the integration of new arms including tanks and aircraft with the infantry assaults. Combined, these factors meant that by the summer of 1918 the BEF had evolved into the most effective fighting force on the Western Front and, through a series of successive battles over the last hundred days of the war, this enabled them to lead the way to victory by comprehensively defeating the German army in the field. The evolution of this development can be traced directly back through the offensive in Flanders at the end of the previous year. Reeling from the hammer blows of the Allied offensives launched between August and November, severely weakened by the toll of their own last-gasp offensives earlier in the year and facing ever worsening political and economic internal strains of war, Imperial Germany finally collapsed and, amidst political turmoil, sued for an armistice which was signed on 11 November.

The Flanders offensive, Third Ypres, Passchendaele, whatever we choose to call it, was a heart-rending tragedy. Hundreds of thousands of men had their lives terminated or ruined for the sake of a few square miles of battered mud. Yet this is not to say that Haig, his subordinate generals and their staff officers were either stupid or donkeys. They had closely argued reasons, many of which were at least partially satisfied, for most of the actions they took, and a considerable number of their attacks can be seen by the grim standards of the Western Front as British 'victories'. But overall, although their reasoning was valid, they can now be seen to be wrong. Like some tottering Hobbsian treatise the whole Flanders offensive was based on a faulty premise – namely that Germany would soon collapse in 1917. But this was in fact simply over-optimistic. The last reasonable hopes of British strategic gains raised by the capture of Broodseinde on 4 October were crushed by the dreadful failure of the Battle of Poelcappelle on 12 October. At that point the offensive should have been suspended. It was not, and thousands of fathers, husbands and sweethearts died in the attacks that followed. They were needless sacrifices for useless ground. Sacrificial ground.

EPILOGUE

Some things happened in France I can only remember in part, there were weeks I can't remember anything about, but the time spent on Passchendaele Ridge was only two days beginning with the bombardment at dawn on July 31st, yet what happened in those two days has seemed to me to outweigh all the rest of the four years.[1]

Private Alfred Warsop, 1st Battalion, Sherwood Foresters

There is little wonder that Ypres could never be forgotten by those who served there. The Stygian nature of the battlefield across which thousands passed on their way to oblivion, and the claustrophobic intensity of the fighting concentrated into such a small area of ground that had been saturated in recent times by a deluge of unbridled slaughter, meant that the scars of Passchendaele were slashed across the psyche of those lucky enough to survive its horrors. Cumulatively, all they had endured, all they had seen, all the terrible things they had done to survive were just too awful to be tucked away neatly in the subconscious on the soldiers' return to civilian life. Like a never-ending loop of film, their traumatic experiences replayed endlessly for the rest of their lives as they tried to make some sense of it all. They had peered through the torn curtain that separates civilized society from the dark, bestial horrors of which man is capable.

> Perhaps no normal infantryman who had been through a 1917 Passchendaele attack would ever be quite the same again. This was the battlefield of all battlefields which exposed the ultimate degradation of fighting and man's inhumanity to man.[2]
>
> Private W. H. A. Groom, 1/5th Battalion, London Regiment (London Rifle Brigade)

From the perspective of the men in the shell holes, the sheer futility of the later attacks made them seethe with deep and anguished resentment at those they considered responsible for their predicament.

> The soldier's general opinion of this battle was extremely bitter. The point at issue was that no infantryman minded one bit being shot about or doing his job on terra firma – somewhere where he could stand to fight. But here we were so hopelessly placed that there was no thought whatsoever of getting to any final objective. So there was this bitter feeling that did prevail among quite a lot of our infantrymen when they saw their lads, not wounded, not wounded but drowned in this filthy mud.[3]
>
> Private Cyril Lee, BEF (Unit not known)

Men struggled to define exactly what had happened to them – why they had been forced to behave as they had; where they had found the strength to keep going – and the bewilderment often lasted for the rest of their lives. Seventy years later, one young artillery officer was still regularly being disturbed by the echoes of the battle.

> Sometimes I don't think about it for months on end, and then I come back and dream about it all. How really extraordinary it was. I still feel I can't quite get it out of my system. I can't sleep sometimes. I just think about it. It was a combination of the awful ground and the shell holes and people being drowned, all trying to struggle towards taking this small village. Horrid.[4]
>
> Second Lieutenant Stephen Williamson, Royal Garrison Artillery

As might be expected, every individual on looking deep inside himself, found different answers that largely depended on his own character, views and outlook. Some took pride just in having been part of it all.

> Though nobody likes it we are making history – not so good as writing an opera, a book or a play, or painting a picture, or making a statue but still if you have the vitality most interesting.[5]
>
> Captain Charles Dudley Ward, 1st Battalion, Welsh Guards

Some seem to have felt that they had been tricked into a situation where the only way to survive was to conform.

> Well then, you will ask, why did men apparently unhesitatingly go forward in an attack and capture strongpoints sometimes with reckless bravery? The answer is simple – I must repeat that there is no alternative to the firing squad but to go forward and you do your damnedest to kill the men who are trying to kill you. If you do not, you just die. In all this fighting when trenches and strongpoints are captured, you are not a hero – you are obeying not man's instinct to kill, but man's instinct to live by killing

> the man who would kill you. Those who believe in the inevitability of war will always emphasise that man has an inherent killer instinct, that it is human nature and little can be done about it. Another 'Old Lie', a perfidious old lie. Man is not born a killer, it is the society in which he grows up which makes him one and that society must continually reiterate the lie to justify the act of killing in war and the profitable manufacture of the weapons to do that killing. I never wanted to kill anyone, but I did . . .[6]
>
> Private W. H. A. Groom, 1/5th Battalion, London Regiment (London Rifle Brigade)

Many were motivated not through the fear of being killed but of letting others down. For them the desperate need to conform was linked more closely to their own self-respect and the desire to be a good, reliable member of their peer group of friends and comrades. These men recognized that they were all equally at risk and faced the hell of war together.

> How did they endure it, how did they get through it? The answer must be partly the old one – the fear of fear. The fear of being found afraid. I think that would run a certain distance. Another very great one is belief in human beings, your colleague, that doesn't necessarily mean he's below or above you in rank – but the one you're with. Any one day you say, 'My job is to be at the cross-roads at such and such a time with the bread or whatever you're carrying and "Old So and So" will be there, he'll be expecting it and there's going to be no letting him down.' That goes a good long way. Then we had the idea of interest in what would come out of this extraordinary titanic fatal performance – who would really win the gloves.[7]
>
> Lieutenant Edmund Blunden, 11th Battalion, Sussex Regiment

Together they endured, clinging to each other and a slightly sentimental vision of home. But most were no longer fooled by the worn-out notions of patriotism, King and Country. The things they had experienced had drained them of such high-flown, abstract concepts and as bitter men they gained strength from an ironic, collective debunking of the nation's symbols and propagandists.

> It was in song – in the billet and on the line of march – that Tommy broke away from the horrors of war. Songs like, 'There's a long, long trail a-winding', that expressed his yearning for home and loved ones. Songs with humour and satire that made light of his burden and the loss of comrades. They picked on Horatio Bottomley whose paper 'John Bull' claimed to have all the answers for victory and sang:

'We always keep our copies by
And that is why we prophesy
The war was over last July
It said so in "John Bull".'

I retain the memory of dirty, tired men, wearing steel helmets, with ground sheets across their shoulders, plodding through the mud and rain of Flanders but singing cheerfully, 'It's always blooming well raining!'[8]

Quartermaster Sergeant Frederick Hunt, 203rd Machine Gun Company, Machine Gun Corps

There was no getting away from the war. It was there and so were the soldiers. Although they might mournfully sing 'We're here because we're here because we're here . . .' to cover up their disappointment, in the end there was no escape from the fact that they were just small cogs in a faceless machine, powerless to affect the course of their own destiny. The stresses, strains, demands and consequences of the war simply flowed over them like the incessant deluge and all they could do was try to deal with them. Consequently many eventually became so inured to the horrors of war that they learned to suppress their innermost feelings, compressing and distorting their pain with the risk of becoming emotionally unstable.

Arms and legs flew into the air like lumps of mud. If anyone had told us before the war that we should witness such slaughter and loss of life and still have kept our sanity I would have told them that they were talking a load of 'bullshit'. Almost every kind of feeling dried up inside of us.[9]

Driver Rowland Luther, 92nd Brigade, Royal Field Artillery

In such a highly pressurized environment, with so many men living on the very edge of their self-control, perhaps strangely their fears do not seem to have found release in direct hatred for those who might have been seen as their natural enemy – the German soldiers who faced them across No Man's Land. Writing in his journal when back in Britain on leave, one padre sadly noticed the gulf between soldier and civilian in this respect.

There is far less hatred of Germany in the front line than at home I think. Here I suppose he is a sort of bogey (such as Boney was in the Napoleonic Wars) who is feared and dreaded – hated because unseen. Out there, we see such a lot of him that we have not that feeling. He is really not too bad and a great fighter and Methodist.[10]

Reverend Maurice Murray, 12th & 13th Battalions, Royal Sussex Regiment

Fellow feeling and common experience bound the two sides together in the line but drove a wedge between the home and fighting fronts. This in turn deepened the soldiers' sense of isolation from the familiar, comfortable world they were fighting to protect.

The misery of the campaign brought a natural increase in cynical and fatalistic feelings. In such an atmosphere the former certainties of organized religion became extremely vulnerable to revaluation. As the inherent contradictions and hypocrisies of religion were clearly exposed by their personal experiences, men began to question their faith.

> The German prayer book found in the pillbox at Poelcappelle – on the cover, 'Mit Jesus in der Feld', and inside a coloured picture of Christ looking with pity on a dead German soldier. The same picture as in our own Field Prayer Book, 'With Jesus in the Field'. The only appreciable difference being in the uniform of the dead soldier – German in one, khaki in the other – and the feeling experienced on seeing that picture compared with one of our own, that the whole War was a horrible mistake.[11]
>
> Signaller Sydney Fuller, 8th Battalion, Suffolk Regiment

Many had previously accepted the given truths of religion without demur but now, faced by so many dreadful things that seemed to conflict with all they had been taught, they became aware of a new scepticism awakening within them. After his dreadful experiences during an attack Groom realised he had lost his religious faith.

> Where, oh where, was God in this earth covered ossuary, this mud swamp receptacle for the bones of the dead? It was I suppose for me the moment of truth. I thought of the patriotic national churches all praying for victory. How could God choose? We Christian killers killing Christians . . . I had doubts before but now I saw clearly, I think for the first time, that the Church's teaching of personal salvation with all the emphasis on sin, forgiveness, confession, absolution was a selfish creed. If I survived, I should have to find a more self-less religion than that of the Church . . . Now on this day, with this traumatic experience, my belief in a Church which condoned killing faded away. I would not again voluntarily attend or take part in the communion or other church services and rightly or wrongly that was that.[12]
>
> Private W. H. A. Groom, 1/5th Battalion, London Regiment (London Rifle Brigade)

Assailed by many of the same sights and conditions as the ordinary soldiers, even the chaplains had to dig deep to find consolation and an explanation as to why their God had allowed the war.

> Although of man's making, much good has and will come out of the war. Sacrifice, love, opportunities for women, love of home after the war, usefulness and handiness in the home, love of land and agriculture, self denial especially after the war to pay for it all and lastly immunity from future warfare.[13]
>
> Reverend Maurice Murray, 12th & 13th Battalions, Royal Sussex Regiment

However sincerely Murray believed this to be so, it seems hard to accept that many of his men would have agreed with him. They had their own reasons for continuing and were forced to find ways of assimilating their experiences to preserve their own sanity. They may have come to accept the war as an evil necessity, and some may have been glad not to have missed it, but few would have regarded it as a positive, beneficial experience.

After the war society was not yet ready or equipped to deal with the vast numbers of survivors suffering from shell shock and other serious psychological disorders. Post-traumatic stress counselling was still many years away and instead most problems of this nature were either ignored or locked away. In a country whose economy slowly spiralled down into a severe depression, those wounded in body as well as in mind found that they were expected to survive with little help for their disabilities except a pittance of a pension which in many cases was bought off with an inadequate lump sum after less than a decade. Little special provision could be made, as they were not special. There were literally hundreds of thousands of men suffering from their wounds, either physical or psychological, or the lingering effects of mustard gas. Soldiers returned to their families with the impact of their experiences seared into their bodies and brains. Like corpses floating back to the surface from the depths of shell holes, in civilian life the terrors and traumas they had tried to suppress gradually returned to the surface and found release in dreadful nightmares that rendered sleep a torment, changed patterns of behaviour and broke up previously happy families.

As ever, different individuals responded in different ways and many claim to have overcome the effects almost immediately. But there was a sliding scale of despair at the bottom of which lay the ultimate release of suicide. Man is, on the whole, a resilient species and for the majority time did heal. Those who survived managed, for the most part, eventually to come to terms with it all. That is not to say, of course, that they emerged unmarked by the experience; merely that it became a central part of who and what they were. Later in life they began to take pride in being a 'Passchendaele veteran'. But time is a two-edged sword and they found that it was not only the sharpness of their pain that had faded.

> I was proud that I had been one who had endured its terrors. In those days I did not guess that there would come a time during my own lifetime when folk no longer gave a tinker's damn whether one had been at Third Ypres or not. In fact, the vast majority of the people of Britain as I write these words have never even heard of Third Ypres and the Passchendaele Ridge.[14]
>
> Lieutenant R. G. Dixon, 14th Battery, Royal Garrison Artillery

To the blighted generation who lived through the First World War and desperately wanted to believe that the horrors they had experienced at least represented the nadir of human civilization, the words 'Ypres' and 'Passchendaele' conjured up a special horror.

> I suppose no name in history has ever had so dreadful a significance for so many human beings as the name of Ypres. It was not so much that you were more likely to be killed there than anywhere else – and from first to last Ypres gathered in a harvest of more than half a million casualties – as that it reduced life to the lowest terms of misery and hopelessness . . . Every yard of that featureless slab of landscape held the menace of death. If you were not there the war films will have told you what it was like; if you were there the war films will make you laugh. For those few miles of ground north and south of the terrible road that runs from Ypres to Menin bear lasting witness to the indestructible tenacity of the human spirit. After the nightmare of Passchendaele there is no conceivable cataclysm of war or nature which civilised man might not endure.[15]
>
> A. J. Cummings

Cummings was writing in 1928 to commemorate the recent opening, by the promoted and ennobled Field Marshal Lord Plumer, of the Menin Gate Memorial to the soldiers lost for ever in the few square miles of the Ypres battlefield. Yet even these 58,896 names did not include the majority of those lost during the long struggle of the BEF to climb the Passchendaele Ridge. A further 34,957 names, recording those lost without trace in the Salient from 16 August 1917 to the end of the war, were engraved on a second memorial that embraces the massive Tyne Cot Cemetery. Containing a further 11,908 individually named graves and encompassing under its Great Cross one of the original German concrete pillboxes, Tyne Cot stands on the western edge of the Passchendaele Ridge not far from the village itself. From there today a beautifully clear vista unfolds back across the Steenbeek Valley to the ramparts of rebuilt Ypres. The proximity of the city, which feels almost within reach, underlines the agony and frustration of what took place there. The scars of the battle have largely faded. The villages have been rebuilt and, as if in a symbolic attempt to project a new identity distinct from that erased by the war, they are now known by their Flemish names: St Juliaan, Langemark, Poelkapelle, even Passendale itself. The farmers have ploughed their myriad furrows across the shell-torn but still fertile land. As it did for the soldiers, time has healed the wounds of the earth as well.

As the whole process of reconstruction was just beginning, the League of Nations offered parents all over the world a glimmer of hope that maybe, perhaps, there would be no more wars and that their sons might never have to risk their lives again in mortal combat. But it was not to be. The Menin Gate Memorial had barely been unveiled and the Salient returned to a semblance of normality before the drums of war began to beat once more. At first the sound was so soft that people, tired and still grieving for those so recently slain, tried to pretend they could not hear it. But throughout the 1930s it became more insistent until at last it could be ignored no longer. Fuelled by the vile bigotry of Nazi ideology and characterized by a stultifying brutality, the Second World War broke out and, defying the agonized pleas of those who had emerged traumatized from the previous one, proceeded to plumb new depths of indiscriminate slaughter. Global casualties, particularly in Germany and the Soviet Union, far exceeded those suffered between 1914 and 1918 and the boundaries of war were eliminated completely to encompass civilians of all ages, races and creeds. The final obscenity of genocide, epitomized by the vast, industrial killing factory of the Auschwitz concentration camp, meant that the spirit of human endurance was tested to even greater limits than before. But for the British and Commonwealth soldiers, despite the many terrible experiences they suffered in North Africa, Italy, north-west Europe and the Far East, the trials of Passchendaele remained a benchmark of unsurpassed horror.

NOTES TO THE TEXT

PRELUDE

1 A. J. Cummings, 'Ypres, The Tragic Story of the Salient', *Daily News*, 23/7/1928

I GESTATION

1 IWM DOCS H. W. Yoxall, letter, 3/8/1917

2 IWM DOCS H. M. Dillon, typescript diary, pp.34–6, 24 October 1914

3 D. Haig, quoted in J. Terraine, *Douglas Haig: The Educated Soldier* (London: Hutchinson, 1963), p.115

4 IWM DOCS J. D. Keddie, letter, 4/5/1917

5 J. E. Edmonds, quoted in J. Charteris, *Field Marshal Earl Haig* (London: Cassell, 1929), p.13

6 E. Ludendorff, *My War Memories* (London: Hutchinson, 1919), Vol. I, p.307

7 D. Lloyd George, *War Memoirs of David Lloyd George*, Vol. I (London: Odhams Press Ltd, 1938), pp.828–29

8 D. Haig, diary, 1/5/1917, quoted in R. Blake, *The Private Papers of Douglas Haig, 1914–1919* (London: Eyre & Spottiswoode, 1952), p.223

9 D. Haig, diary, 4/5/1917, quoted in R. Blake, *The Private Papers of Douglas Haig, 1914–1919* (London: Eyre & Spottiswoode, 1952), p.228

10 D. Haig, quoted in J. E. Edmonds, *Military Operations: France and Belgium 1917*, Vol II (London: HMSO, 1948), p.24

11 D. Haig, quoted in J. E. Edmonds, *Military Operations: France and Belgium 1917*, Vol II (London: HMSO, 1948), p.27

2 MESSINES

[1] IWM DOCS G. Stewart, manuscript account, pp.54–5

[2] IWM DOCS R. Macleod, 'An artillery officer in the First World War' (typescript diary), 13/7/1917

[3] J. Charteris, *At GHQ* (London: Cassell, 1931), pp.227–8

[4] E. Ludendorff, *My War Memories* (London: Hutchinson, 1919), Vol. I, p.273

[5] E. Ludendorff, *My War Memories* (London: Hutchinson, 1919), Vol. I, pp.386–7

[6] IWM SOUND G. Clayton, AC 10112

[7] IWM DOCS O. H. Woodward, 'The War Story of Oliver Holmes Woodward' typescript memoir, pp.81–2

[8] IWM SOUND B. Frayling, AC 4105

[9] IWM SOUND B. Frayling, AC 4105

[10] IWM SOUND Roll, AC 4215

[11] IWM DOCS O. H. Woodward, 'The War Story of Oliver Holmes Woodward' typescript memoir, pp.96–7

[12] IWM SOUND Roll, AC 4215

[13] IWM DOCS O. H. Woodward, 'The War Story of Oliver Holmes Woodward' typescript memoir, p.97

[14] IWM SOUND Roll, AC 4215

[15] O. H. Woodward, 'The War Story of Oliver Holmes Woodward' typescript memoir, p.97

[16] IWM SOUND B. Frayling, AC 4105

[17] R. Hamilton, *The War Diary of the Master of Belhaven, 1914–1918* (Barnsley: Wharncliffe, 1990), pp.303–4

[18] N. Fraser-Tytler, *With Lancashire Lads and Field Guns in France, 1915–1918* (Manchester: John Heywood Ltd, 1922), p.199

[19] IWM SOUND Roll, AC 4215

[20] IWM SOUND A. Hemsley, AC 9927

[21] IWM SOUND F. W. S. Jourdain composite quotes from SR 11214, Reel 4 & 5 plus material from 'A Subaltern's War', *The Ranger*, 7/1968 p. 34.

[22] IWM SOUND F. Collins, AC 8229

[23] IWM SOUND F. W. S. Jourdain composite quotes from SR 11214, Reel 4 & 5 plus material from 'A Subaltern's War', *The Ranger*, 7/1968 p. 34.

[24] N. Fraser-Tytler, *With Lancashire Lads and Field Guns in France, 1915–1918* (Manchester: John Heywood Ltd, 1922), p.199

[25] IWM SOUND J. Crow, AC 9118

3 PLANS AND PREPARATIONS

1 Charteris, quoted in J. E. Edmonds, *Military Operations: France and Belgium 1917*, Vol. II (London: HMSO, 1948), p.426

2 Charteris, quoted in J. E. Edmonds, *Military Operations: France and Belgium 1917*, Vol. II (London: HMSO, 1948), p.97

3 D. Haig, quoted in J. E. Edmonds, *Military Operations: France and Belgium 1917*, Vol II (London: HMSO, 1948), p.425

4 D. Haig, quoted in J. E. Edmonds, *Military Operations: France and Belgium 1917*, Vol II (London: HMSO, 1948), p.425

5 D. Haig, quoted in J. E. Edmonds, *Military Operations: France and Belgium 1917*, Vol II, (London: HMSO, 1948), p.426

6 Madonogh, quoted in J. E. Edmonds, *Military Operations: France and Belgium, 1917*, Vol. II (London: HMSO), 1948), p.98

7 W. Robertson, quoted in J. E. Edmonds, *Military Operations: France and Belgium 1917*, Vol II (London: HMSO, 1948), p.98

8 D. Lloyd George, *War Memoirs of David Lloyd George*, Vol. II (London: Odhams Press Ltd, 1938), p.1280

9 D. Lloyd George, *War Memoirs of David Lloyd George*, Vol II (London: Odhams Press Ltd, 1938), p.1282

10 D. Lloyd George, *War Memoirs of David Lloyd George*, Vol II (London: Odhams Press Ltd, 1938), p.1283

11 J. Jellicoe, *The Submarine Peril* (London: Cassell, ND), p118

12 D. Haig, diary, 20/6/1917, quoted in R. Blake, *The Private Papers of Douglas Haig, 1914–1919* (London: Eyre & Spottiswoode, 1932), pp.240–41

13 IWM DOCS I. Maxse papers, Davidson memorandum, file 35/2

14 IWM DOCS I. Maxse papers, Davidson memorandum, file 35/2

15 IWM DOCS I Maxse papers, Davidson memorandum, file 35/2

16 IWM DOCS I. Maxse papers, H. Gough memorandum, file 35/2

17 H. Gough, quoted in J. E. Edmonds, *Military Operations France and Belgium 1917*, Vol. II (London: HMSO , 1948), p.440

18 H. Gough, *The Fifth Army* (Hodder & Stoughton, 1931), p.194

19 H. Gough, *The Fifth Army* (Hodder & Stoughton, 1931), p.210

20 IWM DOCS M.W. Murray, transcript diary, p.94

21 M. Haldane, *A History of the Fourth Battalion The Seaforth Highlanders* (London: Witherby, 1927) p.218

22 IWM DOCS T. C. Owtram, typescript memoir, p.25

23 IWM DOCS M.W. Murray, transcript diary, p.87

24 IWM DOCS S. T. Fuller, diary, 30/3/1917

25 IWM SOUND W. Grover, AC 10441

26 IWM SOUND M. Dillon, AC 9752

27 IWM SOUND F. Collins, AC 8229

28 H. Gordon, *The Unreturning Army* (London: J. M. Dent & Sons, 1967), p.54

29 H .Gordon, *The Unreturning Army* (London: J. M. Dent & Sons, 1967), p.48

30 IWM DOCS H. W. Yoxall, letter, 3/8/1917

31 IWM DOCS S. Bradbury, typescript memoir, p.29

32 IWM DOCS S. Bradbury, typescript memoir, pp.30–1

33 IWM DOCS S. Bradbury, typescript memoir, pp.33–4

34 IWM DOCS P. Christison, typescript memoir, pp.62–3

35 Sandilands, W. and Macleod, N., *Story of 7th Batt. Cameron Highanders* (Stirling: Mackay, 1922), p.101

36 IWM SOUND W. Collins, AC 9434

37 IWM SOUND J. C. Hill, AC 4135

38 IWM DOCS S. T. Fuller, diary, 28/7/1917

39 IWM DOCS P. Christison, typescript memoir, p.63

40 D. Haig, quoted in H. A. Jones, *The War in the Air* (Oxford: The Clarendon Press, 1922–37), Vol. 5, p.38–9

41 W. R. Ludlow, 'Some Extracts from an Area Commandant's Diary', *The Ypres Times*, Vol. 3, No. 5, pp.123–4

42 N. Fraser-Tytler, *With Lancashire Lads and Field Guns in France, 1915–1918* (Manchester: John Heywood Ltd, 1922), pp.205–6

43 H. Gordon, *The Unreturning Army* (London: J. M. Dent & Sons, 1967), p.57

44 N. Fraser-Tytler, *With Lancashire Lads and Field Guns in France, 1915–1918* (Manchester: John Heywood Ltd, 1922), pp.205–6

45 IWM DOCS R. J. Blackadder, typescript diary, 26/6/1917–30/6/1917

46 IWM DOCS R. J. Blackadder, typescript diary, 29/7/1917

47 R. Hamilton, *The War Diary of the Master of Belhaven, 1914–1918* (Barnsley: Wharncliffe, 1990), pp. 330–1

48 R. Hamilton, *The War Diary of the Master of Belhaven, 1914–1918* (Barnsley: Wharncliffe, 1990), p.346

49 R. Macleod, 'An artillery officer in the First World War' (typescript diary), 20/7/1917

50 R. Macleod, 'An artillery officer in the First World War' (typescript diary), 20/7/1917

51 R. Macleod, 'An artillery officer in the First World War' (typescript diary), 23/7/1917

52 IWM SOUND M. Dillon, AC 9752

53 IWM DOCS M. W. Murray, transcript diary, p.98

54 IWM SOUND R. Beall, AC 4013

55 IWM DOCS S. T. Fuller, diary, 24/7/1917

56 IWM DOCS M.W. Murray, transcript diary, p.98

57 M. L. Walkinton, *Twice in a Lifetime* (London: Samson Books, 1980), pp. 130–1

58 IWM DOCS P. Christison, typescript memoir, p.64

59 IWM DOCS S. T. Fuller, diary, 30/7/1917

60 IWM DOCS G. V. Dennis, typescript memoir, Chapter 10, p.2

61 IWM DOCS E. C. Barton, typescript memoir, p.1

62 IWM DOCS E. C. Barton, typescript memoir, p.2

63 B. Martin, *Poor Bloody Infantry* (London: John Murray, 1987), pp.157–8

64 J. Jack, *General Jack's Diary, 1914–1918: The Trench Diary of Brigadier J. L. Jack*, edited and introduced by J. Terraine (London: Eyre & Spottiswoode, 1964), p.237

65 R. Hamilton, *The War Diary of the Master of Belhaven, 1914–1918*, (Barnsley: Wharncliffe, 1990), p.356

4 PILCKEM RIDGE, 31 JULY 1917

1 IWM DOCS E. C. Allfree, typescript diary, 31/7/1917

2 IWM DOCS S. Bradbury, typescript memoir, pp.35–6

3 J. Jack, *General Jack's Diary, 1914–1918: The Trench Diary of Brigadier J. L. Jack*, edited and introduced by J. Terraine (London: Eyre & Spottiswoode, 1964), p.237

4 IWM DOCS T. C. Owtram, typescript memoir, p.26

5 IWM DOCS J. S. Handley, typescript memoir, p.7

6 IWM SOUND U. Burke, AC 569

7 J. Jack, *General Jack's Diary, 1914–1918: The Trench Diary of Brigadier J. L. Jack*, edited and introduced by J. Terraine (London: Eyre & Spottiswoode, 1964), pp.237–8

8 IWM DOCS A. C. Warsop, typescript memoir, p.13

9 IWM DOCS E. C Barton, typescript memoir, pp.2–3

10 IWM SOUND U. Burke, AC 569

11 IWM DOCS T. C. Owtram, typescript memoir, p.26

12 IWM SOUND U. Burke, AC 569

13 E .Blunden, *Undertones of War* (London: Cobden-Sanderson, 1930), pp.219–20

14 IWM SOUND I. Watkins, AC 12232

15 IWM DOCS A. C. Warsop, typescript memoir, p.13

16 A. Gibbs, quoted in C. H. Dudley Ward, *The History of the Welsh Guards, 1915–1919* (London: London Stamp Exchange, 1988), p.154

17 A. Gibbs, quoted in C. H. Dudley Ward, *The History of the Welsh Guards, 1915–1919* (London: London Stamp Exchange, 1988), pp.155–6

18 IWM DOCS Lord Gage, *Firle, A Memoir* typescript, pp.24–5

19 IWM DOCS S. Bradbury, typescript memoir, p.36

20 IWM SOUND C. Lane, AC 7257

21 E. Blunden, *Undertones of War* (London: Cobden-Sanderson, 1930), pp.221–2

22 IWM SOUND H. Birks, AC 4024

23 J. C. Allnatt, *The Tank*, Part I , p.277

24 IWM SOUND H. Birks, AC 4024

25 J. C. Allnatt, *The Tank*, Part I, p.312

26 J. C. Allnatt, *The Tank*, Part I, p.312

27 IWM DOCS J. S. Handley, typescript memoir, pp.7–10

28 IWM DOCS T. C. Owtram, typescript memoir, pp. 26–7

29 IWM DOCS, J. S. Handley, typescript memoir, pp.7–10

30 IWM DOCS S. E. Gordon, typescript diary, 31/7/1917

31 IWM DOCS J. S. Handley, typescript memoir, pp.7–10

32 IWM DOCS T. C. Owtram, typescript memoir, pp.27–8

33 IWM DOCS, J. S. Handley, typescript memoir, pp.7–10

34 IWM SOUND U. Burke, AC 569

35 J. Jack, *General Jack's Diary, 1914–1918: The Trench Diary of Brigadier J. L. Jack*, edited and introduced by J. Terraine (London, Eyre & Spottiswoode, 1964), p.239

36 M. L. Walkinton, *Twice in a Lifetime* (London: Samson Books, 1980), pp.131–2

37 M. L. Walkinton, *Twice in a Lifetime* (London: Samson Books, 1980), p.133

38 IWM DOCS E. C. Barton, typescript memoir, pp.2–3

39 IWM SOUND U. Burke, AC 569

40 IWM SOUND U. Burke, AC 569

41 IWM DOCS E. C. Barton, typescript memoir, pp.2–3

42 IWM DOCS E. C. Barton, typescript memoir, p.3

43 IWM DOCS A. C. Warsop, typescript memoir, p.13

44 IWM DOCS A. C. Warsop, typescript memoir, p.14

45 IWM DOCS A. C. Warsop, typescript memoir, p.15

46 IWM DOCS E. C. Barton, typescript memoir, p.3

47 IWM DOCS E. C. Barton, typescript memoir, pp.3–4

48 IWM SOUND E. G. Williams, AC 10604

49 IWM DOCS S. T. Fuller, diary, 30/7/1917

50 IWM DOCS S. T. Fuller, diary, 30/7/1917

51 IWM DOCS S. T. Fuller, diary, 30/7/1917

52 IWM DOCS S. T. Fuller, diary, 30/7/1917

53 IWM DOCS S. T. Fuller, diary, 30/7/1917

54 IWM DOCS E. C. Barton, typescript memoir, p.4

55 IWM DOCS E. C. Barton, typescript memoir, p.5

56 IWM SOUND G. Thompson, AC 9549

57 IWM DOCS G. V. Dennis, typescript memoir, Chapter 10, p.3

58 IWM DOCS J. S. Walthew, letter, 31/7/1917

59 IWM DOCS J. S. Walthew, letter, 31/7/1917

60 N. Fraser-Tytler, *With Lancashire Lads and Field Guns in France, 1915–1918* (Manchester: John Heywood Ltd, 1922), pp.214–15

61 IWM DOCS A. J. Heraty, typescript memoir, p.57

62 IWM DOCS R. M. Luther, typescript memoir, p.36

63 IWM DOCS A. J. Heraty, typescript memoir, p.57–9

64 IWM DOCS F. S. Walthew, manuscript memoir, p.2

65 J. C. Allnatt, *The Tank*, Part I, p.313

66 IWM DOCS J. S. Handley, typescript memoir, pp.7–10

67 IWM DOCS M.W. Murray, transcript diary, p.100

68 IWM DOCS M.W. Murray, transcript diary, p.100

69 M. L. Walkinton, *Twice in a Lifetime* (London: Samson Books, 1980), p.134

70 IWM DOCS T. C. Owtram, typescript memoir, pp.27–8

71 IWM DOCS P. Christison, typescript memoir, pp.64–5

72 IWM DOCS G. V. Dennis, typescript memoir, Chapter 10, p.4

73 IWM DOCS A. C. Warsop, typescript memoir, p.15

74 IWM DOCS A. C. Warsop, typescript memoir, pp.15–6

75 IWM DOCS J. S. Handley, typescript memoir, pp.7–10

76 IWM DOCS G. V. Dennis, typescript memoir, Chapter 10, p.3

77 A. C. Johnston, quoted in A. Crookenden. *The History of the Cheshire Regiment in The Great War* (Chester: W. H. Evans & Sons, 1938), pp.115–16

78 IWM DOCS J. S. Handley, typescript memoir, p.11

5 AUGUST DESPAIR

1 IWM DOCS R. Macleod, 'An artillery officer in the First World War' typescript diary, 3/8/1917

2 Operational Memorandum, 1/8/1917, quoted in J. E. Edmonds, *Military Operations: France and Belgium 1917*, Vol. II, (London: HMSO, 1948), p.448

3 IWM SOUND S. Goldsmith, AC 4115

4 D. Lloyd George, *War Memoirs of David Lloyd George*, Vol. II, (London: Odhams Press Ltd, 1936), p.1306

5 J. Charteris, *Field Marshal Earl Haig* (London: Cassell, 1929), p.272

6 E. Gold, *Spectator*, 17/1/1958

7 We are here greatly indebted to the work of John Hussey in his article, 'The Flanders Battleground and the Weather', contained in *Passchendaele in Perspective: The Third Battle of Ypres*, edited by Peter Liddle (London: Leo Cooper, 1997) pp.140–58

8 J. Charteris, *At GHQ* (London: Cassell, 1931), pp.236–7

9 IWM DOCS A. C. Warsop, typescript memoir, p.16

10 IWM DOCS A. C. Warsop, typescript memoir, p.16

11 IWM DOCS A. C. Warsop, typescript memoir, p.17

12 H. Gordon, *The Unreturning Army* (London: J. M. Dent & Sons, 1967), pp.70–71

13 H. Driver, quoted in (Anon.) *The 54th Infantry Brigade, 1914–1918: Some records of Battle and Laughter in France* (Aldershot: Gale & Polden Ltd, 1919), p.110

14 H. Driver, quoted in (Anon.) *The 54th Infantry Brigade, 1914–1918: Some records of Battle and Laughter in France* (Aldershot: Gale & Polden Ltd, 1919), p.110

15 S. Gillon, *The Story of the 29th Division* (London: Thomas Nelson & Sons, 1925) pp.129–30

16 IWM DOCS A. E. Glanville, diary entries, 31/7/1917–16/8/1917

17 G. E. Mackenzie, quoted in W. H. A. Groom, *Poor Bloody Infantry* (London: William Kimber, 1976), p.127

18 IWM DOCS A. E. Glanville, diary entry, 16/8/1916

19 IWM SOUND A. Hanbury-Sparrow, AC 4131

20 IWM SOUND A. Hanbury-Sparrow, AC 4131

21 Edited from W. H. A. Groom, *Poor Bloody Infantry* (London: William Kimber, 1976), pp.117–18

22 Edited from W. H. A. Groom, *Poor Bloody Infantry* (London: William Kimber, 1976), pp.118–19

23 N. Fraser-Tytler, *With Lancashire Lads and Field Guns in France, 1915–1918* (Manchester: John Heywood Ltd, 1922), pp.223–4

24 Edited from W. H. A. Groom, *Poor Bloody Infantry* (London: William Kimber, 1976), pp.119–20

25 Edited from W. H. A. Groom, *Poor Bloody Infantry* (London: William Kimber, 1976), p.120

26 Edited from W. H. A. Groom, *Poor Bloody Infantry* (London: William Kimber, 1976), pp120–21

27 IWM SOUND A. Hanbury-Sparrow, AC 4131

28 IWM SOUND A. Hanbury-Sparrow, AC 4131

29 IWM DOCS S. A. Lane, typescript memoir, pp.13–14

30 W. R. Ludlow, 'Some Extracts from an Area Commandant's Diary', *The Ypres Times*, Vol. 3, No. 5, p.124

31 H. Gough, *The Fifth Army* (London: Hodder & Stoughton, 1931), p.205

32 C. D. Baker-Carr, *From Chauffeur to Brigadier* (London: Ernest Benn, 1930), p.251

33 IWM DOCS R. Macleod, 'An artillery officer in the First World War' typescript diary 20/8/1917

34 Public Record Office WO95/92 A. G. Barker, G Battalion, Tank Corps, Report of Operations, 19/8/1917. We are very grateful to our friend and colleague, Bryn Hammond, for drawing our attention to these reports.

35 Public Record Office WO95/92 E. T. Morgan, G Battalion, Tank Corps, Report of Operations, 19/8/1917

36 Public Record Office WO95/92 H. Coutts, G Battalion, Tank Corps, Report of Operations, 19/8/1917 (originally not in first person)

37 IWM SOUND M. Dillon, AC 9752

38 IWM DOCS P. Christison, typescript memoir, p.66

39 IWM DOCS P. Christison, typescript memoir, p.67

40 D. Lloyd George, *War Memoirs of David Lloyd George*, Vol. II (London: Odhams Press Ltd, 1938), p.1280

6 FOOTSLOGGERS

1 IWM DOCS M. W. Murray, transcript diary, p.100

2 IWM DOCS P. Christison, typescript memoir, p.65

3 IWM SOUND G. Cole, AC 9535

4 IWM SOUND A. Griffin, AC 9101

5 IWM SOUND G. Clayton, AC 10112

6 C. L. Fox, *Narrative of the 502 (Wessex) Field Company, Royal Engineers, 1915–1919* (London: Hugh Rees Ltd, 1920) pp.85–6

7 IWM SOUND J. Dillon, AC 4078

8 IWM DOCS C. H. Dudley Ward, manuscript diary, p.482

9 IWM DOCS R. W. F. Johnston, typescript memoir, p.78

10 IWM SOUND W. Collins, AC 9434

11 IWM SOUND A. Griffin, AC 9101

12 IWM DOCS H. J. Knee, edited together from typescript memoir, pp.3–4 and manuscript memoir, pp.6–8

13 IWM DOCS M.W. Murray, transcript diary, pp.123–4

14 IWM SOUND J. Dillon, AC 4078

15 IWM DOCS S. T. Fuller, diary, 10/10/1917

16 IWM DOCS G. D. J. McMurtrie, typescript memoir, p. 8

17 IWM SOUND W. Collins, AC 9434

18 Sandilands, J. W. & Macleod, N., *Story of 7th Batt. Cameron Highlanders* (Stirling: Mackay, 1922), p.103

19 IWM DOCS S. Bradbury, typescript memoir, p.41

20 IWM DOCS G. Buckeridge, typescript memoir, p.64–5

21 IWM SOUND G. Horridge, AC 7498

22 IWM SOUND S. Sibbald, AC 10169

23 IWM SOUND H. Hopthrow, AC 11581

24 IWM SOUND J. Pickard, AC 8946

25 IWM SOUND E. Blunden, AC 4030

26 IWM SOUND J. Mallalieu, AC 9417

27 IWM SOUND J. Fitzpatrick, AC 10767

28 IWM SOUND G. Greenwell, AC 8766

29 IWM DOCS G. Fleming, typescript memoir, p.16

30 IWM SOUND J. Fitzpatrick, AC 10767

31 IWM SOUND C. Lee, AC 4156

32 IWM DOCS M. W. Murray, transcript diary, pp.102–3

33 IWM DOCS S. T. Fuller, diary, 17/8/1917

34 IWM DOCS G. Fleming, typescript memoir, p.18

35 IWM DOCS G. D. J. McMurtrie, typescript memoir, p.10

36 W. H. A. Groom, *Poor Bloody Infantry* (London: William Kimber, 1976), p.128

37 IWM DOCS G. V. Dennis, typescript memoir, Chapter 10, p.9

38 IWM DOCS S. Bradbury, typescript memoir, pp.38–9

39 IWM DOCS G. D. J. McMurtrie, typescript memoir, p.11

40 C. Lawrence, *Sergeant Lawrence goes to France* (Melbourne: Melbourne University Press, 1987), p.147

41 IWM DOCS C. H. Dudley Ward, manuscript diary, pp.472–3

7 GUNNERS

1 IWM SOUND R. Talbot-Kelly, AC 4242

2 IWM DOCS R. G. Dixon, typescript memoir, p.26

3 IWM SOUND E. W. Stoneham, AC 4237

4 IWM DOCS A. J. Heraty, typescript memoir, p.54

5 IWM SOUND C. Denys, AC 9876

6 IWM DOCS A. J. Heraty, typescript memoir, p.60

7 IWM DOCS R. G. Dixon, typescript memoir, p.131

8 W. J. K. Rettie, quoted in W. W. Wadsworth, *War Diary of the 1st West Lancashire Brigade, RFA* (Liverpool: Daily Post, 1923), pp.91–3

9 IWM SOUND E. W. Stoneham, AC 4237

10 R. Hamilton, *The War Diary of the Master of Belhaven, 1914–1918* (Barnsley: Wharncliffe, 1990), p.369

11 IWM SOUND R. Talbot-Kelly, AC 4242

12 M. C. Walker, *A History of 154 Siege Battery, Royal Garrison Artillery* (Dublin: John T. Drought, 1919), p.38

13 R. Hamilton, *The War Diary of the Master of Belhaven, 1914–1918* (Barnsley: Wharncliffe, 1990), p.368

14 IWM SOUND C. Denys, AC 9876

15 H. Gordon, *The Unreturning Army* (London: J. M. Dent & Sons, 1967) p.55

16 H. Gordon, *The Unreturning Army* (London: J. M. Dent & Sons, 1967), p.55

17 R. Hamilton, *The War Diary of the Master of Belhaven, 1914–1918* (Barnsley: Wharncliffe, 1990), p.359

18 IWM DOCS R. G. Dixon, typescript memoir, p.130

19 IWM SOUND J. Crow, AC 9118

20 IWM SOUND H. V. Doggett, AC 4079

21 IWM SOUND L. Ounsworth, AC 332

22 IWM SOUND M. Rymer-Jones, AC 10699

23 IWM SOUND L. Ounsworth, AC 332

24 IWM DOCS R. M. Luther, typescript memoir, p.37

25 IWM DOCS R. Macleod, 'An artillery officer in the First World War', typescript diary, 27/8/1917

26 N. Fraser-Tytler, *With Lancashire Lads and Field Guns in France, 1915–1918* (Manchester: John Heywood Ltd, 1922), p.234

27 IWM DOCS R. G. Dixon, typescript memoir, pp.90–1

28 IWM DOCS R. G. Dixon, typescript memoir, pp.28–33 (edited)

29 IWM SOUND L. Ounsworth, AC 332

30 IWM SOUND L. Ounsworth, AC 332

31 H. Gordon, *The Unreturning Army* (London: J. M. Dent & Sons, 1967), p.90

32 IWM SOUND C. Denys, AC 9876

33 M. C. Walker, *A History of 154 Siege Battery, Royal Garrison Artillery* (Dublin: John T. Drought, 1919), pp.39–40

34 IWM SOUND L. Briggs, AC 5

35 IWM SOUND C. Denys, AC 9876

36 R. Hamilton, *The War Diary of the Master of Belhaven, 1914–1918* (Barnsley: Wharncliffe, 1990), pp.372–3

37 IWM SOUND L. Ounsworth, AC 332

38 M. C. Walker, *A History of 154 Siege Battery, Royal Garrison Artillery* (Dublin: John T. Drought, 1919), p.39

39 IWM DOCS J. S. Walthew, letter, 25/7/1917

40 IWM SOUND L. Briggs, AC 5

41 M. C. Walker, *A History of 154 Siege Battery, Royal Garrison Artillery*, (Dublin: John T. Drought, 1919), pp.43–4

42 C. Lawrence, *Sergeant Lawrence goes to France* (Melbourne: Melbourne University Press, 1987), p.132

43 IWM SOUND C. Lewis, AC 4162

44 IWM DOCS R. G. Dixon, typescript memoir, p.27

45 C. Lawrence, *Sergeant Lawrence goes to France* (Melbourne: Melbourne University Press, 1987), p.118

46 R. Macleod, 'An artillery officer in the First World War', typescript diary, 24/8/1917

47 C. Smith, 'The Slush at Passchendaele', *The Ypres Times*, Vol. 7, No. 2, p.43

48 IWM DOCS R. G. Dixon, typescript memoir, p.88

8 BITE AND HOLD

1 IWM SOUND W. Bunning, AC 4046

2 E. Ludendorff, *My War Memories* (London: Hutchinson & Co, 1919), p.479

3 E. Ludendorff, *My War Memories* (London: Hutchinson & Co, 1919), p.480

4 IWM SOUND G. Horridge, AC 7498

5 IWM DOCS S. Bradbury, typescript memoir, pp.42–3

6 C. E. Wurtzburg, *The History of the 2/6th (Rifle) Battalion, The King's Liverpool Regiment, 1914–1919* (Aldershot: Gale & Polden Ltd, 1920), p.133

7 IWM DOCS V. R. Magill, manuscript memoir, p.15

8 IWM DOCS V. R. Magill, manuscript memoir, p.35–6

9 IWM DOCS V. R. Magill, manuscript memoir, p.36–7

10 IWM DOCS V. R. Magill, manuscript memoir, p.36

11 IWM DOCS V. R. Magill, manuscript memoir, p.55–7

12 IWM DOCS V. R. Magill, manuscript memoir, p.59–60

13 IWM DOCS V. R. Magill, manuscript memoir, p.65

14 IWM DOCS C. H. Dudley Ward, manuscript diary, p.458

15 Harington, quoted in J. E. Edmonds, *Military Operations: France and Belgium 1917*, Vol. II (London: HMSO, 1948), pp.452–3

16 M. C. Walker, *A History of 154 Siege Battery, Royal Garrison Artillery* (Dublin: John T. Drought, 1919), p.41

17 Harington, quoted in J. E. Edmonds, *Military Operations in France and Belgium 1917*, Vol II (London: HMSO, 1948), p.460

18 Harington, quoted in J. E. Edmonds, *Military Operations in France and Belgium 1917*, Vol II (London: HMSO, 1948), p.461

19 IWM DOCS R. J. Blackadder, typescript diary, 20/9/1917

20 IWM SOUND D. Wimberley, AC 4266

21 IWM DOCS J. F. Bloxam, typescript letter, 23/9/1917

22 C. Lawrence, *Sergeant Lawrence goes to France* (Melbourne: Melbourne University Press, 1987), pp.124–5

23 IWM SOUND S. Sibbald, AC 10169

24 IWM SOUND D. Wimberley, AC 4266

25 IWM DOCS M. F. Gower, manuscript letter, 23/9/1917

26 IWM DOCS S. E. Gordon, typescript diary, pp.307–8

27 IWM SOUND H. Pohlmann, AC 4197

28 IWM SOUND D. Wimberley, AC 4266

29 IWM DOCS H. W. Yoxall, letter 24/9/1917

30 IWM DOCS D. Coutts, typescript diary/memoir, 20/9/1917

31 IWM DOCS J. F. Bloxam, typescript letter, 23/9/1917

32 IWM DOCS A. J. Jackson, manuscript letter, 4/11/1917

33 IWM SOUND C. Austin, AC 11116

34 C. Lawrence, *Sergeant Lawrence goes to France* (Melbourne: Melbourne University Press, 1987), pp.130–2

35 E. Ludendorff, *My War Memories* (London: Hutchinson & Co, 1919), p.488

36 J. McCudden, *Five Years in the Royal Flying Corps* (London: Aeroplane and General, 1918), p.193

37 J. McCudden, *Five Years in the Royal Flying Corps* (London: Aeroplane and General, 1918), p.194

38 V. Cronyn, quoted in A. Revell, *High in the Empty Blue: The History of 56 Squadron* (Mountain View: Flying Machines Press, 1995), p.165

39 J. McCudden, *Five Years in the Royal Flying Corps* (London: Aeroplane and General, 1918), p.194

40 G. H. Bowman, quoted in A. Revell, *High in the Empty Blue: The History of 56 Squadron* (Mountain View: Flying Machines Press, 1995), p.162

41 G. H. Bowman, quoted in A. Revell, *High in the Empty Blue: The History of 56 Squadron* (Mountain View: Flying Machines Press, 1995), p.162

42 A. Rhys Davids, quoted in H. A. Jones, *The War in the Air*, Vol. IV (Oxford: The Clarendon Press, 1922–37), p.189

43 J. McCudden, *Five Years in the Royal Flying Corps* (London: Aeroplane and General, 1918), p.194

44 IWM DOCS R. J. Blackadder, typescript diary, 22/9/1917–7/11/1917

45 IWM SOUND D. Price, AC 10168

46 C. J. Huffield, 'The Zonnebeke Show', *The Ypres Times*, Vol. 4, No. 4, p.104

47 C. J. Huffield, 'The Zonnebeke Show', *The Ypres Times*, Vol. 4, No. 4, p.105

48 C. J. Huffield, 'The Zonnebeke Show', *The Ypres Times*, Vol. 4, No. 4, pp.105–6

49 C. J. Huffield, 'The Zonnebeke Show', *The Ypres Times*, Vol. 4, No. 4, p.106

50 E. Ludendorff *My War Memories, 1914–1918* (London: Hutchinson & Co, 1919), p.489

51 J. Charteris, *At GHQ* (London: Cassell, 1931), p.257

52 IWM DOCS F. P. J. Glover, manuscript diary, 1/10/1917

53 IWM SOUND W. Towers, AC 11038

54 IWM DOCS R. J. Blackadder, typescript diary, 22/9/1917–7/11/1917

55 IWM SOUND K. Page, AC 717

56 IWM SOUND W. Bunning, AC 4046

57 IWM DOCS D. L. Rowlands, manuscript letter, 5/2/1918

58 IWM SOUND W. Bunning, AC 4046

59 IWM DOCS E. F. Trundle, transcript letter, 14/10/1917

60 IWM SOUND E. Rhodes, AC 10914

61 IWM SOUND E. Rhodes, AC 10914

62 IWM DOCS F. P. J. Glover, manuscript diary, 4/10/1917

63 IWM SOUND C. Carrington, AC 4057

64 C. Carrington, writing as C. Edmonds, *A Subaltern's War* (London: Peter Davis Ltd, 1929), pp.163–4

65 IWM SOUND C. Carrington, AC 4057

66 IWM SOUND E. Rhodes, AC 10914

67 E. Ludendorff, *My War Memories* (London: Hutchinson & Co, 1919), Vol. II, p.491

68 E. Ludendorff, *My War Memories* (London: Hutchinson & Co, 1919), Vol. II, p.490

9 JOURNEY'S END

1 IWM DOCS R. W. F. Johnston, typescript questionnaire, p.10

2 IWM DOCS R. J. Blackadder, typescript diary, 22/9/1917–7/11/1917

3 C. L. Fox, *Narrative of the 502 (Wessex) Field Company, Royal Engineers, 1915–1919* (London: Hugh Rees Ltd, 1920) p.84

4 IWM SOUND J. W. Palmer, AC 4198

5 IWM SOUND J. W. Palmer, AC 4198

6 IWM DOCS C. H. Dudley Ward, manuscript diary, p.480

7 RAF MUSEUM, F. J. Ortweiler, AC 88/7, manuscript diary, 6/10/1917

8 C. F. Sharland, quoted in C. E. W. Bean, *The Official History of Australia in the War of 1914–1918*, Vol. IV (St Lucia, Queensland: University of Queensland Press, 1982), p.883

9 Benedict Williamson, *Happy Days in France and Flanders with the 47th and 49th Divisions* (London: Harding & More Ltd, ND) p.55

10 IWM DOCS T. A. Bickerton, typescript memoir, p.15

11 IWM SOUND M. Rymer-Jones, AC 10699

12 IWM DOCS G. D. J. McMurtrie, manuscript memoir, p.9

13 IWM DOCS C. H. Dudley Ward, manuscript diary, p.458

14 Norman Cliff, *To Hell and Back with the Guards* (Braunton: Merlin Books, 1988), p.83

15 IWM SOUND M. Rymer-Jones, AC 10699

16 IWM DOCS T. A. Bickerton, typescript memoir, pp.15–16

17 IWM SOUND N. Macmillan, AC 4173

18 IWM SOUND H. Birks, AC 4024

19 W. H. L. Watson, *A Company of Tanks* (Edinburgh & London: William Blackwood & Sons, 1920), pp.158–9

20 Quoted in C. Williams-Ellis, *The Tank Corps* (London: Country Life, 1919), p.98

21 IWM DOCS B. G. Buxton, typescript memoir, p.4

22 W. G. Fisher, quoted in C. E. W. Bean, *The Official History of Australia in the War of 1914–1918*, Vol. IV (St Lucia, Queensland: University of Queensland Press, 1982), pp.906–7

23 IWM DOCS, S. T. Fuller, diary, 11/10/1917

24 IWM DOCS H. J. Knee, typescript memoir, pp.1–2

25 IWM DOCS B .O. Stokes, typescript memoir, p.7 (quoted courtesy of Lyn Macdonald)

26 W. G. Fisher, quoted in C. E. W. Bean, *The Official History of Australia in the War of 1914–1918*, Vol. IV (St Lucia, Queensland: University of Queensland Press, 1982), p.927

27 IWM DOCS Siegfried Sassoon correspondence, manuscript letter from J. Cottrell, 16/10/1917

28 IWM DOCS F. J. Rice, manuscript memoir, pp.48–9

29 IWM DOCS S. T. Fuller, diary, 13/10/1917

30 IWM DOCS C. H. Dudley Ward, manuscript diary, pp.486–7

31 IWM DOCS R. W. F. Johnston, typescript memoir, p.83

32 W. G. Fisher, quoted in C. E. W. Bean, *The Official History of Australia in the War of 1914–1918*, Vol. IV (St Lucia, Queensland: University of Queensland Press, 1982), pp.931

33 N. Fraser-Tytler, *With Lancashire Lads and Field Guns in France, 1915–1918* (Manchester: John Heywood Ltd, 1922), p.247

34 N. Fraser-Tytler, *With Lancashire Lads and Field Guns in France, 1915–1918* (Manchester: John Heywood Ltd, 1922), pp.247–8

35 IWM DOCS R. W. F. Johnston, typescript memoir, pp.82–5

36 IWM DOCS R. W. F. Johnston, typescript questionnaire, pp.10

37 N. Fraser-Tytler, *With Lancashire Lads and Field Guns in France, 1915–1918* (Manchester: John Heywood Ltd, 1922), p.241

38 IWM SOUND J. Pickard, AC 8946

39 IWM SOUND R. Tobin, AC 4243

40 IWM DOCS M. Yewdall, transcribed letter, 2/11/1917

41 IWM DOCS I. Maxse papers: A. B. E. Cator, 'Report on Operations, 26th and 30th October 1917', file 39

42 IWM DOCS M. Yewdall, transcribed letter 2/11/1917

43 *London Gazette*, VC citation,13/2/1918

44 *London Gazette*, VC citation,11/1/1918

45 J. E. Puley, quoted in R. Hodder-Williams, *Princess Patricia's Canadian Light Infantry, 1914–1919* (London & Toronto: Hodder & Stoughton Ltd, 1923), p.269

46 Major Sullivan, quoted in R. Hodder-Williams, *Princess Patricia's Canadian Light Infantry, 1914–1919* (London & Toronto: Hodder & Stoughton Ltd, 1923), p.270

47 Major Niven, quoted in R. Hodder-Williams, *Princess Patricia's Canadian Light Infantry, 1914-1919* (London & Toronto: Hodder & Stoughton Ltd, 1923), pp.271–2

48 IWM DOCS I. Maxse papers: A. B. E. Cator, 'Report on Operations, 26th and 30th October 1917', File 39

49 IWM DOCS I. Maxse papers: A. B. E. Cator, 'Report on Operations, 26th and 30th October 1917', File 39

50 IWM DOCS J. W. Mudd, manuscript letter, 22/10/1917

51 W. R. Bird, *Ghosts have warm hands* (Toronto: Clarke, Irwin & Company Ltd, 1968), p.82

52 IWM DOCS C. E. L. Lyne, transcribed letter, 4/11/1917

53 IWM DOCS R. J. Blackadder, typescript diary, 22/9/1917–7/11/1917

54 N. Fraser-Tytler, *With Lancashire Lads and Field Guns in France, 1915–1918* (Manchester: John Heywood Ltd, 1922), pp. 249–50

55 Major Shiel. quoted in (Anon.) *The War History of the 1st Northumbrian Brigade, RFA* (Newcastle upon Tyne: J. W. Hindson & Sons, 1927), pp.173–4

56 E. G. Black, *I Want One Volunteer* (Toronto: The Ryerson Press, 1971), p.63

57 W. B. Kerr, *Shrieks and Crashes being memories of Canada's Corps, 1917* (Toronto: Hunter Rose Company Ltd, 1929), p.189

58 J. G. McKnight, Canadian Broadcasting Company interview quoted in (Anon.)

New Brunswick Fighting 26th : A Draft History of the 26th New Brunswick Battalion, CEF, 1914–1919, (New Brunswick: 26th Battalion Overseas Association Inc., 1992) p.61

59 IWM DOCS H. M. McIntyre Hood, transcript of interview, p.13

60 W. B. Kerr, *Shrieks and Crashes being memories of Canada's Corps, 1917* (Toronto: Hunter Rose Company Ltd, 1929), p.191

61 A. W. Pagan, quoted in E .Wyrall, *The Gloucestershire Regiment in the War, 1914–1918* (London: Methuen & Co Ltd, 1931), p.238

62 W. B. Kerr, *Shrieks and Crashes being memories of Canada's Corps, 1917* (Toronto: Hunter Rose Company Ltd, 1929), p.191

63 W. B. Kerr, *Shrieks and Crashes being memories of Canada's Corps, 1917* (Toronto: Hunter Rose Company Ltd, 1929), p.192

64 E. Ludendorff, *My War Memories* (London: Hutchinson & Co, 1919), p.492

65 IWM DOCS, D. L. Rowlands, transcript letter, 5/2/1918

66 C. Harington, 'The Ypres Salient in 1918', *The Ypres Times*, Vol. 2, No. 2, 4/1924, p.34

67 C. Harington, 'The Ypres Salient in 1918', *The Ypres Times*, Vol. 2, No. 2, 4/1924, p.36

68 C. Harington, 'The Ypres Salient in 1918', *The Ypres Times*, Vol. 2, No. 2, 4/1924, p.36

10 EPILOGUE

1 IWM DOCS A. C. Warsop, typescript memoir, p.10

2 W. H. A. Groom, *Poor Bloody Infantry* (London: William Kimber, 1976), p.128

3 IWM SOUND C. Lee, AC 4156

4 Stephen Williamson, interviewed by Nigel Steel, Canterbury, 9 May 1985

5 IWM DOCS C. H. Dudley Ward, manuscript diary, p.527

6 W. H. A. Groom, *Poor Bloody Infantry* (London: William Kimber, 1976), p.134

7 IWM SOUND E. Blunden, AC 4030

8 IWM DOCS F. Hunt, typescript memoir, p.26

9 IWM DOCS R. M. Luther, typescript memoir, p.36

10 IWM DOCS M.W. Murray, transcript diary, p.106

11 IWM DOCS S. T. Fuller, diary, postscript

12 W. H. A. Groom, *Poor Bloody Infantry* (London: William Kimber, 1976), p.122

13 IWM DOCS M.W. Murray, transcript diary, p.129

14 IWM DOCS R. G. Dixon, typescript memoir, p.27

15 A. J. Cummings, 'Ypres, The Tragic Story of the Salient', *Daily News*, 23/7/1928

SOURCES

For reasons of space, only sources from which quotations have been taken or to which reference is made in the footnotes are detailed in the following lists. The authors would like to thank all of those who have given permission for these sources to be used. In particular they would like to acknowledge those individuals who hold the copyright of the collections of unpublished papers held in the Imperial War Museum. Every effort has been made to obtain permission from the relevant copyright holders. But this has not always been possible and the authors would be pleased to hear at the Museum from anyone with whom contact has not been established.

UNPUBLISHED MANUSCRIPT SOURCES

1. Imperial War Museum, Department of Documents (IWM DOCS)

Lieutenant E. C. Allfree, 459pp. typescript diary

Lieutenant Colonel E. C. Barton, 7pp. typescript memoir

T. A. Bickerton, 30pp. memoir, 'The Wartime experiences of an ordinary Tommy'

Lieutenant R. J. Blackadder, 73pp. diary/memoir

Rev. J. F. Bloxam, letters

S. Bradbury, 159pp. typescript memoir

G. Buckeridge, 95pp. memoir, 'Memoirs of my Army Service in the Great War, 1914–1918'

Captain B. G. Buxton, 7pp. typescript memoir

General Sir Philip Christison, 217pp. memoir

J. Cotterell, manuscript letter to Siegfried Sassoon, 16/10/1917, in Siegfried Sassoon correspondence.

Major D. D. Coutts, 132pp. diary/memoir

G. V. Dennis, 314pp. typescript memoir

Lieutenant Colonel H. M. Dillon, typescript diary

Lieutenant R. G. Dixon, 142pp. typescript memoir

Major C. H. Dudley Ward, 865pp. manuscript diary

Sir Gilbert Fleming, 40pp. typescript memoir

S. T. Fuller, 372pp. diary/memoir

Captain Lord Gage, 13pp. excerpt chapter from privately published memoir, 'Firle, A memoir'

Lieutenant A. E. Glanville, diary

Lieutenant F. P. J. Glover, 9 manuscript diaries

Colonel S. E. Gordon, 326pp. typescript diary

M. F. Gower, 179 manuscript letters

Second Lieutenant J. S. Handley, 58pp. typescript memoir

A. J. Heraty, 82pp. typescript memoir

F. Hunt, 52pp. typescript memoir

A. J. Jackson, 7pp. manuscript letters

Lieutenant Colonel R. W. F. Johnston, 107pp. transcript memoir plus 12pp. typescript questionnaire

J. D. Keddie, manuscript letter

Lieutenant H. J. Knee, 4pp. typescript memoir and 118pp. manuscript memoir

S. A. Lane, 22pp. typescript memoir, 'The Great War, Personal Experiences of a Front Line Infantryman'

R. M. Luther, 41pp. typescript memoir, 'The Poppies are Blood Red'

Lieutenant Colonel C. E. L. Lyne, 76pp. transcript memoir, 135pp. letters

M. McIntyre Hood, 35pp. transcript of interview

Colonel R. Macleod, typescript diary 'An artillery officer in the First World War'

Lieutenant Colonel G. D. J. McMurtrie, 83pp. transcript memoir

V. R. Magill, manuscript memoir

General Sir Ivor Maxse, miscellaneous papers

J. W. Mudd, 8pp. manuscript letter

Reverend M. W. Murray, 170pp. transcript diary.

Captain T. C. Owtram, 29pp. typescript memoir

Colonel F. J. Rice, 177pp. manuscript memoir

D. L. Rowlands, 5pp. typescript letter

G. Stewart, manuscript memoir

B. O. Stokes, 8pp. typescript memoir

Captain E. F. Trundle, manuscript letters

Lieutenant F. S. Walthew, manuscript letters

Lieutenant J. S. Walthew, manuscript letters

A. C. Warsop, 17pp. transcript memoir

Captain O. H. Woodward, typescript memoir, 'The War History of Oliver Holmes Woodward'

M. Yewdall, typescript letters

Captain H. W. Yoxall, manuscript letters and diary

2. Royal Air Force Museum

F. J. Ortweiler, manuscript diary (AC 88/7)

3. Public Record Office

G Battalion, Tank Corps, Reports of Operation (WO 95/92)

UNPUBLISHED ORAL SOURCES

1. Imperial War Museum, Sound Archive (IWM SOUND)

Charles Austin, AC 11116

Reginald Beall, AC 4013

Horace Birks, AC 4024

Edmund Blunden, AC 4030

Leslie Briggs, AC 5

W. Bunning, AC 4046

Ulrich Burke, AC 569

Charles Carrington, AC 4057

George Clayton, AC 10112

George Cole, AC 9535

Frederick Collins, AC 8229

William Collins, AC 9434

Jim Crow, AC 9118

Cyril Denys, AC 9876

Jack Dillon, AC 4078

Mark Dillon, AC 9752

H. V. Doggett, AC 4079

Joe Fitzpatrick, AC 10767

Bryan Frayling, AC 4105

Sidney Goldsmith, AC 4115

Graham Greenwell, AC 8766

Walter Grover, AC 10441
Alfred Griffin, AC 9101
Alan Hanbury-Sparrow, AC 4131
Arthur Hemsley, AC 9927
J. C. Hill, AC 4135
Harry Hopthrow, AC 11581
George Horridge, AC 7498
F. W. S. Jourdain, AC 11214
Clifford Lane, AC 7257
Cyril Lee, AC 4156
Cecil Lewis, AC 4162
Norman Macmillan, AC 4173
John Mallalieu, AC 9417
Leonard Ounsworth, AC 332
Kenneth Page, AC 717
J. W. Palmer, AC 4198
Joseph Pickard, AC 8946
Hartwig Pohlman, AC 4197
Donald Price, AC 10168
Mr Roll, AC 4215
Ernie Rhodes, AC 10914
Murray Rymer-Jones, AC 10699
Stewart Sibbald, AC 10169
E. W. Stoneham, AC 4237
Richard Talbot-Kelly, AC 4242
George Thompson, AC 9549
Richard Tobin, AC 4243
William Towers, AC 11038
Ivor Watkins, AC 12232
E. G. Williams, AC 10604
Douglas Wimberley, AC 4266

2. Others

Stephen Williamson, private interview with Nigel Steel, Canterbury, 9 May 1985

PUBLISHED SOURCES

1. Books

Anon., *New Brunswick Fighting 26th : A Draft History of the 26th New Brunswick Battalion, CEF, 1914–1919* (New Brunswick: 26th Battalion Overseas Association Inc., 1992)

Anon., *The 54th Infantry Brigade, 1914–1918: Some records of Battle and Laughter in France* (Aldershot: Gale & Polden Ltd, 1919)

Anon., *The War History of the 1st Northumbrian Brigade, RFA* (Newcastle upon Tyne: J. W. Hindson & Sons, 1927)

Baker-Carr, C. D., *From Chauffeur to Brigadier* (London: Ernest Benn, 1930)

Bean, C.E.W., *The Official History of Australia in the War of 1914–1918,* Vol. IV (Queensland: University of Queensland Press, 1982)

Bird, W. R., *Ghosts have warm hands*, (Toronto: Clarke, Irwin & Company Ltd, 1968)

Black, E. G., *I Want One Volunteer* (Toronto: The Ryerson Press, 1971)

Blake, R. (ed.), *The Private Papers of Douglas Haig, 1914–1919* (London: Eyre & Spottiswoode, 1952)

Blunden, Edmund, *Undertones of War* (London: Cobden-Sanderson, 1930)

Charteris, Brigadier General John, *Field Marshall Earl Haig* (London: Cassell, 1929)

Charteris, Brigadier General John, *At GHQ* (London: Cassell, 1931)

Cliff, Norman, *To Hell and Back with the Guards* (Braunton: Merlin Books, 1988)

Crookenden, A., *The History of the Cheshire Regiment in The Great War* (Chester: W. H. Evans & Sons, 1938)

Dudley Ward, C. H., *The History of the Welsh Guards, 1915–1919* (London: London Stamp Exchange, 1988)

Edmonds, Charles, *A Subaltern's War* (London: Peter Davis Ltd, 1929)

Edmonds, Brigadier James, *Military Operations: France and Belgium, 1917, Vol. II* (London: HMSO, 1948)

Fox, C. L., *Narrative of the 502 (Wessex) Field Company, Royal Engineers, 1915–1919* (London: Hugh Rees Ltd, 1920)

Fraser-Tytler, N., *With Lancashire Lads and Field Guns in France, 1915–1918* (Manchester: John Heywood Ltd, 1922)

Gillon, S., *The Story of the 29th Division* (London: Thomas Nelson & Sons, 1925)

Gordon, Huntley, *The Unreturning Army* (London: J. M. Dent & Sons, 1967)

Gough, General Sir Hubert, *The Fifth Army* (Hodder & Stoughton, 1931)

Groom, W. H. A., *Poor Bloody Infantry* (London: William Kimber, 1976)

Haldane, M., *A History of the Fourth Battalion, Seaforth Highlanders* (London: Witherby, 1927)

Hamilton, Lieutenant Colonel R. G. A., *The War Diary of the Master of Belhaven, 1914–1918* (Barnsley: Wharncliffe, 1990)

Hodder-Williams, R., *Princess Patricia's Canadian Light Infantry, 1914–1919* (London & Toronto: Hodder & Stoughton Ltd, 1923)

Jack, J., *General Jack's Diary, 1914–1918: The Trench Diary of Brigadier J. L. Jack,* edited and introduced by J. Terraine (London: Eyre & Spottiswoode, 1964)

Jellicoe, Admiral Lord, *The Submarine Peril* (London: Cassell, ND)

Kerr, W. B., *Shrieks and Crashes being Memories of Canada's Corps, 1917* (Toronto: Hunter Rose Company Ltd, 1929)

Lawrence, C., *Sergeant Lawrence goes to France* (Melbourne: Melbourne University Press, 1987)

Liddle, (ed.), P. *Passchendaele in Perspective, The Third Battle of Ypres* (London: Leo Cooper, 1997)

Lloyd George, David, *War Memoirs of David Lloyd George*, Vols. I & II (London: Odhams Press Ltd, 1938)

Ludendorff, General Erich, *My War Memories*, Vols. I & II (London: Hutchinson, 1919)

McCudden, Major James T. B., *Five Years in the Royal Flying Corps* (London: Aeroplane and General, 1918)

Martin, B., *Poor Bloody Infantry* (London: John Murray, 1987)

Raleigh, Sir Waller, and Jones, H. A, *The War in the Air*, 6 vols (Oxford: The Clarendon Press, 1922–37)

Revell, A., *High in the Empty Blue: The History of 56 Squadron* (Mountain View: Flying Machines Press, 1995)

Sandilands, J. W. and Macleod, N., *Story of 7th Batt. Cameron Highlanders* (Stirling: Mackay, 1922)

Terraine, John, *Douglas Haig: The Educated Soldier* (London: Hutchinson, 1963)

Wadsworth, W. W., *War Diary of the 1st West Lancashire Brigade, RFA* (Liverpool: Daily Post, 1923)

Walker, Captain Maurice, *A History of 154 Siege Battery, Royal Garrison Artillery* (Dublin: John T. Drought, 1919)

Walkington, M. L., *Twice in a Lifetime* (London: Samson Books, 1980)

Watson, W. H. L., *A Company of Tanks* (Edinburgh & London: William Blackwood & Sons, 1920)

Williams-Ellis, Major Clough, *The Tank Corps* (London: Country Life, 1919)

Williamson, Benedict, *Happy Days in France and Flanders with the 47th and 49th Divisions* (London: Harding & More Ltd, ND)

Wurtzburg, C. E., *The History of the 2/6th (Rifle) Battalion, The King's Liverpool Regiment 1914–1919* (Aldershot: Gale & Polden Ltd, 1920)

Wyrall, Everard, *The Gloucestershire Regiment in the War, 1914–1918* (London: Methuen & Co Ltd, 1931)

2. Journals and Periodicals

Daily News, A. J. Cummings, 'Ypres: the Tragic Story of the Salient', 23 July 1928

London Gazette, various VC citations

The Ranger, Colonel F. W. S. Jourdain, 'A Subaltern's War', July 1968

The Spectator, E. Gold, 17 January 1958

The Tank

The Ypres Times, Vol. 2, No. 2, General Sir Charles Harington, 'The Ypres Salient in 1918'

The Ypres Times, Vol. 3, No. 5, Brigadier General W. R. Ludlow, 'Some Extracts from an Area Commandant's Diary'

The Ypres Times, Vol. 4, No. 4, C. J. Huffield, 'The Zonnebeke Show'

The Ypres Times, Vol. 7, No. 2, C. Smith, 'The Slush at Passchendaele'

INDEX